ERVING GOFFMAN

Few sociologists have commanded a larger readership than Erving Goffman. From his first book, *The Presentation of Self in Everyday Life* (1956), to his last, *Forms of Talk* (1981), his publications were eagerly awaited and his ideas widely discussed. In 1982, when he died at the age of sixty, the response was that a figure of outstanding importance had left the stage of modern sociology.

In this powerful study, Tom Burns provides a meticulous and incomparable examination of Erving Goffman's work. Burns arranges Goffman's writings into a series of themes such as 'Social Order', 'Acting Out', 'normalisation', 'abnormalisation', 'grading and discrimination' and 'realms of being'. This is a useful device because it brings out the richness and diversity of Goffman's preoccupations which are often lost in secondary accounts that insist on labelling Goffman as a sociologist of face-to-face encounters or a 'symbolic interactionist'.

In a painstaking and accurate discussion, Burns shows the meaning and application of Goffman's key concepts. He also guides the reader in the direct influences upon Goffman's thought. He shows more clearly than anyone else how Goffman was influenced by Durkheim, Simmel, the Chicago School, animal ethology and linguistic philosophy. The book ends with a crisp and incisive critical assessment of Goffman's sociology.

Accomplished and exhaustive, this fair-minded study is already being celebrated as a seminal contribution to making sense of Goffman's sociology.

Tom Burns was Professor of Sociology at Edinburgh University from 1964 to 1981.

ERVING GOFFMAN

Tom Burns

London and New York

First published in 1992
by Routledge
11 New Fetter Lane, London EC4P 4EE

Simultaneously published in the USA and Canada
by Routledge
a division of Routledge, Chapman and Hall, Inc.
29 West 35th Street, New York, NY 10001

Typeset by Amy Boyle Word Processing
Printed and bound in Great Britain by
Biddles Ltd, Guildford and King's Lynn

British Library Cataloguing in Publication Data
Burns, Tom 1913–
Erving Goffman.
1. Sociology
I. Title
301.092

Library of Congress Cataloging in Publication Data
Burns, Tom, 1913–
Erving Goffman/Tom Burns.
p. cm.
Includes bibliographical references and index.
1. Goffman, Erving.
2. Sociologists–United States–Biography.
3. Social interaction. I. Title.
HM22.U6G642 1992
301'.092–dc20

ISBN 0-415-06492-9
0-415-06772-3 (pbk)

CONTENTS

AUTHOR'S NOTE

References to those writings which were published in book form, and quotations from them, are incorporated in the text by means of the abbreviations of the book titles used by Goffman himself, and the page number of the edition I have used. In the case of essays republished as collections, the reference is to the title of the book; thus, references to "Role Distance" are to *E* (*Encounters*). The dates when previously published essays first appeared are given in brackets.

The abbreviated form of book titles, the titles themselves, editions used, and the essays included in each published collection are:

PS *The Presentation of Self in Everyday Life* (1956), Doubleday, Anchor Books, 1959.

A   *Asylums: Essays on the Social Situation of Mental Patients and Other Inmates*, Doubleday, Anchor Books, 1961. Includes: "Characteristics of Total Institutions" (1957); "The Moral Career of the Mental Patient" (1959); "The Underlife of a Public Institution: A Study of Ways of Making Out in a Mental Hospital"; and "The Medical Model and Mental Hospitalization: Some Notes on the Vicissitudes of the Tinkering Trades".

E   *Encounters: Two Essays on the Sociology of Interaction*, Bobbs-Merrill, 1961. Includes: "Role Distance" and "Fun in Games".

S   *Stigma: Notes on the Management of Spoiled Identity*, Prentice-Hall, 1963.

BP *Behavior in Public Places: Notes on the Social Organization of Gatherings*, Free Press, 1963.

IR *Interaction Ritual: Essays on Face-to-Face Behavior*, Doubleday, Anchor Books, 1967. Includes: "On Face-Work: An Analysis of Ritual

Elements in Social Interaction" (1955); "The Nature of Deference and Demeanor" (1956); "Embarrassment and Social Organization" (1956); "Alienation from Interaction" (1957); "Mental Symptoms and Public Order" (1964); and "Where the Action Is".

SI   *Strategic Interaction*, Univ. of Pennsylvania Press, 1969. Includes: "Expression Games: An Analysis of Doubts at Play" (1966) and "Strategic Interaction".

RP   *Relations in Public: Microstudies of the Public Order*, Allen Lane, 1971. Also contains, as appendix: "The Insanity of Place" (1969).

FA   *Frame Analysis: An Essay on the Organization of Experience*, Harper & Row, 1974.

GA   *Gender Advertisements*, Macmillan, 1979.

FT   *Forms of Talk*, Blackwell, 1981. Includes: "Replies and Responses" (1976); "Response Cries" (1978); "Footing" (1979); "The Lecture" (1976); and "Radio Talk".

Quotations from Goffman are marked by single quotation marks (thus: '...'); quotations from other sources are provided with double quotation marks ("..."), and these are also employed in all other cases for which quotation marks are the conventional sign.

In the present text, the discrepancies between the actualities of sex difference and the grammatical conventions of gender are not significant. However, the reader is asked to observe that "he", "him" and "his", when they refer to an antecedent noun of common gender, like "individual" or "person", should be read as "he or she", "him or her" and "his or hers".

ACKNOWLEDGEMENTS

I am indebted to Randall Collins and Sheldon L. Messinger for their comments on an earlier draft of the main text.

1
PRELIMINARIES

I

Erving Goffman's last book, *Forms of Talk*, was reviewed at length in the *New York Review of Books* and, three months later, in its English clone, the *London Review of Books*.[1] Given their authors (Christopher Ricks, then Professor of English at Cambridge, and Alan Bennett, playwright and erstwhile member of the *Beyond the Fringe* quartet), and the journals in which they appeared, the two reviews together amount to dealing the author a reviewing "natural". Both reviewers are warm in their praise, making much of the 'grace' and 'wit', the 'untiring perspicacity' and 'humour and imagination (intimately related)' of his writing, and of the sheer enjoyment they found in reading Goffman. These observations do not refer just to *Forms of Talk*, for both are at pains to show how well acquainted they were with his other books.

The breadth of Goffman's appeal and the popularity of his writings outside the special interests of social scientists had been apparent for many years. Well before these reviews appeared, sales of *The Presentation of Self* were over half a million, *Stigma* was reaching towards its thirtieth reprinting, and translations existed in over a dozen languages. But the reviews, and the reviewers, are useful markers of the extraordinary range of interest in his writings – although there had been other indications, sometimes in odd places. It was surprising to find the theatre critic of *The Guardian* adopting the term "Goffmanesque" for occasional use and, what is more, leaving it unexplained. Mr Bennett made the same discovery from the opposite end, so to speak. He reported that he found it disconcerting to realise that "the books I once thought so private are piled promiscuously on any campus counter at the start of every term".

I have begun by remarking on the two reviews because, as well as signalling the enthusiastic warmth with which Goffman's work had

1

come to be received, they also revealed certain misconstructions, prejudices or simple ignorance as more pervasive, even at this late date, than I would have thought likely. Perhaps most of his popularity did come from the rich harvest his writings contain of the revelations – which close inspection of the trivial mistakes and innocent deceptions of ordinary conduct can yield – of how the blemishes and improprieties we conceal complement the merits and virtues we flaunt, of how self-regard can make cowards and bullies of us all. There is also the rich bonus of the pungent and nicely turned prose in which all this is conveyed. Yet, judging by these reviews, his work seems in danger of being treated as a compendium of notes and observations of "manners", many of them witty but all of them about commonplace and familiar things. The best that Goffman offers, apparently, is a treasury of portable quotations, of one-liners, all subversive, satirical, perceptive, and so on, but buried, unfortunately, in a bran tub of rather over-elaborate and far-fetched visions of social behaviour, personal identity, and of the arbitrariness of the common distinctions we draw between normal and abnormal, sanity and insanity, masculine and feminine.

This, at all events, is how Frank Cioffi evaluated Goffman's work. Twelve years or so earlier than the reviews in question, his Royal Institute of Philosophy lecture provides copious examples taken from writings by Everett Hughes, David Riesman and, at greater length, Erving Goffman to illustrate how it is that instead of giving us information – which is what he implies they are supposed to do – they, like many of their colleagues, fill their pages with observations and insights about matters we already know well enough, and which, in any event, have been made available to us for ages by novelists and essayists: "Goffman's theses concerning the problems involved in stigma management are as truistic and as insusceptible of an information-rationale as those concerning impression-fostering in *The Presentation of Self*."[2]

Despite the diametric opposition between their assessments, the construction Cioffi puts on Goffman's writings parallels the impression that both Ricks and Bennett manage to convey. The suggestion in both reviews is that, though he writes "like an angel" and is "untiringly perspicacious", what he is concerned with is not of central importance – not about what most of us see as essential to one's existence as a social being, nor about "the framework of society" itself – but a sideshow, the quirks and mishaps ("the common predicaments and awkward moments") of existence, and of the existence of *individuals* at that. This is an old charge, and perhaps one tends to be hypersensitive about it; there are remarks in Goffman's own writings which can be used in evidence, although the remarks ought properly be seen to be selected from the wardrobe of mantles of (mock-)modesty he liked to assume on occasion. Here, though, the charge is given special weight in that both reviewers seem to be at pains to distance Goffman from other sociologists and from sociology in general. Bennett does it by mildly jeering references to "Schegloff et al." and to "Goffman's heavy-footnoted helpers"; Ricks more objectionably by identifying "a principled dissatisfaction with his profession" as one of Goffman's "humane impulses".

Original and talented as Goffman was, celebrated as he became, and distinctive as his writing is, he can hardly be said to stand in isolation from other social scientists, nor his work from other developments in social science. Clifford Geertz names Goffman as "perhaps the most celebrated American sociologist right now, and certainly the most ingenious" in an essay which sets out to draw a kind of sketch-map of some of the more interesting of the recent developments in social science. These developments, he argues constitute a

> challenge . . . to some of the central conceptions of mainstream social science. The strict separation of theory and data, the "brute fact" idea; the effort to create a vocabulary purged of all subjective reference, the "ideal language" idea; and the claim to moral neutrality and the Olympian view, the "God's truth" idea – none of these can prosper when explanation comes to be regarded as a matter of connecting action to its sense rather than behaviour to its determinants.[3]

Given that seeking the explanation for action in its meaning for others rather than in its causal origins provides the key to Goffman's work, his name (as any social scientist would expect) figures fairly large on Geertz's map of the new territories and altered boundaries of social science.

Both reviewers profess to see Goffman's true affinities to be with novelists, essayists and "literary" writers in general – to see him, in short, as "one of us". Christopher Ricks pulls in Swift, Paul Goodman, and, stretching to the point of overbalance, Thomas Carlyle. Bennett recruits Tolstoy, Proust, and Kafka. Such observations can be dismissed fairly easily as the usual kind of reviewers' hype. But considered in the light of Clifford Geertz's remarks about the interpenetration – or "blurring" – of the modes of thought which now prevail in the humanities and the social sciences, they also reveal the rather depressing parochialism that has afflicted English letters over the past few decades. It had shown itself in rather more seemly fashion some years previously, when Richard Hoggart expressed a yearning for some established and acknowledged tie-up or *rapprochement* between social scientists and "critics in the humanities", naming Goffman as a sociologist whose writings showed a marked affinity with the kind of thing produced by "critics of the arts".[4] The suggestion (repeated in the introduction he wrote for the English edition of *Gender Advertisements*) was that both sides would profit by a closer association. Hoggart's proposal seemed to me at the time to be rather otiose; social scientists of Goffman's generation had long since adopted Clyde Kluckhohn's reading of his own vocation of anthropologist as a licence to poach. It looks more now as if he was aiming in the wrong direction, and that it is the "critics in the humanities" who stay so obstinately locked in their closet.

True, the kind of insights that such reviewers seem to look for in his work, to the exclusion of anything else, are the kind that one also finds in certain novels and short stories published at the time he started writing – those, for example, by Ivy Compton-Burnett, Mary McCarthy and William Sansom. But the point is that he was totally a sociologist, so that whatever he read was read with a sociological eye and an eye for sociology. Most of us, for example, found Stephen Potter's "Gamesmanship" and "Lifemanship" articles, which appeared in *Punch* around 1950, positively inspirational. What Stephen Potter did was to disclose an elaborate code of conventions which operated in everyday social intercourse, which was nevertheless tacit, even secret, but which we were all aware of once it was made public. It was in Goffman's writings, though, that this kind of perceptiveness was put in context, and so took on new life.

It was not that such reading "put ideas into his head"; after all, Georg Simmel had long before examined a much wider range of dimensions and aspects of social encounters and sociable relationships, and *The Presentation of Self* is much more than "Lifemanship" or the section on sociability in Simmel's *Grundfragen der Soziologie* writ large. What Potter's articles perhaps did, by their oblique but recognisable affinity with Goffman's own ideas, was to provide the kind of licence or mandate that even the boldest beginner needs.

4

The slightest acquaintance with Goffman's writings shows how wide, how miscellaneous, and yet how purposeful his reading was. His writing style was consciously and deliberately worked at – how could it not be? – although it would be hard to pin down the models he used. Novelists like Compton-Burnett "influenced" his style of writing just as much as Durkheim and Simmel "influenced" his style of analytical thinking, but there were in both cases plenty of other models and influences. His handling of words, the tongue-in-cheek primness of style, the sudden insights which come from matching incongruities, the 'plonking' opening paragraph, the deadpan witticism, the throwaway aphorism, and even the rather awful passages of sententious moralising, are all much more in keeping with the very careful prose one found in the better contributions to the *New Yorker* than anything one can find in professional texts. Like them, they are the product of much editing and re-editing – though, in his case, strictly by his own hand. The carefully composed idiosyncrasy of style was matched by the equally painstaking eclecticism of the sources he used for purposes of illustrative quotation: sociological studies of occupations, books of etiquette, diplomats' reminiscences, descriptions of manners and customs in Britain and elsewhere, memoirs and autobiographies, newspaper articles, and the like.

II

The main purpose of this book is expository. I want it to present a straightforward, clear and basically sympathetic survey of Goffman's work as a whole. This is perhaps sufficient reason, but there are two additional concerns behind it.

The first is that, as I have probably made obvious enough by now, I believe there has been a tendency to pass judgement on too narrow or too superficial an acquaintance with his work, perhaps on too hasty a suspicion of the swift popularity of his first publications. At all events, he has, I think, been too often dismissed as entertaining, stylish, full of perspicacious insights and diverting comments, but essentially lightweight, uninterested in the weightier concerns of social science, not a true contender in the intellectual stakes at least at heavyweight standard. It seems to be a view shared by those who applaud him most heartily, like the two reviewers I began with; by those, like Frank Cioffi, who do not; and by others, like A. W. Gouldner and Alasdair MacIntyre, who are both appreciative and critical, and who also have to be taken more seriously.

As my second concern, I want this account of Goffman's writings to stand apart from the tendency to dismember someone's life work in order to put the pieces together again, trimmed or re-jigged, so as to represent or fit some favoured theoretical construction or critical target of the author's choosing. I have in mind here what seems to be a fashion best known to us in its "director-theatre" guise but also frequently encountered in recent decades in new interpretations of philosophical writings, although I suppose the recent treatment of history and biography would serve just as well.

This is not to say that the account will be uncritical. In his preoccupation with unravelling the rules of the game of social interaction in general and conversation in particular, and of revealing how closely the latter was embedded in the first, he did tend to underrate – or even to overlook – the manifold ways in which people's behaviour towards each other, or in each other's company, is preformulated in terms of social structure and individual interests and appetites. The conceptual apparatus he made use of proved defective on occasions – especially those parts he took too unquestioningly from Durkheim. There are also missed opportunities, passages which broach major themes but leave them unexplored.

I shall, on the other hand, try to steer clear of the worst mistake of trying to fit him into one or other "school" of thought in sociology: structural-functionalism, or existentialism, or symbolic interaction, or phenomenology, or Marxism – all of which, and more, have been applied to Goffman. There are three reasons why it would be wrong. The first (to which one may perhaps give the least weight) is that he did his best to avoid being classified in this way, even to the point of declaring a belief in conceptual eclecticism. The second is that, as Gilbert Ryle maintained in the case of philosophical "schools", when any particular set of ideas about the subject-matter of social science reaches the point of becoming a "school of thought" and having a label attached to it, any merits it may have had become suspect.

It is, though, the third reason which counts. It is that Goffman saw the practice of social science as discovery. This is not to say that he brought new facts to light or revealed information which was previously unknown, but that he made clear what was previously unclear, pointed to the significance of things which had been regarded as of little or no consequence, and disentangled what was previously an indiscriminate muddle.

III

Goffman's writings amount to some two dozen books and articles. Almost all the articles were later republished in four collections of essays – *Asylums, Interaction Ritual, Relations in Public,* and *Forms of Talk* – on (more or less) compatible themes. Two other books, *Encounters* and *Strategic Interaction,* each consisted of two essays either previously unpublished or revised from their first published form and retitled. Lastly, there are the five monographs which were published separately as books: *The Presentation of Self in Everyday Life, Stigma, Behavior in Public Places, Frame Analysis,* and *Gender Advertisements.*

The eleven books form a singularly compact body of writing. All his published work was devoted to topics and themes which were closely connected, and the methodology, angle of approach and, of course, style of writing remained characteristically his own throughout. The most obvious changes occurred in the terminology ("conceptual apparatus") he brought to bear on his analysis of the subject-matter he had decided on. To begin with, he stuck close to the ideas and methodological approach of Durkheim and Simmel, but he tended to leave them behind during the 1960s, took to making free with concepts developed for the study of animal behaviour, and dipped into the backwater of the phenomenological tradition which had opened up in sociology. "Neurath", says Quine, "once likened science to a boat which, if we are to rebuild it, we must rebuild plank by plank while staying afloat in it." Goffman does not seem to have been satisfied with replacing a plank here and there to keep his microsociological craft afloat; towards the end, it is almost as if he set about rebuilding it entirely out of the planks of linguistic philosophy still floating in America. But, to drive the simile to the point of self-destruction, all this repair work, whatever the scale, was done on the superstructure rather than the hull; or to put it better, perhaps, whatever the materials he built his boat out of, he kept it on course.

Sorting his writings into distinct categories is not easy, and while it is possible to group the whole body of writings into subsets, in each of which a common or central preoccupation is discernible, it involves some arbitrary (and therefore dubious) decisions.

There are no clear-cut lines of division between any one subset and the others; there are many connections which have to be restated after making them. This is in part because, apart from his PhD dissertation on his sojourn in Shetland (which was never published), he did not follow what is for most academic social scientists the conventional practice of writing up his researches in any particular field of study or location in the form of a comprehensive report. His notes on Shetland, on the three years he spent as a visiting researcher with the National Institute of Mental Health and on the shorter period as a working member of the staff of casinos in Las Vegas were kept as a repository of research material to draw on for illustrative and demonstrative purposes. Shetland provided the first-hand empirical research material that went into *The Presentation of Self*, but occasional references to his Shetland notes turn up in his writings over the next fifteen years or so. The years at the National Institute of Mental Health proved an almost inexhaustible resource.

Each of his published writings was, in fact, built out of a systematic analysis of some aspect of, or perspective on, the kinds of social behaviour, or social interaction, which he saw prevailing in contemporary (American) society. Yet while what he called the "microsociology" of social interaction was central, he did of necessity devote a good deal of attention to the individual self in many of its aspects and to certain aspects of social order, social structure and organisation which bore directly on his main theme. These three themes provide the basic categories, but during the last dozen or so years of his lifetime, he regrouped his conceptual forces, so to speak, for a new attack on the problems of social interaction, social order, and the self, which suggests that it is advisable to compromise by making room for a fourth category.

The three categories that define themselves most clearly are social interaction, the self, and social order. The largest, of course, is directly concerned with social interaction, and this comes first, occupying the three chapters which follow this one. The next, Chapter 5, is about individual conduct, roles and role-playing, and includes the view of individual behaviour as histrionic performance given in his first and best-known book, *The Presentation of Self in Everyday Life*; but two later essays, "Role Distance" and "Where the Action Is", supplement and, to a large extent, reshape the book's account of the individual self. The *Asylums* papers – together with two others, "Mental Symptoms and Public Order" and "The Insanity of Place", which are discussed in Chapters 6 and 7 – stand fairly clearly on their own, although there are passages in the other earlier writings which bear just as directly on the same subject-matter of mental illness and mental hospitals. Following these is a chapter about *Stigma* and *Gender Advertisements*, which deals with other aspects of generic discrimination and subordination. The next four chapters (9-12) deal with his renewed attack – in *Frame Analysis* and *Forms of Talk* – on the principal subject-matter of social interaction, but with consideration of the "self" featured more prominently and more intertwined with the analysis of social interaction.

IV

This is not the place for even the sketchiest of biographies beyond the bare facts of Goffman's career (a collection of extracts translated from his writings recently published in France is prefaced by a biographical sketch of about eighty pages[5]), but there are points in that career which might be illuminated by some indication of the context of ideas in which he moved during his formative years – those spent at Toronto, Chicago, Edinburgh, and Paris – before his first academic appointment in 1954, when he was 32.

Erving Goffman was born in 1922 in Manville, Alberta, Canada. He came of a family of Ukrainian Jews who had joined the great influx of Russians into Canada just before the turn of the century. The family later moved to Dauphin, in Manitoba, where his father ran what must have been a fairly successful tailoring business. He himself thought, or at least said, that being a Jew, and a Russian Jew at that, explained a lot about him, but I doubt that. Like the rest of us, he saw origins more as a way of indexing others than of accounting for himself, although – again like the rest of us – he used his own, on occasion, to turn a conversational trick or two. (There were times – when visiting England, of course – when he would even refer to himself as 'a colonial'.)

After three years at high school in Winnipeg, he enrolled as a student at the University of Manitoba (with chemistry as his "major" subject) in the first year of the Second World War, but dropped out to go to Ottawa to work for the National Film Board of Canada, which John Grierson had set up. He did for a time, I believe, think seriously of making a career in films, but moved back to finish his degree, majoring in sociology (he had met Dennis Wrong at the Film Board, and went back with him to Toronto for their senior year). Among his teachers when he was a senior undergraduate were C. W. M. Hart and Ray Birdwhistell, both of whom were instrumental in pointing him towards the new possibilities opening up in sociology and cultural anthropology. He graduated in 1945, having performed well enough academically to be accepted for the graduate school at Chicago.

The years at Chicago, which at that time ranked with Columbia as the leading American school of sociology, were undoubtedly the biggest influence in the formation of what has usually been read as an idiosyncratic approach to the study of society and social behaviour – although it did not seem all that strange in the fifties.

Goffman's graduate studies were in social anthropology at least as much as in sociology; one of his PhD supervisors was Lloyd Warner. But sociology and social anthropology were very closely affiliated in the Chicago school. The lectures Radcliffe-Brown gave there in the thirties had a great deal to do with the dominance of functionalism in American sociology during the fifties; but what seeds he sowed then fell in very fertile ground. The urban sociology to which Park, Burgess, and Wirth gave a central position was instinct with functionalism, albeit of the pluralist kind that Robert Merton later made his own. More to the point, there was a big programme of "investigative" research which had been moulded back in the thirties by Park and Burgess. (It was Park who thought his sociology graduates could learn a lot from, and perhaps should try to become, journalists.) Many of the studies of inner-city milieux, occupational "types", and the like relied on methods of empirical research now dubbed 'participant observation' – which in fact closely resemble those developed by social anthropologists. Lloyd Warner, who moved to Chicago after the war, had conducted his Harvard-based 'Yankee City' studies along much the same lines, although they were made more academically respectable by being tied in with anthropology and orthodox studies of social stratification. Lloyd Warner had also been involved in the Hawthorne studies before moving to Chicago, being directly responsible for the "Bank Wiring Room" study, still the most protracted observational study of social conduct and interaction ever carried out in industry.

Goffman was at Chicago later than all this, but the strategy of the urban studies research was extrapolated into the series of studies of individual occupations conceived along much the same methodological lines – *The Jackroller*, *The Saleslady*, and so on – which, after a much-needed intellectual reinforcement by Everett Hughes, were followed by the *Boys in White* series of studies. All this was going on, or in the making, while Goffman was at Chicago, and there is no doubt that, while the Chicago years could hardly be said to have 'programmed' his later work, they did undoubtedly have much to do with the kind of social scientist Goffman became. There were some very intelligent and imaginative people among the academic staff – and among his fellow-students too.

If one is looking for "influences", the most influential of his teachers was undoubtedly Everett Hughes. The concept of 'total institution' was coined by him. Goffman's early paper, "On Cooling the Mark Out" is an exercise on the theme of Hughes' repeated injunction to the effect that basic patterns of behaviour and institutional structures were best looked for in the analogies which underlie seeming incongruities – "learning about doctors by studying plumbers, and about prostitutes by studying psychiatrists".[6] There is much else in Everett Hughes's seminar series on institutions which prefigures Goffman's later writings. But talk of 'influences' is misleading where, as in this case, it is the positive effort to take up ideas and develop them in entirely new ways which counts.

For a rather inconsequential chain of reasons, it was decided that the fieldwork for his Chicago PhD should be done in the Shetlands (Unst). He was attached to the Department of Social Anthropology at Edinburgh largely because Lloyd Warner (who had made ethnographic studies of Australian aborigines) knew Ralph Piddington, an Australian, head of the newly created department there. Goffman's brief from Lloyd Warner was to make a study of the "social structure" (what else?) of the island community, but this offered him precious little scope. He soon became much more intrigued by, and perhaps saw a more profitable line of enquiry in, the interplay between locals and visitors in and around the hotel he stayed in. This is often a rather exploitative business (mutually exploitative, that is), masked by – and sometimes expressed through – overtly patronising or covertly ironic put-downs. He was also taken by the rather cryptic, or coded, means of communication used by the islanders among themselves – the kind of thing which is conducted in Gaelic in the Hebrides; in Shetland, surreptitious communication with fellow islanders in the presence of outsiders (higher class islanders as well as incomers, or tourists) has to be done by gesture, stance, demeanour, and intonation – *except* in the hotel kitchen, "backstage", where the hotel staff were their own audience.

His first ideas about what might be called a rhetoric of conduct were undoubtedly being worked up (rather than worked out) during the Shetland period. His first paper, "Symbols of Class Status" is best seen as a departure-point, a 'good-bye to all that' – to Lloyd Warner in particular. Even before that paper was published, he was talking about the kind of study-material he was to use in the earlier papers on interaction published in the late 1950s – how people tried to control the situations they were in, instead of merely defining them, and the failures and mishaps they encountered in the attempt. (The first paper on this sort of theme, "On Cooling the Mark Out", was published before he had handed in his PhD thesis.) The same sort of material also went into the first full-dress monograph, *The Presentation of Self in Everyday Life*, in which the ideas he had worked up in Shetland about the rules of social interaction and the modes of self-presentation were more fully – though by no means exhaustively – deployed.

After a few spells of fieldwork, interspersed with terms spent in Edinburgh and trips to Chicago, he fled the rigours of Shetland (and, for that matter, Britain, which was still under "austerity" management) for the fleshpots of Paris (or Washington-sur-Seine, as it was for a time).

He completed his PhD thesis ("Communication Conduct in an Island Community") in 1953. The next year brought his first academic appointment, as "visiting scientist" in the National Institute of Mental Health (NIMH) in Bethesda, near Washington. There, he conducted his research as "participant observer" in the guise of ward orderly or hospital porter.

He spent three years at Bethesda and then, in 1957, joined the Department of Sociology at Berkeley, rising fairly rapidly to full professor status in 1962. His interests seem to have broadened after he arrived in California, and, to some extent, to change direction. No academic of his generation could, even (or especially) during the MacCarthyite years, have altogether escaped the Marxist and Marxisant ideas of the first, and biggest, intellectual "new wave" to spread out from France after 1945, but Goffman showed precious little sign of their having affected his own ideas or his approach to his work. On the other hand, two new interests (in phenomenology and ethology) and the revival of an old one (linguistics) are very clearly reflected in the work he was producing towards the end of the sixties and into the seventies.

The relevance of Alfred Schutz's writing to the study of behaviour in terms of its significance and meaning rather than its causation began to be taken up around 1960, and social psychologists and sociologists who had been attracted to "symbolic interaction" and other derivatives of G. H. Mead's writings began to arm themselves with a background in phenomenology (and, to a lesser extent, hermeneutics). The second new departure was more specific. Given Goffman's work for the NIMH, the working relationship he came to establish at Berkeley with Gregory Bateson's group – who were studying mental illness and were stationed in the Veterans' Administration Hospital in Palo Alto – was more or less inevitable. So was his attraction into animal behaviour studies, to which Bateson's attention was turning during Goffman's first years at Berkeley. Third, the interest he had found in linguistics at Edinburgh revived under the impact of Chomsky's revolutionary "transformational grammar", to which a number of social scientists were beginning to respond by the early sixties; in Goffman's case, this was reinforced by the presence at Berkeley of John Searle and, later, H. P. Grice, who cultivated an offshoot (which proved to be longer lived there than on its home ground) of the Oxford school of "linguistic" philosophy.

All three "influences" were beginning to be reflected in his writings towards the end of the sixties. A third, and final, stretch of fieldwork occurred during the same decade, again in the acceptably professional guise (acceptable, that is, in social anthropology) of participant observer, when he worked for a time in the casinos at Las Vegas.

He stayed at Berkeley until 1968, when he moved east, to the University of Pennsylvania, working closely with the large sociolinguistics school there. He was sixty when he died.

V

I want, finally, to treat a very early paper, "On Cooling the Mark Out",[7] as a kind of trailer for the main body of writings. It is an account and analysis of procedures designed to reconcile people with failure. The title itself is taken from the special cant of confidence tricksters, the 'mark' meaning their victim, and 'cooling out' referring to the practice, which they sometimes think necessary, of calming him down so as to minimise any unwelcome publicity and, especially, to reduce the risk of his informing the police.

There are places in almost all Goffman's writings where his propensity for sardonic comment shows through. This is fairly obvious to most readers, but it is for the most part no more than a recurring undertone or an occasional throwaway remark. Of course, 'satire' is

13

not a usable term for social scientists; nor is it, for that matter, in the lexicon of any academic practice. Yet it would be silly totally to ignore this aspect of Goffman's writing, or its appeal. Much of *The Presentation of Self* and many of the earlier papers had the appeal of the kind of subversive writing which became fashionable in the fifties. He explored pretension and embarrassment; the treatment accorded the mentally handicapped, the defective and the mutilated, as well as the defensive strategies to which such persons resorted; failure, loss of face, and loss of dignity; and the vulnerability of everyday living and its underworld. He did so with a scholarly (at times ponderous) gravity combined with an exuberant display of verbal dexterity (and, at times, of sheer verbosity) which kept him a safe distance from current conventions of academic writing. The combination of clinical approach, sensational content, deadpan stylishness, and bizarre juxtapositions was perfect for a generation whose culture heroes included Tom Lehrer and Lenny Bruce.

The satirical edge shows itself only fleetingly in the first paper he published, "Symbols of Class Status"; the English public school system is bracketed with Chicago's twenty-six "Charm Schools" as 'a machine for systematically re-creating middle-class people in the image of the aristocracy'. His second paper, "On Cooling the Mark Out", though, went the whole hog.

The paper is a perfect example of Goffman's manner of working. For him, the attraction of books like D. W. Maurer's *The Big Con* and *The Professional Thief*, the oral reminiscences which Edwin Sutherland took down from a convicted pickpocket, and their revelations about the tricks, strategic operations and argot of the criminal underworld did not lie – as they did for many of his fellow students – in the promise of more adventurous exploration into the nature of criminality; he was never much interested in the academic study of crime. What mattered more was that, like Everett Hughes, Goffman was fascinated by the stratagems and specialist skills, the standards of morality and codes of conduct, the occupational definitions, the demarcation rules, the snobberies and, of course, the argot of thieves, whores, hustlers, con men, and tricksters of all kinds. It was a looking-glass world which reflected, in caricature form, but revealingly, the postures and antics of the world of politics, business, industry and, especially, the professions. Nowadays, of course, the comparison has become tedious – done to death and unbearably cliché-ridden. But Goffman, like Hughes, meant it seriously.

The point of the paper lies in using the 'cooling-out' stratagems adopted by confidence tricksters as a model for the widespread adoption throughout society of analogous "damage-limitation" procedures. "Society" has devised these procedures because the fuss which may be made by those who fall victim to what they see as deprivation, discrimination or unjust treatment, or whose expectations or hopes suffer disappointment, is 'bad for business' (p. 452). In other words, a certain amount of repair work has to be done by others to restore the order which keeps us going, the order being (in this case) a system of rights and duties, obligations and privileges, beliefs and ideas in which we have invested our lives and careers, and in which are established our relationships, status, roles, jobs, and livelihood.

But there is more to the analogy. We are all potential marks, and therefore all liable, some time, to need cooling out. For, living as we do in a society dominated by possessive individualism and market competition, we live in a society in which failure is common, and certainly more frequent than success, if success means "coming first" or "getting the job" or "getting the girl". But aspiring to success means committing oneself to a venture, which means first of all committing oneself to a self-image of someone better, cleverer, smarter or somehow superior to what one has hitherto thought of, or been accepted as, being. Committing oneself to such ventures means risking the destruction of the image one now has of oneself. The *fact* of failure is essentially the loss of self-esteem which comes from loss of "face" which, in turn, is the result of failing to live up to the image one has of oneself. Hence the subtitle: "Some Aspects of Adaptation to Failure", and the analysis of 'consolation as a social process'.

The paper, although it was published in *Psychiatry* – the journal in which many of his earlier essays first appeared – does not fit into any of the categories appropriate to the rest of his work; and it was omitted from the four volumes of collected papers. But in the choice of topic, the angle at which the central theme is approached, the moralising tone and style of writing, it bears the clear imprint of what became recognisable as characteristic of his work. What is more, they are present, in this particular paper, in neat and undiluted form. And they are present as the appropriate mode for his bent for satirical observation of – and critical moralising about – "society" as a kind of supra- or extra-human presence or force, and its "victims". 'Poise', for example, a favourite word in later papers, occurs here as a quality exploited by confidence men, talented actors who build up social

15

relationships for the sole purpose of abusing them. Failure to live up to one's self-image is extended to include fatal illness as well as failing an examination; ways of refusing to be 'cooled out' include suicide and fantasy – 'the last stand of the defeated self'; and the burden and fuss of consolation may be dodged by 'carrying' the mark as a passenger. This last, he remarks, is frequently practised by business offices, government agencies, and spouses – and 'perhaps, is the most important source of private charity in our society' (p. 460).

There is perhaps something a little contrived, even 'cute', about using the ways of confidence tricksters as a model for the range of procedures available for limiting or repairing damage to self-esteem and, thereby, to the fabric of society. The metaphors, similes and analogies he later put to use had a rather more respectable provenance. But the heuristic strategy employed in the way the paper is organised persisted and became what is perhaps the most characteristic – most "Goffmanesque" – feature of his work. It consisted in uncovering what happens in trivial and commonplace, or peripheral or bizarre, corners of social conduct, depicting its mechanism and its working in almost painfully elaborate detail – and then peeling off more and more of the covering of seemingly normal behaviour and relationships to reveal similar or analogous structures and processes at work throughout the whole order of society.

NOTES AND REFERENCES

1. C. Ricks, Review of *Forms of Talk*, in *New York Review of Books*, 16 July 1981, pp. 42-4; A. Bennett, *idem*, in *London Review of Books*, 15 October-4 November 1981, pp. 12-13.
2. F. Cioffi, "Information, contemplation and social life", in *The Proper Study* (ed. G.N.A. Vesey), Royal Institute of Philosophy Lectures, vol. 4, 1969-70, Macmillan, 1971, p. 126.
3. C. Geertz, "Blurred genres; the refiguration of social thought", in *Local Knowledge*, Basic Books, 1983, p. 34.
4. R. Hoggart, Review of Tom Burns, *The BBC: Public Institution and Private World*, in *The Times Higher Education Supplement*, 7 October 1977.
5. Yves Winkin, *Erving Goffman: Les moments et leurs hommes*, Eds du Seuil, 1988.
6. E. E. Hughes, *The Sociological Eye; Selected Papers*, Aldine-Atherton, 1971, p. 316.
7. "On cooling the mark out: some aspects of adaptation to failure", *Psychiatry*, vol. 15, 1952, pp. 451-63.

2
SOCIAL ORDER-
INTERACTION ORDER

From first to last, Goffman's principal concern was with what is called "social interaction" – which could well comprehend virtually the whole of human activity. Economics, sociology, social anthropology, politics and social psychology, as well as history, could all be said to be dedicated, in their different ways, to the study of social interaction, if this is taken to mean how people behave towards each other. By convention, however, the scope of reference of social interaction is restricted to actions which are immediate – i.e. carried out either in the physical presence of other people or within sight or earshot of them – and reciprocal. Thus social interaction includes behaviour in public places as well as social encounters, public meetings and theatrical performances as well as conversations, physical assault and theft as well as buying and selling, driving a car in a city as well as sexual intercourse in bed. Telegrams, telephones and radio have extended the means and opportunities for social interaction of a strictly verbal kind.

As we shall see in Chapter 12, Goffman makes a case for including radio and television broadcasts at one end of the range of social interaction, and talking to oneself at the other. But this chapter, and the two which follow, are concerned with what he has to say about social interaction in ordinary, everyday, social life in Western society.

It is easy enough to specify the publications which belong to this first group. In a prefatory "author's note", *Relations in Public* was announced as continuing the consideration of face-to-face interaction developed in three previous books: *Encounters, Behavior in Public Places,* and *Interaction Ritual*. The first of the papers republished in *Interaction Ritual* appeared in 1955, and the last book of the series, *Relations in Public*, was published in 1971. So the complete set brackets *Asylums* and *The Presentation of Self in Everyday Life* and the essays which appeared later as corollaries to them. However, I shall omit "Role

Distance", the second essay of *Encounters*, which could be said to extend and to some extent modify the argument of *The Presentation of Self*, and include *Strategic Interaction*, which expands the scope of social interaction to include aspects of hostile, competitive, and adversarial encounters in general.

These dozen or so essays are central to the body of Goffman's writings as a whole. They are also the source of a number of problems and difficulties about his work. Not the least of these is the fact that, in some cases at least, the solutions to them are also to be found in his writings, although they have to be put together from scattered references and asides.

This calls for some explanatory preamble to begin with, which occupies the next three sections of this chapter.

I

Even today, as Goffman remarks in one of his later essays, it is in social interaction that 'most of the world's work gets done' (*GA*, x). One can safely assume that even more of "the world's work" was done by way of social interaction in the past, and all of it in prehistorical times, since social interaction in the conventional sense mentioned earlier must then have comprehended virtually all "the ways in which people behave towards each other". But the ways in which people behave towards each other have been immeasurably extended and complicated by what is usually called technological progress.

The consequences of advances in material technology are all too familiar: people living thousands of miles apart can now talk to each other, work, trade with and visit each other – and kill each other. Yet the advances in social technology have been just as momentous, as Arthur Stinchcombe once pointed out in a notable essay.[1] The origin and growth of literacy and the advent of printing led to the progressive expansion and strengthening of organisation, government, and systems of law. Division of labour (functional specialisation) laid the foundations of economic and political organisation and, indeed of civilised life. Using money instead of barter vastly extended the network of human relationships, accelerating the division of labour, promoting the growth of cities, and facilitating rulership. The extrapolation of the uses of money by credit went further, extending contractual relationships into the future, amplifying potentialities for trade and the production of goods, and generating industrialisation.

All these changes have produced a growing quantity and variety of institutions and organisations and, along with them, a *re*-distribution of rights and privileges, and also of duties and obligations. This, in turn, has made for an unequal distribution of resources – material and immaterial – among societies and among people within the same society. And, lastly, the variety of institutions and organisations, and the relationships between them, together with the inequality between individuals and their interrelationships, constitute what is called the "social structure" of a society.

It is understandable, therefore, that it is the proliferation of institutions and organisations in relatively recent times that takes up the foreground of any view we have of society. We tend nowadays to think of the world as peopled by organisations and institutions, and of individuals as ordered according to structures of relationships of power and authority or influence, of inheritance, wealth, income, or some other derivative of their placement in the social structure. And the study of the life of society by economists and political scientists, as well as sociologists, has become largely a matter of investigating the size, constitution, character, power, and durability of these large institutional lumps of social being – of economic, political, or social systems – and of explaining how they relate to each other. The detailed empirical study of how economic transactions are executed, of the minutiae of interpersonal behaviour, or of the everyday conversations and interchanges between relatives or neighbours, has tended to be bypassed or overridden by social scientists of all persuasions – sociologists, psychologists and anthropologists as well as economists and political scientists – in their preoccupation with the macroscopic problems which, by their nature, have to be formulated in abstract terms.

This was not always the case. Two or three hundred years ago (the period in which, significantly enough, Bury discerned the origins of the "idea of progress") some of the more striking advances in social technology occurred, making the new social superstructure possible and, to begin with, one supposes, more vividly apparent. At all events, students of political, economic and social behaviour were still capable of analysing and evaluating the larger institutional and organisational constructs, old and new, while holding on to a lively awareness of how they were founded on the practicalities of everyday social intercourse. This is most clearly visible in the work of English and Scottish philosophers from Hobbes and Locke to Hume and Smith – although it is Condorcet who seems to have conceived "the progress of history" in its more monumental aspects as truly understandable only in the minutiae of social action when he wrote: "What happens at any particular moment is the result of what has happened at all previous moments, and itself has an influence on what will happen in the future."[2]

But, by one of the most rapid and most radical of transitions in the history of thought, this comprehensive view of society and of social action virtually disappeared within a generation. Almost before they had died, Adam Smith was being treated as the apostle of the new ethos of individual self-interest and David Hume as the apologist of individualism's darker, sceptical, side.

II

Sociology began as virtually a resistance movement against the trend towards individualism which set in near the very end of the eighteenth century. Since then, it seems to have drifted into conformity with the ethos of individualism which had infused political, economic and moral thought – as it still does. The case of sociology is further complicated by a kind of chiasma with which it has been afflicted during the course of its own historical development. Some years ago, Peter Blau pointed to the way in which empirical sociological research had turned what is a fairly common categorical separation between mental constructs and the empirical data held to be relevant to them into a dilemma, and so dug a trap for itself: "As sociology became transformed into an empirical science from the social philosophy in which it originated, methods of research had to be devised", and, since social institutions and structures are only observable – i.e. only reveal themselves empirically – in the characteristics and actions of individuals, the object of study was individual behaviour. But this was not the end of it. Empirical studies became more and more – in some respects, solely – dependent on survey interviews.

> Interviewing surveys make the individual [in isolation, that is] the unit of analysis, particularly, though not only, if samples are used in which each respondent represents many other individuals with similar characteristics. . . . Investigators confronted by empirical data that reveal differences in individual behaviour are naturally inclined to seek to explain these differences, and if they are

sociologists they will search for social conditions that can account for the variations in individual behaviour, such as socioeconomic position or religious affiliation.[3]

Marx, Weber, and Durkheim, like their predecessors, set out to describe and explain the major institutions and other features of society, and to account for their origin. But, Blau goes on to point out, when individuals, their attitudes, opinions, beliefs and behaviour in specific circumstances become the primary object of study, the nature and causal origins of the institutional structure of society – which it used to be the concern of sociology to account for – become the means by which individual behaviour can be explained. The dependent variable (the *explicandum*) becomes the independent variable (the *explicans*), and the true subject-matter of sociology – social institutions, and how they originate, grow, change, fossilise or die – is lost sight of.

In the process, the nineteenth-century conceptual glossary of social institution, class structure, power relationship, organisation, and the rest, remained in constant use, becoming fixed – given. But new facts and variant forms are always being turned up, not least through social research. So, in order to accommodate both their glossary of terms and their individualistic preoccupations, sociologists tend to keep their notions of social structure and of social institutions vague and fluid. In fact the concepts of mainstream sociology, well worn as they are, have become – have had to become – infinitely elastic and all-inclusive. The new is assimilated into the old, taking on the shape and characteristics which fit into our familiar image of society. Almost a hundred years after the publication of Weber's and Durkheim's first essays, our ideas of how society is constituted and of how it works are virtually unchanged; as against this, the work of one man, Freud, has utterly revolutionised our ideas of our own individual personalities.

To repeat, while the subject-matter of sociology, properly speaking, is social institutions, relationships, social structures, organisations, social change, social movements, and the like, the empirical evidence about their character and history lies in the conduct of the individuals who constitute them, and through which such abstractions (for that is what they are) manifest themselves. What confronts the sociologist is not a *choice* between, on the one hand, studying "societal concepts", which Maurice Mandelbaum (in a paper[4] published in the same year as Goffman's first essay in *Interaction Ritual*) regarded as "irreducible", and, on the other, the empirical analysis and explanation of the minutiae of social interaction but the *problem* of how to close the gap between the two.

It is to this problem, I believe, that Goffman's studies of social interaction were initially addressed. *Relations in Public*, for example, carries as a kind of frontispiece a quotation from Herbert Spencer (of all unlikely people) which fits the general theme of this first group of Goffman's writings on social interaction so well that it is worth repeating in full:

> If, disregarding conduct that is entirely private, we consider only that species of conduct which involves direct relations with other persons, and if under the name government we include all control of such conduct, however arising; then we must say that the earliest kind of government, the most general kind of government, and the government which is ever spontaneously recommencing, is the government of ceremonial observances. More may be said. This kind of government, besides preceding other kinds, and besides having in all places and at all times approached nearer to universality of influence, has ever had, and continues to have, the largest share in regulating men's lives.

Spencer's view of the nature of social, or public, order, as well as of its importance, seems in tune with Goffman's general approach – in his early writings, at least. The overall purpose of *Behaviour in Public Places* and the four essays on closely related topics is precisely to identify and describe the "ceremonial observances" out of which this "government" is constructed. These earlier essays (and *Stigma* and *Gender Advertisements*, too) are studded with references to the ways in which social relationships, power and authority, organisation and the other larger topographical features of the social landscape may be seen reflected in social encounters. The connectedness of social interaction and the structure of society is in any case implicit in the repeated references to Durkheim.

Goffman was, of course, by no means alone in taking as his principal object of study the small change of social interaction which could be said to constitute the physiology of the social institutions and organisations which make up what we see as "society". His time at Chicago was also the period when it was becoming, at the hands of followers of G. H. Mead (notably Herbert Blumer) who taught there, the nursery of the school of behavioural studies known as "symbolic interaction". Elsewhere, principally at Yale and MIT,[5] psychologists were starting up the laboratory studies of small groups which mushroomed so astonishingly in the 1950s. Goffman was not unsympathetic to the symbolic interaction school, but tended to keep his distance; he was not particularly interested in the clues that expressive behaviour provides for the study of individual psychology, the development of the self, role-taking, and the like.

As for small-group laboratory experiments, he dismissed the whole corpus as the product of 'A sort of sympathetic magic . . . , the assumption being that if you go through the motions attributable to science, then science will result. But it hasn't' (*RP*, xviii). By 1971, when the movement had petered out, Goffman could perhaps afford to be dismissive. Psychologists had themselves become even more so. Such experiments, it was said, often compelled people "to behave not only like rats but like *solitary* rats".[6] Worse still for the scientific pretensions Goffman picked on, it all too often proved impossible to replicate experiments and get the same results. Having learned these lessons themselves, psychologists had already developed research strategies involving a wide array of procedures, from observations of the kind Goffman relied on and the analysis of video-recorded sequences to modifications of the kind of procedures developed for projective tests and psychodrama.

All of which leads up to the point that Goffman's work stands apart from, rather than midway between, the approaches characteristic of the "symbolic interactionist" school of social psychology and studies of social interaction among small groups by experimental psychologists (or the studies of "non-verbal communication" which followed them). In Goffman's hands, the study of the minutiae of social interaction took a very different shape. Unshakably empiricist as all his studies are, they necessarily applied to the conduct of individuals, since it is only in individual behaviour that it is possible to observe the nature and working of the social institutions and structures we have – or have had – fabricated for ourselves. But he observed, and analysed, the conduct of individuals as an attribute of social order, of society, not as an attribute of individual persons.

Goffman's "ultimate behavioural materials" consisted not simply of verbal statements but also, and often more significantly, of 'the glances, gestures, positionings . . . that people continuously feed into the situation (*IR*, 1). People have, in fact, an enormous fund of knowledge about what to do and how to conduct themselves in all the manifold social circumstances in which they find themselves. But knowledge of this kind is implicit, tacit, unthought of – although easily recognised for what it is when our attention is called to it. By far the greater part of the procedures we follow when it comes to our moment-to-moment behaviour is largely unconscious, not in the Freudian sense but as being left to virtually automatic processes to which we need not and usually cannot attend. This kind of unthinking, virtually unconscious, "practical" ability, obviously emanates directly from – is rooted in – our physical make-up, our animal nature. But it includes more than our physical endowment, which we think of as inherently unalterable, and subject only to improvement and deterioration. What counts in social interaction are the movements and adjustments we constantly make in order to amplify, adapt, refine and reapply the elementary functioning of what physical capabilities we have. These modes of adjustment can, of course, be itemised and examined, analysed and discussed, if we are compelled or impelled to do so, but in the ordinary way we feel no call to do so, at least so far as our own expressive behaviour is concerned. We are conscious of other people acting "out of character" or "being at a loss", or of their acting "naturally" or seeming "at home" in a new situation; to be conscious of these things in ourselves is to be embarrassed.

Goffman's preference (during the early part of his career, at any rate) for looking at how people behaved rather than listening to what they said about how they behaved led almost inevitably to the overt adoption, by the time he came to write *Relations in Public*, of the methodology (the mental approach and conceptual glossary) of students of animal behaviour. But his "direct method" approach has deeper roots. Remarks and acts which are unattributed, or are treated as somehow disembodied – that is, as independent or regardless of whosoever uttered or executed them – have always served as study material for social observers, and for novelists and playwrights, as well as for linguists, jurists, and others. More largely, they are incorporated in the way we speak and in how we behave in the company of others. For styles of speech, demeanour and performance are manufactured out of the miscellaneous bits and pieces of talk and activity appropriated, casually or sedulously, for individual use. The currency of everyday conversation and interaction is a *bricolage* of words, phrases and inflections, and of gestures, postures and facial expressions picked up from others.

To begin with, Goffman's studies of social interaction were mostly to do with what he called the 'grammar and syntax' of social interaction. It has some resemblance to what Chomsky made of linguistics; the kind of microsociology Goffman practised in these earlier studies is best thought of, I believe, as the study of the "surface structure" of social interaction. Greater concern with semantic content came later.

He leaned heavily on strategic ideas worked out a generation before him by Durkheim, as well as Freud. What he took from Freud was his insistence on the significance – the meaning – that can be read into what appear to be superficial and transient thoughts and imaginings, and also into what are taken to be trivial slips and mistakes: 'the ways of our errors'. From Durkheim came the conception of what constitutes the essential, first-hand, data for the study of society. Durkheim's own method did not involve him in the collection of first-hand data – in anthropological "fieldwork". Durkheim was a scholar, not an empirical observer; the empirical observations he used were second hand – the monographs of missionaries and other early anthropologists, and government statistics. But his definition of what he called a "social fact" is the foundation of Goffman's own method. A "social fact" is "every way of acting, fixed or not, which is general throughout a given society, while existing in its own right, *independent of its individual manifestations*".

His indebtedness to Durkheim is anchored in this proposition. If the objects of sociological study, being impossibly abstract or impossibly large or impossibly numerous, are out of reach of empirical observation, then we have to make use of something which we can treat as if it were a kind of Leibnizian monad, a constituent particle which both reflects and prehends the cosmos of which it is a constituent particle. Most sociologists have plumped for individual persons, taking their circumstances and their relationships to others, and what they are asked, or choose, to tell about their attitudes, beliefs, ideas and opinions, as representations of the society whose members they are. Goffman's monad was the social act itself – the encounter *between* individuals. His proper study was 'not the individual . . . but rather [the syntactical relations among] the acts of different persons mutually present to one another' (*IR*, 2).

This brings us to another connection. All Durkheim's major writings acknowledge the existence of an explicit social order composed of rational beings each competing and cooperating with others for their own advantage, for domination, or for protection. But this jural,

25

gesellschaftliche, world of contractual and quasi-contractual relationships and power struggles coexists with – indeed, is founded on – an implicit, substructural "moral" order on which each and every individual relies, if only as guarantee of the rational order based on contract, if only as the repository and source of the rituals which guide behaviour and govern relationships. Goffman adopted this Durkheimian notion of a moral order pervading society and sustaining individual conduct, but came up with a different picture from Durkheim's. The moral order which constituted the social reality that Durkheim explored served as a durable, consistent and all-sustaining underlay for individual existence and individual behaviour; for Goffman, it was fragile, impermanent, full of unexpected holes, and in constant need of repair.

III

Studies of social interaction, even in the narrower sense of concern with surface structure, bulk much larger than any other kind in his writings. But it has also to be said that although his interest in the study of social interaction was sustained throughout his career, by the time he came to write the paper he prepared (just before he died) for his presidential address to the 1982 meeting of the American Sociological Association as its new president,[7] the scope he claimed for his 'interaction order' was far more limited than it was throughout the years when he was engaged on the writings considered in these first chapters.

However, while the writings discussed in this chapter and the next two all deal with social interaction, and all rely on much the same evidence and methods of study, Goffman brings into play different conceptual frameworks or intellectual approaches – "brings into play" rather than "employs" or "relies on", because the ways in which his procedure relates to them differs. In *Behavior in Public Places*, Goffman announces early on that he proposes to use 'social order' as a conceptual mode, being more appropriate than 'natural system' or 'game'. 'Natural system' (or "closed natural system") is a formulary proposed by A. W. Gouldner[8] to reflect the emphasis increasingly placed by social scientists (influenced by von Bertalanffy's "General Systems Theory"[9]) on the way in which organisations, once established on a durable footing, appear to take on a life of their own. 'Game' refers to "game-theory", the analytical apparatus developed by von

Neumann and Morgenstern,[10] in which the game of chess is taken to be paradigmatic of adversarial encounters in which what is won by one side is equal to what is lost by the other. It was applied enthusiastically by students to the competitive and conflictual interrelationships thought to be typical of economic and political systems and some social situations, as well as to international relations and to military and para-military affairs. Goffman's later book, *Strategic Interaction*, does make frequent reference to game-theory as a model, but the book is rather more about its limitations than its uses as a conceptual framework. As for ethology, of which he makes so much in *Relations in Public*, the terminology developed in animal behaviour studies is used sparingly, and dropped altogether when it comes to the critically important essay, "Remedial Exchanges".

"Social order", the conceptual framework explicitly adopted as a "model" in *Behavior in Public Places*, is the most problematical and troublesome of the lot. The word "model" in this connection usually implies explanation in terms of a formal statement of the set of entities and relationships required to produce the phenomenon in question or an analogue – an actual working system, mechanical, biological or social, that embodies the relationships in an obvious way. "Social order", as Goffman represents it, is neither. It is defined simply as 'the consequence of any set of social norms that regulates the way in which persons pursue objectives'.

Put this way, the reference of the term is to the recognition by people of an obligation to display what used to be called "civility" or "good manners" – socially acceptable or "proper" behaviour – in the presence of others. It is taken to apply to any kind of encounter, including business dealings, disputes and rival claims as well as sociable meetings, behaviour in public, business affairs, and extends to those conducted in an "impersonal" manner by telephone, correspondence, and so forth, as well as face-to-face. The highest common factor, so to speak, is no more than the practice of behaving predictably, or refraining from causing offence to other people, or not obstructing or interfering with their presence, passage or utterance, either actual or intended. This goes along with the idea that orderliness in this sense is supposed to prevail in all possible circumstances and in all kinds of encounters. Social order, in other words, is a fundamental element of social existence – one of the features which define a society, as Goffman says at one point.

Yet, even this early, Goffman's commitment to the universal

27

applicability of his social order "model" seems to have wavered. There is a passing reference to the existence of other *types* of social order, such as economic, political, legal, and so on (*BP*, 8). *Strategic Interaction* opens with a declaration of intent that could well stand as epigraph to the whole body of writings. It is, writes Goffman, the author's 'ultimate interest to develop the study of face-to-face interaction as a naturally bounded, analytically coherent field'. Even so, he ends the sentence by calling it 'a *sub*-area of sociology'. And when he came to write his last completed essay, "Interaction Order", he withdrew still further, suggesting that the political, economic and other orders had the same sort of significance as what he now called 'interaction order'.

But such cautionary moves raise more questions than they settle. The word "order" in connection with economic order, legal order, political order and so on may differ from interaction order in one categorical sense – namely, as regards the *kind* of things which are dealt with, the kind of vocabulary deemed appropriate, the kind of conventions for conducting debate, negotiation, bargaining, and exchange. But this is not really pertinent to the distinction Goffman is making. His rules of orderly conduct apply to *all* types of encounter. The main distinction between these other orders and his "interaction order" lies in the fact that the kind of aims pursued by the parties engaged in legal disputes, economic transactions, or political debate are specific, or even prescribed – and aims are precisely what Goffman rules out: observing the rules of orderly conduct, he says at one point, applies not to the ends sought but to the way in which they are pursued.

"Social order" is admittedly a difficult term, like many others which make up the conceptual currency of social science. But its difficulty does not lie in its being amorphous, like "power", or slippery, like "social class", but in its being both complex and elastic. The difficulties which arise from reducing "social order" to "interaction order" and relegating it to a place among several other orders of equal consequence are not simply terminological.

For sociology, the orderliness which prevails in face-to-face interaction reflects and supports all other kinds of social order. Social order is central to the fundamental question of how it is that society is possible – of "why, if man is simply a gifted animal, men refrain from unlimited resort to fraud and violence in pursuit of their ends and maintain a stable social system".[11]

The idea of social order may well be peculiar to European thought.

It is certainly an idea actively discussed by Western philosophers after Hobbes had pointed out what life would be like without it, but it is clearly a notion we derive, ultimately, along with so much else, from classical Greece. Obviously, if we search for the Greek counterpart to our notion of social order, abstract as it is, we come up with an abstract noun – *politeia* – as the nearest. The word, Ehrenberg remarks, stood not only for the totality of individual citizens but for the solidary body of citizens, not only the sum of the individuals but the living body of the citizenry, both rulers and ruled, and also for its political life and nature.

The use of the same word for participation in the state and for its general structure shows that the participation was in the main not a purely legal act between individual and state; it reflected the vital adherence of the individual to the citizen body, as also to the other communities within the state, and therewith was bound to them, bound to religion and soil.[12]

All the same, it pays to tread carefully. Although modern scholars seem for the most part to construe the Greek notions of *polis* and *politeia* in a rather abstract, normative, sense – a legal and moral entity rather than a community of individuals – the Greek *polis* was essentially an arena of action. The whole notion of a primary concern with action – with things done, and the way in which moral obliquity, or, especially, "the Gods" or "fortune" affected the outcome – rather than with motive, intention, character, or any personal attributes or relationships is, as John Jones has said, "desperately foreign" to us.[13] If, however, we take Greek society to be the archetypal face-to-face society of European history,[14] then this essential fact is grasped.

Conceptions of social order have almost always been two-sided. The idea of social order as constituted by the action of individuals may go back as far as Aristotle or beyond, but it was nearly always confronted – or sometimes complemented – by an equal and opposite notion. When we come to David Hume, Francis Hutcheson, and Adam Smith, man was the creature of society for them, too; the manifold achievements of man in building the material, cultural, spiritual and economic environment of a civilised life, the plenitude of activities in which man engaged, were only possible because of the existence of social order and organisation. On the other hand, ordered society and social organisation, in turn, were possible because of the presence in man of specific needs, propensities, feelings, emotions ("passions"), *and,* corresponding with these, an understanding of the existence of similar or parallel needs, feelings, etc., in others. The word they used for such mutual understanding was "sympathy",[15] which is best rendered as "fellow-feeling". For Hume, the individual is both creature and creator of society, the means by which he can remedy his deficiencies, satisfy his needs, and realise his values. To quote Duncan Forbes:[16]

> Hume's awareness of man's social interdependence is so striking a feature of his thought, in the *Treatise* especially, that it would be nearer the mark to say that for him society is the "natural unit". Not only is man so peculiarly helpless by himself, his needs so many compared with other animals and his ability to satisfy them so feeble that "it is by society alone that he is able to satisfy his defects".
>
> (*Treatise*, p. 485)

And Adam Smith's writings show clearly enough that he shared the same view, as Amartya Sen has pointed out in his strictures on the "overenthusiastic admirers" of Smith, who, "contrary to what he actually said", have made him "the 'guru' of self-interest".[17]

But, since the eighteenth century, we seem to have lost our hold on that half of the two-sided conception of the relationship between the individual and society which saw society as a historical creation for which its present members have to assume responsibility. Common to a number of historians of political and social ideas, like J. G. A. Pocock, Quentin Skinner, and John Dunn, and to historically minded moral philosophers like Alasdair MacIntyre, is the notion that somewhere in the course of history (English or Western European history, of course) we have lost control of our situation and our destiny. The picture of individual man as the creator of the society from which he draws so much of his attainments as well as his support has been swamped by the notion of control by supra-human forces or by unconscious drives. John Dunn speaks of "the increasingly alienated vision" of social order we now have, in which the individual has become the overburdened inheritor of a vast array of political and social relations which it is futile for him to try to affect, still less to alter.[18] For MacIntyre, we have reached a point where we can no longer realise the nature of the catastrophe we have suffered – which is the loss of any comprehension, theoretical or practical, of our moral situation.[19]

Whatever the reason, it is a truncated, one-sided, conception of

30

social order that is conveyed by modern writers such as Dunn and MacIntyre and is generally reflected in contemporary accounts of social order – especially that given by Erving Goffman. It is presented as a finished system which we individually acknowledge by obeying its rules, quite different from the idea of social order that prevailed in early modern times, as well as in the distant past, a social order with which members of a society felt obliged to conform, but which they also were responsible for maintaining and, if they saw need, changing.

Social order – his version of it – bulks much larger in his writings than the view of individual behaviour as histrionic performance given in his first and best-known book. (*The Presentation of Self in Everyday Life* is best regarded, I think as a kind of rider to his account of the social order which sustains the everyday life the self is presented in. It was in any case an interpretation which was substantially revised in his longest and most ambitious book, *Frame Analysis*.) There are many dimensions of social order, some of which Goffman wants specifically to include within the scope of his own model: the kind of order which prevails changes, as society changes; also, while social order – of a sort – is maintained in every society (that being one of the features which define a society), the kind of social order maintained and the ways in which it is maintained differ from society to society; it can also vary, in the case of a larger society, between different regions, communities, social milieux, and classes of the same society – and between different social occasions involving the same sort of individuals, or even the same individuals.

Social order comprehends the accommodations arrived at between all these variations and contingent circumstances, as well as the overall orderliness we normally expect, or hope, to encounter in everyday public life – an orderliness which is characteristic of any society with some claims to stability. There are, of course, plenty of times and occasions when it breaks down or is broken; plenty of individuals who flout it, and a few who exploit it for ulterior purposes; but what is important, Goffman insists, is that there is a readiness on the part of most people to see order restored, whenever it has been disrupted.

In this first phase of his career, it turns out that Goffman's conception of the comprehensiveness and importance to be attached to social order is not very far removed from what social philosophers and most sociologists have accorded to it, and still do, even when it became the one-sided version we now have. And this opens the door to all the traditional problems: not only "how is society possible?" but how is social order, once established, maintained in face of all the entrenched inequality, flagrant injustice, discriminatory practices, political dissension, blatant acquisitiveness, dis-order and violence which pervades society – our own, as well as virtually all others, past and present? How – or how far – does social order reflect the complex attachments and hostilities within the family, in kinship systems, in the neighbourhood or the community; or the exploitative relationships embodied in power and authority in the organisations and institutions which constitute the scenes and settings of individual lives – and of social interaction?

Questions of this kind were undoubtedly implicit, if seldom quite explicit, in the criticisms made by some reviewers and commentators during the sixties and seventies. There are answers which might be made, but Goffman did not give them. Instead, when he returned to the general theme of social interaction in his presidential address to the ASA, he used the occasion to reduce the scope of what he had earlier variously (and fairly indiscriminately) called 'social order', 'public order' or 'social organisation' to the more modest 'interaction order'. The interaction order is merely one of several domains. The economic order is another domain. Social interaction itself is now defined as 'that which uniquely transpires in social situations, that is, environments in which two or more individuals are physically in one another's response presence'.[20]

To make sure that the baby really has been thrown out with the bath water, he reduces the significance of the interaction order still further. As the notion that the interaction order is to be construed as either the manufacturing plant or the shop window of the macroscopic features of society is found to be 'uncongenial', he urges his audience to regard social interaction as a somehow autonomous order of social action, only loosely connected with the major organisational or institutional building blocks of the social structure:

> In sum, to speak of the relatively autonomous forms of life in the interaction order . . . is not to put forward these forms as somehow prior, fundamental, or constitutive of the shape of macroscopic phenomena.[21]

IV

Despite the problems with Goffman's glossary of terms (and his later uncertainties about the connection between the study of "societal" factors and his chosen field of "microsociology"), it is useful to start with *Behavior in Public Places*. It is the longest of this first group of essays, and, having the broadest coverage, it serves as a kind of central lobby for the early essays on social interaction reprinted in *Interaction Ritual*. There are exits and entrances in its pages which connect it with these earlier essays. In them one finds bravura treatments and more detailed explorations of the rules and rituals of conduct and of the ways in which they may be broken, or may break down, and initial sketches or detailed miniatures of many of the themes incorporated in the book.

Behavior in Public Places is easy to read, as all his writings are, yet is one of the most difficult to come to grips with. The first chapter is filled with classificatory definitions which seem to promise a catalogue *raisonnée* of the details of everyday sociability. This is not, in fact, on offer. Detailed as his analysis can be, Goffman's writings on face-to-face encounters do not, as I have already said, constitute anything like a complete taxonomy either of encounters themselves or of the constituent elements he proposes for analysing them; for this, one has to go to a text like Michael Argyle's *Social Interaction*. There are fewer entertaining curiosities, and the mock pedantry, when it comes, can descend into heavy-handed (and, sometimes, slightly erratic) facetiousness – as with the 'assistance to developing hilarity, sadness or grimness' offered by 'pharmacological agencies such as alcohol' (p. 175). The opening chapter devoted to definitions, besides being mildly offputting, also contains some inconsistencies and confusions. And, at first reading, keeping track of the minutiae of sociable interaction does become a little tiresome.

So it takes some persistence, and a second reading, before one grasps how novel an enterprise in sociography *Behaviour in Public Places* is. Everyday social behaviour – "manners" – is taken as itself systematically constituted, as subject-matter worth studying for its own sake, and not as evidence of either primitive or sophisticated mentality, or of human variability or ethical relatively, nor as the surface manifestation of the structure of kinship or power relationships. The main thrust is towards the elucidation of the principles by which social order is maintained.

Goffman, in the preface to *Encounters*, as well as in *Behavior in Public Places*, is careful to distinguish his subject-matter – encounters, gatherings, and the social interaction that occurs in them – from what is called 'collective behaviour' (crowds, mobs, panics, riots and the like), from social groups and religious or political movements, and from laboratory studies of small groups. It is the unfocused interactions and spontaneous involvements that constitute everyday social life which are his main concern.

Making up a terminology for this particular purpose faces him with the familiar difficulty of choosing between technical terms, neologisms of his own making, and familiar words in common currency. Since the social experiences he wants to discuss are familiar and commonplace (and also, perhaps, because he wants to steer clear of the terminology developed for psychological experimentation), he adopts the second alternative. A number of pages are devoted to shaking off the looseness and imprecision of common usage. The set of terms he worked out in this book was retained throughout his writing career, so it is worth while rehearsing them briefly.

The public order he proposes to deal with in *Behavior in Public Places* is that which prevails in *social gatherings*, a term which stands for 'any set of two or more individuals who are in one another's immediate presence' (p. 18). It may be a committee meeting, a political rally, a *tête-à-tête* conversation, a lecture, a party, the people (all of them, customers and waiters) in a restaurant, or the people (patients, nurses, physicians, technicians, paramedical and domestic staff) in a hospital ward. There is very often an occasion for a social gathering, making it a *social occasion*, with a motive, purpose or function which accounts for people's copresence. Some of the terms used for the different kinds of gathering are in fact names for different sorts of occasion for gatherings; others refer to places like restaurants and hospitals with a specific and familiar social function. So, what constitutes proper conduct and demeanour in different kinds of gatherings is a question decided for the most part by the kind of social occasion they denote.

Not all gatherings are "occasioned". The same social space – the streets, parks and other open spaces of a city – may serve as the location for a variety of gatherings, some with specific, though different occasions, but all mingling with each other or with boundaries which are vague or easily crossed. Nevertheless, a social gathering, wherever or however it occurs, necessarily takes place in a specific setting (*situation*); by definition, anyone present in that situation, or entering it, is automatically a member of the gathering. But the presence of others *in* the same situation – workmen engaged

34

in repair work in a street or in an office building, for example – may be relatively, though never quite, inconsequential.

So a distinction has to be made between 'merely-situated' and 'situated' interaction. The first is characteristic of *unfocused* situations, where the presence of others may be incidental and irrelevant to any individual's activities; interaction in such cases typically amounts to no more than passing awareness of the presence, appearance and behaviour of others who happen, perhaps momentarily, to be within seeing or hearing distance. In 'situated' activities, the presence of others is actually a prerequisite. 'Situated' activity is 'intrinsically dependent' on the conditions that prevail in the situation.

This is fairly clear; but trouble arises when he goes on to give examples of what he means, the nuances he introduces making the distinctions well-nigh indecipherable. However, it is enough that, however situated or merely-situated social activity might be, as soon as persons are in the presence of others, their conduct comes under some sort of rule of public order: 'Copresence renders persons uniquely accessible, available, and subject to one another. Public order, in its face-to-face aspects, has to do with the normative regulation of this accessibility' (*BP*, 22). The most obvious kind of normative regulation, and that which has received by far the most attention, has to do with the safety of persons and property. But Goffman's concern is

> with the fact that when persons are present to one another they can function not merely as physical instruments but also as communicative ones. This possibility, no less than the physical one, is fateful for everyone concerned, and in every society appears to come under strict normative regulation, giving rise to a kind of communicative traffic order.
>
> (*BP*, 23-4)

It is this kind of communicative order, too, against which symptoms of mental illness are, for the most part, regarded as offences – as 'situational improprieties'.

Towards the end of the introductory chapter of definitions, Goffman lists four general properties of what is reckoned to be situational propriety. One intriguing aspect of these four "general" properties of situational propriety is how very specific they are. The first ('an air of controlled alertness') is one of the distinguishing marks of the managerial and professional middle class that he gave as his general area of reference. The *absence* of the last (attentiveness, and 'readiness to respond to any new developments and new departures in the situation') is said to be a familiar pointer to the improprieties of conduct characteristic of the mentally defective and the mentally ill. The account of these "general properties" introduces an element of caricature into his picture of situational propriety; they are not so preposterous, certainly, as that of the norm of American masculinity he pictures in *Stigma* (see p. 216, below), but the flavour of overeager sociability is entertainingly authentic.

V

Our familiar and commonplace experience of the behaviour of people in public, or in the company of others, are characterised for the most part by orderliness – as, of course, it has to be. This orderliness, says Goffman, is maintained by the observance of rules governing behaviour in public. These rules apply not to the ends sought by participant individuals nor to any consequent patterns of relationships, but to the ways in which those ends may be pursued. In this they are rather like traffic rules, which are concerned with how you go, not with where you are going.

Goffman in fact uses traffic rules as a paradigm for the systems of rules which uphold public order. The traffic rules he has in mind are not, or not so much, the code of rules pertaining to motor cars, which has the force of law, but the observances followed by pedestrians in busy streets, even though both laws and observances have much the same purpose. Pedestrians form traffic lanes on the pavements; overtaking is permissible, but there is an overall, and usually well-observed, requirement that people make their own way along crowded pavements without colliding, obstructing or interfering with other people's passage. This they do by making their own intended moves readable by means of continuous, though unobtrusive, 'overall body-signals' and, conversely, by continuously scanning the signals given out by other pedestrians.

The topic of vehicular and pedestrian traffic rules, which is touched on only briefly in *Behavior in Public Places*, is resumed and dealt with more extensively in *Relations in Public* (pp. 5-18). If the traffic code for pedestrians in crowded streets is taken to be one small, though significant, aspect of the requirements by which public orderliness is maintained, then the social order that people sustain when they are together is visible as a matter of the observance of rules of conduct and demeanour which people regard as obligatory whenever and wherever others are present. The rules governing conduct in social interchanges, while employing much the same sort of communicative mechanisms, are generally less immediately obvious and more complex than those observed by pedestrians; they are also more exacting and far more numerous. They concern not merely the avoidance of collisions, obstructions, interference and other kinds of disruption and awkwardness but the observance of social propriety.

The fundamental importance which attaches to the rules governing social interaction is not spelled out at much length in *Behavior in Public Places*, perhaps because it had already been enlarged upon in earlier papers. 'The rules of conduct which bind the actor and the recipient [of deference] together', we are told, in "The Nature of Deference and Demeanour", for example, 'are the bindings of society' (*IR*, 90). In fact, the exhaustive analysis of deference and demeanour is as good a demonstration as any of the bonding effects which the rules of social order produce. They are, to begin with, complementary observances. Deferential behaviour has a reference external to the interaction, tacitly invoking the place in the wider society occupied by the other, or others, present. Demeanour refers more to the way in which a person manages his own part in an encounter rather than the rank of the others relative to his. Each mode of conduct serves as 'warrant or justification' for a display of the other; the complementarity of the two makes them mutually reinforcing: 'by treating others deferentially, one gives them an opportunity to handle the indulgence with good demeanour' (*IR*, 83), thus spreading 'a constant flow of indulgences . . . throughout society'. Through them, 'the world tends to be bathed in better images than any one deserves' (*IR*, 91).

Observing social propriety is as much a matter of general demeanour as of behaviour, and here the whole conception of comportment, or demeanour, is translated from the static (and banal) significance attached to it in ordinary discourse to become a complex of technical skills by which an individual is credited with being an acceptable, socialised, person. In short, the individual is expected to display 'poise'. The word has acquired an altered meaning – a less specific reference – since "On Cooling the Mark Out". It is now simply a capacity to retain composure, not the skilful exercise of tact or graciousness. 'During interaction, the individual is expected to possess certain attributes, capacities, and information which, taken together, fit into a self that is at once coherently unified and appropriate for the occasion' (*IR*, 105).

Just as the rules which have to be followed for social intercourse to be orderly are more elaborate than those which obtain for pedestrian traffic, so the flow of information exchanged is more detailed and complex – immensely so, in fact. Non-verbal communications – which have to do with physical appearance, facial expression, gesture and bodily movement – have a significance ascribed to them in all situations. (Indeed, as Michael Argyle remarks, "interpersonal attitudes are communicated far more effectively by non-verbal than by verbal signals; where the two are in conflict the verbal message is virtually ignored."[22]) In company, an individual is always at least half-aware that some aspects of his appearance and actions are available for anyone else present to read and interpret (just as theirs are to the individual), and, with this in mind, tends to modify them, so that they are in conformity with the impression the individual wants to convey. Such communications are broadcast. They cannot easily be shielded, or focused on particular recipients, but may be seen and, what is more, interpreted, by everyone present, because they are conveyed through 'body idiom' – a conventionalised form of non-verbal discourse – which is by far the most significant component of behaviour in public. For although 'an individual can stop talking, he cannot stop communicating through body idiom; he must say either the right thing or the wrong thing. He cannot say nothing' (*BP*, 35).

'Body idiom' is the all-inclusive term Goffman uses for 'dress, bearing, movements and position, sound level, physical gestures such as waving or saluting, facial decorations, and broad emotional expressions' (*BP*, 33). Broadcast for everyone present to see these may be, but they are often enough directed consciously and specifically at an individual or group. Employing it to express deference is one kind of ceremonial convention by which an individual conveys his appreciation of others present and, at the same time, places himself in the social context they represent. Deferential behaviour, which is often a matter of mutual exchange, is as much a matter of communication through demeanour and body idiom as it is of words and action.

Again, to take a slightly more recondite example, "catching someone's eye" across a room is an extraordinarily fleeting and minute matter, yet somehow quite unmistakable. An even more lightweight item of body idiom is involved in what Goffman calls 'civil inattention', which belongs to the same communication code, but lies at the other end of its range, so to speak. 'Civil inattention' is the mutual 'eye-catching' exchange with which one person admits seeing another but makes it prefatory to 'at the next moment withdrawing one's attention from him so as to express that he does not constitute a target of special curiosity or design'. Unfortunately, he goes on to assert that, in pedestrian traffic, the signal takes the modified form of 'eyeing the other up to approximately eight feet, during which sides of the street are apportioned . . . and then casting the eyes down as the other passes – a kind of dimming of lights' (*BP*, 84). This constitutes a rare, though not unique, instance of his overreaching himself in his dedicated trawling of the minutiae of observed behaviour; a perpetual alertness for recognition signals may be warrantable on the Berkeley campus or a useful precaution in disreputable urban quarters, but anyone attempting this in a crowded city-centre street would run the risk of colliding with a dozen other passers-by – or perhaps of being arrested.

Despite this lapse, civil inattention is something of a prize addition to Goffman's conceptual armoury. It is a refinement of Simmel's notion of ritual space ("ideal sphere") alluding to the adjustment of distance that people tend to make when they approach or pass by others. It also connects with Durkheim's conception, invoked in previous papers, of the sacredness of the human person. But it transcends the rather generalised levels of both Simmel and Durkheim in pointing to the positive, paralinguistic uses to which body movements of all kinds are put. Civil inattention, which requires so delicate an adjustment, carries a relatively heavy load of significance – something clearly evident when the rules which apply to it are broken – when an individual 'looks through' another, and so treats him as non-existent, a 'non-person'. Ostentatiously 'looking through' someone is as much a breach of civility as staring at him. Between calls to display deferential appreciation and polite avoidance, there is, in fact, as he remarks in "The Nature of Deference and Demeanor", an 'inescapable opposition, and therefore a 'peculiar tension . . . held apart, yet realised together' (*IR*, 76).

VI

There is throughout the whole sequence of writings discussed in these three first chapters a thoroughgoing effort to define social, and public, order, to identify what is meant by them, and to classify the elements and characteristic features of the rituals and rules through which order is sustained. In so doing, Goffman sketches out a rationale for those elements and their characteristics, a rationale which is essentially Durkheimian.

The grounding of Goffman's work on social interaction in an essentially Durkheimian view of society is (since it is stated and restated in almost every one of the earlier papers) familiar enough. "The Nature of Deference and Demeanor", for example, refers to the codes of rules of behaviour which obtain in every society, codes which *guarantee* that everyone acts appropriately and receives his due. Among these codes are some which are elevated into systems of substantive rules, and become law. Others, equally binding when it comes to face-to-face interaction, govern morality (and ethics, he adds at one point!) and, of course, the ceremonial behaviour towards others which is encoded in etiquette.

If social encounters have a structure – and they unquestionably do – then rules provide it. 'I fall back on the assumption that, like any other element in social life, an encounter exhibits sanctioned orderliness arising from obligations fulfilled and expectations realised, and that therein lies its structure' (*E*, 19).

In "The Nature of Deference and Demeanor" he writes of rules imposing a kind of "oughtness" on people, rules of conduct being a guide for action which is 'recommended not because it is pleasant, cheap, or effective, but because it is suitable or just' (*IR*, 48). In this context, maintaining a rule tends to commit one to an image of self, so that one becomes, to oneself and to others, "the sort of person who . . .". Following a rule thus becomes a communicative act, expressive of the self the individual is presenting on that occasion.

At its crudest, Goffman's conception of these rules treats them as a regulatory system imposed on individuals by some ultimate authority called "Society". Thus, in the characteristic moralising end-piece which concludes "On Face-Work" – an essay which dates from the same year, 1956, as "The Nature of Deference and Demeanor" – one finds:

> Throughout this paper it has been implied that underneath their difference in culture, people everywhere are the same. If persons have a universal human nature, they themselves are not to be looked to for an explanation of it. One must look rather to the fact that societies everywhere, if they are to be societies, must

mobilise their members as self-regulating participants in social encounters. One way of mobilizing the individual for this purpose is through ritual; he is taught to be perceptive, to have feelings attached to self and a self expressed through face, to have pride, honour, and dignity, to have considerateness, to have tact and a certain amount of poise. . . .

Universal human nature is not a very human thing. By acquiring it, *the person becomes a kind of construct, built up not from inner psychic propensities but from moral rules that are impressed upon him from without* (emphasis added). . . . And if a particular person or group or society seems to have a unique character all its own, it is because its standard set of human-nature elements is pitched and combined in a particular way.

(IR, 44-5)

None of this is very satisfactory. Even at the level of interpreting – "making sense of" – individual behaviour in ordinary social intercourse, the idea of conduct as entirely rule-bound is difficult to swallow. This is especially so when one comes across some of the qualifications Goffman inserts.

The code followed by pedestrians in busy streets is put forward as a useful paradigm of the rules he has in mind. This, he says, is because he is, in *Behavior in Public Places*, dealing 'not so much with a network of rules that must be followed as with rules that must be taken into consideration, whether as something to follow or carefully to circumvent' (p. 42). This last phrase, 'carefully to circumvent', catches an ambiguity which dogs Goffman's notion of rules throughout this group of writings. "Circumventing" rules has a delinquent air about it, less perhaps than breaking them or cheating, but still of disobedience to the spirit in which the ruling authority – "Society" – means us to obey them. The impression of society as a governing authority, superior and alien to the individuals who constitute it, is heightened rather than diminished.

The ambiguities multiply when one finds that the onus can shift towards individual participation as a matter of "tacit agreement", implying, as it does, something in the nature of a social contract: 'A person's performance in face-work, extended by his tacit agreement to help others perform theirs, represents his 'willingness to abide by the ground rules of social intercourse. Here is the hallmark of his socialisation as an interactant' *(IR, 31)*. References to the individual's 'willingness to abide by the ground rules' seem to imply conformity

41

with the general will of society, a sense, almost, of a social contract after the manner of Rousseau, rather than of obedience to impersonal authority.

But the whiffs of contractualism are faint and rare. It is, after all, difficult to reconcile a contractualist view with one that regards the individual, in the words quoted earlier, as 'a kind of construct, built up not from inner psychic propensities but from moral rules that are impressed upon him from without'. Mostly, in these early papers, one's impression is of governing power exerted by a reified, even deified, "Society".

The trouble is that although "rules are rules", as they say, the meaning of the word hardly has the inflexibility that the common saying seems to attach to it. One finds a variability in different contexts and situations. Goffman exploits the variability but does not come clean about it. In games, which he makes so much of, breaking the rules either attracts penalties or makes it impossible to continue. They are hardly something one 'takes into consideration, whether as something to follow or carefully to circumvent'.

Decisions about whether to follow the rules of social order or to circumvent them *do*, however, rest on the weight given to different sets of considerations. Which throws a different light on the rules of conduct, making them rather more a matter for the kind of assessment and adjudication implied in Goffman's later remarks about them than for the compulsive obedience he suggested in the first place. And this, in turn, gives back to the individual some of the autonomy of which those earlier pronouncements deprived him.

VII

If following a rule becomes a communicative act, expressive of the self the individual is presenting (above, p. 38), this raises the question of the nature of the self that is simply an expression of the rules governing individual behaviour. The answer supplied by Goffman is uncompromising and drastic. His vision of a rule-governed social order has its counterpart in the image of a socially constructed self. The original entity of autonomous selfhood which one feels (perhaps for no good reason) one was born with surrenders its uniqueness and significance. It manifests itself in appropriate responses to the company it keeps and to the physical setting, the mental configuration, the emotional charge, of the social situation in which it finds itself. The rational conclusion comes in a passage in one of the essays in *Asylums*, where he suggests that even in 'free' society, all that is left of the individual self is often what 'resides in the cracks . . . of the solid buildings of the world' (*A*, 320). And again, 'Universal human nature is not a very human thing. By acquiring it, the person becomes a kind of construct, built up not from inner psychic propensities but from moral rules that are impressed upon him from without' (*IR*, 45).

"Rule" is of course a very Durkheimian term, but it was also, thirty years ago, favoured by linguists. Social interaction typically involves conversation after all, and references to "the grammar and syntax" of social encounters and of social order show clearly enough the source of Goffman's usage. And the same usage seemed positively authenticated by the currency that Wittgenstein's notion of language games and their "rules" enjoyed. But since then its appropriateness for both linguistic and social behaviour has been put to question.

The picture we now have is, I believe, rather too complex to be covered by rules. To go back to his own starting-point, the account of pedestrian traffic on busy city streets treats the whole process very much as if it was a straightforward communication system, with signals exchanged between individuals conversant with the rules of pedestrian traffic. But what each person is looking for and reading in the faces and 'overall body-signals' of other pedestrians are very specific messages about the direction they are aiming for and how swiftly or forcefully they mean to get there. It is their *intentions* in these very limited respects that are being read – not their character, their mood, or anything else that might well engage our attention in other circumstances.

The fact that it is intentions (as well as other kinds of meanings, including indexical) that we read in pedestrian traffic – or in any kind of encounter – introduces a further set of complications. Utterances and non-linguistic expressions have (at least) two levels of meaning. If we follow H. P. Grice,[23] there is a margin between the "natural" or "timeless" meaning of an utterance (i.e. when heard or read independently of any other specific social connection between utterer and recipient), and the "non-natural" meaning it bears when it is directed to specific others on a specific occasion. The margin is filled with the intentions of the utterer and also with the recognition of them by the recipient, such recognition being part of the intentions of the utterer. "Non-natural" utterances, in fact, often mean no more than a vague *something*, a something which is not contained altogether

43

in the words but requires recognition of the utterer's intention.

More steps towards clarification are supplied by a well-known paper of Gilbert Ryle's, "The Thinking of Thoughts",[24] one of several which appeared as a sort of serial appendix to the *The Concept of Mind*. This introduced the term "thick description" to denote the multiplicity of layers of meaning which can accumulate on any kind of physical act which lends itself to being employed and construed as expressive social action. "Thick description", admittedly a not very precise expression, suffers also from having been taken up and used in a number of different ways, often at some remove from what Ryle had in mind.

Ryle's interest, like Grice's, is in intentions, especially the nuances and complexities we seem able to read in them. The illustrative example he uses is the way we attach a quite different meaning to, say, a wink as against a blink. There is a difference we *know* to exist between the involuntary twitch of one eyelid, a nervous response to some irritation or nervous impulse, directed to nobody at all, and a wink, which is a signal, a coded message to someone in particular. Yet they are, to all appearances ("objectively"), both precisely the same. It is in the *significance* we read into the one and into the other that the difference lies. Nor is this all. A third possibility is for a wink to be parodied; a fourth for a novice at winking to practice before a mirror, a fifth for a novice parodist to practice "taking-off" someone else's wink.

There are other levels in what Ryle calls the pyramid of learned accomplishment – for none of these higher level winks can be attempted or brought off without knowledge of, or skill at, reading precisely the same physical action at a "lower" level. At the end of the paper he points to the corresponding difference which obtains between a statesman writing the letters of his name and signing a peace treaty. In both examples, an identical physical action carries widely differing interpretations. This is where description has to acquire "thickness". What is involved is akin to the notion of keying which Goffman introduces in *Frame Analysis*, but incorporates the step-by-step process of experiential learning by which what we call sophistication is acquired. This is essential. "By no pedagogic ingenuities could you teach a child what stealing is before teaching him what owning is; or teach a boy to parody a wink before teaching him to wink and recognise winks."[25] It is not a matter of learning rules. The variety of expressive meanings (and understandings) that can be read into exactly the same physical action is something which has to be built up by experiencing successive – and progressive – interaction between individuals.

In situations where two persons come into contact (or operate "within the same social field") for the first time, what one of them does is important largely as an indication of what he "seems to be up to". Very often, it is reading intentions that matters rather than straightforward indexical or other meanings – and this, as Grice shows, is no easy matter. What seems to happen between passers-by, or in sudden encounters or first meetings between strangers, is that knowledge of each other's intentions is followed, if things go right, by the realisation that this knowledge is mutual, and so on. What could develop is an infinite regression of mirrored awareness of intent and purpose – "I know that you know that I know . . . etc., etc.", with any possibility of action foundering in a psychological impasse.

But this kind of regression, although it can happen (as when two pedestrians dither between passing by each other to the left or the right), hardly ever does. Instead, awareness becomes imputed, as it were, to social orderliness and the desire to sustain it. In place of the impossible overload of signal decoding, information-reading, analysis, and decision-making in single one-to-one relationships between strangers, something akin to Ryle's "pyramid" of sophisticated awareness based on previous experiences takes over. For simplicity's sake, one can group them into three levels. *Routines, conventions*, or *understandings* are developed which guide, or prompt, behaviour in situations involving people whose relationship is of varying degrees of distance or familiarity. They are impersonal, but only in the sense that it is on them that one relies *in the first instance*, rather than going through the complexities of interpreting the other's intention or purpose. At the "lowest" level, so to speak, *routines* are learned in the first place by observation and replication; *conventions* embody guidelines which people see themselves and others as "following", but which are applicable in analogous, not merely identical, situations; *understandings* are purpose-built, constructed by acquaintances, by friends and by enemies, lovers and rivals, husbands and wives, children and parents, among themselves. The three are, naturally, selections from a much more complicated "pyramid" of mutual comprehension; they are, that is, conjugated in some layered arrangement, with understandings providing the necessary base, but overlaid by conventions and they, in turn, by routines. All are susceptible to upset by some untoward circumstance, and so to displacement and search for a new reciprocity of meaning and comprehension, or to replacement by some other routine, convention, or understanding.

These notions taken from Grice and from Ryle are being interpolated not as contradictory evidence to Goffman's main theme but to supplement it, and to point towards a modification of his Durkheimian explanation. This is a matter which will be resumed later, and some final remarks appended in the final chapter. For the time being, it is I hope sufficient to see in Grice's idea of intentionality and Ryle's conception of a "pyramid" of sophistication in reading intentions a suggestion that there is more *structure* to be reckoned with in encounters than Goffman's two levels of "situated" and "merely-situated".

NOTES AND REFERENCES

1. A. L. Stinchcombe, "Social structure and organizations" in *Handbook of Organizations* (ed. J. G. March), Rand McNally, 1965, pp. 142-93.
2. Marquis de Condorcet, *Sketch for a Historical Picture of the Progress of the Human Mind*, 1795; trans. J. Barraclough, Weidenfeld & Nicholson, 1955, p. 4.
3. P. M. Blau "Objectives of sociology", in *A Design for Sociology* (ed. R. Bierstedt), American Academy of Political and Social Sciences, Monograph No. 9, 1969, pp. 50 and 51.
4. M. Mandelbaum, "Societal facts", *British Journal of Sociology*, vol. 6, 1955, pp. 305-17.
5. See, for example, R. F. Bales, *Interaction Process Analysis*, Addison-Wesley, 1950, and H. V. Leavitt, "Some effects of certain communication patterns on group performance", *Journal of Abnormal Psychology*, 1951, pp. 28-50.
6. M. Argyle, *Social Interaction*, Methuen, 1969, p. 18.
7. E. Goffman, "The interaction order", *American Sociological Review*, vol. 48, 1983, pp. 1-17.
8. A. W. Gouldner, "Organizational analysis", in *Sociology Today* (eds R. K. Merton, L. Broom and L. S. Cotrell Jr), Basic Books, 1959, pp. 400-28.
9. L. von Bertalanffy, "General systems theory", *General Systems*, vol. 1, 1956, pp. 1-10.
10. J. von Neumann and O. Morgenstern, *Theory of Games and Economic Behaviour*, Princeton Univ. Press, 1944.
11. D. H. Wrong, *Skeptical Sociology*, Heinemann, 1977, p. 33.
12. V. Ehrenberg, *From Solon to Socrates*, Methuen, 1968, pp. 38-9.
13. H. J. F. Jones, *On Aristotle and Greek Tragedy*, Chatto & Windus, 1962, p. 33.

14. P. Laslett, "The face-to-face society", in *Philosophy, Politics and Society: First Series* (ed. P. Laslett), Blackwell, 1956, p. 162.
15. See G. R. Morrow, "The significance of the doctrine of sympathy in Hume and Adam Smith", *Philosophical Review*, vol. 32, 1923.
16. D. Forbes, *Hume's Philosophical Politics*, Cambridge Univ. Press, 1975.
17. Amartya Sen, *Ethics and Economics*, Blackwell, 1928, p. 24. See also "Adam Smith's Prudence", in S. Lall and F. Stewart, *Theory and Reality in Development*, Macmillan, 1986.
18. J. Dunn, "The concept of 'trust' in the politics of John Locke", in *Philosophy and History* (ed. R. Rorty, J. B. Schneewind and Q. Skinner), Cambridge Univ. Press, 1984, p. 284.
19. A. MacIntyre, *After Virtue*, Duckworth, 1981, p. 4.
20. E. Goffman, "The interaction order", *American Sociological Review*, vol. 48, 1983, p. 4.
21. E. Goffman, "The interaction order", *American Sociological Review*, vol. 48, 1983, pp. 8-9.
22. M. Argyle, "Non-verbal communication and language", in *Communication and Understanding* (ed. G. Vesey), Royal Institute of Philosophy Lectures, vol. 10, 1975-6, Harvester Press, 1977, p. 65.
23. H. P. Grice, "Meaning", *Philosophical Review*, 1957, pp. 377-88, and "Utterer's meaning and intentions", *Philosophical Review*, 1969, pp. 147-77.
24. G. Ryle, "The thinking of thoughts: What is 'le penseur' doing?", in *Collected Papers*, vol. 2, Hutchinson, 1971, pp. 480-96.
25. G. Ryle, "The thinking of thoughts: What is 'le penseur' doing?", in *Collected Papers*, vol. 2, Hutchinson, 1971, pp. 494.

3

INVOLVEMENT, INTERDEPENDENCE, AND ALIENATION

Clifford Geertz, in the review of developments in the social sciences and the humanities quoted earlier, places Goffman firmly among those influenced principally by what he calls "the game analogy". Despite his frequent use of dramatistic language, "as his view of the theatre is that it is an oddly mannered kind of interaction game – ping-pong in masks – his work is not, at base dramaturgical", Goffman draws instead, says Geertz, on game-imagery, which is applied "to just about everything he can lay his hands on, which, as he is no respecter of property rights, is a very great deal".[1] Game-imagery, he says, comes from a number of different sources, but the most important "are Wittgenstein's conception of forms of life as language games, Huizinga's ludic view of culture, and the new strategies of von Neuman's and Morgenstern's *Theory of Games and Economic Behaviour*".[2]

As well as making free with "everything he could lay his hands on" to use as illustrative material, Goffman was quite prepared to pick up and put to use any number of analogies (the confidence trick, for one) and classificatory systems of ideas drawn from other disciplines (e.g. animal behaviour studies). He did use all three prime sources of imagery Geertz mentions – theatre, ritual, and games – but he also went to some trouble to distinguish their uses and application. Further, he uses the notion of 'play' developed by Huizinga (and by Piaget and Jerome Bruner) in ways quite distinct from those to which the 'theory of games' is applied.

That said, it has also to be said that Goffman does seem on occasion almost to treat 'ritual' and 'game' as interchangeable terms. But this is not because he was slipshod in his use of words. It has to do, I believe, with a central ambiguity in his treatment of social order, and this, in turn, with his preoccupation with what I have called "discovery" rather than with ordering what his empirical pursuits discovered in terms of some comprehensive "theory".

The ambiguity lies in the relationship of the individual to society (sc. "the social order"). In most of his early writings, as I have already said, he tended to extend and amplify the essentially Durkheimian view of the individual as the creature – almost the puppet – of "society" (or "societal facts"). "Society" is seen as taking an operationally very positive part not only in social intercourse between individuals, but in their affairs, their careers and the formation of their characters. Play, games, and ritual become – almost – means devised by "society" to enliven its creatures' lives with absorbing interests ("Fun in Games"), to provide the rich glow of "character" so as to encourage them into achievements which exemplify traits useful to society ("Where the Action Is"), and to endow their behaviour with a significance for the maintenance of social order which goes far beyond the polite amenities of every day ("The Nature of Deference and Demeanour"). One mark – which I take to be significant – of this propensity is the frequent use, throughout the bulk of his earlier writings, of 'society' and 'societies' as the subject of transitive verbs. The collection of papers published under the title *Interaction Ritual*, for example, begins with an account of ritual as one of the ways in which '*societies mobilise their members* as self-regulating participants in social encounters' (*IR*, 44; emphasis added). It ends with a lengthy essay on gambling, risk-taking and 'character-contests', all of which are important '*if society is to make use of the individual*' (*IR* 259; emphasis added).

Rules of the kind which do indeed obtain in games and play govern the social order of Goffman's early writings, but they are for the most part imposed on individuals by "Society" acting as supreme and impersonal legislative authority. They are not presented to him as something arrived at through the operation of intersubjective consciousness between ordinary individuals or of the peculiar configuration of human minds, still less as the formal, written, or made-up rules of board games, cards, sporting contests, or the unspoken 'frame' which discriminates playing from serious activity.

But in *Strategic Interaction*, the relationship of the individual to social order is seemingly reversed. Social order is made to appear the *consequence* of the 'organizational necessity' (*SI*, 130) of trust. In fact, Goffman comes close to John Locke's[3] and Niklas Luhmann's[4] perception of trust as a cognitive, rational, indeed calculative, mechanism, though not as a means to cooperation (Locke), or as a buffer against disappointed hopes and expectations (Luhmann), but simply to provide a basis for individuals to deal with – even talk to – each other (*SI*, 135).

So, rather than trying to identify the source of Goffman's idea of society among the metaphorical images of ritual, drama, play, and games, it is simpler to acknowledge that he had little respect for the boundary fences that their followers have erected around the ground staked out by the more adventurous lateral thinkers who, by pursuing analogical and metaphorical lines of thought beyond the point their predecessors and most of their contemporaries have thought reasonable, have discovered new and fertile territory.

II

There are of course gradations in the extent to which conduct is 'situated', and therefore required to be appropriate in ways specific to the situation. Gatherings in the street – or a restaurant, or a large church, or an entrance hall or lobby – may comprehend two or more occasions occurring simultaneously. Consequently, those present in the same situation and in the one gathering may yet be involved wholly or partially in one occasion out of two or more; they may indeed be involved in more than one of the occasions.

Because there may be two or more occasions in the same gathering, the involvement which makes participating in the social interaction proper to one rather than some other occasion has to be demonstrated. At the same time, the presence of others who may not be involved in the same occasion has to be acknowledged; and this acknowledgement, too, needs to be expressed. Here, and in other instances, the conduct of people present in a gathering has to accord with the social proprieties appropriate not only for the situation and the gathering as a whole, but also for the occasion which entitles them to be present. They have to be involved as participants *and* as bystanders, and to show that they are.

A good deal of attention, and space, is devoted to involvement in *Behavior in Public Places*; even so, much of the point will be missed unless that treatment is coupled with the discussion of involvement in "Fun and Games", published two years earlier. This essay is also a consideration of the structure of gatherings, but, because it deals exclusively with focused gatherings, involvement is a central topic: hence games, since these characteristically *demand* the involvement of participants. It is in games that participants, professing obedience to the rules, immerse themselves in the same little world to the point of appearing to discard any other consideration or interest – pecuniary, emotional or aesthetic. Games put a "frame" around a particular set of objects or sequence of events, with the "frame" determining what sense has to be made of everything within it (p. 20).

The same concept of 'framing', which Goffman took from Bateson, was later elaborated into a complicated interpretative account of experience and perception in his longest book, *Frame Analysis*. In this context, however, 'framing' means 'adhering to rules of irrelevance'. These determine the properties of the situation at large which are to be treated as irrelevant, out of frame or simply not happening.

There follows a notable instance of Goffman's tendency to overbid on the hand he claims to have been dealt by Durkheim. While Durkheim argued that society was imbued with a collective moral consciousness from which individuals drew their own consciousness of the regulatory norms it was proper to observe, Goffman credits "society" with sovereign command over human affairs. For the fact that attention can be so withdrawn from the world "outside" the game, he says, is a striking tribute to the way in which human propensities may be made subject to social organisation (*E*, 20). This really is to get things back to front. So far as attention and inattention are concerned, 'human propensities' come first, and social organisation has little to do with it. For it is a psychological commonplace that (to use a familiar reference),

> It is of the essence of attention that it is selective. We can focus on *something* in our field of vision, but never on *everything*. All attention must take place against a background of inattention. A heightened awareness of reality as such is something mystics may dream about, but cannot realise. . . . To see at all, we must isolate and select.[5]

Second, games generate 'a matrix of possible events and a cast of roles' which admit of only certain properties of the events, persons and actions which fall within the boundaries set by the rules of irrelevance. Certain actions ('plays' or 'moves') are given special meaning; participants are given special identities. The elements and properties designated in this way Goffman calls 'realised resources'.

Lastly, we have 'transformation rules'. If one thinks of committee meetings, concerts, public ceremonies, games and sports, and the like, it is clear that the participants ignore much of what is going on around a gathering or encounter. This is not so much a matter of lack of interest as of conscious disregard – of treating them as of no account. Quite often, too, differences of status, rank, age, gender, and so on are put aside, so far as the people directly involved are concerned. On the other hand, while many of the properties of events and characteristics of participants may be treated as non-existent, it is also possible for other properties and characteristics of theirs to be taken into account, in which case they may act so as to predetermine the way in which the realised resources of the encounter are allocated among the participants. Some participants who possess special social qualifications or competences may, for instance, play a recognised part in the proceedings as chairman or secretary of a meeting, instrumentalist, partner at cards, etc.

Even so, there is a necessary discrepancy between the way 'realised resources' are distributed in many kinds of gathering and are distributed in the world at large. For one thing, the boundaries, structure and resources of encounter simply cannot accommodate the span of differentiation prevailing in the larger society.

So it is that the properties of things, events and persons which are valid for the world at large outside the encounter undergo a kind of transformation when they become resources for realisation within the encounter. This may amount to the temporary, make-believe, egalitarianism which consists in the reduction or elimination of 'outside' differences that one finds in prayer meetings, carnivals, clubs and legislative assemblies as well as games and committees – or even to their reversal, as in the Saturnalia and similar calendar events.

What this adds up to is that the barrier to externally based properties is more of a screen than a solid wall, and that the screen not only selects but also transforms and modifies what passes through it. All three sets of rules – inhibitory rules that tell participants what they must not attend to, facilitating rules that tell them what they may recognise and attend to, and transformation rules which govern transactions across the boundary between the two – are therefore related not only to the encounter but also to the "outside" world. For encounters are always in fact *occasioned* in the broader world of events and of the structure of society. 'Together, these rules represent one of the great themes of social organisation, being one basic way in which every encounter is embedded in society' (*E*, 33).

Nevertheless, it is, I think, of central importance that the involvement which is intrinsic to social encounters – albeit to a varying extent – is bound up with the reduction of social values, distinctions, and concerns in general to what can be handled locally. It is this *localisation* of social forms and forces which both makes for and is called into being by social interaction.

It is apparent that we are some distance from the notion of a game as it is rendered in game-theory. Goffman underlines the difference by drawing a distinction between 'playing' and 'plays' on the one hand – where the only considerations are the rules relating to the game itself, good and bad stratagems, and results (all of which are the theme of 'game-theory') – and 'gaming' and 'gaming encounters' on the other, in which what matters is the different kinds of interaction among people who are there for the game. The distinction is crucial to the point he wants to make in "Fun in Games", because focused gatherings of all kinds share the unique and significant properties of 'gaming encounters' which a consideration of interaction in terms of game theory tends to leave out. The most important of these properties is what he calls the 'organismic' nature of participants' psychological involvement, when perception and mind are almost wholly involved in the game, and they are correspondingly almost totally unaware of anything else.

> By this spontaneous involvement in the joint activity, the individual becomes an integral part of the situation, lodged in it and exposed to it, infusing himself into the encounter in a manner quite different from the way an ideally rational player [in the perspective adopted for game-theory analysis] commits himself to a game move in an ideally abstract game.
>
> (*E*, 38)

A move in accordance with a game strategy, and ("ideally", at least) unencumbered by involvements, is something quite other than the mobilisation of the self which occurs in the execution of the move during a gaming encounter.

Much of the importance of involvement in gaming encounters, and in all kinds of interaction for which they are the model, lies in co-involvement. For involvement has to show itself. And what shows through (is 'betrayed' by) a display of involvement is one's intentions which are identical with theirs in asserting the reality of the world prescribed by the transformation rules and the unreality of other worlds. Feelings of security, exclusive solidarity, closeness, mutual regard are all provided with reassurance by a display of involvement.

In this way, involvement – to the appropriate extent – is not only possible but obligatory.

There are nevertheless degrees of involvement, which may be 'tight' or 'loose'. The degree of co-involvement of two in an intimate encounter like making love may demonstrate the success (or sometimes, he notes, the failure) of an interaction in engrossing a pair of individuals. On the other hand, there is everywhere a host of multi-situated games and game-like activities available, which makes for what he calls a 'reality-market' – a fun-fair world available whenever or wherever the individual decides to immerse himself in it.

Allowance has to be made for secondary (or side-)involvements (smoking a cigarette, doodling, chatting with a friend during a lull) which are extraneous to the main ('dominant') involvement and have to be clearly demonstrated as subordinated to it. Some minimal declaration of main involvement by way of dress, demeanour or action is usually obligatory, but this varies in degree and can be overdone. Except on very special occasions, involvement must *not* be total. 'Whatever the main involvements, and whatever their approved intensity, . . . the individual is required to give visible evidence that he has not wholly given himself up to this main focus of attention' (p. 40). There has to be some margin of self-command and (simultaneous) involvement, ways of shielding involvement, allocating different amounts of attention to different involvements, and so on.

III

The impression conveyed by representing the individual as 'a kind of construct, built up not from inner psychic propensities but from moral rules that are impressed upon him from without', tends to be reinforced by the absence of reference to any other sort of power operating *within* society. This is something which is missing in all Goffman's work on the structure and nature of social interaction. (It is also missing from Durkheim, incidentally.) There is hardly any mention of power relationships between categories and groups of people, or between individuals. Since for many – perhaps most – sociologists, non-Marxist as well as Marxist, the structure of society is determined by power, I am inclined to think that it is this omission which lies at the bottom of criticism such as Gouldner's (below, p. 116) about the subordination of 'underlying essences' to 'appearances' – criticism which was perhaps best, or at least most succinctly, put by

Edward Shils in a conversation I once had with him about Goffman and his writings, when he said, "There's no blood".

It could be argued that the kind of observation made by Gouldner and Shils (and by other critics) proceeds out of a less than careful reading of what Goffman was in fact writing about in these early essays. For one thing, it leaves out of consideration altogether the treatment of power and authority in the *Asylums* essays, and of status and discrimination in *Stigma*. Yet there undoubtedly are ambiguities – even contradictions – about his handling of how the larger implications of what is meant by social order are reflected in everyday social behaviour. What is more, Goffman seems almost to have surrendered to this kind of criticism by the rather defensive tone of his 1982 presidential address, in which he tried to "de-contextualise" social interaction from macroscopic and other sociological considerations. Denying any substantive connection between the two (or treating it as unfathomable) seems the least satisfactory way of resolving the issue.

What is really provoking, though, is that the beginnings of a strategy for connecting his "microsociology" with the orthodoxies of "macrosociology" are discernible in two of the essays discussed in this chapter: "Fun in Games" and "Strategic Interaction". Later essays – notably "Where the Action Is" – sketch in some other major features, and a good deal of supporting evidence shows up elsewhere in his writings, once the main outlines become discernible.

In "Fun in Games" Goffman goes to some lengths to emphasise how much the 'rules of interaction' – and the involvement of participants – are directed towards turning a face-to-face encounter into a little world of its own, curtained off from the larger society. The curtain is transparent, of course, but it acts as a filter. It does so in two ways. While admission to the occasions, the gatherings, the situations in which face-to-face interaction occurs is determined well beforehand by the power structure, status system and the religious, cultural and intellectual affinities prevailing in that society, the 'outside world' is thereafter treated as 'irrelevant', in accordance with the 'rules of irrelevance', by which 'certain properties of the participants' will be treated as non-existent, along with 'properties of the material context' which are 'held at bay' (*E*, 20-1). Partly because this filtering process is among the assumptions on which an encounter is founded and partly because of the rules governing the encounter itself, encounters tend, *normally*, to suppress or greatly to reduce the overt exercise or even the manifestation of power – physical, political, economic or any other kind.

The essay on "Embarrassment and Social Organisation" puts the matter more positively. The rules governing social interaction in general (i.e. the rules pertaining to the maintenance of social order) have this in common with games, that they seal the encounter off from the social differences which obtain outside it; at the very least, they minimise social differences to an extent which qualifies each individual as an acceptable self for the purposes of the encounter, with the attributes, capacities, and information which, taken together, fit a self that is a coherently organised unit appropriate for the occasion. 'The elements of a social encounter . . . consist of effectively projected claims to an acceptable self and the confirmation of like claims on the part of others' (*IR*, 105-6).

Mutual acceptance, according to the rules of the game which hold good for a great deal of social interaction, makes for at least a pretence of equality, a temporary balance of power. Politeness itself, in fact, amounts simply to the elimination of social distinctions, to this 'democratising' of deference' (*IR*, 60). Deferential behaviour, which might be thought of 'as something a subordinate owes to his superordinate', is in reality something one individual offers an equal; there are even 'deference obligations' owed by superiors to inferiors (*IR*, 59). For the ritual deference paid to others is not intended to express respectful awe so much as to ease social contacts and social situations, everyone according everyone else the treatment modelled on deference to superiors.

In fact, the egalitarian spirit which is proper to certain kinds of face-to-face encounter has a far wider significance than is accorded it by, for example, Simmel, whose treatment of sociability as 'mere play' Goffman dismisses as 'embarrassing'. For the presumption of equality, which Simmel (rightly) describes as a first rule of sociable gatherings, applies to other occasions and situations. Goffman goes on to quote Weber and Parsons to underline the fact that 'a crucial part of the conduct of business, government and the law has to do with the way in which an official handles clients or customers in direct face-to-face dealings' (*E*, 22) and this, if the 'handling' is to be proper, is on the basis of equality. Much the same rule, it could also be said, applies to meetings of committees, when their members – as is often the case – are of unequal standing, power or influence in other contexts.

So the filtering and transformation processes which Goffman

dissects and examines with such care in "Fun in Games" are devices for excluding, minimising, or sanitising properties of the 'outside world' or of individual participants, all in the interests of making them sufficiently compatible for interaction – polite interaction – to take place.

But if "most of the world's work gets done" in social encounters, how does this show of egalitarianism fit in with the structure of the society in which encounters occur? What is supposed to happen to the institutional, organisational, and structural features of the "real" world which are thus excluded?

One can point to two ways – one temporary, one permanent (or virtually so) – in which the institutionalised structure of society enters into encounters. In the first place, the presumption of equal footing for those persons present in a "situated" gathering is a special device which comes into operation so as to serve special functions in circumstances where structural differences (inequalities of power, authority, age, status, prestige, and so on), differences in familiarity, length of acquaintance, closeness of kinship, or even mutual liking, are put aside, either formally or tacitly, but in either case temporarily, so as to ease proceedings for everyone present. Differences, that is to say, are concealed and held in abeyance for the time being, not cancelled.

Social occasions and situations sterilised in this way have in fact long been put to use by powerful individuals and groups in many ways. Diplomacy is a political process which was invented precisely to extend the forms of politeness already obligatory between kings and princes, however disparate their power or resources, to their representatives, so as to cloak the advancement of interests in which they were spectacularly involved in the world outside the encounter. The same is true of negotiations between representatives of two opposed groups, of bargaining, petitioning, and the adversarial process which operates in courts of law. In short, 'strategic interaction,' along the lines appropriate to the models developed in the theory of games, can develop within the framework of polite encounters. The point is that the framework of polite encounters holds good, even when the motives of the participants, having passed through the screen laid down by the 'rules of irrelevance', remain unchanged and have to be presumed as involvements hardly less than dominant.

Although Goffman does not develop the theme of diplomatic manoeuvring between negotiators, he has plenty to say about poise, savoir-faire, aplomb, and other aspects of the social skills by which individuals take commanding positions in encounters, diplomatic and other, from which the presumption of equality, the 'democratising' of politeness, has removed other expressive aspects or manifestations of power and social difference. The quotation in "Fun in Games" from *Pride and Prejudice* (*E*, 52-3) shows Elizabeth putting down D'Arcy, her social superior, by expounding the rules of encounter involving polite (i.e. empty) conversation proper for a particular 'focused gathering' (a local ball).

In the second place, there are strict limits to how far people are prepared to go in admitting others to the "little worlds" and the egalitarian sociability within them created by sealing off encounters. Goffman has a lot to say in *Stigma* about the pervasive and seemingly ineradicable inequalities and forms of discrimination which confront the physically and mentally disabled, blacks, "ethnics", and old people. Most of these inequalities are not covered by any kind of temporary functional accommodation. The stigmatised are simply not admitted – or tactfully exclude themselves. Encounters are for "people like us".

In the case of women, of course, structural inequality – discrimination – is no bar to social interaction. What happens, as he spells out at length in *Gender Advertisements*, is that specialised ritual displays have been developed in order to preserve these particular structural inequalities *within* the framework of social encounters.

Nevertheless, both the temporary and the more durable institutional and structural constraints are not themselves part of the action of encounters; indeed, their very potency consists in their remaining invisible and tacit. We have in fact to conceive of them as mental constructs. This does not, of course, make them unreal. Power, authority, and influence remain as they were; so do differences of wealth, income, status, prestige, and so on, legal and other rights and obligations, loyalties, commitments, and the contractual bonds which tie people to organisations. But the *kind* of reality they represent is different. So is the world of being in which they exist. Social institutions, organisations, and the social structure are the creatures of social interaction, actually present in the minds of immediate participants – and only in them.

IV

Strategic Interaction, the third of the quartet of books in which Goffman said he was setting down what he had to say about social interaction, presents something of a poser. The first essay, "Expression Games", amounts to a description, analysis, and classification of all the ways in which the information ordinarily conveyed through speech or, often unconsciously, through expressive behaviour may be manipulated, distorted or concealed, and of the ways in which it may nevertheless be uncovered or extracted and interpreted – or misinterpreted. 'Concealment, fabrication and pointed display are possible on one side; correct and incorrect discoveries are possible on the other.' But the supporting evidence for this habitual "Goffmanesque" line consists of lengthy quotations from what has been written about espionage, smuggling and its detection, criminal conspiracies and so on, and is somewhat tedious and distinctly old hat; we have had a plethora of such stuff thrust at us throughout the 1980s. Much of the time, the level hovers somewhere between *True Detective* and *Reader's Digest*.

The second essay, "Strategic Interaction", starts off even more depressingly, with a protracted 'miniature scenario; featuring "Harry". Harry is in turn a forest ranger beset by a brush fire, to begin with, and then by a hungry tiger, next an aeroplane pilot faced with engine failure and equipped with a defective parachute, and, last, a native (sic) spearman cut off from his home ground by another spearman from a hostile tribe. All these predicaments are presented as exemplary ('tight and pure') instances of the kind of situation for which "game-theory" was designed. For 'once nature, self-interest and an intelligent opponent are assured, nothing else need be; strategic interaction follows' (p. 102).

But perseverance in reading beyond this point (admittedly, this is more than two-thirds of the way through "Strategic Interaction") pays off, and handsomely. For in the last twenty or thirty pages of the book is an outline of a realistic, empirically based, explanation of the orderliness prevailing in social interaction. It is an explanation alternative to the earlier thesis of obedience to the rules imposed by "society" and is in cognitive terms.

The book operates at different levels, in fact. There are several links between the first essay, "Expression Games", and other writings of his on social interaction. It expands what the "Tie-Signs" essay in *Relations in Public* says about the expressive elements of social relationships, and adds some touches to the account he gives of concealment and deception in "Normal Appearances" in the same book. "Expression Games" could also rate as a set of corollaries to the theme of expressive behaviour broached in *Behavior in Public Places* about the impossibility of anyone's *not* communicating through expressive behaviour: 'he must say either the right thing or the wrong thing. He cannot say nothing.' And again, it also harks back to the basic assumption underlying his 'principles of dramaturgical perspective' spelled out (in a footnote) towards the beginning of *The Presentation of Self*, namely, 'that in all interaction a basic underlying theme is the desire of each participant to guide and control the responses made by the others present' (*PS*, 3).

At another level, the book could be meant to be read as a critical assessment of the limitations of the theory of games outside of what had become its conventional realm of war, economics and experimental social psychology. Or it might be taken as an attempt to qualify, modify, and supplement game theory so as to make it applicable to social interaction of any kind. In both essays, it is the conscious and deliberate moves and counter-moves of planned ("strategic") behaviour rather than the subroutines of impression-management that are at issue – although 'informal' (non-serious) social interaction is not altogether excluded, and is brought in to clinch the final argument.

Still, as I have said, it is in the culminating argument that the interest of the book lies. And this is built solidly on theses already developed in previous writings. The three major theses are, first, that, in face-to-face interaction, the information which the participants wish expressly to communicate is never the total amount of information communicated; people constantly 'exude' expressions, which contain other information, including information about themselves. Second, if information has to be communicated, this is done mostly in face-to-face interaction between people. Lastly, the channels by which information is transmitted are a matter of social arrangements.

"Expression Games" deals with the individual's capacity to acquire, reveal, and conceal information in dealings which are calculative, in the game-theory sense. There is a wider reference. If, as he says at the beginning of the book, 'face-to-face conduct is never merely and not always a form of communication' (*SI*, ix), communication, too, has to be qualified in much the same way. More than communication is at issue:

In every social situation we can find a sense in which one participant will be an observer with something to gain from assessing expression, and another will be a subject with something to gain from manipulating this process. A single structure of

contingencies can be found in this regard which renders agents
a little like us and all of us a little like agents.

(SI, 81)

The implication running through a great deal of Goffman's writings
that there is something exploitative, competitive, or both, about all
encounters, perhaps all relationships too, is now made explicit. And
this means that assessment of other people's intentions and motives
must play a major part in encounters.

"Harry's" predicaments which fill the early pages of the second essay
are, of course, exemplary of game-theory proper. And one essential
prerequisite of game-theory is that the player be committed to the
game being played, in the first place, and thereafter to each and every
move the player makes. In "Harry's" case, where his life is at stake, he
could hardly be anything else, of course, but the same absolute
commitment is one of the presumptions of game-theory.

Absolute commitment entails a number of constraints. There is a
'*constraint to play*', for even doing nothing is a course of action which
will affect the way the game develops. Second, the number of positive
moves open to him at any stage is limited: '"Harry's" situation, in
other words, is *structured*.' Third, once a move is initiated, he is
committed to it – he has to go through with it and take the
consequences. Fourth, the payoff is intimately connected with the
moves of the game: actions and the allocation of gains and losses are
'part of the same seamless situation'. In other words, the payoff is
intrinsic to the course of action taken.

All four factors, taken together, can be thought of as an
'*enforcement system*'.

For the critically important fourth and fifth sections of "Interaction
Strategy" (pp. 113-36), we move outside the limits of the 'pure and
tight' games of "Harry's" assorted predicaments. In the social life of
every day, as opposed to the kind of thing that game-theory deals
with, there are social norms which impose constraints – but which also
open up possibilities. In real life, the 'enforcement system' is usually
not vested in physical or "natural" circumstances but in some
specialised system invested with authority to make judgments about
actions ("moves in the game") and to allocate outcomes. Gladiatorial
displays may be transformed into contests which 'could equally be
carried out over a Ping-Pong table' (p. 115). In other words, the
degree of success of moves and the kind and amount of payoff to be
awarded are calculated according to an arbitrary scale; they are linked

together *'extrinsically'* by a system of sanctions which is organised socially. In these new circumstances, those verbal and non-verbal communications (expressive behaviour) which in most 'pure and tight' games are categorically different from strategic moves, may now count as effective moves.

All kinds of new possibilities now enter. Is a move "real", i.e. to be taken seriously, or is it a feint, a practice shot, a fumble, a joke? Equally, serious moves may be misperceived ("misframed") as non-serious. Someone may be unauthorised to make some particular move, which means that it is revoked or discounted, or a penalty exacted from the offender. Cheating becomes a feasible possibility; so does bribery, bringing undue influence to bear on the outcome, and so forth.

These new factors transform the whole game situation. What really counts in this new, "loose", "impure" game is not so much, or not only, the move but whether or not it reflects the player's true intention. This matters not at all in the pure and tight category of games; only actions count. Now, assessment enters. Intentions have to be read. Reading the intentions that lie "behind" actions requires some assessment of what the action "expresses" – whether or not to take what an individual is saying or doing at face value; how to respond in one case or the other. Hence, as Goffman remarks in *Relations in Public*, 'there is created in connection with relationships what is true of any event that can support or undermine the image of an individual, namely, a game of expression' (*RP*, 212).

Which raises the question of what kinds of constraint, what enforcement system, could possibly apply in games played according to this "real life" code. In games of cards, chess, sporting contests and so on, moves are connected up with outcome through a set of explicit rules; steps are taken, also, to ensure that all moves are visible. When the payoff of games of this kind is a financial or other kind of reward, there is ordinarily an authorised enforcement system, with officials appointed to ensure fair play. The law enters as something of an all-purpose enforcement system. But the great majority of "real life" games are played outside such institutional provisions, and some other sanctioning process has to come into force in order to insure against disruption, deception, or irresponsible behaviour.

In the ordinary way, of course, players do "play the game" and 'act so that their placements are, in fact, commitments' (*SI*, 123). Guilt, shame, fear of losing reputation and thus of the possibility of entering into similar situations in the future also play some part in holding a player to his commitment. Nevertheless, it is not especially cynical to suppose that when the stakes in the game are very substantial, unless they are matched by the "objective" basis of commitment, it becomes less likely that players will feel entirely bound by normative considerations or by the disapproval his action might arouse. All too obviously, if a player thinks the gains from opting out outweigh any intrinsic payoff, that player may indeed opt out – and often in fact does. This is notoriously the case in situations where there is a conflict of interests. But it also happens that there are instances in which there is a mixture of motives as well. This is particularly true of bargaining, in which there is both conflict of interests between the two parties *and* a desire to reach a mutually satisfactory outcome.

Goffman's line of argument here may owe something to T. C. Schelling's exercises in restyling, or remodelling, game-theory in order to obtain a closer approximation to the "real-life" bargaining and negotiation situations that arise in business, industrial relations and foreign policy. But it is more likely that both of them had for some time recognised parallels, even convergence, in the way their ideas were developing. Schelling makes good use of Goffman's early essay on face-work in *The Strategy of Conflict*; Goffman spent a year working on *Strategic Interaction* in the Center for International Affairs at Harvard, where Schelling was.

Both focus on those situations in which, in Goffman's words, 'the participants must themselves provide the enforcement, or where they must rely on a vague and shifting public for this purpose' (*SI*, 126). 'What we find', he goes on, 'is a mosaic of ill-understood, varying practices.' In Schelling's terms, these "practices" are characteristically "coordination games", in which there is a mixture of interdependence and conflict, of partnership and competition.[6] For Goffman, they are situations which call for mutual assurance; and this in turn has to be based, first, on a belief that the way he behaves 'provides a window into his intent', and, second, on the knowledge that it is very often more rewarding *in the long run* to abide by one's word, even in the absence of any formal enforcement.

Considerations such as these open up a range of possibilities for interpreting interaction encounters and the connection between them and the larger structural features of society. But these are best pursued in the context of the wider discussion of Goffman's view of social order outlined in the final chapter.

V

Running through the whole of *Behavior in Public Places* and most of the papers in *Interaction Ritual* is a second theme within the general thesis formally presented and in terms of which the conceptual framework and the definitional glossary are worked out. This second theme is the exploration of the world of the mental patient. It is a central concern of the *Asylums* essays, which will be discussed in later chapters, but the observations on the behaviour of mental patients derived from his NIMH research are of direct relevance to his treatment of social interaction. For one way of determining the precise nature of the rules of social intercourse is to note the ways in which they are broken, by conduct which is condemned as 'uncivil', 'unmannerly', 'disorderly', 'embarrassing' or 'disruptive' – and the behaviour of the insane can be all of these things.

A whole chapter of *Behavior in Public Places* is given over to the ways in which people transgress the rules of interaction. Since such transgressions have observable consequences, and by looking at the manifold ways in which things can go wrong – rules transgressed, ignored or challenged – one can point to what is needed for things to go right, i.e. demonstrate the existence and the operation of the rules governing social gatherings and individual conduct in them.

To begin with, people may behave in ways usually labelled 'abstracted' or 'preoccupied'. These are classified as 'auto-involvements' (eating, dressing, picking one's teeth, cleaning one's fingernails, dozing, and sleeping); 'aways' (giving oneself up to solitary participation in a play-like world, while outwardly participating in an activity within a social situation – a kind of 'inward emigration from the gathering'); and 'occult involvements' (episodes of preoccupation in which the individual gives others the impression, whether warranted or not, that he is not aware of being 'away'). These last are distinguishable from 'aways' by what happens after discovery ('snapping out' of a reverie, as against noticing that one has been talking to oneself, for example).

Second, there are failures in propriety. The mildest are those occasions when people find themselves wrongly identified, or treated impersonally, or with less regard than they think is their due. Other departures from the rules are in themselves notoriously ambiguous in intent and interpretation: mock solemnity, mock politeness, mimicry, 'sending up', and so on can vary from the unserious kind of impropriety which occurs between friends, acquaintances, colleagues, or workmates (and are a familiar standby of music-hall comics in the past and television entertainers nowadays) to malicious taunting or a display of defiance or contempt.

This brings us, thirdly, to those transgressions which seem to be committed on purpose.

> The idiom through which modes of proper ceremonial conduct are established necessarily creates ideally effective forms of desecration, for it is only in reference to specified proprieties that one can learn to appreciate what will be the worst possible form of behaviour. Profanations are to be expected, for every religious ceremony creates the possibility of a black mass.
>
> (IR, 86)

Intentional transgressions vary in the degree of offence they provoke, as well as in the form they take. Some draw retribution on the offender and some do not, being regarded as permissible or, often, simply being condoned. ('Every round of life provides at least a few places for getting away with being away' (BP, 70).) At the other end of the scale, though, there is the face-to-face ritual profanation which is a constant phenomenon in some psychiatric wards (IR, 88).

'Patients may profane a staff member or a fellow-patient by spitting at him, slapping his face, throwing faeces at him, tearing off his clothes, pushing him off his chair, taking food from his grasp, screaming into his face, sexually molesting him, etc.' While these acts may conceivably be the product of blind impulse or perhaps imbued, for the patient, with some special symbolic meaning,

> from the point of view of the society at large and the ceremonial idiom, these are not random impulsive infractions. Rather, these acts are exactly those calculated to convey disrespect and utter contempt through symbolic means. Whatever is in the patient's mind, the throwing of faeces at an attendant is a use of our ceremonial idiom that is as exquisite in its way as is a bow from the waist done with grace and a flourish. Whether he knows it or not, the patient speaks the same ritual language as his captors. . . .
>
> (IR, 89)

There are also patients who inflict the same kind of profanation on themselves. Here, the reaction of fellow-patients reveals the same sort of awareness of rules of public order being implicit in the disruptive behaviour which defies them. 'These self-derogations, carried past the limits of polite self-depreciation, were considered a tax upon the others', who, prepared as they were to ignore any shortcomings among their fellows, 'felt it was unfair to be forced into contaminating intimacy with the individual's problems' (*IR*, 90).

In other words, when even the worst improprieties are being committed, mental patients still show that they are aware, at some indistinct but fundamental level, of the rules they are breaking and of the public order they have disrupted. Goffman's explanation measures such behaviour by standards which apply to the purposeful efforts of individuals well acquainted with high standards of politeness, and aware of their significance, to use that knowledge to present themselves in the worst possible light. What Goffman seems to be arguing is that, in so doing, they contrive to preserve the integrity of the social world they are turning upside down.

There are occasions when people could be said to be using 'situational improprieties' as a way of expressing their resentment against a community or a social class or, specifically in the case of mental patients, against the social establishment or institution in which they find themselves. A fairly protracted list of them is offered in Chapter 14 of *Behavior in Public Places* (p. 224). These acts of sabotage directed against the self and the situation in which mental patients find themselves, Goffman suggests, may be interpreted as self-defence: 'It seems that the patient sometimes feels that life on the ward is so degrading, so unjust, and so inhuman that the only self-respecting response is to treat ward life as if it were contemptibly beyond reality and beyond seriousness' (*BP*, 225).

The interpretation of mental patients' behaviour in terms of self-defence could, in fact, apply just as well to the response it meets with from hospital staff. They, too, turn the tables on improper conduct *and* acknowledge the rule of public order in doing so. Affronts get labelled as 'aggression' or 'hostile outbursts'. The labels are in themselves defences against interpreting such 'proclamations of alienation' in any other way than as directed against their professional selves or their institutional identities. Goffman calls it covering them up 'with a psychological tent' (*IR*, 88), although one might be forgiven for thinking that words like "aggression" and "hostile" convey much the same interpretation as the one he gives. What I am suggesting – more as an extension of his interpretation than an amendment – is that, regardless of the outrageous extremes of mental patients' behaviour (regardless, too, of the inhumanity of some of the methods used to restrain them), a sense of public order and an awareness of the rules by which it is sustained is implicit in the way in which both sides behave. The further suggestion is that the kind of behaviour Goffman is reporting, however obnoxious, stays nevertheless within limits – "structural" limits imposed by the society in which the institution is lodged. If one considers that such behaviour, again on both sides, stops short of the beastliness we know men are capable of (in wartime, for example), this interpretation may not seem utterly unrealistic. At all events, it is an interpretation which provides some rationale for the "community care" policy which gained widespread acceptance later.

Goffman's purpose, in these passages in the interaction essays, is to show how breaches of them demonstrate the existence, the nature, and the strength of the rules of public order. They also repeat the message so forcibly conveyed in *Asylums*, which is that treating patients simply as non-persons, let alone inhumanely, or offensively, makes some such reaction almost inevitable among a sizeable proportion of them. 'When a mental patient checks into a hospital, an itemised account is usually made of every one of his belongings; this requires his giving himself up to others in a way that he may have learned to define as a humiliation.' The same goes for other practices: searches for liquor, drugs, and other contraband, the use of concealed microphones in wards, censoring mail, discussing intimate details about a patient's person or condition as if he were not there, unlockable toilets, violent constraint and treatment, forced feeding, forced medication, and so on.

Furthermore, patients are sorted out into grades according to the degree to which they seem to violate 'ceremonial rules of social intercourse'. There are very good practical reasons for so doing (and in fact only backward hospitals do not). But grading often means that individuals who are desperately uncivil in some areas of behaviour are placed in the intimate company of those who are desperately uncivil in others. Thus, 'individuals who are the least ready to project a sustainable self are lodged in a milieu where it is practically impossible to do so', and:

> When the individual is subject to extreme constraint he is automatically forced from the circle of the proper. . . . Others may show ceremonial regard for him, but it becomes impossible for him to reciprocate or to act in such a way as to make himself

worthy of receiving it. The only ceremonial statements that are possible for him are improper ones.

(*IR*, 92-3)

The passages which deal with mental patients tend to become longer and more frequent towards the end of all the essays. And while his accounts of the conduct and treatment of mental patients may in general serve to demonstrate the existence of rules of social behaviour in normal society, Goffman also turns the connection around. The analysis of interaction rules in normal society is used to challenge the justice not only of many features of their incarceration and treatment but of the verdicts which segregate them from society at large. Towards the end of *Behavior in Public Places*, in fact, he does so openly.

The transgressions committed against, as well as by, mental patients are not only useful illustrations of the rules of social interaction; they provide, at the same time, additional ammunition for the long campaign of attrition which Goffman wages against the apparatus of "normalisation" (below, pp. 157-66) and the power structure it sustains, and, especially, against the rules concerning discrimination and segregation. The final sentences of *Behavior in Public Places* read:

> The ultimate penalty for breaking the rules is harsh. Just as we fill our jails with those who transgress the legal order, so we partly fill our asylums with those who act unsuitably – the first kind of institution being used to protect our lives and property, the second to protect our gatherings and occasions.

Goffman's work on interaction was begun well before his years with the NIMH, but his researches in mental hospitals provided empirical evidence for much of what he wrote later on interaction. Indeed, the choice of mental hospitals as a field of research gives some indication of why Goffman adopted the approach to the study of interaction that he did. For, from a psychoanalytic standpoint, it is virtually axiomatic that there is something artificial, fabricated, about the rules and the judgments by which the behaviour of particular individuals is regarded as rendering them unfit for civil society – flexible and liable to be ignored or circumvented as we know those rules to be.

This is made explicit enough in Freud's writings, especially the later ones. Interest in the literature of psychoanalysis and general psychiatry had grown since the 1920s, and was especially strong among social scientists during the years after the Second World War. Goffman read through this literature more thoroughly than most. His observations on the ways in which social order may be disrupted or threatened by the kind of behaviour which others defined as evidence of mental illness date from the time he spent in Shetland. He saw early on how such behaviour, *and* the judgments passed on it, can be useful indicators of the existence and the nature of the rules governing behaviour in public places and of social orderliness in general.

In the group of writings on social interaction, mental patients, their behaviour, and their treatment fall to be considered under two heads. First, they enter into accounts of how the rules of interaction come to be transgressed, how encounters break down, and so forth. Second, they are used to illustrate the ability of mental patients to interpose their own 'rules of irrelevance' between outer circumstances and themselves and the focused interactions in which they are involved, to invoke their own 'transformation rules', and so forth – rules which are strikingly different from what is supposed to obtain ordinarily or 'normally'. The two are closely connected.

The point is best considered later, when we come to review *Asylums*, but it is worthwhile saying now that there is little in his work of the ideological commitment to the challenge to 'normalcy' one finds in R. D. Laing and Thomas Szasz. If there is any indebtedness to others besides those he met at Bethesda it is to Gregory Bateson's group in California. There is, on the other hand, some approximation to the notion of madness as a social construct which has been ascribed to Foucault. This, in brief, is to the effect that modern society sees itself as a society of 'reasonable' beings committed to the accomplishment of works and the transmission of meaningful speech. Society, therefore – rightly or wrongly, but inevitably – has to defend itself against people whose actions are pointless in terms of constructive work (culminate in nothing) and whose speech is empty of meaning (refers to nothing).

Goffman is not so much concerned about 'society's' reasonableness or rightness in taking defensive measures but does question the grounds of the judgment and, more especially, challenges both the effectiveness and the harshness of the measures. The challenge is, once again, essentially Durkheimian. For it is Durkheim who wrote, in his 1906 paper "The Determination of Moral Facts":

> The human personality is a sacred thing; one dares not violate
> it nor infringe its bounds.

The sentiment is echoed throughout Goffman's writings on mental hospitals and the people consigned to them.

VI

This brings us back to a consideration touched on earlier (above, pp. 28-31). For, continuing the selfsame sentence, Durkheim also remarked that, "at the same time the greatest good is in communion with others". For the wrong perpetrated by deliberate transgressions of propriety lies not in the offence given to others so much as in what it betokens, namely, the desecration of communality, a purposeful sabotage of the essential infrastructure of all social action.

It is this, after all, which marks the distinction between behaviour which is sometimes permissible, or at least pardonable, and sometimes, even when it is exactly the same kind of behaviour, not. Auto-involvements, 'aways' and occult involvements, for example, lead others to suspect that the apparent involvement of the individual in an encounter is in fact false, and that 'he has been all along alienated from their world' (*BP*, 78). This kind of misjudgment can be easily avoided by ostentatious displays designed to demonstrate that one is hailing somebody, searching for a lost coin, or simply waiting to meet another, or is properly preoccupied with abstruse matters (the "absent-minded professor" is the stock example).

The significance of the distinction lies, of course, in its showing that the rules governing social behaviour are accommodated to the specific occasion, gathering or situation. And this, in turn, means that 'the fact that others regularly interpret the activity of an individual as "meaningless" or "crazy" is not proof that it is, nor even proof that meaning will have to be sought by reverting to the kind of extended symbolic interpretation sometimes attempted in psychoanalysis' (*BP*, 79). Such activity, in short, can scarcely be liable to sanction because it is intrinsically offensive; it must be so because it is so defined by some specific group of people.

But the difference in the way activities of the selfsame kind are treated has its own, deeper, significance. Whether to condemn or condone depends entirely on whether the behaviour in question threatens to weaken or destroy that 'firm sense of reality' which comes from involvement in an encounter. What Goffman is invoking here is the most fundamental of social ties – that 'kind of trust-in-the-other that is necessary if people are to be in each other's presence and get on with their separate affairs' (*BP*, 78).

The idea of society as a moral order is fairly commonplace. But the notion that the lives, feelings, and behaviour of individuals are not only, like language, an essentially social construct, but are dependencies of a collective moral consciousness, has been taken to be somewhat too 'metaphysical'. It hypostatises society. On the other hand, the idea that society depends for its existence on mutual trust and the fellow-feeling that subtends it has a respectable ancestry, looking back well beyond Durkheim to people like David Hume, Francis Hutcheson, and Adam Smith. It is perhaps still necessary to emphasise this quite fundamental aspect of the system of ideas associated with their names, especially that of Hume, the central figure; for it is diametrically opposed to what was for a very long time the established view, which seems to have taken hold early in the nineteenth century, or even before. According to this view, Hume and Smith figured as the apostles of individualism (with individual man as the 'natural unit'), with civilisation, distributive justice, economic welfare, and civil society all, by some miracle accomplished by a 'hidden hand', the product of self-interest, which played the paramount role in individual behaviour and, therefore, in the social (and economic) system.

With a sociologist less averse to anything approaching "grand theory", one would look for some pursuit of this idea, some discussion of the way in which the traffic of social interaction – which is the stuff of social order – organises itself, or is organised, so as to constitute society. In "Alienation from Interaction" he does remark on the mutual and sympathetic awareness with which participants in an encounter must watch out for 'the things in which others present can become spontaneously and properly involved, and then attempt to modulate his expression of attitudes, feelings, and opinions according to the company'. And there even follows a reference to Adam Smith, who, he says, argued that

> the individual must phrase his own concerns and feelings and interests in such a way as to make those maximally usable by the others as a source of appropriate involvement; and this major obligation of the individual *qua* interactant is balanced by his right to expect that others present will make some effort to stir up their sympathies and place them at his command. These two tendencies, that of the speaker to scale down his expressions and that of the listeners to scale up their interests, each in the light

71

of each other's capacities and demands, form the bridge that people build to one another, allowing them to meet for a moment of talk in a communion of reciprocally sustained involvement. It is this spark, not the more obvious kinds of love, that lights up the world.

(*IR*, 116-17)

Another instance occurs in his notes on what he calls 'drift', which is the spontaneous growth within a group of involvement in an engrossing task, in talk or in a game. A common, or mutual, involvement which takes a group figuratively away from a larger gathering while remaining physically part of it predicates the existence of 'sympathy', 'fellow-feeling', and 'identification with the other' well beyond the obligations imposed by any rules governing social interaction. Most pertinent of all is a statement, towards the end of the paper on deference and demeanour, which includes, but also goes beyond, the reaffirmation of a Durkheimian view of society as bound into a moral order by normative obligations imposed on the individual.

The rules of conduct which bind the actor and the recipient [i.e. of deferential behaviour] together are the bindings of society. But . . . opportunities to affirm the moral order and the society could . . . be rare. It is here that ceremonial rules play their social function, for many of the acts which are guided by these rules last but a brief moment, involve no substantial outlay, and can be performed in every social interaction. . . . Through these observances, guided by ceremonial obligations and expectations, a constant flow of indulgences is spread through society. . . . The gestures we sometimes call empty are perhaps in fact the fullest of all.

(*IR*, 91)

But such larger views make an appearance only in fleeting references and asides; he seems, almost, to slide away from the larger implications of his references to 'trust-in-the-other' – although there are times, as with the reference to Adam Smith, when he seems to come close to it. Much more frequent, and typical, are the references to the negative aspects of interpersonal concordance. There is the ostentatious denial of contact: waitresses or barkeepers who refuse to have their eye caught, motorists and passers-by in contests for priority who refuse to accord each other the 'civil inattention' by which their claims, as well as their presence, would be acknowledged. By contrast, beggars and prostitutes trade on the universality of those pedestrian traffic rules which make it obligatory for everyone to catch the eye of others and to signal either civil inattention or 'the mere exchange of friendly glances'. But even in these cases it is not simply that the existence and the character of rules of social intercourse becomes most easily detectable when they are infringed, flouted, betrayed or exploited. The delinquencies themselves are testimony to the interpersonal concordance, the understanding of "the other", which derives from our capacity to put ourselves in his place and fit our actions to his, which is of such supreme importance to human society, and on which its individual members are so dependent.

There are nevertheless clues, and more than clues, to a concern with what might be called the bonds of communality, rather than the rules of public order, in his account of the various social bonds assumed or acknowledged by people who make up social occasions by their mere presence at them. Social bonds of some kind establish themselves at the very outset of an occasion, but may alter in scope, intensity and duration, and in the way they develop or fade. Ties of some kind cover all those present, but may coexist with others between sets, subsets, and pairs of individuals. They may be symmetrical or asymmetrical, instigated mutually or one-sidedly, and may be so independently of what obtains on other occasions or in other settings.

The terms he uses in this connection – 'collusion' is a favourite – carry a suggestion of underhandedness, even conspiracy, which is slightly misleading. What can be said, though, is that in general, and among fully adult members of society, the social ties which underwrite appropriate conduct, demeanour and talk on any occasion depend for their validity – and indeed for their existence – on their being unspoken. There is a multiplicity of different *kinds* of ties, all of them with their own set of rules calling for appropriate conduct, utterances, comportment, and expressiveness. Among persons who are presumed to be 'socialised' (i.e. competent adult members of society), compliance with such rules has to be tacit. They are tacit not merely in the sense of not needing explicit statement but because to voice them would be to destroy their applicability; the occasion could only continue in existence with a different set of ties and of rules. 'Tact' and 'complicity', which also occur in his writings, likewise bespeak tacit understanding, unspoken acceptance, mute assent.

He comes closest of all to the view which I am superimposing on (rather than elucidating from) his work in a quotation[7] from a study of surgical teams which – quite frequently – can become so well coordinated that commands, directives or prompts are unnecessary when emergencies arise. In the quoted passage he cites, the accidental cutting of a small artery during an operation is read as a signal for the immediate performance of appropriate and complementary tasks by all the members of the team. No one tells anyone else what to do; no one needs telling.

The same might be said of the performance of their different tasks in complete concordance with each other by the expert crews who man fishing vessels or racing yachts, by established ensembles of actors or acrobats or musicians, or by gun-crews. Over and above the trained skills involved, tasks involving the cooperative *and coordinated* effort of two or more persons depend for their performance on the minimal signals communicated between the members of the team through 'body-idiom' and, of course, the ability to read them instantaneously. It is this special human capacity for interpersonal concordance which is the essential prerequisite of all human organisation, including – though this is almost always missed – power structures and authority systems. It is a capacity which comes directly not so much from a propensity to identify with others as from an ability and readiness to assume their point of view and interpret their intentions. It is this which, in Humean, "communitarian" terms, forms the basis of social life.

I have suggested that there are, in the observations about social behaviour, social encounters, and social relations which are to be found scattered about in Goffman's writings, at least the makings of a taxonomy of social interaction. They could all add up to something much bigger, of the kind I have touched on in the references to Hume and Smith. He makes sudden dives underneath Durkheim's "social facts", his "ways of acting, fixed or not", which are general throughout society, soundings for a quick look at 'the ultimate behavioural materials': 'the glances, gestures, positionings, and verbal statements that people continuously feed into the situation'.

The issue is whether it is the meanings and feelings which people attach to these things which make up the *'moral* order' of society, the warp on which all social institutions and all social relationships are woven, or whether the same meanings and feelings are epiphenomena, a psychological gloss imposed on the experience of individuals in order to facilitate compliance with society's rules. It is the second of these interpretations which Goffman seems to favour.

NOTES AND REFERENCES

1. C. Geertz, *Local Knowledge*, Basic Books, 1983, p. 24.
2. C. Geertz, *Local Knowledge*, Basic Books, 1983, p. 24.
3. See J. Dunn, "The concept of 'trust' in the politics of John Locke", in *Philosophy in History* (eds R. Rorty, J. B. Schneewind and Q. Skinner) Cambridge Univ. Press, 1984, pp. 279-301.
4. N. Luhmann, "Trust", in *Trust and Power* (eds T. Burns and G. Poggi), Wiley, 1979.
5. E. Gombrich, *The Image and the Eye*, Phaidon Press, 1982, p. 15.
6. T. C. Schelling, *The Strategy of Conflict*, Oxford Univ. Press, 1963, p. 89.
7. The passage quoted is from T. Burling, *Essays in Human Aspects of Administration*, New York State School of Industrial and Labor Relations, Cornell Univ., Bulletin 25, 1955, pp. 10-11.

4
FRIENDS, POLITE FICTIONS, AND ENEMIES

Early on, in keeping with his self-conscious (or self-righteous) abdication from any grand theoretical pretensions, Goffman described himself as an 'urban ethnographer', a journeyman collector of facts about human social behaviour. When he came to write *Relations in Public*, however, he adopted the title of 'human ethologist'.

The close attention to the minutiae of behaviour, which shows up in all Goffman's work, is the hallmark of the methods followed by students of animal behaviour. Biology had always found a place for behavioural studies, but one of the consequences of the Darwinian revolution was to deliver such studies from most of their anthropocentric bias; ethology emerged as a distinct branch of biological studies around the turn of the century. Ethologists distinguished themselves from earlier naturalists by seeking a more fundamental, more constrained, empiricism. The question they asked was not "What is this thing like?" but "What is going on here?" This question was also, and essentially, Goffman's. Nevertheless, while he helped himself generously to the fund of concepts and insights made available by animal behaviour studies, he did so for the most part with his customary choosiness; there are long passages, too, in which he parts company altogether with ethological terminology.

I

Relations in Public is a collection of six essays. There is also an appendix, "The Insanity of Place", but the essay belongs more to the *Asylums* papers than to those discussed here. The six essays which make up the book proper are, this time, not only all interconnected thematically but also ordered in sequence, later ones making use of definitions spelled out and propositions established on empirical evidence earlier in the book. So, despite what the author says in his preliminary "Note", it is safer to treat them as the chapters of a book rather than as if each had 'its own perspective' and started 'from conceptual scratch'.

The six essays vary in length (and quality). Some are largely taken up with definitions and a taxonomy not of relationships so much as of the ways in which relationships are displayed, observed, and preserved in interaction. "Remedial Exchanges" is an exercise in showing how violations and infringements declare the existence and the characteristics of the social order, and how it is that so much of our behaviour is best seen as repair and maintenance work on its behalf. This is in line with the kind of approach he adopted in his earlier work, and there are some references back to it. Yet *Relations in Public* is more than a development of the taxonomy of the analytical elements and rules of social interaction laid out in *Behavior in Public Places* and *Interaction Ritual*. Before, the focus of interest was not the individual but what he called the syntax of the interactions between different persons when they are together (*IR*, 2). This time, it is social relationships ('an element of social structure'), or rather the connection between social relationships and the face-to-face behaviour of individuals in public.

In the first essay, which deals with 'two things that an individual can be', we have the individual, to begin with, treated as 'a vehicular unit' (it is here that the observational *tour-de-force* on pedestrian traffic already mentioned occurs). The rest of the essay makes some play with the idea of the individual as a 'participation unit', broaching one of Goffman's more problematic theses concerning the nature of the self. In this first essay, however, the notions he wants to get across are that an individual can behave as though he embodied two selves, or perhaps more, and also can act with another person as if both constituted but one individual.

Relationships that are on public display include some that are, so to speak, "intra-individual". There are occasions when, in apologising for his behaviour (or even his presence), an individual acts as if he stood aside from his offending self. Second, a couple often behave as if they were one (which hardly requires stretching the imagination beyond the world of popular songs). Both kinds of brief behavioural sequence are familiar enough, and what suggests itself immediately is that they might be more simply – and better – envisaged, or interpreted, as part and parcel of the resort to 'as if' entities and situations which so permeate everyday thinking and talk. Resort to the world of 'as if' is an utterly commonplace element of ordinary talk and conduct, as well as serving as an indispensable resource for the 'practical thought' which we employ in morality, business, law, organisation, politics, and so forth.[1] It is also exactly the kind of feature which Goffman might have been expected to seize upon and explore through all its ramifications. Instead, he chose, in this and other places, to treat the notion of the individual as so lacking in rigour as to be useless, or a convenient fiction, despite the almost unique precision of the root meaning of the word. This does not, of course, prevent his using the word in its ordinarily received sense, any more than in other cases when he chooses to pick a quarrel with the vocabulary of ordinary speech, or of social science.

It is when we come to the second essay that he starts helping himself to the concepts and terms made available by animal behaviour studies, announcing the principle which sets the strategy of the whole book: 'At the centre of social organisation is the concept of claims'. Claims are made, in this connection, not to specific objects but to a preserve, to a designated field and whatever lies within it; also, the preserve moves around with the claimant.

But the scope of the concepts he takes over from animal behaviour studies is immediately broadened. The notion of territorial claims is extended, when it comes to human beings, to matters which are either scarcely or else not at all territorial in any ordinary sense. The notion of territoriality seems to have encouraged him to annex more elements of everyday social intercourse into the world of 'as if': taking turns, and the use of items of clothing and other possessions as 'markers' in order to stake a claim to occupancy, are both subsumed under the heading of territoriality, which is fair enough; but 'territoriality' also covers 'information preserves' (facts about oneself and one's life, thoughts and feelings, etc., commonly thought of as 'private'), and 'conversation preserves' (the right to some kind of control over who can engage one or break into conversation, and when).

We then come to the kind of theme which is integral to so much of his work, namely, deviations from and violations of the social rules (principles) governing social interaction. Infringements are put to use, as they were in earlier essays, to highlight the existence, the potency, and the characteristics of the rules governing territoriality. Touching others, even proximity to them, can constitute a transgression; so can staring – sometimes even glancing – at others; so can noise, smells, loud talk, or intrusions into a conversation. Self-violations are included: smearing oneself with excrement, or eating it ('heroic' types of self-violation) are now rare, but milder forms persist.

There is, though, a complication: a couple intimately involved with each other may be said to possess the same territory jointly. So, what counts as intrusion, exposure, or obtrusion when performed by one 'individual' to another may well be perfectly acceptable when performed by one of a couple sharing the same territory. For relationships, if they are to be 'close', must require giving up some of the boundaries and barriers that ordinarily separate people; what is an invasion of privacy between strangers or mere acquaintances is an expression of intimacy between persons intimately involved with each other. So the conception of an individual behaving as though he embodied two selves is matched with the counterpart notion of couples behaving as if they were one person.

The third essay opens with yet another definition of ritual: 'Ritual is a perfunctory, conventionalised act through which an individual portrays his respect and regard for some object of ultimate value to that object of ultimate value or its stand-in' (*RP*, 62).

This looks very Durkheimian but in fact the footnote references to this pronouncement (on p. 62) are all taken from writings by ethologists. And for them, ritualisation is concerned primarily with communication, which serves as the basis for a number of other functions – e.g. channelling certain behaviour patterns, notably aggressive ones, into specific areas; the avoidance or prevention of interbreeding.

Despite the ethological references, there follows immediately a quotation from Durkheim on 'positive' rituals (paying homage through offerings) and 'negative' ones (interdicts and avoidance). The twofold classification provides the basis for his division of interchanges into 'supportive' interchanges ('positive rituals') and remedial interchanges ('negative rituals').

The essay on "supportive" interchanges is a comparatively lightweight affair; it is to some extent a reworking of material dealt with in *Interaction Ritual*. Supportive interchanges are brief episodes of interaction concerned with establishing, continuing, or renewing relationships. They may be classified in a number of ways, but here Goffman refers to two: by theme and by function.

Classifying by theme gives us, first, what he calls 'rituals of identificatory sympathy', by which he means those gestures and expressions of concern by which one person acts as if he were assuming the situation and experiencing the selfsame feelings (of loss, injury, desolation, etc.) as another. 'Identificatory sympathy' is at any rate a thematic subclass rather weightier than the others he proposes. 'Grooming talk' (a term coined by Desmond Morris) consists of conventionalised and often perfunctory phrases enquiring after someone's health, welcoming someone's return after a lengthy trip – or after illness. There are, too, those positive ritual courtesies between passing acquaintances or in encounters between the 'anonymously related', in which 'small offerings are received as though they were large, and large ones, when made, are often made with the expectation that they will be refused' (*RP*, 66). Another subclass could be taken as an exemplary specimen of 'identificatory sympathy'; it amounts to the 'tactful avoidance of open exclusion', and includes such minor courtesies as those – like offering to share 'minor comforts and comestibles' – which children are so often admonished by their parents to observe.

Classifying supportive interchanges by function, he comes up with greetings ('passing greetings', 'surprise greetings') and leave-takings, which, besides opening and closing an encounter in more or less definitive and unambiguous style, serve to maintain, sometimes to instigate, an enduring relationship. Also included are 'ratificatory rituals', which serve to acknowledge a new status – congratulations for marriages, careful commiserations for divorce, doleful condolences for funerals, and other verbal gestures. Such rituals can offer confirmation that a new organisational rank, social status, or presentation of self, etc., is accepted and approved.

II

The fourth essay is central to the whole book. It concerns the second, "negative", category of rituals, those which, according to Durkheim, have to do with interdicts and avoidance. In Goffman's adapted version, "remedial interchanges" consist of routines and rituals, verbal and non-verbal, which are commonly used to assuage injury, insult, or offence, and so restore relationships endangered by behaviour which might be taken to be offensive.

But remedial interchanges are far more consequential in social life than their function as compensatory or appeasement rituals might suggest. In the first place, the apologies, pleas for forgiveness, regrets, and so forth which are so frequently inserted into conversation are the means we commonly employ to change the content, focus, direction, or implication of what we are doing or saying. They mark a fresh paragraph in behavioural discourse, or propose a change of frame for the interaction in which we and others are engaged. There is also a second function, the reciprocal of the first, which is to promote the resumption of normal traffic-flow in social intercourse which has been cut off or broken into by some untoward incident, apparent impropriety, or mistake.

It is the sheer deftness and imaginative grasp in reading the subtle social constructions which underly the utterly commonplace, and conveying their significance in a way which is both lucid and striking that made Goffman so brilliant a social scientist and so rewarding to read. Insights such as these bring the "shock of recognition" we get from perceptive writing (Wilson's phrase, so frequently used in comments on Goffman's work, is entirely justified). But they also blind one to alternative interpretations and, in the present instance, to a possible misdirection implicit in the line of argument in which these observations are embedded.

The first two sections into which the essay is divided have to do, naturally enough, with the rules of social order and 'the process of social control by which infractions are discouraged' (*RP*, 108). Norms are 'enforced', says Goffman, by social sanctions, which are themselves 'norms about norms' – socially approved methods by which conformity may be assured.

The maintenance of orderliness in society at the level of everyday, brief, and transitory interactions, so runs his argument, is hardly a matter of law enforcement agencies. On the other hand, 'When individuals come into one another's immediate presence, territories of the self bring to the scene a vast filigree of tripwires which individuals are uniquely equipped to trip over' (*RP*, 106). The wrong committed may be trifling and retribution negligible, even if any is offered, but the trouble is that transgressions of the social norms governing interaction are, almost by definition, patently obvious or easily discoverable. Even so, what seems intentional or malicious may be entirely accidental, or incidental to a sequence of actions in which purpose, intention or function is unknown to bystanders. Mistakes can be made. The assortment of tripwires combined with the fallibility of others' judgments and, ordinarily, the triviality of the offence, means that there is less concern to lay blame correctly than to get everyone going about their business again.

And this prompts the obvious question: If the wrongs committed are so trivial and so patently manifest to all, why bother about making amends? The question is underscored rather than answered when Goffman goes on to observe that the primary function of remedial interchanges is to encourage the resumption of the flow of ordinary social intercourse.

It could be argued, surely, that what the whole of this "Remedial Interchanges" essay is driving at is the way in which individuals are constantly at work not only promoting, reinforcing, repairing or restoring the social order but creating, recreating and rearranging it. Which also means that the social order is not a finished system which we individually acknowledge by obeying its rules, but a *modus vivendi* which operates in so far as – and only in so far as – we, also individually, take the time and trouble to keep it going.

Goffman himself provides some support for this alternative interpretation in later passages. 'When an interactional offence occurs, everybody directly involved may be ready to assume guilt and offer reparation' (*RP*, 108) – even to the extent of their assuming the worst possible reading of what has happened, this being, he says, *the swiftest way of restoring normality*. Again, there is a section on "remedial work" which is designed, apparently, to substantiate one major contention of the essay, which is that the purpose of remedial work is to assert or reassert an individual's support of social propriety in general, not simply to make amends for an offence: '[T]he job of the offender is to show that it was not a fair expression of his attitude, or, when it evidently was, . . . to show that whatever happened before, he now has a right relationship – a pious attitude – to the rule in question' (*RP*, 118). In other words, one important function of remedial interchanges is a demonstration of our readiness to shoulder social obligations – obligations which, as Bernard Williams says, work "to secure reliability, a state of affairs in which people can reasonably expect others to behave in some ways and not in others"[2] – hence the offering of seemingly pointless apologies, the gratuitous assumption of responsibility for avoiding embarrassment or for turning a conversation, and the like.

One feature of social norms that Goffman stresses is that they apply to individual items of conduct as instances of a *class* of actions to which the norm applies. Thus an individual's actions are liable to be read as symptomatic, as expressions of that person's individual character. This is relevant to the working of the sanctioning system since, by his actions, the individual proclaims his success or failure in realising the person he and others feel he is, or should be. There is, in short, an important set of norms (perhaps an important aspect of all norms), deviation from which may be relatively harmless but which may put at risk the individual's tacit claim to be a person of normal competence and worth.

So, success in pleading mitigation often depends on establishing the fact that what was done is not to be taken as representative of one's true self. This feature of remedial work, which consists in shedding or reducing moral responsibility for an offence, is in fact intrinsic to apologies. To apologise for one's actions is in effect to disown the self (or part of the self) responsible. It is as if the self were split into 'a blameworthy part and a part that stands back and sympathises with the blame giving, and, by implication, is worthy of being brought back into the fold' (*RP*, 113).

Obviously, apologies are central to 'remedial work', but 'accounts', which amount to exculpatory utterances or gestures, may serve instead, since 'there is no act whose meaning is independent of reasons for its occurring, and there seems to be no act for which radically different reasons cannot be provided, and hence radically different meanings' (*RP*, 110). 'Accounts' do indeed vary, and Goffman provides a convincing illustration of how they can, in a footnote on a previous page (p. 102); this offers no less than twenty-four plausible accounts of "what was really happening" in a case where someone has driven through a red traffic light, and so seems clearly enough to have committed a traffic offence.

Both 'Accounts' and 'Apologies', while usually thought of as occurring after the event, may be offered beforehand, but "Requests", the third mode of remedial work, occur typically at or before the beginning of what might be an infringement of social norms. "Requests" ask licence to commit what might be thought a violation of someone else's rights, territorial or other. "May I . . .?", "Do you mind . . . ?", "Excuse me", and the like seek permission to engage in potential violation.

A characteristically "Goffmanesque" passage follows this exploration of seemingly trivial polite formulae. For, as he says, people in our kind of society are so familiar with the possibility and the usefulness of turning potential violations into requests that it becomes possible for all sorts of compulsion to be 'clothed, however lightly, as requests' (p. 115). So, personal searches in police stations and customs posts are routinely carried out by *asking* subjects to empty their pockets or purses; even body searches are usually prefaced by requests for permission.

The same kind of thing is said to go on in the more macabre setting of executions, and he adds, in a footnote, 'How clever, if not obscene, are the workings of society that occasions of ultimate coercion can be used to affirm ritually the respectfulness of the coercers and the free will of the coerced', (p. 115, n. 12). The moralising turn is beautifully executed, but it could be argued that what we have here is the reciprocal of people's tendency, with which he has made a good deal of play, to project a second self which they can disown or withdraw from. Even the worst of criminal offenders, he says, may want to be divorced from that previous or 'other' self responsible for the crime, and be aligned on the right side of the moral order. But this capacity, which is presumed to be universal, must also be something which everybody is aware of, at least intuitively, as existing in others as well as themselves. It is also, therefore, a capacity which may be exploited by others. 'For every territory of the self there will be a means of requesting permission to intrude' (*RP*, 115), and this by virtue of the known capacity the individual has of 'splitting' into two selves as a way out of awkward social situations. So it is that the offender, prisoner, or condemned criminal may be split by others into two, in order to ease their task, with one of the two 'selves' allowed to participate in the courtesies of everyday interaction.

If there is "obscenity" in this, as Goffman makes out, it must surely lie in the ultimate facts of compulsion, interrogation, imprisonment or execution, not in the scanty clothing of social amenity in which they may be dressed up. In other words, it is a matter which pertains to the structure, especially the power structure, of society rather than, as Goffman implies, to the rules of polite conduct which *sometimes* apply to the way these things are managed.

"Body Gloss", the fifth section in the essay, returns to the theme of 'body idiom' which was first explored in *Behavior in Public Places*. This time, gestures, facial expressions, glances, and movements are presented as a 'gloss' (explanatory or critical comment) on his situation offered by an individual who, conscious of transgressing some norm, has no means of shutting himself and witnesses off in a remedial interchange encounter. He is therefore obliged to 'provide a broad gesture for anyone who cares to receive it. . . . He provides a gloss on his situation' (*RP*, 125). Remedial acts broadcast in this way are not directed at making amends to others for offending them so much as at legitimating conduct which might conceivably seem odd or offensive to others. 'Orientation gloss', for example, consists of making gestures or assuming attitudes which define one's actions, or mere presence, as oriented to some everyday, or harmless, or necessary, purpose in cases where they might possibly be interpreted as aberrant or suspicious. A person standing alone in an otherwise empty street may feel called upon to consult his watch or to throw an occasional impatient glance along the road to demonstrate that he is waiting for a bus, or an acquaintance, to show up. 'Circumspection gloss' has the same purpose of disarming suspicion among possible onlookers by converting a misdemeanour into something similar but innocuous (replacing a stare by a scanning glance, for example). 'Overplay gloss', on the other hand, consists in minimising any intrusive or awkward act by overacting; given the expressive character his actions would wear if he were driven by some overwhelming compulsion, 'the individual throws himself into what would thus become of him, but in unserious manner' (p. 135).

The next section, "Dialogue", rounds off the analysis of remedial work by incorporating the responses of others into the interchange: 'a reply allows a request to be granted, an account to be credited, an apology to be proven sufficient, an acknowledgement that the remedial message has been clearly received.' All the same, although this makes for participation by both the giver and the receiver of an offence, we are not to suppose that this is 'communication in the narrow sense of the word' (by which one supposes is meant the transmission and reception of information); 'stands are being taken, moves are being made, displays are being provided, alignments are being established. Where utterances are involved, they are "performative"' (the term for a class of non-propositional utterances coined by J. L. Austin, who here makes his debut in Goffman's writings).

The last sections in the essay concern what might be called the syntax of remedial interchanges. The section on the structure of remedial interchange repeats the sequence of offence and ritual work, the latter capable of being pursued through apology, account or request ('remedy'), acknowledgment or response ('relief'), on to, possibly, appreciation from the offender and, finally, to ways in which an offence may be "minimised" in deprecatory fashion. Rapid attenuation of the interchange is the rule, for otherwise these rituals would take up the whole of everyone's time. For the same reason, each part ('turn') of the alternating sequence might be omitted, after the opening exchange.

But the basic structure of the interchange is now treated as a theme available for transformation into a number of variations. Apart from abbreviating the sequence, reversing the order, substituting minimal expressions, gestures, or 'almost anything' in place of an utterance, both sides of an interchange take on responsibility for the offence and the role of offender simultaneously, so as to get over the incident as quickly as possible. At the other extreme is the denial of either 'remedy' or 'relief' after an offence, thus provoking a direct challenge – a 'run-in'.

'This disruptive possibility', says Goffman, 'is endemic to the ritual organisation of encounters, created by the very frame of reference whose purpose seems to be to protect occasions from such discord.' This comes as something of a surprise. So far, we seem to have been living in a moral universe in which some all-wise social deity had enacted legislation to cover all foreseeable social encounters. The term 'organisation' has also gained admittance, bringing with it implications of encounters being arranged, even designed, by people with some purpose of their own in mind. I suppose it could be argued that displays of anger in retorts, gestures or facial expression are 'ritualised' too, but this is to dilute the notion of ritual until it becomes indistinguishable from expressive behaviour in the broadest sense, and we find ourselves with nothing outside ritual to hold on to.

The concepts of ritual, social control, and moral social order seem hardly capable of performing their architectural duties for the whole design. Some alternative interpretation seems at any rate to be required to fit the rather problematical variations which occur between equitable termination and 'run-in'. A swift transition from the opening move in a remedial interchange to a 'run-in' must depend largely on the instant recognition accorded a whole range of expressions, movements, gestures, and inarticulate utterances, too, as well as words. So, it could be argued, the variable structure of remedial interchanges is a consequence of the ability of members of any society to read the intention behind any given act or expression at least as much as a matter of variations in ritual; and ability of this kind depends on the way in which specific patterns of behaviour and speech become familiar as stereotypes.

Witnesses of some individual's transgression often seem to feel obliged to reassure the offender by acknowledging acceptance of any remedial move he offers 'that his message has been received and the viability of his line granted' (p. 159). So one encounters the 'little sympathetic grimace, that is, a smile, accompanied by a slight shaking of the head', which bystanders give when they become witnesses of an 'overplay gloss' gambit, such as an unserious run performed by a latecomer (p. 159-60). And the characterological aspect is caught in the observation that to engage in overplay gloss of this kind requires the performer to 'split himself in two', and requires evidence from onlookers that 'the disassociation is perceived and accepted as he defines it' (p. 161) although the individual is still 'dependent' on a reply, or a response from onlookers, when he 'plays himself straight'. Goffman includes smiles that do service as thanks among such 'appeasement gestures' (the term is Konrad Lorenz's.). And we also have this: 'Passing a parent and infant, an individual holds a smile, suggesting that as a member of the league of child-lovers he is to be trusted fully' (p. 160).

What he calls 'overlays on the ritual base' constitute another class of variations on the basic remedial cycle. These are utterances, or their equivalent in gesture or body gloss, which amount to giving a lifemanship twist to the remedial cycle – saying 'thanks' when an expected or routine courtesy is not performed, or by an augmented response when courtesy extends beyond the bounds of usage customary in any particular milieu. 'Overlays' also comprehend teasing, playful or provocative responses, and the kind of byplay in which an apparently neutral question or a seemingly conventional response contains a reproof, both representing the purposeful obstruction or obfuscation of a conventional remedial interchange, as in:

Wife: "I dented the fender again coming into the garage."
Husband: "You what?"
Wife: *(with inflexion and volume rising above her husband's):* "You heard what I said."

Snippets of conversation like this lead directly into the ninth section, 'Structural Speculations', which takes us further into sociolinguistics territory. The section is something of a curiosity. It sets out to 'sketch in the framework that might be necessary if we are to begin to deal with the complexities of ordinary verbal give and take' (p. 171), but turns out to be a brief attempt at the analysis and classification of repartee: 'cracks, comebacks, squelches' and what have come to be known as "one-liners".

In effect, the analysis turns on the possibilities of asserting some kind of superiority over the other party to an encounter. These possibilities are opened up by revoking or altering the course of the encounter which the opening conversational gambit seemed to call for. Since a conversational interchange is normally assumed to follow a conventional course, the opening remark will ordinarily allow that course to be predicted with some safety. But possible next moves also admit of an assortment of comebacks, deadpan squelches, and other miniature displays of verbal *savate*, classified as 'set-ups', 'cut-offs', 'decoupling', 'one-liners', 'comebacks', and 'post-terminals' (pp. 173-80). Goffman's examples are gathered from a miscellany of sources which include the comic paper *Mad*, Paul Goodman and Lawrence Durrell, and Charles Schutz's "Charlie Brown" cartoon strips.

The last section, 'Conclusions', ruminates on some of the implications of what the essay has explored, and ends by once more cruising around the notion of the individual as the creature of society, and self-determination as a figment of the requirements of social interaction (above, pp. 42-3) – but not quite taking it on board. It also includes an utterly preposterous declaration (seeing that it is made by a man who scarcely ever betrayed the slightest interest in the history of anything) about the importance of the history of manners, and some head-shaking over the neglect of this kind of history by other students of social behaviour.[3]

III

'Tie-Signs', the title of the next essay, refers to the ways in which individuals who relate to each other reveal their identities, social and private (because 'mutual treatment occurs within a framework of identification') and so on to displays, alignments and expressions.

Goffman's account of 'frameworks of identification' is drawn directly from the analysis of public ('social') and private ('personal') identity he developed in *Stigma*. 'Social identity' is revealed by signs and marks which place an individual according to social categories: age, sex, social class, and so on. Identification signs of this sort suffice for passing (and usually anonymous) relationships, essentially those between categories of persons rather than individuals. All that is needed is to establish how individuals will treat each other, should they have occasion for closer acquaintanceship.

Private ('personal') identity, on the other hand, being something unique (or uniquely imputed) to the individual, is more a matter of marks which distinguish individual persons as such and of the *display* of mutual familiarity with names, appearance, past happenings, and so on (p. 189). There have to be signs, in short, which provide – consciously or unconsciously – evidence for others that an individual has an established ('anchored') relationship with one or more of those present. Anonymous and anchored relationships are meant to represent polarities, with many variant forms between the two.

People tend to classify anchored relationships – which are the only sort dealt with in the essay – according to three attributes: name, terms, and stage of development. The conventional *names* of given relationships – brothers, kin, married couple, colleagues, and the like – are, he says, good enough for most purposes, including the present one, although there are ambiguities about them. The *terms* of a relationship, though, refer to its strength rated in various ways, such as 'close', 'estranged', etc.; strength, in this connection, represents a compound of different attributes: familiarity, confidence, sympathy (sense of mutual identification). The third criterion, *stage of development*, has a significance equivalent to age-grade, and arises from the circumstance of a relationship having a history – even a career.

When people meet each other, either for the first time or when they are already acquainted, they 'are under subtle obligation to treat each other in a way that makes such intelligence incidentally available' (p. 194). Of course, such incidental intelligence – the 'tie-signs' of the title – is discoverable in the form of photographs, letters, telephone calls, and so forth, as well as in gatherings, but the present concern is with the evidence made available by those present to each other through tie-signs – body-placement, posture, gesture, voice.

Equally, of course, evidence of this kind tends to be diffuse, and also rather ambiguous, so that mistakes are always possible in interpreting it. Yet, despite the awkwardness of possible error, the connection which exists between social relationships and public order means that, in Western society at least, there is a 'right and duty' to display tie-signs, even if only at minimal level. There is an expectation, Goffman goes on, that there will be some degree of fit between social and personal identity, choice in relationships, and rectitude of conduct. This also follows, presumably, from the fact that acting out social relationships in public has to be done in conformity with the rules of public order.

Interpersonal rituals are included among tie-signs, since they attest to a relationship; unwittingly displayed, they may even reveal hidden relationships. Evidently, public life can be treacherous for those who would conceal relationships, but what is more important, Goffman observes, is that 'these signs make it possible for individuals in public to engage in encounters without too much fear that their innocence will be misunderstood and that compromising will occur'.

There are also 'relation markers', the sort to be seen when a young couple enter a larger gathering, the hand squeeze and the exchange of smiles serving to fortify them for the occasion, but also to issue notice to the gathering to respect their special relationship. Goffman, having defined markers as acts or arrangements that exhibit or establish claims to territory, has now stretched the notion of territory to include a close relationship with another person. The link between territory and relationship, in this context, is, he says, 'exclusivity'. This could perhaps be better rendered as possessiveness, especially when he goes on to remark that issuing such notices is especially true when they denote relationships with subordinates.

Changes in relationship are usually marked by acts and events that serve to signal and to establish the new state of affairs. These acts and events are occasioned most obviously by births, marriages and deaths, when change signals tend to be most clearly ritualised; but they are also prescribed for celebrating homecomings, the renewal of former acquaintanceships, and so on down to interchanges in which the ritual itself may be, 'as it were, ritualised' (p. 205) – by which is meant that it is accorded a 'merely perfunctory' performance and answers to what, in a borrowing from the terminology of animal behaviour studies, is called a "display".

However, the primary concern of the "Tie-Signs" essay, we learn on page 205, is with relationship formation; and the change signs to which most significance attaches are those which mark the initiation of a new, closer, more intimate, more affectionate relationship. These first moves always involve 'familiarities', or taking minor liberties with the other's belongings, personal space and so on. What Goffman is driving at is that all 'anchored' relationships presuppose prior acquaintanceship (and thus the existence of an "understanding"), and this seems mostly to come into being for reasons 'outside itself' - i.e. as a direct and immediate result of institutional arrangements - sibling, customer, co-worker, etc. Others are intrinsically discretionary. In Western society, it is these discretionary relationships that most immediately involve considerations of public order as expressed in rules about co-mingling. Relationships are for the most part formed during 'social occasions', when participation by itself confers the right to initiate talk with anyone present and to be received in a friendly manner. However, this particular implication is qualified by what follows, because we now come to the initiator's risk in being exposed to rejection: hence 'strategic tact' (p. 207), by which an attempt at initiating a relationship is made tentatively, and with the circumspection needed to deal with rejection without loss of face. 'An ambiguity thus results, but this derives not from some lack of consensus, failure of communication, or breakdown in social organisation, but from competent participation in the relationship game' (p. 207).

Competence in the kind of strategic tact which can take discreet advantage of the ambiguities inherent in the change signals which initiate relationships is also brought into play outside parties and the like - notoriously so, in street pickups, and so on. The point is that this sort of thing is a direct consequence of the way pedestrian traffic is organised by the exchange of visible signs of intention; it constantly provides openings for using strategic tact to take advantage of expressive moves which are necessarily ambiguous. 'And since these openings exist, there must be countervailing norms to prevent the populace from falling through them' (p. 210).

'Encounter-groups' and the like, as Goffman pointed out earlier on in a footnote (p. 58), set out to disregard such ambiguity traps. Territorial violations and tie-signs which proclaim a strong relationship (familiarity, trust, sympathy) are actively promoted between first acquaintances. The claim is that stimulating close relationships in this manner - taking the deed for the will, in other words - either serves actually to promote intimacy and friendship or induces emotional rewards of the same kind.

Goffman clearly regards this version of taking the deed for the will as psychological chicanery of an unpleasant kind. Yet "taking the deed for the will" turns up in another essay, where it is put forward to challenge the existence of free-will and volition. It arises in this way. Although, he says, it is 'traditional' to think of threats to the rules governing behaviour in terms of claimants and potential offenders, it is perhaps better to think of *all* participants in encounters as engaged perpetually in avoiding or warding off violations and contingencies which might gave rise to them. The implication is that the maintenance of social order and the preservation of the structure of social relationships depends on everybody's being in a state of constant wariness when they are in the presence of others.

There is a final twist to the argument. Central to the whole issue of territoriality is the 'ego', the positive feelings which the individual thinks of as identical with his actual self. It is here, he says, that we ('traditionally') locate the conception of self-determination and free-will, which supposedly come into play in deciding what and whom to avoid (so as to gain or maintain respect), and what and whom to accede to or engage with (so as to gain or maintain self-regard). If, however, the management of territoriality is the simultaneous and constant concern of everyone, might it not be that we should regard 'personal will and volition . . . not as something which territorial arrangements must come to terms with and make allowances for, but rather as *a function which must be inserted into agents?*' (emphasis added).

This passage resumes the theme broached at the end of the fourth essay, "Remedial Exchanges". The point of remedial interchanges – all the manifold explanatory accounts, excuses, requests, and pleas we give in order to make amends for omissions, errors, and accidents of the most trivial, as well as serious, kind – is that they are 'a central organisational device of public order'. Their function is not to make reparation to others for our misdeeds but to repair possible damage to the fabric of society. We are impelled to do so because of our awareness of the unending need to repair damage or forestall threat to social order. Creatures of society as we are, it is this which we have to regard as of paramount importance. And this awareness comes, in turn, from our recognition of these remedies as something prescribed by society. The very fact that apologies, accounts, and pleas may be directed to chance acquaintances or strangers, or even broadcast to any one within sight or hearing, must mean that we are conscious of their ultimate function.

Even if the individuals choose not to offer the 'correct' response, they still have to take the trouble to show awareness of what has happened and to manage themselves, so as to dispel or withstand disapproval, and to maintain some plausible relationship with others. And while it may seem that some degree, or level, of self-determination is involved in remedial actions, the repertoire of responses available to individuals, whatever they do, is culturally determined, a *donnée* of our culture. So society closes the range of choices open to us even as it opens up the possibility of choosing. 'And even more deterministic is the need, the obligation, the compulsion, to take some kind of stand relative to the perceivable deficiency in question' (p. 187).

In other words, we feel compelled to express regrets, excuses, requests so as to 'keep station' in society, rescue our social identity or self-respect from possible danger, or preserve the regard of other people.

Declaring, in effect, that there is no such thing as the individual (in the universally accepted sense, that is) seems as *outré* as the much-quoted pronouncement by a British prime minister that there is no such thing as society. But it is in fact more outrageous, in that his argument leads round not just in circles but in ever-diminishing ones. For what it adds up to is that individuals are endowed with the feelings of self-respect and self-regard which are enshrined in personal will and volition (and endowed too, presumably, with goals to aim at and desires to satisfy) so as to fulfil the two functions of the maintenance of territorial preserves. In so doing they are, however, restricted to the repertoire of conduct and utterances they receive as bequests from society; the personal initiative and free choice we think we exercise in all this is simply a necessity laid on us (by "society") to maintain the social order as a going concern. And the two functions served *by* maintaining territorial preserves are none other than, first, to avert threats to individual self-respect and, second, to court associations which enhance individual self-regard.

IV

"Normal Appearances", the last of the six essays which make up *Relations in Public* (not counting the appendix), also rounds off the exploration of social interaction in general which he had pursued for some fifteen or more years. It is a paper which shows Goffman at his unorthodox, offbeat, and subversive best. The subject he deals with is an utterly familiar part of everyone's life, is touched on, referred to, exploited, discussed endlessly in newspapers and journalistic pieces and in both popular and up-market fiction – but totally passed over by social scientists, or virtually so. This is what seems to be an alarming increase in our vulnerability to physical assault, to theft, larceny, burglary, and vandalism, and to invasions of our private lives – in all of which we tend to be deceived by the 'normal', natural-seeming scenery and goings-on around us. The ethological framework (Goffman style) is fully developed and artfully deployed. The conception of social order as a set of moral incumbencies is pushed to its Hobbesian limit. And the essay ends by quoting a lengthy piece of reportage by Lévi-Strauss on the merciless importunity of Calcutta beggars, a pointer to the true awfulness of a world in which the rules governing social intercourse have been totally eroded. The argument is superbly organised and presented, and there are any number of aphorisms, saws, pithy asides, and snide comments.

The first part of the essay works through the terminology of ethological studies to do with the behaviour of hunter and prey, and its applicability to human beings, especially city-dwellers. Human beings, it is assumed at the outset, have the same two basic modes of activity as animals: 'either they go about their business grazing, gazing, mothering, digesting, resting, playing, attending to easily managed matters at hand – or, fully mobilised, a fury of intent, alarmed, they go to attack or to stalk or to flee.' Keeping the two states of being separate and distinct is a matter of vigilance – not a full-scale alert, for this is impossible to sustain for long, but a 'running reading' of the situation. And, 'by a wonder of adaptation these readings can be done out of the furthest corner of whatever is serving for an eye, leaving the individual himself free to focus his main attention on the non-emergencies around him' (p. 238).

For the most part, then, so long as the world around one carries no hint of some unusual presence or occurrence, vigilance amounts to no more than a 'side-involvement', leaving the individual feeling safe enough to carry on with his own affairs. "Feeling safe enough" is a deliberately imprecise way of putting it: adequate – or appropriate – as an account of subjective awareness, but not, of course, for the circumstances to which it is a response. For while, in the case of human beings, 'normality' or 'naturalness' is equated simply with the absence of danger or threat or fear of the unexpected or untoward, 'normal' appearances, in the animal world, do not signify absence of risk (or opportunity) but the level of risk an individual is prepared to cope with, or of opportunity not worth attempting. The "normality" or "naturalness" of a situation for animals, then, is an adjustment – precarious and subject to instant disturbance – arrived at between those who are present to each other's senses. It is, in short, an artefact, *created* by those cohabiting within the same physical setting. Each individual typically comes to terms with whatever range of risk and opportunity an environment contains, withdraws his main attention from them, and gets on with other matters.

But, according to one of the conclusions arrived at in one of the preceding essays, "Tie-Signs", the normality and naturalness we find in situations always have to be contrived. Indeed, we are often aware that 'acting normally' or 'naturally' has sometimes to be achieved by self-conscious effort. And although, in human society, it is *usually* the case that normal appearances, typical appearances, and proper appearances are much the same, 'this agreement conceals the adaptive social processes that produced it and the inevitable possibility that these appearances will not coincide' (p. 240). So, if the naturalness and normality of social situations (or, by extension, social settings) has to be thought of as manufactured, then, obviously, the appearance of normality or naturalness may be manufactured too, and so be false. The rather protracted argument is brought to a conclusion on page 282, where we find,

> In this paper, we deal with a normalcy show, with one individual seeking for warnings while concealing his suspicions and the others concealing the threat and opportunity they constitute for him while searching for signs that they are suspected.

The drift of the argument so far has been to draw a much closer parallel between arousal, alarm, vigilance and adjustment in the animal world and human society than we commonly think is the case. One could go on; there is, for example, the possibility, in the animal world, of individuals reading signs made by other animals, even by members of other species, as alarms. This holds good for human society, too, even short of panic, where the connection is all too obvious. Of course, there are differences. While in certain animal species there may be individuals who are treated by their fellows as especially alert, or who keep position as look-outs, and so reduce the need for vigilance by everyone else, who have merely to keep an eye on them, this hardly amounts to the provision made in modern Western societies for protecting individuals going about their ordinary lawful business against attack or interference.

Further, there exists in some people a trained capacity for effective action in alarming situations. If one starts with the notion of an individual's acquired experience or skill as a factor in determining what he would sense as alarming, it is apparent that the capacity of a diver, an aircraft pilot, a skier (or a sword-swallower), to be at ease with his activity is attained only after 'a period, often long, when catastrophe seemed everywhere and all attention given to saving his own skin'. To do these things with ease and confidence requires more than acquiring the relevant technical information and learning the specific skills or procedures involved. But this is merely to 'intellectualise' the process. To be at ease in what were formerly alarming situations means that the individual has built up a fund of specific competence out of his experiences. He has, that is, become practised in procedures of his own devising for coping with the threats and opportunities which that kind of activity throws up at him. This is not a matter of routine skills acquired through practice. 'He acquires a survivably short reaction time – the period needed to sense alarm, to decide on a correct response, and to respond' (p. 249).

Extrapolating from this, it is possible to see that, for all of us, almost every activity we now perform with unthinking ease 'was at some time something that required anxious mobilisation of effort – walking across a road, uttering a complex sentence' (p. 248).

So we are all, to a greater or lesser degree, "experts". Although coping with the world around us, in this positive sense, amounts to more than just knowing it, it also includes knowing the limits of such competence. Both the expert and the ordinary individual, adult or child, acquire a fund of knowledge about the things, activities, and occurrences which are to be avoided, either altogether or at certain times. Again, there are institutionalised procedures in modern societies for encouraging this. Particular signs and alarms are often positioned so as to encourage avoidance. Yet, as all parents know, the efficacy of such alarms and warnings depends on the individual's having acquired some understanding of the motives and intentions of the persons or agencies who put them there. For the world around the individual is, especially nowadays, a socially determined world. 'Its features are there by virtue of the socially organised training the individual has obtained and by virtue of some kind of collective guarantee regarding the material and human elements in the situation' (p. 250). The guarantee is never absolute, and frequent false alarms serve to dim vigilance, but, on the whole, individuals – animal and human – acquire some kind of adaptive competence which allows them to set a margin between the alarm sign itself and the object or happening which is the

96

source of alarm – between what we may call "fight or flight" distance and "orientation" distance, a margin which varies with the experience or expertness of the individual. Ethologists have adopted Uexküll's term, *Umwelt*, for the space within which *potential* sources of alarm may be found.

We now approach the nub of the essay's thesis:

> I take it as a central fact of life that they who might through their doings alarm someone will very often be concerned about this fact themselves. As predators, they will want to get close enough to pounce; as prey, they will want to stay out of the line of untender attention.

In any event, normal appearances, what they consist in, and how they may be sustained, will be of the greatest concern. Hence the need for cover, or disguise; what is normal appearance to an intended victim or to an intending predator 'becomes the cloak that his others must discern, tailor, and wear . . . To disappear from sight, to melt from view, is not, then, to hide or sneak away; it is to be present but of no concern' (pp. 256-7).

Ordinarily, the normality of the appearance of the everyday world we move around in is not a matter of conscious awareness, and the amount of what we can cope with grows with experience. It is the exceptional that triggers awareness. But for predators or prey, both seeking to avoid drawing attention to themselves, conscious awareness of what makes for normal appearances is of paramount concern – 'not normal appearances *for them* but normal appearances *of them* for the enemy'. They will need to know what seems natural for the subject (i.e. prey or predator) in order to preserve it.

Alarms may, of course, prove false, or reassurance may come quickly; if so, concentration will decay quickly. When other persons are the reason for alarm, though, reassurance has a special role. 'For individuals who cause alarm can, in the face of this reaction, provide evidence that the alarm is false – with an account, underlined by a request or apology.' Furthermore, people often hold off responding to an alarm until the person who provoked it has a chance to offer an account and possibly an apology. 'And it seems that no matter how bizarre and threatening an alarming sight may be, an effective account may be discovered for it' (p. 266) – effective in that, true or false, it will allay fears.

This last theme is pursued into the world of criminals and their police antagonists, where a premium is placed on 'presence of mind': the instant ability to produce effective accounts (which need not, of course, be true accounts). There are actually two dramaturgic tasks they may have to perform: they can play out roles that are alien to them (as when a police spy acts like a Trotskyite student so as to penetrate a radical organisation); a second task is to conceal their own concern lest they give themselves away – i.e. they must "act natural", which in fact means to act out a style of behaving which is really their own.

"Acting natural" in this way is a virtually universal social skill which we put to frequent, and legitimate, use. Anyone who occupies a role in a way that is recognised, legitimated and supported by others often comes to act it out in a 'genuinely forthright manner'. Yet it also 'functions as a display to convince audiences' (as the "sincerity" cultivated by politicians and other public figures on television has taught us). 'He is still doing that which he has had to learn to do (often what he felt unnatural in what he was doing), . . . and that which, when something goes wrong, he can become self-conscious about.'

What this all adds up to is that the protagonists on both sides in an alarming, or potentially alarming, situation have a need to act natural – to act as though there were no need for apprehensiveness. And this may hold good even when, perhaps especially when, there is true cause for alarm: for signs of suspicion could make those on the other side suspicious. Individuals are prompted to "act out" normal behaviour, for a variety of reasons. Acting nonchalantly is a means of saving face, of convincing others that he or she is not rendered helpless by hostile intrusion, disconcerted by challenge, or embarrassed by an untoward occurrence or unwelcome presence. Behaving naturally becomes a form of deceit when it comes to masking the planned disruption of a relationship – as in the case of a husband or wife having a secret affair or contemplating divorce. Third, there is the "set-up", a kind of moral ambush designed to entrap, but again requiring someone to "act natural" in order to conceal from others what he knows, or intends. And, fourth, self-enactment may be enforced under threat – 'at the point of a gun', as Goffman says. In all these cases, a lie is enacted. What makes these particular performances false, though, is not the creation of a new, false, routine but the continuation of an old, valid one in altered circumstances. Not only the individual centrally concerned, but certain others will, in part, have the same task – that of enacting one's own self – though in different degrees and for different reasons. And this makes for a kind of convergence between innocence and treachery.

The section ends with what might be taken as an argument for the reasonableness of wholesale paranoia, or at least a plea for paranoiacs. 'Since it is possible for normal appearances to qualify as reason for alarm, alarming signs will ever be available' (p. 282). However, the leading edge of argument is now concerned with vulnerability itself. Just as we learn that social situations, which may be falsified, are therefore always to be regarded as contrived, so the possibility that normal appearances may be faked leads to the suggestion that *Umwelte* are also constructs. The assumptions an individual makes about his *Umwelt* are vulnerable to a sharp reminder that, in certain circumstances, they are mere assumptions, and possibly unfounded.

In modern society, the individual's *Umwelt* is often prescribed by the built environment – his room, his house, workplace, office, or some familiar haunt other than these. These are likely to be assumed to be unhazardous and innocent – although they might not be so. Further, such 'furnished frames', even if they are not the individual's own possessions, tend to be regarded as part of his own 'fixed territory'; any damage to it can be a damage to him. Indeed, possession of a 'furnished frame' subjects the possessor to extra grounds for alarm even when he is absent. Defilement by burglars is *said* to be common (Goffman is rightly cautious here), but in any case even a 'clean' burglary is seen as a desecration.

Moving on from 'furnished frames', one comes to the vulnerability which derives from the limitations of human perceptual equipment. Not only is there always a zone 'behind one's back', but danger can lurk behind a partition, and in the dark; Goffman calls these thresholds of perceptibility 'lurk lines'. With the increasing prevalence (or reporting) of physical assault in American, and now British and European, cities, 'lurk lines' have multiplied, and the city-dweller has now acquired experience of the 'sentry problem' (in which exactly those sounds that everyone discounts and disattends are for him matters of intense concern), and the 'sniper problem' (in which streets hitherto treated as innocent become fraught with danger).

Of course, the multiplication of lurk lines is an effect produced by a changed social rather than physical environment; for every *Umwelt*, however closed off by walls, has points of routine access and impingement. Access may be restricted, but these conventional restrictions are indeed conventional, or largely so, and points of access can easily become points of alarm. There is perhaps more significance than Goffman allows in the frequent exploitation of the notion of lurk lines in children's play, which often seems designed for training experience in alertness to danger, in accounting for it as a perpetual possibility, and in dealing with it. Still, given his own preoccupations, he sees the major significance of the notion in the extreme fragility of the *Umwelt* of paranoiacs, with vulnerability extended to the belief that friends and acquaintances are linked in collusive betrayal, and so best avoided.

Finally, there are the special vulnerabilities which lie in the individual's 'social net' (which, in this context, signifies those actually co-present with him – friends, acquaintances, strangers – a kind of social *Umwelt*). These vulnerabilities are, of course, the familiar stuff of much popular writing, but, Goffman, suggests, 'what is insufficiently appreciated is the bearing of the information given off by expressive behaviour on these contingencies' (p. 303).

When with others, i.e. those in his immediate view (his 'social net'), an individual has to assume that a supply of social information will be available to him. Ordinarily, this information is enough for him to judge whether or not to be alarmed, and so put a limit to the dangers contained in the social net around him. But it is precisely these expectations which will be manipulated by potential predators – pickpockets, spies, con-men, surveillance teams. Moreover, ample opportunities for supplying false social information are available in what Goffman calls 'stocked' (as against "stock") characters, i.e. figures in public places whose presence is rendered legitimate or acceptable by reason of their official duties or familiarity, such as policemen, newspaper sellers, road menders, etc. All are treated as 'non-persons' – as not really there.

How, then, can we ever be sure that things are what they seem, and that there is nothing or nobody in our immediate surroundings which is threatening, or may prove harmful? For if, as we have just seen, the absence of anything unusual in a situation does not necessarily mean that it is safe, neither does the unexpected necessarily give rise to alarm or unease. The resolution of this perpetual – and rather paralysing – dilemma, Goffman argues, lies in the fact that one feels at ease, and safe, if nothing untoward is occurring, or present, in one's surroundings which is *connected* with one's current undertaking, purpose, task, or project. There are plenty of things and happenings in public places which are indifferent to one's own concerns and designs, and are consequently ignored as merely incidental.

'The individual, then, divides his *Umwelt* into the designed and the undesigned, into project and setting, into the self-oriented and the incidental' (p. 312). Connectedness is all. He can even dismiss all sorts of otherwise alarming incidents as fortuitous: lucky or unlucky, sheer coincidence or pure accident. The only proviso is that they are, or seem, undesigned.

All of which allows apparently fortuitous happenings to be contrived which later have harmful or threatening consequences for the individual centrally concerned. By way of illustration, Goffman harks back to the world of "Cooling the Mark Out". In the 'big con', for example, the mark is centre stage, but must be convinced that all the others are merely incidentally present and that he, too, is an incidental user of the place. 'Playing the world backwards' is the somewhat mystifying term he uses for contrivances of this kind, in which the seeming happenstance presence of others has in fact been planned.

> It should now be plain that as the individual moves through the course of his day, the changing surround that moves with him is likely to contain many minor dealings with others that could have alarming consequences for him. At many points he will be vulnerable to having his world played backwards.
>
> (p. 319)

In addition to this kind of hazard, the possibility that the individual's world can be played backwards is matched by the possibility that it will be "played forward" improperly. For the individual assumes that the minor dealings he has with persons passing on their several ways will not be used by them to lay the basis for unanticipated costs to him in the future. Pickpockets, thieves, confidence tricksters, and others engage in forward playing when they 'finger' a potential victim. What is really important, Goffman goes on, is that, given that an apparently undesigned contact turned out in retrospect as the first visible move in a well-designed game being played against the individual, it follows that *any* current incidental contact that has so far not led to anything alarming might yet do so. Hence, the very idea of someone being 'merely present' involves vulnerabilities.

The final position we reach in this section concerned with

connectedness and contrivance is that 'even perfect appearances can be suspect'. Normal appearances become, as it were, a broad cover under which persons and agencies may try to monitor the individual, approach him for attack, conceal things vital to him, attempt to make secret contact with him, and the like. 'His *Umwelt* becomes hot for him' (p. 328). So, instead of the standard image of a continuum which leads from 'the peace that usually obtains in public and semi-public places', and from people 'quietly going about their business', to places less secure, and so on 'until we are in the battlefield . . . we might better ask of the most peaceful and secure [situation] what steps would be necessary to transform it into something that was deeply unsettling. And we cannot read from the depths of the security the number of steps required to reverse the situation' (p. 329) – for the probability of alarm has to be distinguished from its structural feasibility.

V

The tenor of the last pages of the essay is bleak and menacing, though perhaps they are meant not so much as awful warning as to underline the importance of the study of public order and its mechanics. We are, he writes, more and more conscious of the vulnerability of public life – and things are getting worse. People have unavoidably to expose themselves both to physical settings over which they have no or little control and to the close proximity of others over whose selection they have little to say. Public places are protected by laws, but it has become impossible to rely on the police for the prevention of crime. And the possibility that those present will lend a hand, raise hue and cry, serve as witnesses has been drowned by the spectacular growth in civic apathy. So, 'in place of unconcern there can be alarm – until, that is, the streets are redefined as naturally precarious places, and a high level of risk becomes routine' (p. 332).

But it is not simply the multiplication of criminals and the diminishing reliability of publicly organised urban defence systems which put public order at risk. He ends the essay with a lengthy quotation from Lévi-Strauss on the experience of being beset, from the moment he set foot outside his hotel in Calcutta, by crowds of hawkers, beggars, shopkeepers, peddlars, rickshaw-boys, pimps.

"One dare not meet a gaze frankly, for the simple satisfaction of making contact with another man; the slightest pause will be interpreted as weakness, as purchase for an importunity. . . . You are thus at the very outset compelled to deny in others that specifically human quality which makes possible good faith and a sense of contract and obligation. . . ."

(p. 333)

It is all very distressing, but it is an experience which could be matched by any traveller in the early twentieth century who disembarked at Suez, any well-dressed nineteenth-century tourist in Rome, or, for that matter, any inexperienced visitor to Hogarth's London. A high level of risk in public places, outside as well as inside cities, was accepted as routine right up until the last century. The public order we know has possibly to be viewed as a temporary product of the invention of police forces and street lighting, which are now proving to be not the safeguards they once were.

Goffman's disregard of any historical dimension is typical and unsurprising. But it takes one aback to find Lévi-Strauss unable to recognise that what he is describing is not anarchy, nor a system of public order which has fallen into ruin, but a particular kind of public order which is indigenous, so to speak, to modern Calcutta (though by no means exclusive to it). It exists in disregard of the social barriers – erected to protect the haves from the have-nots – which, in our society, replace those provided first by bodyguards and then by police. Interpreting the slightest pause "as weakness, as purchase for an importunity", bespeaks not total disorder but a set of conventions within a public order which still makes the haves, when they venture into public, immediately accessible to the have-nots as legitimate prey.

Public order is not a finished system which we individually acknowledge by obeying its rules but a *modus vivendi* which operates in so far as – and only in so far as – we, also individually, take the time and trouble to create it and to keep it going. In Merleau-Ponty's words:

> The human world is an open or unfinished system and the same radical contingency which threatens it with discord also rescues it from the inevitability of discord and prevents us from despairing of it, providing only that one remembers its machineries are actually men and tries to maintain and expand man's relations to man.[4]

Public order may be regarded, as Goffman regards it, as a body of rules to which we subject our behaviour and on whose correct observance our acceptability as members of society depends. But it is also, and much more, a system which is contingent upon the dues paid it by the members of society – or, rather, the majority of them. The use of the word "government" for what we understand by social, including public, order in the quotation from Spencer which prefaces the book – while it may seem odd to the modern reader – provides a clue to the essentially political nature of social norms. "Political", because if social order is a kind of elementary government, one must also reckon with pressure groups, parties in opposition, and rebels, as well as with the disenfranchised, the miscreants, the outlaws, and the traitors.

It is in *Relations in Public* that one becomes most aware not so much of a discrepancy as of an uncomfortable imbalance between the methodology (the intellectual approach) Goffman professes and the methods of enquiry and analysis he uses. There are, on the one side, the repeated affirmations of the primacy of social rules and norms – of the grammar and syntax of social action. On the other, one finds him relying, much of the time, on intuitive awareness – sympathetic understanding – of the meanings, intentions, and motives of the actors he observes. He is not alone in this. All social scientists, not excepting neo-classical economists of the stricter sort or the almost forgotten school of behaviourist psychology, attempt to construct models of situations which are logically coherent and so may stand as objectively valid representations of what they have observed and recorded. But in order to do so they must inevitably draw on the awareness they have of other minds – an awareness which comes from the fact that, as Hume put it, "the minds of men are mirrors to one another".[5]

In his ethological mode, Goffman is capable of creating an account of pedestrian traffic on busy city streets that captures perfectly the mutual observation and rapid sucession of signals between passers-by which enables them to go on their several ways without impediment. But it is not only the grammar and syntax of the conventional rules governing visual interaction between pedestrians – the parsing of a "critical sign" (p. 13), the analysis of a "body check" (p. 12) – which is at issue, but the intentions and interpretations of the pedestrians themselves. Goffman naturally – unavoidably – refers to them too, but his prime concern is with the "grammar and syntax" of the conventional rules.

The point I am trying to make may be underlined by the device (slightly underhand, perhaps) of again quoting from Lévi-Strauss, this time from *The Savage Mind*, in order to interpret what Lévi-Strauss wrote in the article published in the *New Left Review*, from which Goffman's quotation was drawn.[6] For Lévi-Strauss, too, had the idea of using urban traffic as an archetypal specimen of interaction rules – although, in his case, it is the training, skill, and heightened tension of the car-driver which is at work, rather than experiential competence of ordinary pedestrians. Lévi-Strauss likens the trained acuteness of perception required of the car-driver to the "procedure of the American Indian who follows a trail by means of imperceptible clues or the Australian who unhesitatingly identifies the footprints left by any member of his tribe". He argues that this involves "a reciprocity of perspectives, in which man and the world mirror each other".[7]

It seems that when Lévi-Strauss looked at traffic, what he saw in it was not Goffman's rules of public order but a series of dialogues between drivers whose intentions are translated into signs which, precisely because they are signs, demand to be interpreted.

NOTES AND REFERENCES

1. The world, or worlds, of 'as if' was a topic which seems to have fascinated a number of people before the middle of the century, but dropped out of fashion after the Second World War. See, for example, C. K. Ogden on Jeremy Bentham's theory of fictions, and Hans Vaihinger's *Philosophy of 'As If'*.
2. B. Williams, *Ethics and the Limits of Philosophy*, Fontana, 1985, p. 187.
3. Norbert Elias *Über den Prozess der Zivilisation* (1939), although not published in translation until 1978, was not unknown before then; and while *The Civilizing Process* is one of the most thoroughgoing, and certainly the most "sociological" treatments of the history of European manners, it is not by any means the only one.
4. Quoted by Stanford Lyman in his review of *Relations in Public (Contemporary Sociology*, vol. 2, 1973, pp. 360-6). The words are taken from Merleau-Ponty's *Humanism and Terror*.
5. *Treatise of Human Nature*, Book II, Part II, Section V.
6. C. Lévi-Strauss, "Crowds", *New Left Review*, XV (May-June 1962), pp. 3-9.
7. C. Lévi-Strauss, *The Savage Mind*, Weidenfeld & Nicholson, 1966, p. 222.

5
ACTING OUT

Most cultures, past and present, and at whatever stage of civilisation they have reached, seem to accommodate some idea of the divisibility of the individual self. For our part, we have become accustomed to the partitioning of the individual which psychologists have arrived at for the more convenient study of mental processes. By this one refers not merely to the familiar Freudian ego, superego, and the id, but to the way in which the special attributes of a person – intellectual attainment, emotional response, memory of the past, and more – may be examined and analysed independently of each other and of the whole person, so that one can speak meaningfully of the psychology of a person and mean something different from what we mean by "a person". There are plenty of other partitionings on offer, few quite so familiar but none which seem therefore unacceptable.

According to Durkheim, for example, the indwelling "I" of a person, the active principle of will and choice which makes the individual self-consciously unique is an implant from the "mana" of the social order of which the self is part. The individual becomes – almost – a mere particle of society. Equipped with this notion, Durkheim could go on to treat major social processes like social change as the consequence of some inner dynamic working within society, such as the division of labour, rather than of man's perpetual endeavour to construct and reconstruct social order around him.

This is true of much of Goffman's writings, too, but when it comes to *The Presentation of Self in Everyday Life*, and the essays associated with it, the individual is partitioned along different lines and becomes something else – or rather, some things else.

What we encounter in the dramaturgic model he adopted in his first book (a model altered a good deal later on; but never entirely abandoned), is a series of selves, one "inside" the other, after the

106

fashion of a Chinese box, or Russian doll. There is an inner self lurking inside the self which is present, or presented, to the outside world of others. The divisions match those between playwright, producer, actor, and part. There is a social self ("producer") which measures the appropriateness of the individual's role to the social position in which it is fixed ("part"), and also adjusts the distance between them – i.e. the degree to which it seems rewarding to measure up to performance of the role at its most typical ("actor"). But there is also an inner "I" which distinguishes between his self-image and the misconceptions of himself which he feels his behaviour must be sowing among others, or retreats even from the self-image into wondering "is this really me?" It *manages* the social self. It is both tactician and strategist, directing the social, role-playing, self into and through social situations, establishments, settings.

I

The idea that 'all the world's a stage', is as old as the theatre itself. Plato, in the *Philebus*, writes of 'the great stage of human life' on which men act out both comedy and tragedy; Petronius' *'totus mundus agit histrionem'* became a familiar motto in the Renaissance, expressive of a sense of the unreality of life.[1] By Shakespeare's time, the *theatrum mundi* topos had become a commonplace; it was its *over*-familiarity that he used to such effect in a number of plays.

As always, Shakespeare worked within the framework of established ideas – in this case, the analogy's two classic referents: the manipulation of human affairs by superhuman forces ("as flies to wanton boys, so we to the gods"), and the conscious deceptions which men practise on each other ("seeming a saint when I most play the villain"). Thereafter, with no extension of reference, and the secularisation of a divine puppeteer into "social forces", the theatre metaphor for human existence and conduct descended into cliché.

Its resurrection by social scientists in the present century owes much to their adoption of the term 'role' to represent routines or codes of behaviour appropriate to (and thus expressive of) specific social positions – as father, mother or child; as worker, salesman or manager; as priest, physician or politician; as neighbour, spectator, host or guest. It was not until later, though, that the full content of meanings contained in the analogy began to be unpacked in elaborate models which went beyond the odd allusion and the poaching of terms like "role" and "actor". The opening-up came from initiatives – notably by Marcel Mauss and Victor Turner among social scientists and by Kenneth Burke among humanists – which were independent of each other but almost certainly the product of the re-arming of social enquiry and humanist ideas which happened in France, Britain, and the United States during the inter-war years, and burst into active life after the end of the Second World War.

In Goffman's case the most influential of these new initiatives was Kenneth Burke's. His *Grammar of Motives*, first published in 1945, laid out a comprehensive *schema*, hinted at in his earlier *Permanence and Change*, for the interpretation of human action and social intercourse which he called "dramatism". The book does not pretend to be an analysis of motives *per se* – i.e. a psychology of social action. What Burke is careful to say that he offers is a key to the way in which we normally and habitually interpret behaviour and impute motives. In the words of his opening paragraphs:

> What is involved when we say what people are doing and why they are doing it? An answer to that question is the subject of this book. The book is concerned with the basic forms of thought which, in accordance with the nature of the world as all men necessarily experience it, are exemplified in the attributing of motives. These forms of thought can be embodied profoundly or trivially, truthfully or falsely. They are equally present in systematically elaborated metaphysical structures, in legal judgments, in political and scientific works, in news and in bits of gossip offered at random.
>
> We shall use five terms as generating principle of our investigation. They are: Act, Scene, Agent, Agency, Purpose. . . . [Any] complete statement about motives will offer *some kind* of answer to these five questions: what was done (act), when or where it was done (scene), who did it (agent), how he did it (agency), and why (purpose).[2]

"The titular word" for the method he is employing, he says a little later, "is 'dramatism', since it invites one to consider the matter of motives in a perspective that, being developed from the analysis of drama, treats language and thought primarily as modes of action."[3]

Burke's "dramatism" is not an instrument for the analysis of social behaviour in objective terms any more than it is for the psychological study of motivation. It in fact involves not so much an exploration of the motives as of the intentions and purposes we read into others' actions, as if we were members of a critically aware theatre audience.

Goffman, when he came to adopt the terminology of stage theatre for his "dramaturgic" rendering of social behaviour, also distanced himself from any positivist claims by asserting that he was using that terminology metaphorically. In fact, both his and Burke's approaches, by using the mirror of metaphor or analogy to unfamiliarise the familiar and thus make it more knowable, reveal something of the hermeneutic twist which Goffman deployed more fully in his later work. There is an essay by Helmuth Plessner which provides almost cook-book directions for attaining deeper understanding (or *better* knowledge) by making ourselves "exiles from the familiar", distancing ourselves from the all-too-well known. Before we can understand what other people (and to some extent ourselves) are up to, before we can come to a fresh appreciation of what we experience, and, through that, actually come to *know* something instead of "knowing *about*" it, we have to "see with different eyes".[4] And indeed, using theatricality as a means of analysing human action and social intercourse does involve turning away from the attempt to explain the world in terms of a description of the world of objective fact "out there", in favour of the phenomenologists' search for the universal structures of subjective orientations to human existence.

Even before Kenneth Burke had deployed his 'dramatist' thesis, Marcel Mauss had given a lead in a parallel direction, this time linking the theatrical analogy with ritual. In a 1938 lecture to the Royal Anthropological Institute,[5] he suggested that, in modern, industrialised, urban societies, the "social self" (*personne morale*) is able to express itself in its entirety only through a multiplicity of roles and situations. These are commonly quite unconnected with each other. What makes it possible for the individual to realise an aspect of himself (a role) in these performances is the operation, on specific social occasions, of a ritual process. The occasions are endowed with type-meanings ("typifications") which impart commonly understood significances and meanings to actions, events, utterances, demeanour, expressions. It is only through the aggregation of such occasions for role-playing that the individual, in modern society, is able to realise the totality of what he sees as his *personne morale* and become a *personnage*.[6]

During the fifties, Victor Turner took up and developed Mauss' theme, working up an interpretative schema into which he could fit both dramaturgical expressiveness and the ritual meanings it utilised and sustained.[7] The way in which tribal societies handled the conflict situations which arose within them periodically, and which could occur at any level of social organisation – a family quarrel, a village dispute between rival factions, a regional uprising – is portrayed as a repeat performance, a new "production", of a social drama. As the conflict grows and emotions are aroused, people surrender to common moods and common purposes. Consequent action proceeds to crisis and denouements which involve resort to public performances which accord with conventions of appropriate behaviour – litigation, feud, sacrifice, prayer. These are in effect ritualised forms of expression which contain the conflict and render it orderly. Resolution of the conflict means that the order of things that obtained previously, or something like it, is restored *and* that the measures taken have proved successful. If not, as Clifford Geertz puts it, "all sorts of unpleasant consequences follow, and the old order falls apart".[8]

The focus of interest for Mauss lay in the parallel array of "sacred self" and "*personnage*" which he thought obtained in primitive societies; he saw ritual as the means whereby the individual was able to realise the totality of this sacred self. Otherwise, the self stayed fragmented, dispersed among the roles which the kinship system allocated to him. Turner, on the other hand, fitted ritual into the larger framework of "social drama".

Lastly, there is a suggestion in Lévi-Strauss' *The Savage Mind* that ritual by itself serves much the same reconciling or reunifying function that Turner gives to his "social drama". The function of ritual, he suggests, it to "bring about a union (one might even say communion in this context) or in any case an organic relation between two initially separate groups". Contrasting this with the disjunctive effect which is the product of games, he goes on: "There is [in ritual] an asymmetry which is postulated in advance between sacred and profane, faithful and officiating, dead and living, initiated and uninitiated, etc., and the 'game' consists in making all the participants pass to the winning side by means of events, the ordering of which is genuinely structural," i.e. replicating, and thereby reconstituting, the relationships and values enjoined by society.[9]

II

The Presentation of Self in Everyday Life was first published in 1956. Two later essays, published at intervals of some years, "Role Distance" (1961) and "Where the Action Is" (1967), share much the same area of interest (the way in which the individual manages his roles and the various selves he presents in them) as well as the same angle of approach that he adopted for *The Presentation of Self*. There are some differences. The essays do 'develop their own conceptual perspectives' (though not quite 'from scratch'), and the dramaturgical principle which provided the framework for the book is dropped. But, on the whole, they may be taken as elaborations of themes lightly sketched out in the earlier book. "Role Distance" is a further exploration of the relationship of the individual to his several selves and their roles, with the individual as the central concern:

> The model of man according to the initial role perspective is that of a kind of holding company for a set of not relevantly connected roles; it is the concern of the second perspective to find out how the individual runs this holding company.
>
> *(E, 90)*

"Where the Action Is" takes up the suggestion made in the book concerning performance which 'highlight the common official values of the society in which it occurs' *(PS, 35)* and explores in some detail the way in which 'activities that are consequential, problematic, and undertaken for what is felt to be their own sake' *(IR, 185)* are precisely those which exemplify highly prized values, and so lend themselves to the creation of exemplary 'character': 'Plainly, it is during moments of action that the individual has the risk and opportunity of displaying to himself and sometimes to others his style of conduct when the chips are down. Character is gambled' *(IR, 237)*.

Behind all these three notions – the composition of 'selves' which the individual presents on a series of stages; the individual as a kind of enterprise engaged in managing a whole stable of roles and social selves to the best advantage; and individuals gambling their stables of selves in hazardous ventures in order to prove (to themselves at least as much as to others) that they possess the kind of special virtues ('character') most highly prized in society – stands the singular conception which animates this whole section of Goffman's writings. This is the idea of treating the individual as an institution with its own structure, cultural values and interests, and *internal* relationships, as well as social relationships with others, and all subject to normative controls.

It is the business of sociologists to enquire critically into the nature of social institutions and to arrive at an understanding of them which is better – deeper – than that of the people through whose conduct the institutions exist. In *The Presentation of Self* and the two supplementary essays, Goffman examines the individual exactly as if he were a social institution, and with the same purpose in mind. I do not, by this, mean to suggest that Goffman set out on the study of individual conduct with the idea of considering the individual as an institution in the forefront of his mind, but his adoption of the dramaturgical metaphor for this first and major study of individual conduct proved to be a brilliantly successful strategic device for doing so. It provided him with a ready-made set of technical terms, in familiar use throughout history, for the analysis of the individual and the self. It is, however, best thought of as a heuristic device, rather than a "conceptual framework" or "theory".

Goffman puts the world of the theatre and its terminology to use as "different eyes", and does so with skill and subtlety. One of the major achievements, and pleasures, of *The Presentation of Self* is the way the basic theme of behaviour as stage performance – which is set out in the first, and longest, chapter – is elaborated in the five succeeding chapters into a complete apparatus of ideas for the analysis of the ways in which people conduct themselves in society. And it is in these later chapters that the basic *topos* of life as theatre which Goffman took over pays off. By pursuing the theatrical metaphor beyond the commonplace notion of "putting on an act", he pulls out a series of images and builds an analogical superstructure with them which enables him to exploit the analytical resources of the metaphor much more fruitfully than anyone before him. The key element is the introduction into the whole schema of two notions, which are in fact implicit in the theatricality *topos*: one is that there has to be an audience to which performances are addressed, and that the part played by the audience is important; the other is that performances of all kinds require a "back-stage" – some time and space for the preparation of procedures, disguises or materials essential to the performance, or for the concealment of aspects of the performance which might either discredit it or be somehow discordant with it.

This divides the total dramatistic schema (Kenneth Burke's Act, Scene, Agent, Agency, and Purpose) into two twice over: once between performers and audience, and again between 'front-stage' and 'back-stage'. With this relatively simple analytical device, Goffman assembles extraordinarily diverse collections of behavioural routines, everyday observations, and easily recognisable characteristics and, merely by juxtaposing them in an unfamiliar classification, reveals them in a newly significant light. Audience complicity, 'breaking role', 'discrepant roles', the moral obligations of membership of a team of performers, playing as member of a team, and a number of other categories, most of them derived from the terminology of the theatre, are put to use as manifestations of the individual's management of his conduct and situation. Goffman's own way of putting things, although intrinsic to his whole procedure, and more than a stylistic gloss, is really an added bonus. The essential achievement is a matter of organisation.

The conviction these sections convey does not come just from the stage metaphor – although that helps the process of mental digestion. It comes, for the most part, out of the sheer technical virtuosity Goffman displays in reframing a host of observations about 'common humanity' – all of them familiar, but present to our minds, usually, as a heterogeneous, incoherent, clutter – in an elaborate taxonomic scheme derived from one or other of his organising principles.

What he has to say about gossip, for example, hardly rises above the level of common knowledge. The fact that individuals are spoken to relatively well to their faces and spoken about relatively badly behind their backs ('one of the basic generalisations that can be made about interaction') is hardly news; nothing could be more banal. But, taken up and repositioned in first one context of other pieces of folk-wisdom and common observation, and then another, its significance – though not its meaning – becomes transformed.

Having brought up the commonplace contrast between "speaking fair" to people and "speaking ill" behind their backs, he goes on to dismiss the idea, which is just as commonplace, that the explanation lies in 'our all-too-human nature' (p. 172). Derogatory remarks, he goes on, made within a 'team' of performers about others (the 'audience') who are, for the time being, out of sight and out of earshot, serve to maintain solidarity, demonstrate mutual regard and compensate for any loss of self-respect*. Furthermore, gossip – while one aspect of what he rightly calls a 'well-worn notion' – is catalogued among a broader class of 'staging talk' (sc. 'backstage' talk) which includes outright criticism (of the 'audience' – here, typically, shop customers), mimicking, cursing, ridiculing them, and so forth. There is also, however, a third frame, broader still; for what we know familiarly as 'talking shop' is also something which is reserved for backstage conversation. The connection is worth stressing, he says, 'because it helps point up the fact that individuals with widely different social roles live in the same climate of dramaturgical experience. The talks that comedians and scholars give are quite different, but their talk about their talk is quite similar.' Talking shop, like gossip, turns out to be a kind of insurance policy – and sometimes a security-blanket.

A second instance of the same kind of procedure is his identification, definition, and classification of secrets. It is all quite elementary and straightforward to begin with. As we all know, there are facts about themselves which individuals, or teams of individuals, may want to "keep dark" because they think them incompatible with the image of themselves they are trying to convey. Dark secrets such as these are in fact double secrets, because not only are crucial facts hidden, but the fact that they are being hidden is also kept secret. But there are also strategic secrets: intentions and capacities concealed so as to prevent an audience – or a potential audience – preparing themselves for, or pre-empting or preventing, developments an individual or team is preparing to bring about. Obvious instances of such teams are business concerns and the military, who are – or see themselves as – perpetually engaged in thwarting opponents. Then there are 'inside' secrets, which mark an individual as a member of a group; 'inside' secrets serve to make the group feel "different" and its members "special" because they are "in the know". Inside secrets, Goffman goes on, may have little strategic importance, and may not

---

*Cf. "In essentials, gossip is passing judgments – disapproving, depreciating, or condemning – on the behaviour of others. It is an indispensable instrument for fixing one's own occupational prestige, or for finding an acceptable style. Collusion in gossip offers the guarantee that, because one is united with at least one other in judging A to be deficient in technical knowledge, B to have made a stupid gaffe, C to be too sycophantic, D to spend too much time chatting in the canteen, the speaker and his hearer – compared with these others – are at least free from such faults. In gossip, speakers' and hearers' status claims are underwritten."[10]

be particularly dark – but dark secrets and strategic ones serve very well as inside secrets 'and we find, in fact, that the strategic and dark character of secrets is often exaggerated for this reason' (p. 143).

This is not the end of it, however, for there are also other kinds of secrets – 'secrets about secrets'. These consist, in the first place, of 'entrusted' secrets (the clearest instance being the 'rule of confidentiality' which doctors and lawyers apply to their dealings with clients) and 'free' secrets (secrets which concern someone other than oneself, but which 'one could not disclose without discrediting the image one was presenting of oneself'). Lastly, there are 'latent secrets'. 'All destructive information is not found in secrets, and information control involves more than keeping secrets'; it may be necessary to keep enquiry away from potentially damaging revelations, which amount to 'latent secrets, and the problems of keeping secrets are quite different from the problems of keeping latent secrets latent' (p. 144).

What Goffman has done is to collect a number of scattered bits of common knowledge and reorganise them into a coherent and logical framework which, so to speak, reframes and so recodes and redefines them. The passage in which secrets are described and classified occurs in the chapter on "Discrepant Roles", which discusses the importance of information control: 'the audience must not acquire destructive information about the situation that is being defined for them. In other words, a team must be able to keep its secrets and have its secrets kept' (p. 141). The contents of the passage are no more than fairly commonplace observations about the way people behave, but their presentation within this new framework, juxtaposed and illuminated in an unfamiliar manner, enables – forces – us to see them with different eyes.

III

The Presentation of Self, in addition to being Goffman's most popular book, has also attracted the most criticism (and perhaps for these two reasons has tended to overshadow his other work, including, and in particular, the two later essays, "Role Distance" and "Where the Action Is"). Sustaining a metaphor actually to book length has, unavoidably, something of the air of an elaborate conjuring trick, and there does seem to be a lurking suspicion of this behind much of the criticism of *The Presentation of Self* – criticism which has spread to Goffman's overall thesis. One of the more familiar, and substantial, criticisms appeared in what has (unfortunately) become Alvin Gouldner's best-known book, where he takes Goffman's 'dramaturgical' exercise to task.[11] Goffman's sociology, he suggests, is really a sociology for the new, college-educated middle class, aware of the irrationalities of the modern system of rewards and anxious to take advantage of them (a sociology for 'yuppies', that is, although the tag wasn't invented then). "Goffman's is a social 'dramaturgy'", says Gouldner, "in which appearances and not underlying essences are exalted." More seriously (and more recently), there is Alasdair MacIntyre's interpretation of what Goffman's work stands for, which is a world that is "empty of standards of achievement". "Success in Goffman's social universe is nothing but what passes for success. There is nothing else for it to be." For MacIntyre, "Goffman has liquidated the self into its role-playing, arguing that the self is no more than 'a peg' on which the clothes of the role are hung."[12]

No doubt Goffman himself is partly to blame for this sort of thing. The "new, college-educated middle class" may well be Goffman's audience (as it presumably has to be for his kind of book), but it provided him with his subject-matter, as he so often made clear. There is, too, a curious ambivalence about his discussion of the metaphor of the stage which he is using as the foundation of his whole thesis. One finds him at the very beginning insisting on the inadequacy of the stage metaphor (p. xi) and this goes on throughout the book – but he never altogether disowns it. 'All the world is not, of course, a stage', he says at one point (p. 72), and then continues, 'but the crucial ways in which it isn't are not easy to specify.' And, at the very end, when he says he is dropping the language and mask of the stage (p. 255), he nevertheless insists that successful theatre involves the use of *real* techniques, and these are 'the same techniques by which everyday persons sustain their real social situation'.

Again, there are references to the notion of people 'acting' themselves, in the sense of an individual living up to the conception he has formed of himself, the self he would like to be and which, in the end, becomes second nature, his 'truer' self. All of which adds to the impression of falsity, of human action as founded on pretence, even deceit. This impression is heightened by his actually underplaying the part played by the social order or by social organisation at certain critical points in *The Presentation of Self*. This is odd, in view of the emphasis he continually places in his interaction studies on the dominant part played by the social order and what he calls 'society' in the way people behave towards each other.

Most of the passages which convey this contrary emphasis (on the individual, rather than society, as puppet-master) are in the first section of the book. This itemises the constituent elements of his rendering of individual behaviour as performance. So, if the evidence is "stacked" in the way I have suggested, it is almost bound to reinforce the importance of the individual's desire, or need, to define the situation, control the responses of others, and show himself to the best advantage.

'Front', for example, the subject of one of the eight sections of the chapter on 'Performances', is concerned with what is the permanent, fixed, part of an individual's performance. It has two aspects. The first is 'setting', which amounts to stage scenery and visible equipment ("props") including furniture – the whole of what the theatre knows as "decor". The second is 'personal front', which again has two aspects: 'appearance' – sex, age, clothing, size and looks, and so forth, all of which in general are expressive of the individual's social position; and 'manner' – posture, demeanour, facial expression, speech pattern, etc., which announce the interaction role he expects to portray.

The part played by 'setting' is sketched briefly, and lightly; also, both here, and later in the book, it is presented as if it were contrived by the individual himself, an extension of the individual's own 'appearance' and 'manner'. Admittedly, this is often the case with domestic settings, of course, and in other cases where the individual assumes control of setting, appearance and manner. As Goffman says, all three elements *should* fit together. But most social encounters outside people's homes also take place in settings which are taken to be appropriate to them – indeed, are so designed. For, as Kenneth Burke insists at the very outset of his *Grammar of Motives*, encounters take much of their characteristic style and pattern of development from their settings:

> Using "scene" in the sense of setting, or background, and "act" in the sense of action, one could say that "the scene contains the act". And using "agents" in the sense of actors, or actors, one could say that "the scene contains the agents".
>
> It is a principle of drama that the nature of the acts and agents should be consistent with the nature of the scene.[13]

Since scene and situation are, when we can contrive it, composed to fit each other and the actions, words, and demeanour with which we fill them, it is all too likely that when we find ourselves in settings devised by others, we compose our behaviour, and even our purposes and feelings, so as to be in compliance with the settings enclosing us – or perhaps in revolt against them, but in any case in some designedly meaningful relationship to them. The relationship between scene and act is perhaps not quite synecdochic (the word Burke uses), but rather a matter of promptings towards those kinds of action for which the scene is designed and deprecation of any which are not.

The manifold settings we find ourselves in which prompt us towards conduct that conveys impressions in accordance with the generalised impression for which the setting is designed are, of course, provided by organised institutions. And here, as elsewhere, Goffman omits economic, political, religious, cultural, and social organisation in general, as well as specific organisations, from the account. He refers to the places provided by these organisations often enough, but always as places where 'a particular performance is usually given, as well as the performers and performances usually found there' (p. 124). The examples he cites are cathedrals and schoolrooms, but it is as though what was under discussion was the choice of habitats suitable for bird-watching. The decorations and permanent fixtures in such a place, we are told, 'tend to fix a kind of spell over it; even when the customary performance is not being given in it, the place tends to retain some of its . . . character' – which is surely to be expected, seeing that they were purpose-designed by specific organisations for those kinds of performance. But it is not simply a matter of cathedrals built by organised churches and schools built by departments of education. The whole occupational world certainly, and most of the rest of our urban worlds to a large extent, provide us with purpose-built settings. Once within them, we tend to fit in "naturally"; and we do so in premeditated fashion, spending our working lives, for example, in well-defined networks of rooms and working spaces connected by passages, stairs, lifts, streets, telephones and vehicles, each one of which actually is in "synecdochic" relationship with the whole milieu of work.[14]

This is not the only miscue in the chapter on "Performances". There is the frequently quoted passage which occurs in the section on 'Dramatic Realisation':

A *Vogue* model, by her clothing, stance, and facial expression, is able expressively to portray a cultivated understanding of the book she poses in her hand; but those who trouble to express themselves so appropriately will have very little time left over for reading.

(pp. 32-3)

Goffman's comment only holds good on the unlikely assumption that the choice of both pose and book was the lady's. (Incidentally, the reviewer who came to the lady's defence, suggesting that her reading the book was not so unthinkable as all that, was just as far off the point; *Vogue* models seem to have an especially distracting effect.) There are other lapses, like reading the mandatory standards of hospitality in eighteenth-century Scotland as pretentiousness ('a claim for higher status than would otherwise be accorded'). They are all relatively trivial; the trouble is that all such errors fall on the discreditable side of the moral balance-sheet and this, by the end of the book, reaches a formidable total. It is this, as much as anything, which has contributed to the adverse assessments of Gouldner and MacIntyre, and may account for the touches of hostile criticism which one finds in even the more laudatory reviews of the book.

More to the present point, however, all these revelatory instances, correct or mistaken, of conduct which is less admirable than those acting it out would have us think, go to support the notion of the individual as a responsible, autonomous, agent. This is entirely in line with the traditional moral belief which credits the individual with free will, a capacity for self-determination and independent action. But it is the selfsame set of beliefs at which the writings on interaction whittle away, and which, as I have pointed out, Goffman openly challenges in *Relations in Public*. The patent cynicism which shows up in *The Presentation of Self* is quite compatible with an individualist ethic; but in order to mount the radical critique of selfhood which comes in later books, free-will and individualism have to be revealed as illusory, as an ideological superstructure devised by "Society" so as to render individuals more willingly obedient to its rule. The Diogenes of *The Presentation of Self* turns into the Thrasymachus of *Behavior in Public Places*, in which identity and individual will are what "Society" makes them.

Not that, in this earliest of his books, Goffman adheres to some kind of traditional "natural law" position, with ultimate sovereignty attached solely to the individual. He floats about, somewhere between the two extremes. Beginning the chapter on "Teams", for example, he says that 'it is easy to assume that the content of the presentation is merely an expressive extension of the character of the performer'. The suggestion is that such an assumption is a mistake – but when we come to alternative interpretations, what we find are performances (by individuals) which: (1) 'express the characteristics of the task that is performed', (2) are 'part of a projection that is fostered and sustained by the intimate cooperation of more than one participant', or (3) involve taking on distinctive roles prescribed by the needs of the occasion. Each and every one of these interpretations must mean that performances are either prescribed by other individual selves or assumed by one individual in order to accommodate others.

Thus far, what we have is two or more performers, each concerned with his own special performance but joined together (through 'collusion' or 'understanding') as a team in cooperative performance. But cooperative activity such as this, he says (p. 80), 'seems too important to be handled merely as a variation on a previous theme'. He follows this with a proposal that 'an emergent team impression' be presumed ('which can conveniently be treated as a fact in its own right') at an intermediate level 'between the individual performance on the one hand and the total interaction of participants on the other'. But for the rest of the section, indeed of the book, there is no reference to team performance as an "intermediate level of fact". It is a little dismaying to find Goffman laying the hideously familiar trap for himself and his readers which consists of working up a complicated apparatus of concepts, with the relevance of each to the whole theoretical construction worked out in careful definitions, and then leaving it unused.

Team performance is left as a matter of *individuals* performing in cooperation, or collusion, with each other, or according to some mutual understanding which allows each to rely on the others to foster 'a given definition of the situation'. There is even a strong suggestion that team cooperation itself is an expression of the joint self-interest of team-members. For what impels them to refrain from correcting, punishing or even disowning mistakes, inappropriate moves, or downright derelictions of the loyalty owed the team is the interest of each and every individual in preventing complete breakdown, or in shielding the view of the performance reserved for team-members from the audience or outsiders. And self-interest is the *ultima ratio* of individualism.

So, while the methodology employed for this group of studies is much the same as that used in the interactionist studies, the angle of approach is somewhat different. The unit of analysis is the individual (sometimes a group of individuals), and the way he conducts himself in encounters, rather than the encounter itself. This shows up at a number of points. In the first pages of *The Presentation of Self*, for example, he argues that, 'Ordinarily, the definitions of the situation projected by the several different participants are sufficiently attuned to one another so that open contradiction will not occur.' It is not a matter of consensus (which, he says, is anyway a rather optimistic ideal); usually, 'a kind of interactional *modus vivendi*' is reached, which is 'not so much a real agreement as to what exists but rather a real agreement as to whose claims concerning what issues will be temporarily honoured' (p. 9). This, he says, avoids incessant conflict; but it also seems to impute to the individual a capacity for self-determination which the interactionist writings take away.

IV

This impression is reinforced by the "Role Distance" essay, which, like the book, conveys the idea of the structure of social encounters as something approaching mutual understanding reached between *individuals* who are engaged with each other in interaction, an understanding which conjoins the participants and steers the course which interaction follows. In "Role Distance", furthermore, there is a passage in which Goffman argues that there is a difference, and a substantial one, between the prototypical (and therefore rather formal and idealised) idea we have of role and actual role performance. The typical performance of a role is a kind of "aim-off" mark for any actual performer – and the same latitude applies to the responses made by other people in the encounter. For each of them there is, ordinarily, a rather small number of modes of dealing with other people appropriate to their social classification (age, sex, mode of speech, etc.) status, role, and so forth.

> We say, loosely, that legal entitlement to the term of address, 'Doctor', determines how the person so entitled is addressed, when, in fact, we usually merely mean that if we know how a person is usually addressed, we will know which of the available modes of treatment will be accorded him.
>
> (*E*, 94)

We choose the generic mode of treatment that seems about right –

and then, presumably, extemporise. Later in the same essay we find the contrary assertion: that variation from the 'typical' role is, after all, *determined* for the individual by the roles he plays in other situations (as colleague, family man, golfer, political party member, and so on). Even so, there is a degree of individual autonomy left him in that he does have actually to invoke these variant forms of conduct in order to help him out in the particular situation confronting him.

There is in fact a pointer in *The Presentation of Self* to the individual's having a credit balance of autonomy left him. In the final section ("Reality and Contrivance") of the first chapter, the reader is assured that the common-sense dichotomy drawn between honest, sincere performances and false, fabricated ones may serve as 'an ideology for honest performers' but is fairly useless for purposes of analysis. For "real" performances have to be just as painstakingly put together as those which are meant to deceive. 'This is so because ordinary social intercourse is itself put together as a scene is put together' (p. 72). The process of socialisation which fits us for adult membership of society and, secondarily, for filling specific roles, is not a matter of learning in detail and as if by rote the single concrete parts we are called upon to play; there simply is not time or energy enough for that, he remarks. (Nor, one might add, is it all that predictable which roles one will eventually occupy.)

So the individuals' autonomy extends beyond the managerial responsibility they have for the company of selves they hold, and for the several roles each of them may be called upon to play. Playing a role means more than simply reproducing some ideal performance – or copying an expert performer. As Goffman puts it, 'details of the expression and movements used do not come from a script but from command of an idiom' (p. 74). It has to be *realised*. Some capacity for improvisation, even invention, is essential: 'What does seem to be required of the individual is that he learn enough pieces of expression to be able to "fill in" and manage, more or less, any part that he is likely to be given' (p. 73).

What we have in role performance, then, is a special combination. There is, first of all, contrivance – inventiveness, and a capacity for improvisation in "filling out" and connecting up familiar 'pieces of expression' – which, because they are 'pieces of expression' familiar to his audience (for they too have learned them) are recognisable and easily understood by them. Second, there is the meaningful content:

the 'pieces of expression' – skilled phatic routines of posture, movement, gesture, and symbolically loaded formulae of wording, intonation, etc. – which he has learned (by imitation, practice, experience). The situation is defined (controlled) by the way the performer makes his improvisatory or inventive contribution, stringing the routine and formulaic details together.

To illustrate the point, Goffman cites an account by Métraux of possession by a voodoo spirit, instances a young middle-class American girl playing dumb for the benefit of her boy friend, and quotes at length Sartre's description of a Paris waiter "playing the part" of being a waiter (pp. 74-5). All three seem supremely appropriate to his purpose. This is especially true of the last, a quotation which extends over more than a page.

But, if one looks at these three illustrative examples a little more closely, we may note that Métraux's account is one of "possession" performed as a spectacle. The performance has above all to be "convincing". Conviction comes from the masterly improvisation of a sequence of grimaces, cries, gestures, dance-movements, mimed acts. Correct portrayal of possession by a god that has entered the performer comes from "'the knowledge and memories accumulated in a life spent visiting congregations of the cult'" (p. 74). But "correct portrayal" is also a function of its recognisability by the audience as manifestations of the spirit at work; and his actions are recognisable because they have seen them before, at other performances, by other performers. Goffman's "middle-class American girl" is really putting on a show for her companion, stringing together the bright smiles, slow-wittedness (we have to remember that this is America, *c.* 1955), giggles, and limited vocabulary that – she imagines – will be recognised by her companions as emblematic of feminine inferiority, dependence, and "appeal". The example of Sartre's waiter is even more striking and, seemingly, pertinent. His movements are

a little *too* precise, a little *too* rapid . . . his eyes express an interest a little *too* solicitous for the order of his customer. . . . Finally there he returns, trying to imitate in his walk the stiffness of an automaton while carrying his tray with the recklessness of a tightrope-walker by putting it in a perpetually unstable, perpetually broken equilibrium which he perpetually reestablishes by a light movement of the arm and hand.

In fact, he is, while acting as a waiter, 'playing at' acting as a waiter

– producing for his audience an exemplary demonstration of what it is to be a waiter.

None of these three can be read as instances of deception. Belief in the part he is playing – one has to presume – is intrinsic to the role of the person possessed by a god. The girl – presumably – is concerned not so much with pretending to be "dumb" as with "making out". It is true that Sartre included the description of the waiter in the chapter of his book headed "Bad Faith", and designated overdoing the role in this manner as being somehow imprisoned by it. A waiter could sustain his role by waiting at table, and no more. But "acting out" in this way is as much a staged performance for his fellows (especially those watching, however impassively, from behind the bar) as it is a demonstration of superlative professional competence for the customers and a surrender to the social exigences of role-playing.

Performance at this level of intensity involves the individual's committing himself to the performance in a way which goes beyond what is ordinarily required by the social interaction of everyday life. Bearing in mind the two elements of contrivance (i.e. expert improvisation and invention, and a repertoire of "pieces of expression"), there is a more than faint structural resemblance to the kind of performance which is now held to account for the survival in oral tradition of the great epics. To quote Robert Darnton:

> Milman Parry and Albert Lord have shown how folk epics as long as *The Iliad* are passed on faithfully from bard to bard among the illiterate peasants of Yugoslavia. These "singers of tales" do not possess the fabulous powers of memorization sometimes attributed to "primitive" peoples. They do not memorize much at all. Instead, they combine stock phrases, formulas, and narrative segments in patterns improvised according to the response of their audience. Recordings of the same epic by the same singer demonstrate that each performance is unique. . . . In each case, the singer proceeds as if he were walking down a well-known path . . . He creates his text as he goes, picking new routes through old themes.[15]

It is of course hardly surprising that performances such as these bear some resemblance to role-performances in general. On the other hand, if one regards them simply as role-performances, the idea that they are substantially equivalent in all respects is a little hard to credit. For the recital of epic poetry – even the telling of a folk-tale to an audience – is a much more 'stagey' affair than the role-performances of everyday life which Goffman is dealing with. At the very least, since it is a performance with something of the quality of a staged show, 'defining the situation' in such a case requires both the situation to be more compelling and the definition to be more dominating.

Beyond the "prose" of everyday social action, then, it is possible to posit a "poetry" of performance which transcends the performance, committing the individual proper as well as the performed self. It is more consequential, even more fateful, for the individual than everyday role-performance can ever be. It is a more deeply committed performance – a more fully embraced role – and therefore more closely involved with the audience. And, finally, it takes on enhanced significance by expressing, portraying, or exemplifying, social or cultural values of central importance to society.

The selfsame difference in tone, or intensity, distinguishes stage acting from the "acting-out" which goes on in everyday social conversation, a difference which overlays their fundamental resemblance, both of which Goffman elaborates on in *Frame Analysis*.

V

The idea that performance, interaction, and action have more than one level of intensity, momentousness or significance, which is touched on only briefly in *The Presentation of Self*, is explicated fully in the essay, "Where the Action Is".

"Where the Action Is", published in 1967, was one of the products of the "field research" he undertook when he moved to Berkeley. Once again, "fieldwork" meant participant observation; he took a job as a dealer in Nevada casinos – not without encountering some problems with the Regents of the University of California. The sources of funds for the research are worth mentioning: they were, *inter alia*, the Youth Development Program of the Ford Foundation, the President's Committee on Juvenile Delinquency and Youth Crime (through the Office of Juvenile Delinquency and Youth Development of the US Department of Health, Education and Welfare). They point to the fact (one which has been almost totally ignored) that his Las Vegas research was undertaken as part of a programme of studies of criminality. One of the major findings (also largely unnoticed) of his study is that crime involves taking risks, and "proving oneself"; and it

125

provides excitement, 'action', as well as gain. Crime, in short (and as Jean Genet, and others, have said), can be "fun".

Crime is one of the occupations which he lists as 'extraordinary niches in social life where activity is so markedly problematic and consequential that the individual is likely to orient himself towards fatefulness prospectively'. It is then that fearful situations undergo a subtle transformation. . . . 'Instead of awaiting fate, you meet it at the door. Danger is recast into taken risk; fatefulness into grasped opportunity' (IR, 171).

The full list is:

Roles in commerce that are financially dangerous or at least unsteady – market and property speculators, prospectors.
Mining, high construction work, test-piloting.
'Hustling' jobs in business.
Performances by politicians, actors, and other live entertainers.
Soldiers and policemen.
Criminals.
Professional spectator sports.
Some recreational non-spectator sports like mountaineering, big-game hunting, parachuting.

'Action' he defines as 'activities that are consequential, problematic, and undertaken for what is felt to be their own sake' (p. 185). The prototypical form of action is, of course, gambling, which is where the term originated. Goffman's 'action' is a fairly complex notion, definable only at the end of a sequence of preconditions. One begins with gambling as the archetypal way of taking chances; but gambling, properly speaking, demands prior commitment: 'No commitment, no chance-taking' (p. 152).

This holds good even in those activities – car-racing is one – in which skill, daring, knowledge, perseverance, and other 'relevant orders of humanly directed determination are involved' (p. 153), and in a later footnote (p. 204) he quotes Sterling Moss to this effect:

The fastest driver is the one who can come closest to the point at which the car's tyres will break adhesion to the road and let the machine go into an uncontrolled slide. ("Uncontrolled" is the key word. Much of the time, the driver has deliberately broken the car loose and is allowing it to slide, but under control.)

It is factors like skill and daring which make contests different from games of "pure" chance. On the other hand, what makes games of chance different from the numberless occasions of everyday life when people take chances and bet on the outcome of decisions is that games are played in sequence, one being completed before another begins. 'Real life' decisions ordinarily have a long

> determination phase – the period during which the consequences of his bet are determined . . . sometimes over decades, followed by disclosure and settlement phases that are themselves lengthy. The distinctive property of games and contests is that, once the bet has been made, *outcome is determined and payoff awarded all in the same breath of experience.*
>
> (p. 156)

What is more, the bets and prizes the gambler is playing for have subjective values as well as 'socially ratified' values, partly because of what winning or losing allows the gambler to do later. 'This is the gamble's *consequentiality*, namely the *capacity of a payoff to flow beyond the bounds of the occasion in which it is delivered and to influence objectively the later life of the bettor*' (pp. 159-60).

Most of our working lives and much of the rest is of course spent in activities which are consequential, but their consequentiality is hardly noticed, since the probability of their having an expected outcome tends to be rated fairly high. If, however, an activity which is consequential is also "problematic" (i.e. is something as yet undetermined but about to be resolved), it becomes what Goffman calls 'fateful'. And the crux of the essay is the transition from consequentiality to fatefulness. Fatefulness is the mark of the threshold between retaining some control over the consequences of one's actions and their going out of control.

Fatefulness can be adventitious; indeed, as he says, it is always a possibility, the human condition being what it is. Ordinarily, though, the individual manages his life so as to avoid this so far as possible – and most of the circumstances of his life are organised to do this for him. But circumstances can also provide a double ration of fatefulness – as it does for unsuccessful thieves, those Keystone Krooks favourites of Goffman's, whose exploits are chronicled by American newspapers in such rewarding detail, and, when he recounts them, always give service twice over, once as clinical specimen and again as cue for some waggish turn of phrase:

> What is special about criminal enterprise (and other military-like

127

operations) is the narrowness of this reserve [i.e. the latitude that allows time for correcting mistakes in the undertakings of everyday life] and hence the high price that must be paid for thoughtlessness and bad breaks. This is the difference between holding a job down and pulling a job.

(p. 166)

But going over from consequentiality to fatefulness also marks the investment of the individual in his self's "character". Character is something achieved in, and through, action (pp. 214 ff.).

Those whose occupations commit them to taking fateful chances and those who deliberately seek out opportunities for doing so tend to prepare themselves by exercising certain capacities – physical condition and stamina, or timing and judgment – so as to improve them, and to accumulate experience. Such capacities can often be augmented by organised training, dry runs, target practice, rehearsals, and so forth, in which the results are problematic but not consequential. However, there are other essential elements which are incapable of being augmented by training, although the demeanour which is held to go with them may be cultivated. These are what Goffman calls 'maintenance properties'. Capacities such as these do not relate specifically to this or that kind of fateful action but to how the individual will manage himself during it. They appear under 'perceivedly fateful circumstances', which are both consequential and problematic – and *only* in connection with them. This is simply because it is when the individual is on the brink of losing control that these qualities are called for: sudden awareness of what might shortly occur may either break the individual's hold over 'principled behaviour' or confirm his principledness by persevering in the face of his knowledge of the high cost of correct behaviour.

It is these 'maintenance properties' which add up to what is popularly (and by Goffman) called 'character' (p. 217). They include gameness (as in boxing) and gallantry. There is also the reciprocal of gallantry (by which the forms of courtesy are maintained even when there is substantial advantage to be lost), which consists in the exigence of courtesy (he cites the 'excellent illustration' of this theme provided by the police, 'since they sometimes feel they must pledge their fists, their clubs, and even their guns to ensure a nice deference from those they arrest or otherwise accost' (pp. 221-2)). Integrity, which consists in resisting temptation where there would be much profit and some impunity in departing momentarily from moral standards, counts for more, however, since 'no society would long persist if its members did not approve and foster this quality'.

Finally, 'of all the qualities of character associated with the management of fatefulness, the one of most interest for this essay is *composure*'. This, the erstwhile hallmark of the aristocrat, is now universally available in the demotic guise of staying "cool". It includes presence of mind (i.e. staying calm and alert), and stage confidence (the ability to 'act natural' before a critical audience).

These qualities of 'character' born of fateful events, Goffman claims, carry a heavy load of moral significance. 'Because persons in all societies must transact much of their enterprise in social situations, we must expect that the capacity to maintain support of the social occasion under difficult circumstances will be universally approved' (p. 229). An individual's capacity for mobilising himself for the moment is therefore always subjected to moral evaluation by those who observe it – and report on it.

Much of what we have up to this point of the essay has to be read, it seems to me, as an assertion of the continued existence, and the importance to modern society, of *some* of the distinctive features of the *virtū* of Renaissance Italy and the *aretē* of ancient Greece, namely, the pursuit of excellence in the role one has adopted (or been accorded) and, *by so doing*, upholding the good order of society. Goffman has of course addressed himself to the 'moral order of society' fairly frequently in his writings on interaction. But there is here a difference. Whereas in his other writings 'society' as a moral order is represented as imposing its rules on its members, and they as managing their behaviour so as to be in accordance with (or at least acting in awareness of) them, we now have behaviour which is highly valued in moral terms but which cannot be regarded as governed by rules. For one can never hope to excel at any activity by following rules.

Yet, interspersed with those which support this notion of an ethical, as distinct from moral, order,[16] there are others which revert to the notion of a moral universe subject to rule by "society", and relegate ideas of an ethical foundation for right conduct to a 'fundamental illusion' planted in us by society in order to ensure conformity with its rules:

> It should be clear that our illogic in this matter has its social value. Social organization everywhere has the problem of morale and continuity. Individuals must come to their little situations

with some enthusiasm and concern, for it is largely through such moments that social life occurs. . . . To satisfy the fundamental requirements of morale and continuity, we are encouraged in a fundamental illusion. It is our character. . . .

Hypostasis – the reification of "society" – is carried to its extreme: 'We are allowed to think there is something to be won in the moments that we face so that society can face moments and defeat them'.

I am not at all sure that Goffman was alive to the discrepancy between the ethical – almost teleological – view of the importance of 'character' which he was advancing in "Where the Action Is" and the strictly deontological assumption of a social order founded on moral obligation and obedience to norms and rules one finds uncompromisingly stressed in his other writings. The ethical viewpoint is rephrased again and again towards the end of the essay, as if reflecting an increasing anxiety about getting the message across: 'And now we begin to see character for what it is. On the one hand, it refers to what is essential and unchanging about the individual – what is *characteristic* of him.' On the other, it refers to attributes that can be generated and destroyed during fateful moments. 'Plainly, it is during moments of action that the individual has the risk and opportunity of displaying to himself and sometimes to others his style of conduct when the chips are down. Character is gambled' (p. 237). 'The self, in brief, can be voluntarily subjected to re-creation.' . . . 'Statements (including mine) that action is an end in itself must be understood as locutions. The voluntary taking of serious chances is a means for the maintenance and acquisition of character' (p. 238).

VI

"Where the Action Is" credits the individual with being the freely self-determining agent that the moral tradition of Western society makes him out to be: 'the unaided individual is here the efficacious unit of organisation', he says at one point (*IR*, 244). It is the only one of his writings in which this position is held (more or less) consistently. "Role Distance", which is in many ways the analytical counterpart of the later essay, puts the individual firmly back in place as a social construct. It declares itself in the final paragraphs as a challenge to the 'touching tendency to keep a part of the world safe from sociology' (*E*, 152). There is in social thought, he says, a seeming compulsion to exclude that part of individual conduct which has to do with '"personal" matters and "personal" relationships' (i.e. with what an individual is "really like"), from the 'obligatory world of social roles' which belongs to society and to sociological study and analysis. (This is Goffman in one of his more insufferable poses, claiming unique perceptiveness for himself and ignoring the tidal waves of ideas which have moved across the social sciences from Freudian psychology, phenomenology and existentialism, cultural anthropology and other fairly turbulent areas of twentieth-century human and humanist studies, and from which he was by no means the only social scientist to profit.)

"Role Distance" could in fact be said to be an exercise on a theme stated by Edward Sapir in a contribution on "Fashion" to the 1931 *Encyclopedia of the Social Sciences*, from which an extract is quoted towards the end of "Role Distance". Sapir is concerned with the "petty truancies from the officially socialised self", which he says are to be observed in a society in which "the individual has ceased to be a measure of the society itself". Sapir's last clause has resonances which are not explored by Goffman. This is understandable enough, since it flies in the face of the thesis which he seeks to establish in the essay.

There are episodes, expressive features, and the like which are discrepant with the normative prescription of behaviour fitting the role – with 'typical' role behaviour. Such discrepancies, he argues, may be made to fit in with the way a role is in fact acted out in face-to-face situations (what Goffman calls 'situated' role behaviour involving a 'situated' self) in two ways. The first stems from a disinclination of the individual fully to accept the self that the role prescribes; the second comes from the frequent failure of the individual to achieve complete control of what is happening in the situation, and hence of the information about himself that he makes available to others. In either case, there is some need for the individual to deny the role (here 'typical' becomes 'virtual') in which he is projecting information about himself that he feels falsifies his 'true' self.

'Explanations, apologies and joking are all ways in which the individual makes a plea for disqualifying some of the expressive features of the situation as sources of definition of himself' (*E*, 105). 'This "effectively" expressed pointed separateness between the individual and his putative role I shall call *role distance* – the individual is actually denying not the role but the virtual self implied in the role for all accepting performers' (p. 108). He applies the term specifically to behaviour which is directly related to the individual's role, and related 'in such a way as to suggest that the actor possibly has some measure of disaffection from, and resistance against, the role'.

All this is familiar enough, but the point Goffman wishes to establish is that we do not need to see the individual's attempt to disembarrass himself of certain unwanted implications of his 'situated' role as a withdrawal 'into some psychological world that he creates himself', but as an endeavour to act, and to present himself, in terms of some other social identity which has been created for him (i.e. is no less a product of "Society"). 'This . . . is easiest done by invoking an aspect of self clearly relevant to other social situations or settings. The liberty he takes in regard to a situated self is taken because of other, equally social constraints (*E*, 120).

This otherwise rather arid piece of analysis is beautifully illustrated – illuminated – by detailed observations of role behaviour, principally of two situations. The second of these concerns the conduct of members of surgical teams in an operating theatre – something he was able to watch as a privileged spectator during his period of research with the NIMH. The first, however, is, or could have been, drawn from ordinary everyday happenings available to any bystander: it is of the way in which children of different ages (and some attendant adults) behave on a merry-go-round. It is a quite superb piece of work, finely attuned to his purposes, clinically accurate in its perceptions, beguiling – and just saved from teetering over the edge into charm. Thus:

A two-year-old can find the prospect of riding a merry-go-round horse too much from him, despite the ministrations of parents, since it is 'a thing of some size, some height, and some movement', and can also be very noisy. Here, Goffman observes, 'we have one of the classic possibilities of life', namely, a 'flustered failure . . . to keep command of oneself, both as a person capable of executing physical movements and as one capable of receiving and transmitting communications'. What is more, failure to manage both demands for poise threatens to damage the whole system around him and any others who might be involved in it. So, qualifications which permit one to attempt a role may not, in practice, be the same as having the attributes required for performing suitably once the role has been acquired – a quandary familiar to neophytes of all kinds and ages.

A three or four year old, however, though still finding a wooden horse a challenge, appears to find it 'a manageable one, inflating the rider to his full extent with demonstrations of capacity'. Accordingly, he is now prepared to, so to speak, *embrace* his role. 'Just as "flustering" is a classic possibility in all situated systems, so also is the earnest way these youngsters of three or four ride their horses.' There are three aspects of this way of relating to a 'situated' role: attachment to the role, demonstration of qualifications and capacities, and engagement (spontaneous involvement) in the role activity at hand. When all three are present, one may say that the role is 'embraced'. To embrace a role, therefore, is to be embraced by it – 'to disappear completely into the virtual self available in the situation, to be fully seen in the image, and to confirm expressively one's acceptance of it' (*E*, 106).

It is of course possible to pretend to be embraced by a role in order to conceal an actual lack of attachment, just as disdain may be affected to insure against any damaging implications that might be read into actual attachment. At five, 'to be a merry-go-round horse-rider is now apparently not enough', and the role, and the situation, may be 'treated with some irreverence. 'The child says by his actions, "Whatever I am, I'm not just someone who can barely manage to stay on a wooden horse."' And so on, until, at eleven or twelve, he is just old enough to achieve role distance by defining the whole situation as a lark, a situation for mockery.

Turning to the operating theatre and the surgical team, Goffman observes that the role of surgeon, when situated in the setting and activity proper to an operating theatre, is above all one which we would expect to be embraced. 'If the [conventional] role perspective works, then, surely it works here, for in our society the surgeon, if anyone, is allowed and obliged to put himself into his work and get a self out of it' (p. 116). Yet role distance is, he finds, clearly and routinely expressed in the operating theatre.

This is the problem to which the whole essay is addressed. It is essentially the problem of the nature of the self and of personal identity. To embrace a role (which is what one would expect of a surgeon engaged in the action central to his professional role, his social and economic status, and much of the rest of his life), is also to "lose" oneself in it. And the loss is real. For what is lost amounts to one's personal identity *and* one's ego.

The answer which Goffman comes up with lies in his definition of personal identity as itself a social construct. There is a multiplicity of roles other than that which is presently occupied, all of which go to make up personal identity. There are age and sex categories by which we are identified, and by which we identify ourselves. In families, neighbourhoods, circles of friends and acquaintances, clubs, political parties, associations – to name only the most obvious and conventional situations and settings – there is a variety of situated roles waiting for each individual to occupy them for a time. And even in his place of work, the individual becomes involved in social relationships and group formations which may or may not coincide with the boundaries of various administrative units or work teams. In the surgeon's case, all such sources of self-identification 'penetrate the surgical activity system in a diffuse way, qualifying and modifying conduct where this can be done without threatening the task that controls the situation' (p. 137). This means that the individual must attend to the management of his working relationships with his fellow participants, apart from the role demands of the situated system. Hence, requirements such as those imposed by administrative regulations, or teaching, which tend to weaken any established social solidarity with others or to work against its formation, may have to be moderated, so as to preserve working solidarity. This can be done only – or most speedily and effectively – by momentary *expressive* withdrawal from his situated role.

For Goffman, the fact of individual identity being socially ascribed is underlined by the further fact of the need, and the capacity, to sustain a multiplicity of selves simultaneously. While an activity system situated in a social establishment may provide a fairly coherent self-consistent bundle of tasks for a given participant, he will, at the same time, be *officially* involved in (connected up with) other multi-situated matters that have a relevant claim on his time. It may well be that he can honour this claim only by diverting to it some of the concern that is owed the situated activity. In the surgeon's case, diversionary claims include teaching, making future appointments through speaker-phone, rearranging the day's schedule. And there are other more "social" claims which stem from his social identity (age, sex, social class, and the like), and from non-specific affiliations and obligation, such as those which apply to encounters which include strangers. 'These various identificatory demands are not created by the individual but are drawn from what society allots him. He frees himself from one group, not to be free, but because there is another hold on him.'

Situated role behaviour may be modified not by something intrinsically more "human" or "personal" but by conduct pertaining to other formalised modes of conduct available in society for interaction. So there is always something about the context in which a situated role is being played that leads systematically to the appearance of alternative identifications. There is always some discrepancy between the self emerging from a situated activity role (when one is obliged to sustain the system while "on duty", so to speak) and the broad social title in the name of which the activity is carried out.

> Given a situated system as a point of reference, role distance is a typical, not a normative, aspect of role. But the lightness with which the individual handles a situated role is forced upon him by the weight of his manifold attachments and commitments to multi-situated social entities
>
> (E, 142)

Or, one might add, it is allowed for because others regard him as someone, like themselves, with other roles and other commitments, which may sometimes supervene.

There is what Goffman calls a 'clue' offered to our understanding in the latitude allowed to youngsters and to beginners in general, a period of grace during which they are allowed to be not yet quite the persons they will be – a period marked by twitting by seniors and by their own readiness with excuses and apologies. Besides the clue to the actuality of role distance this observation provides, it is also a link with the notion of there being different intensities of commitment to action, with a more fully 'embraced' role at the highest level, which is developed in "Where the Action Is". In that essay, he argued for there being special 'niches' in social life marked out for 'action', which are more consequential, even more fateful, for the individual than everyday role-performance can ever be. They commit the individual proper, as well as the performed self. An audience may be even more closely involved. In "Role Distance" different levels of commitment relate to commitment to the role itself, with the peak represented by 'fully embraced' performance of an 'official' role. In this case, though, the operative force is supplied by 'society'. It is the accomplished, machine-like performance in a role, with no allowance for role distance, which is the prescribed ideal.

VII

There is yet a third dimension to this new-found elasticity in the concept of role-performance. This is mapped out in the sections of *The Presentation of Self* devoted to 'Discrepant Roles' and 'Communication out of Character'. Both labels, it should be said, derive from the notion, which is perhaps worked a little too hard, of a performance being divided into front region and back region, and of the participants between team and audience (with outsiders a possible third party). All the 'discrepant' and incompatible role-performances Goffman describes are just as recognisably socially prescribed as those pertaining to performers and audience – indeed, he says so at one point (p. 169). What is special about them is that, rather than discrepant, they mediate (sometimes legitimately, sometimes illegitimately) between front and back regions, team and audience.

Although, he says, the roles of performers, audience and outsiders are 'crucial',

> there are points of vantage relative to the performance which complicate the simple relation between function, information, and place. Some vantage points are so often taken and their significance to the performance so clearly understood that they can be referred to as roles, though, relative to the three crucial ones, best called discrepant roles.
>
> (p. 144)

Two such roles are essentially those of the *impostor* (one who poses as a member of the team and so is allowed backstage, where he may acquire information which can damage the impression the team seeks to create) and the *shill* (someone who acts as a member of the audience but is in fact in league with the performers). There are also what might be called accredited impostors: those who police the goings-on at performances and displays as the official or unofficial agents of an otherwise unsuspecting public.

But there are other roles, involving no deception whatever, which are also classed by Goffman as 'discrepant'. One group consists not only of roles generally acknowledged as intermediary – 'go-between, agent, broker, foreman, chairman (representing a speaker to the audience, and audience to speaker) – but also "service specialists". The examples given of these range from furniture salesmen and architects (who deal in settings), to hairdressers and dentists (who deal with personal front), and, third, corporation employees such as economists, lawyers, and researchers whose job it is to frame a line of argument for the client (i.e. the corporation) or to establish a legal or factual or intellectual position for him. Confidants are another group, which covers not only priests and psychotherapists, whose role of confidant has been institutionalised to the point of being sanctified, but also other 'service specialists' who are often pressed into the role by their clients. And, last, the role of colleague is even more insistently subsumed under the discrepant role heading, on the grounds that colleagues present 'the same routine to the same kind of audience but do not participate in the same performance'. The implication, presumably, is that merely by being privy to the procedures and devices of impression management, doctors, lawyers, clergy and other professionals share the secret information concerning the same backstage region, but communicate on their own, privately, with different 'audiences'.

The chapter on "Communication out of Character" puts an even greater strain on the original framework of definition, both of impression management as a means of 'controlling the situation' and of the functional separation of team, audience and outsiders and of front region and back region. To begin with, the instances he gives are of awkward or stressful incidents in which the wrong identification of someone, or some similar mishap, may disrupt a performance. In consequence, the performer *behind the character* often 'forgets himself and blurts out a relatively unperformed exclamation' (p. 168).

Apart from such momentary crises, it is quite usual for there to be other 'currents of communication' between team and audience which are incompatible with the official definition of the situation. Goffman then comments:

> When a social situation is studied, these discrepant sentiments are almost always found . . . showing that while a performer may act as if his response to a situation were immediate, unthinking and spontaneous, and think this is so, still it will always be possible for situations to arise in which he will convey to one or two persons present the understanding that the show he is maintaining is only and merely a show.
>
> (p. 169)

It is, I think, fairly clear that we are now well inside the kind of discussion of disparate role-performance which the essay on "Role Distance" subsequently covered. This seems to be confirmed when he goes on to consider 'other standard ways' of breaking front, which include 'referring to aspects of their routine in a cynical or technical way, to give forceful evidence to themselves that they do not take the same view of their activity as the view they maintain for the audience'. Among the 'other standard ways' are: derogatory remarks about the audience; 'staging talk'; utterances and actions which denote both 'a collusive arrangement' with other members of the team and 'affirm a backstage solidarity even while engaged in performace'; and, finally, 'communications which function chiefly to confirm for the performer the fact that he does not really hold with the working consensus, that the show he puts on is only a show'.

> Whatever it is that generates the human want for social contact and for companionship, the effect seems to take two forms: a need for an audience before which to try out one's vaunted selves, and a need for teammates with whom to enter into collusive intimacies and backstage relaxation.
>
> (p. 206)

And there are times when people other than team-mates and audience perform both functions together.

> Each of these kinds of conduct directs attention to the same point: the performance given by a team is not a spontaneous, immediate response to the situation, absorbing all of a team's energies and constituting their sole social reality.

There are two observations which Goffman makes by way of comment on these accidental, incidental or intentional occurrences. Both put large question marks against the whole tenor of the book – not the insights themselves, of course, nor the critical sociological viewpoint they display, nor yet the dramaturgical principle itself, but the assumptions on which the organisational framework and the concepts fitted on to it are based.

The first is that 'the performance is something the team members can stand back from, back far enough to imagine or play out simultaneously other kinds of performance attesting to other realities' (p. 207). Or, to put it in terms Goffman would arrive at later: role-performances are carved out of the 'social reality' of the individuals who perform them, and are 'framed', with the knowledge that a lot is going on outside the frame, and that more will have to go on afterwards.

The second almost gives the whole game away by letting in the possibility of there being, between actors and audience, a kind of sympathetic understanding which proceeds simply from their common humanity: something I have labelled "communality", and which Goffman calls 'a fundamental democracy'. It comes after a recital of the kind of defensive measures taken by teams (or individual performers), and of protective measures which audiences can supply to guard against, cover up or pass over disruptions and embarrassing incidents which can threaten the reality 'sponsored' by the performers.

When such an incident occurs, the members of an audience sometimes learn a important lesson, more important to them than the aggressive pleasure they can obtain by discovering someone's dark, entrusted, inside, or strategic secret. The members of the audience may discover a fundamental democracy that is usually well hidden.

(p. 235)

NOTES AND REFERENCES

1. See E. Burns, *Theatricality*, Longman, 1972, esp. Chap. 2.
2. K. Burke, *A Grammar of Motives*, Univ. of California Press, 1969, p. xv.
3. K. Burke, *A Grammar of Motives*, Univ. of California Press, 1969, p. xxii.
4. H. Plessner, "With different eyes", in *Phenomenology and Sociology*, (ed. T. Luckmann), Penguin, 1978, pp. 25-41.
5. M. Mauss, "Une categorie de l'esprit humaine", *Journal of the Royal Anthropological Institute*, vol. 67, 1938, pp. 256 ff.
6. See E. Burns, *Theatricality*, Longman, 1972, pp. 122-5.
7. His conception of social drama was first outlined in V. W. Turner, *Schism and Continuity in an African Society*, Manchester Univ. Press, 1957.
8. C. Geertz, *Local Knowledge*, Basic Books, 1983, p. 28.
9. C. Lévi-Strauss, *The Savage Mind*, Weidenfeld & Nicolson, 1962, p. 32.
10. T. Burns, "The reference of conduct in small groups: cliques and cabals in occupational milieux", *Human Relations*, vol. 8, 1955, pp. 477-8.
11. A. W. Gouldner, *The Coming Crisis of Western Sociology*, Basic Books, 1970, esp. pp. 378-90.
12. A. MacIntyre, *After Virtue*, Duckworth, 1981, p. 109.
13. K. Burke, *A Grammar of Motives*, Univ. of California Press, 1969, p. 3.
14. See T. Burns, *The BBC: Public Institution and Private World*, Macmillan, 1977, Ch. 3, "Settings".
15. R. Darnton, "Peasants tell tales", in *The Great Cat Massacre*, Penguin Books, 1985, p. 26. See also J. B. Hainsworth, "Ancient Greek", in

Traditions of Heroic and Epic Poetry, Modern Humanities Research Assoc., 1980, pp. 31-3.
16. For the difference, see B. Williams, *Ethics and the Limits of Philosophy*, esp. pp. 6-18, and A. MacIntyre, *After Virtue*, esp. pp. 139-41.

6

"NORMALISATION"

Asylums, Goffman's second book, was published in 1961, just two years after the commercial publication of *The Presentation of Self* had won him the first award of the MacIver Prize. Its impact was as substantial as that of his first book – perhaps more so. For here again, but applied now to something completely different, were the special talents that had revealed themselves in the first book: the sharpness of observation; the revelatory discoveries in what had been taken for well-trodden and over-familiar territory; an intellectual capacity for arranging his observations and analyses according to a coherent and carefully constructed conceptual scheme which gives new meaning to what were commonplace facts and underwrites the whole exercise intellectually.

There are, however, some differences between the *Asylums* essays and his other writings, both earlier and later. The first is stylistic – something which is a weightier consideration in Goffman's case than with other social scientists. Beginning with the title, which one soon discovers is heavy with irony, the sheer skill in writing wins over the reader, once again, by its fluency in exposition, sheer dexterity, and occasional pungency. But the style is generally much plainer, more direct, and (comparatively) economical. This would hardly be worth mentioning except that the style is, I think, a reflection of the fact that he is addressing matters which are of general concern, and presenting views which have a direct bearing on public policy. The moralising tone, too, which elsewhere makes its appearance in brief acerbic comments and interpolations, is sustained throughout the whole book; critical analysis now and again turns into polemic. Over and above the critical attacks on the immediate targets there are occasional bouts of social criticism of Voltairean dimensions. In two of the essays, for example, there are lengthy passages on the way in which organisations control the people who work for them or are confined to them which bear a striking resemblance to Foucault's treatment of "normalisation" as the characteristic means of exerting power in modern society.

However, the immediate targets are located clearly enough in the world of mental illness and its treatment. There are four: custodial treatment; managerialism in the context of the mental hospital; the subjection of mental patients to physical constraint and humiliating treatment as well as to surveillance and moral discipline of a peculiarly intrusive kind; and the rationales of psychiatric diagnosis and mental hospital treatment.

I

As I have already remarked, the term "total institutions" was coined by Everett Hughes. Goffman heard it first in a graduate seminar on institutions which he attended in 1952. It is clear from Goffman's course notes (he gave me a copy of them) that it must have been a remarkable teaching enterprise – enlivened with allusions, encyclopedic in its coverage, and radically critical and innovative in its approach.

First, Hughes argued, since group behaviour and group control were the great historic problems of sociology, the study of social institutions is at the heart of sociology. Social institutions have to be looked on as "mobilisations", not only of persons but of things like rule-making, ideologies, and claims for mandates. Second, he went on to refer to Durkheim, Simmel, and others as all concerned with rule-making and rule-enforcing. But, in contrast to the way Goffman saw it later, the rules of social interaction did not "make" interaction; they "arose" out of it, and conditioned future interaction. Lastly, in one of the seminars, Hughes introduced the term "total institutions" for those social institutions which were much more shut off from the outside world; the example he gave was nunneries.

All Goffman's work reflects the same conviction of the central importance of social institutions, but there is one radical difference. Hughes, like most sociologists, took "social institution" to mean an established social arrangement (a "going concern") whose membership, resources, powers, technical procedures, and "rules of the game" were well known and easily recognised by all – or most – people in a society, whether or not they were members of it, or participants. A complete inventory for a country like the United States would have been impossibly long – the sample list in the notes runs from the US Senate to the corner drug-store. The social institutions which engaged Goffman's attention almost exclusively were those pertaining to everyday social order. In this he follows the usage common among anthropologists; they use the term just as loosely as other social scientists, but, being concerned for the most part with small communities, typically those in pre-literate societies, social institutions for them meant all those customary arrangements by which the social structure of a society operates as a self-perpetuating, or self-renewing, system. Social anthropologists, that is, envisage social structure as the total 'physiology' of a society rather than as its more durable 'skeleton'. Goffman's complete inventory would not perhaps have been much longer than Hughes', but his samples would have included cocktail parties, restaurant meals, pedestrian traffic, friendship, and university lectures and seminars.

The term "total institutions" fitted Goffman's purposes far too well for him to pass it over. So, while he would have preferred to call them "social establishments" – the label he had previously adopted – he took over the term "social institution", in what he called its 'everyday sense'. A little more confusion is added by his using the word "establishment" or "institution" indiscriminately. Still, what counted was tying his observations and analysis of the situation of those "extruded" from society as unfit for it to an all-out assault on the degradations, restraints, and deprivations suffered by mental patients in institutions supposedly created for their care, if not their cure.

Moreover, adopting the term "total institutions" was a very successful move. It caught the imagination. It also, perhaps, helped to diffuse much of the resentment which might have been aroused in the psychiatric profession by a damaging attack on them into a more general reformist assault on the impersonal defects attributable to the characteristics of "total institutions". Psychiatrists could see themselves, too, as the victims of "institutionalisation". At all events, as well as becoming one of the few lasting best-sellers to come from academic sociology, *Asylums* became obligatory reading for psychotherapists.

The term became for a time quite widely used, without becoming established in standard usage. This is perhaps just as well, since its slightly melodramatic flavour invites misuse. Habermas, for one, has applied it to – of all things – the kinship systems of tribal societies,[1] thus compounding the "pernicious" error denounced by Lévi-Strauss of treating primitive peoples as communities living in total isolation from all other communities, whether "primitive" or "advanced", shut in on themselves, each with its own particular assemblage of ritual, aesthetic experience and myth which is presumed to belong exclusively to it.[2]

Goffman begins the essay by noting that one way of classifying institutions is to rank them according to the degree to which they are "closed". "Total institutions" are those, like monasteries and such, which are totally, or almost totally, closed to the outside world. These make up a 'natural and fruitful' category of institutions which have a great deal in common – 'so much, in fact' (and here he adopts a strategy which Hughes made peculiarly his own), 'that to learn about one of these institutions we would be well advised to look at the others'. He then suggests five ('rough') groupings within the overall category, each with rather different characteristics.

They are a rather heterogeneous lot. The first two 'rough groupings' comprise establishments set up to care for those felt to be incapable of looking after themselves and (a) harmless (blind, aged, orphaned, indigent), or (b) posing a possible threat to others (i.e. the inmates of sanitaria, leprosaria, mental hospitals). Third comes the kind of place established so as to protect the community at large 'against what are felt to be intentional dangers to it' and in which the welfare of the inmates is not the first concern (e.g. jails, penitentiaries, PoW camps, and concentration camps). The fourth group is of those 'purportedly established the better to pursue some worklike task and justifying themselves only on these instrumental grounds' (army barracks, ships, boarding schools, work camps, and the like). And, last, there are cloistered retreats and monastic establishments, which serve also as training establishments for the religious.

Goffman offers no very precise definition of "total institutions". All he claims is that 'what is distinctive about total institutions is that each exhibits to an intense degree many items in this family of attributes'. It is a formula which gives him a great deal of latitude, resembling in this Weber's "ideal type" formulation, although it is hardly the same. But Goffman stretches its scope even further, advising the reader that 'none of the elements I will describe seems peculiar to total institutions, and none seems to be shared by every one of them.'

In the event, what one finds is that, since the 'elements' he mentions were in the first place derived from his research, they all of course apply to mental hospitals. But some of the structural features and characteristic practices of mental hospitals can be found, he points out, in merchant ships, army barracks, and English public schools. Expanding the category of "closed" institutions from those which are clearly "custodial", in the narrow sense, to his designation of "total" pays off handsomely in two contrasting ways. In the first place, it all goes to show how unexceptionable, even "normal", such practices have come to be – something to which his contemporary, Michel Foucault, gave central importance. For the most part, however, these other institutions are mentioned simply to provide back-up evidence, which is put to good use. The critical stance he adopts to the practices he encountered in mental hospitals is made firmer, and sharper, by reports of identical, or very similar, practices reported of prisons, concentration camps, and other places to which society condemns its miscreants and outcasts.

There are a dozen or more distinguishable characteristics of mental hospitals, in their total institution guise. But it is the first three which count most. They provide not so much the foundations for the whole system as the basic materials from which the other characteristics are manufactured or assembled.

The first major characteristic is "closure". While total institutions are not completely sealed off from access by, or to, the world outside, social intercourse between those inside and people outside is restricted – severely so, for most of those inside. There is a 'barrier to social intercourse with the outside and to departure that is often built right into the physical plant' (p. 4).

The notion of closure gives all the institutions he names a kind of family resemblance, but it is no more than that. Closure, of itself, is not special to total institutions; factories and, for that matter, homes have walls and fences designed specifically for protection and privacy – to keep some people (thieves, strangers, casual passers-by) out, and some people (children), and pets, in. General hospitals (which the essay leaves completely out of account) certainly do their best to keep patients in for as long as they think fit, and control access to them. They, too, shelter behind a physical barrier which is also social and psychological; it is recognised, approved, and supported as such by the attitudes of the establishment and its institutional context, and by the general public or "society at large". What counts in the case of Goffman's chosen "total institutions" is what he would probably have called "moral closure" (with "moral", as usual with him, carrying the "state-of-mind" reference the word has in French).

The next feature, the "rationalisation" of everyday living, is one he calls 'central'. It consists in the reconstruction of the everyday life of their inmates so that the major sectors of it – work, play, and sleep – which are ordinarily carried on in different places, in different company, under different auspices and without an overall rational plan, are brought together in the same place and under the same authority. A kind of *Gleichschaltung* is forced on individuals and activities. Inmates are marshalled through every phase of their daily round along with everybody else according to a tight, uniform schedule which is 'purportedly' determined by the prescribed aims of the hospital (p. 6).

Of course, universities, colleges, and training schools commonly provide sleeping, eating, and recreational facilities for students, and big corporations have opened up cafeterias and recreational facilities for their employees. What is distinctive about total institutions is that those inside are not free to choose to go outside for these things.

The third important factor is what Goffman calls 'bureaucratic organisation'. While at this stage it may well seem merely irritating, it does need to be pointed out (because it does assume some importance later) that although all the total organisations he mentions could certainly be said to be organised, and even to have a management or administration, hardly any of them qualify as "bureaucracies", however wide the term is stretched.[3] For one thing, the presence of psychiatrists, many in senior administrative positions, means that mental hospitals, which are his main concern, contain a sizeable element of collegial organisation. Again, in most – though not all – of his total institutions there is a group of members responsible for keeping it a "going concern". This makes for a clear line of distinction in membership between "staff" – administrative, professional, technical, custodial or service – and "inmates" – blind persons, passengers, schoolchildren, prisoners or patients. Third, those aspects of the conduct of nurses and others (loosely described as "assistants") which suggest that there was among them a tendency, to put it no higher than that, to use their legitimate powers as a basis for the assumption of illegitimate powers and so become petty tyrants on their own account, betray organisational features which are anything but bureaucratic, properly speaking; the word "bureaucratic" is not synonymous with "authoritarian", still less with "tyrannical".

However, the point Goffman wants to make is clear enough. In almost all closed institutions, custodial or not, the distinction between staff and inmates becomes a line of demarcation. Living arrangements are separate; staff enjoy a freedom of communication with, and access to and from, the outside world denied to inmates. The staff-inmate split is the direct consequence of the combination of, first, the degree of "closure" to which the inmates, as against members of staff or "the establishment", are subject, and, second, the way in which the authority of those in command is interpreted and their power implemented. It makes for a fundamental divide between the two; they belong, in fact, to different worlds.

This "them-and-us" divide is not, of course, confined to total institutions; it is not unknown in factories and other workplaces, and, more generally, underlies social class divisions and other systematic forms of invidious distinction. More to the point, it is something experienced even in the most benign of total institutions, such as general hospitals (which do not figure in Goffman's sample list), or homes for the blind (which do). Even in them, it can breed irritation and mutual resentment. At the extreme, the divide leads almost inevitably to lasting hostility. Each side 'tends to conceive of the other in terms of narrow hostile stereotypes, staff often seeing inmates as bitter, secretive, and untrustworthy, while inmates often see staff as condescending, highhanded, and mean' (p. 7).

The staff-inmate split is the first consequence of the three conditioning elements of closure, rationalisation, and disciplinary control. It has to be said that while this had been widely accepted as necessary, inevitable or even "rational", by the mid-fifties there was a sizeable body of dissenting opinion. Indeed, there was a good deal of practical experience of alternative arrangements to show that it was neither inevitable nor rational. Towards the end of the Second World War, T. C. Main, W. R. Bion, John Rickman, and other psychiatrists (then on the British Army medical staff) had begun the "Northfield Experiment" which turned a military hospital at Northfield, Birmingham, into a "therapeutic community", with patients and all staff officially on an equal footing. This was followed up in a civilian setting by Maxwell Jones, who set up "therapeutic communities" in England, Scotland, California, and elsewhere.[4] American initiatives followed, and by 1957 a large-scale symposium on therapeutic communities was organised at the Walter Reed Army Institute of Research. Goffman (who was well acquainted with the Tavistock Institute, where the Northfield group made its post-war base) in fact read his "Total Institutions" paper at this conference. So his book, when it appeared, was consciously addressed to a public which included an influential number of professional psychiatrists who already wore white hats.

II

The three elements of "closure", "rationalisation", and "bureaucratic organisation" in combination lead into, or are made manifest in, a string of practices and arrangements which diminish the social and personal identity of the inmate, whose freedom has already been drastically curtailed. Much is accomplished during the process of admission itself. Passing through the "barrier" from the outside world and becoming an "inmate" is inevitably a matter that calls for some routine administrative arrangements; but its symbolic significance goes well beyond administrative requirements.

Admission is accomplished by means of procedures which are, in effect, degradation rituals. The routines prescribed for admission in mental hospitals (and prisons) amount to a *'rite de passage'* which involves systematic mortification. Even when it may be unintentional, it appears as if designed to give the recruit a clear notion of his plight: 'a leaving off and a taking on, with the midpoint marked by physical nakedness' (p. 18). The staff who are present are busy

> taking a life history, photographing, weighing, fingerprinting, assigning numbers, searching, listing personal possessions for storage, undressing, bathing, disinfecting, haircutting, issuing institutional clothing, instructing as to rules, and assigning to quarters.
>
> (p. 16)

Of course all this may well be regarded as administratively necessary, and therefore borne with, like the business of admission to a general hospital (and it may even be welcomed by neophytes entering a monastic establishment). But there is usually in mental hospitals (and prisons) an accompaniment which it is impossible to misread or treat as ambivalent. Because a custodial institution takes over control of so many aspects of its inmates' lives,

> staff often feel that a recruit's readiness to be appropriately deferential in his initial face-to-face encounters with them is a sign that he will take on the role of the routinely pliant inmate.

The occasion on which staff members first tell the inmate of his deference obligations may be structured to challenge the inmate to balk or to hold his peace forever.

And this observation is backed up by an 'engaging' illustration taken from Brendan Behan's account of the losing battle he fought with two warders on his admission to prison (pp. 17-18).

The degrading connotations of admission procedures are reinforced, perhaps prepared for, by the sense of deprivation which attends the patient's removal from his former surroundings, social life, and familiar round of activity, however unstable or disorganised they may have been. Outside, however defective his "home world", in short, he could usually manage to sustain a 'tolerable conception of self' (p. 13); there were at least no impenetrable boundaries, nor any absolute prohibition on face-saving gestures.

It is not that total institutions destroy this 'tolerable' self-conception and replace it with something they have themselves fabricated. We are dealing, Goffman argues, 'with something more restricted than acculturation or assimilation'. All kinds of opportunities for action and interaction, of participation in the events and the changes taking place in the larger society outside, are lost to him, and the motivations, reactions, and feelings connected with them are worn away by attrition or overcome by obsolescence. So, if the inmate stays inside long enough, he tends to suffer a sort of training in unfitness for the world outside, rendering him 'temporarily incapable of managing certain features of daily life on the outside, if and when he gets back to it' (p. 13). Goffman's observations are entirely congruent with the findings of a detailed study made in England in 1944-6 of the "deculturation" exhibited by repatriated prisoners of war.[5]

The deterioration in the inmate's capacity for life on the outside is furthered – or perhaps complemented – by what Goffman calls 'role dispossession'. We are used to the notion that, in ordinary life, the individual invests a kind of psycho-social capital in the different roles in which he presents different versions of his self. In most circumstances, moreover, he has some need to keep the settings in which he performs these several roles (and the audiences for them) physically apart. This calls for a certain amount of skill in managing a programme of performances so as to avoid confrontations which might prove embarrassing and to promote encounters that might be rewarding. Scheduling roles in this way is now out of the question for mental patients; the world of the mental hospital is too small, their round of daily activities too routine and too uniform. The skills needed for switching roles in the circumstances of ordinary social life degenerate, and patients may come eventually to lose possession, so to speak, of some of the roles they once habitually filled.

It is a diminished self which emerges from admission procedures, and, after admission, the inmate's self-image is kept under fairly constant attack. 'Given the expressive idiom of a particular society, certain movements, postures, and stances will convey lowly images of the individual and be avoided as demeaning. . . . In total institutions, such physical indignities abound.' To this are added the obligation to address certain staff members as "sir", having to ask permission to use the telephone, light a cigarette, get a drink of water, all forcing the individual into a submissive or suppliant role which an adult is bound to feel is not merely irksome but "unnatural". There is an extra turn which may be given to this particular screw, for staff members may quite possibly take it into their heads to make an issue, or a game, out of it. 'He may be teased, his request denied, or questioned at length, ignored, or put off' (p. 41).

Nor is it possible to dismiss the humiliations of the regimen as confined to submitting to this kind of petty tyranny – as regrettable, but not intrinsic to the system. For it is in what are regarded as the better, "more progressive", mental hospitals that the patient is likely to have a high-ranking staff persuading him

> that his past has been a failure, that the cause of this has been within himself, that his attitude to life is wrong, and that if he wants to be a person he will have to change his way of dealing with people and his conception of himself.
>
> (p. 150)

The hostile edge which encounters between staff and inmates takes on is sharpened by the part played by supervisory staff as intermediaries. Some communication between inmates and supervisory and service staff is obviously necessary, but control of communication from inmates to higher professional and administrative staff level is, or easily becomes, one of the functions of supervisory staff. Characteristically, the inmate is excluded from knowledge of the decisions taken concerning his fate, and this serves to stress the distance between staff and inmates and the difference in the power they can exercise over their circumstances. Inevitably, this reinforces the antagonistic stereotypes they have of each other. 'Two different social and cultural worlds develop, jogging alongside each other with points of official contact but little mutual penetration' (p. 9).

III

The categorical difference between the ordinary round of everyday life and 'batch-living', as Goffman calls it, in total institutions, is nicely illustrated in the different significance which attaches to work.

Inmates in most total institutions are given work to do, and for some of it there is a small amount of pay usually forthcoming. Some kinds of work may provide training, but much of it is in connection with essential, though lowly, services – cleaning, gardening, helping in kitchens, and minor housekeeping chores – tasks which derive from the working needs of the establishment. The low-pay system reflects, or is rationalised by, the view that paying inmates for any work they do is unnecessary and pointless, since all their essential needs are catered for.

This "sensible" point is none the less an infraction of the basic rationale implicit in the everyday world of work outside, of which inmates were once part. Whatever incentive for work is offered in place of payment, this incentive will not have the structural significance it has on the outside. There is, then, a dual incompatibility between the contractual bargain struck between work and pay in society and the supernumerary, though not superfluous, nature of work done by inmates in total institutions. The meaningful relationship between working, being paid for it and spending one's pay, and the differential relationship each has to workplace authority, are both abrogated – *but incompletely*. The economic rationale of the outside world is not completely foregone inside; a few loopholes are conceded through which some fragments of the everyday model of earning a living by work may be imported. There is a canteen and a shop, and things to be bought in them; but few have any money to spend, which means that the provision of this "amenity" can lead to the kind of demoralisation exemplified by "bumming" nickels.

Even though the economic rationale of the wider society, and with it the approved motives and attitudes to do with work, may be, as it is often claimed, factitious, heavily institutionalised and obsessively pursued, such motives and attitudes, and the implied frame of reference, do by their very existence tend to exclude other types of interpretation. Places where they are regarded as inapplicable, as they

151

are in total institutions, become 'dangerously open to all kinds of interpretive flights and excesses and, in consequence, to new kinds of tyranny' (p. 91).

One potential tyranny is implicit in the interpretation put on work as having therapeutic value; it becomes "industrial therapy" or "work therapy". The claim presented to the inmate of a mental hospital is that these tasks will help him relearn to live in society and that his capacity and willingness to handle them will be taken as diagnostic evidence of improvement. But the rationale which "therapeutic values" give to work has another side. It means that work, along with other aspects of inmate behaviour, can be built into the reward and punishment system.

Early on, the inmate is instructed in the "privilege system". Against the rather bleak background of instruction in the house rules, which inform him of the main requirements of inmate conduct, the newcomer is told that there exist certain clearly defined privileges which he may earn. These are held out as "merit awards" for conformity with the rules, including, in particular, obedience to staff. There are also punishments for breaking the rules. One set of punishments consists in the temporary or permanent withdrawal of privileges, or the abrogation of the right to try to earn them.

The existence of such a system of punishments, for such offences, and in such terms, is in itself, Goffman points out, a form of mortification and deprivation. For, consisting as it does merely in the removal or re-imposition of deprivations, it is alien to the normal world of adults, being regarded 'as the sort of thing meted out to children or animals'. The very nature of total institutions, moreover, means that it does not end there. Shifting inmates from one sleeping place or work place to another is used as punishment for recalcitrance or reward for cooperation, so that the reward and punishment system is built into the residential and work system. 'Places to work and places to sleep become clearly defined as places where certain kinds and levels of privilege obtain' (p. 51). So, after the stripping process which begins on admission has detached him from his civilian self, the privilege system obliges the inmate to revise his strategies for living, and so becomes a means of reorganising his life.

The patient's precise location in the hospital has therefore a complex set of meanings which operates at two levels, meanings which are nevertheless all understood well enough by inmates. The "ward system" consists of 'a series of graded living arrangements built around wards, administrative units called services, and parole statuses' (p. 148). At the worst level, the inmates are provided with nothing but wooden benches to sit on, indifferent food, and a small sleeping area. At best level, there may be a room of one's own, what is regarded as good food, and relatively good facilities for recreation; contacts with staff tend to lose much of the abrasiveness that occurs elsewhere, and privileges may include access to the grounds and even the town.

The implications – the moral implications – of this grid of residential amenities and deprivations are made quite clear to those consigned to it.

Once lodged on a given ward, the patient is firmly instructed that the restrictions and deprivations he encounters are not due to such blind forces as tradition or economy – and hence dissociable from self – but are intentional parts of his treatment, part of his need at the time, and therefore an expression of the state his self has fallen to.

(p. 149)

Beyond this, a form of double jeopardy is involved. It becomes clear that the all-important decision concerning the time of release is built into the privilege system. There are acts which become known as ones that will lead to a lengthier stay, or at least to no remission, and others as ways of shortening it. The effectiveness of the system depends on the special meaning to the inmate of "getting out" (i.e. release) or "getting on the outside" (town visits). It therefore both derives from and reinforces the meaning for the inmate of being "in" or "on the inside". By building on the peculiar tension between the world their inmates have left and the institutional world to which they now belong, total institutions provide themselves with a useful instrument for managing men.

It may well be that in the outside world people are often faced with situations, or instructions, which they see as a personal affront. But at the same time, there are some face-saving responses to which he can often resort with impunity. The combination of actual compliance and half-surreptitious defiance of the "dumb insolence" kind is no more common in total institutions than it is elsewhere, but in them may well be penalised by staff. Simply to respond to staff by doing what is required in silence, as a way of keeping aloof, or "answering back", making some minimal gesture, verbal or non-verbal, and the like, to offset submission, may be discounted – or it may be treated as symptomatic. 'Inmates may find a dual language exists, with the disciplinary facts of his life given a translated ideal phrasing by the staff that mocks the normal use of language' (p. 45). Verbal responses may be checked by search, anyone suspected of giving offence may be pushed or pulled along by a guard, or frog-marched. Thus, staff members whose actions provoke resentment, and lead to some kind of defensive response – sullenness, *sotto voce* asides, fugitive expressions of contempt, irony, derision – may take this selfsame response as an incitement to fresh provocation.

There is also, specifically in connection with mental hospitals of 'the advanced type', a sense in which the privilege and punishment system is still further built into the system of control. A "permissive" atmosphere may prevail, so as to encourage the inmate to "project" or "act out" his typical difficulties in living. But acts of aggression or disobedience are nevertheless reported as a matter of official routine, to be brought later to his attention during therapeutic sessions. The term Goffman uses for this system of entrapment is "looping".

IV

The immediate object of his Washington research, Goffman says in the preface to *Asylums*, 'was to learn about the social world of the hospital inmate, as this world is subjectively experienced by him'. Elaborating the notion of the total institutions in the way he did was a marvellously effective way of conveying the meaning of that social world as experienced by the hospital inmate, and the impact it has on him, his attitudes, his idea of his past and his future, and the conception he has of himself. But, as Goffman notes, a total institution is 'a social hybrid' (p. 12). It is both a residential community and what he calls (following the nomenclature current at the time) a 'formal organisation' – characteristically, a collection of people engaged in specified tasks and organised so as to achieve specified ends. It is the kind of organisation familiar in industry, business, and government which is directed and controlled by a hierarchy of managers or administrators, usually thought of as a bureaucratic structure.[6] His account of the character of total institutions, therefore, has to be supplemented by an analysis of the structural features of formal organisations which have some additional bearing on the nature of the subjective experience of mental hospital patients. There are several passages in which he turns aside to review those features.

Given the reasons he has for bringing the nature of "formal organisations" into the discussion, the features he enlarges upon have to do, naturally, with power and control. But the kind of power and the kind of control he has in mind as characteristic of organisations in general are altogether more all-embracing and more insidious than what is usually accorded them either in the social science literature or in ordinary discourse. There is in the third essay ("The Underlife of a Public Institution") a fairly lengthy excursus on the extent to which every organisation seems obliged to impress on its members or participants a conception of themselves which more or less faithfully reflects the values it upholds and wants to see embodied in itself, and in them:

> A formal organisation does not merely use the activity of its members. The organisation also delineates what are considered to be officially appropriate standards of welfare, joint values, incentives and penalties. These conceptions expand a mere participation contract into a definition of the participant's nature or social being. These implicit images form an important element of the values which every organisation sustains, regardless of the degree of its efficiency or impersonality. Built right into the social arrangements of an organisation, then, is a thoroughly embracing conception of the member – and not merely a conception of him *qua* member, but behind this a conception of him *qua* human being.
>
> (p. 179)

Acceptance by the members of an organisation of pay, incentives, rewards, and so forth, amounts to tacit acceptance of the organisation's idea of what motivates him. It is of course an idea he may well feel is entirely natural and unexceptionable, and may be quite unaware of his acceptance of a number of assumptions that are being made about him. But for him to be unaware of them does not mean that they do not exist. *All* organisations, Goffman claims, seek to impose an identity on their members, allocating to each of them a character and a conception of self which is consonant with the organisation's values, requirements, and expectations. 'Starting with aims, regulations, offices, and roles, establishments of any kind seem to end up by adding depth and colour to these arrangements. Duties and economic rewards are allocated, but so, at the same time, are character and being' (p. 111).

155

Goffman's real concern, then, is not what the participant is expected to do but the organisation's conception of him which is implied in its expectations.

> An organisation should be viewed as a place for generating assumptions about identity. . . . To engage in a particular activity in the prescribed spirit is to accept being a particular kind of person who dwells in a particular kind of world.
>
> (p. 186)

When it comes to total institutions, 'to accept privileges like yard exercise or art materials while in jail is to accept in part the captor's view of what one's desires and needs are' (pp. 180-1). In mental hospitals, *a fortiori*, the attempt is made not merely to induce conformity but to compel acceptance of a conception of self which incorporates the values and standards for which the organisation sees itself existing. The total institution regime of what Goffman calls 'regimentation and tyrannisation' is designed, explicitly and implicitly, to this end.

> In a total institution, minute segments of a person's line of activity may be subjected to regulations and judgments by staff; the inmate's life is penetrated by constant sanctioning from above, especially to begin with. Each specification robs the individual of an opportunity to balance his needs and objectives in a personally efficient way and opens up his line of action to sanctions. The autonomy of the act itself is violated.
>
> (p. 38)

By representing formal organisations, which are almost universally thought of in terms of structures, in terms of action and meanings, Goffman is able to argue that the same process of social control operates throughout society. The three characteristic features of total institutions which are fundamental, in that the ten or more other distinguishable 'elements' derive from them (see above, pp. 145-8), are closure, rationalisation (which he later calls 'regimentation'), and disciplinary control ('bureaucratic organisation'). By the end of the "Total Institutions" essay, however, it becomes apparent that the causal sequence which was implied may – perhaps should – be reversed. Instead of the closure, regimentation, and bureaucratic organisation which is imposed by power and authority being expressed, amplified, and supplemented in the humiliations of admission procedures, in mortification, role dispossession, 'looping', and so on, these modes of interaction (for that is what they are) are in fact the empirical ingredients which go to make up the notional structure represented by abstractions like closure, regimentation, and administrative control. The stress is on social action rather than the elements of structure one finds in conventional accounts of organisations.

V

It is at this point that there begins to emerge a quite remarkable coincidence between Goffman's conclusions and what Foucault, later (but almost certainly, quite independently), was to say on the same specific topics. Both of them, to begin with, point out that total institutions like prisons and asylums exist as establishments maintained in and by society at large as, in Goffman's words, 'rational organisations designed consciously, through and through, as effective machines for producing a few officially avowed and officially approved ends'; and in Foucault's, as "instrument(s) comparable with – and no less perfect than – the school, the barracks, or the hospital, acting with precision upon (their) individual subjects". Both also remark that they are in fact storage dumps.[7]

Goffman sees evidence for the contradiction between the declared correctional or therapeutic purposes of total institutions and their undeclared use as dumping grounds in the day-to-day activities of mental hospital staff. The staff of total institutions are engaged in "people-work" – the material for the staff to work on consists of people – which gives a special character to the work they do. For while there are ways in which people can be looked on as inanimate objects, 'the crucial determinants of the work world of the staff derive from the unique aspects of people as material to work on' (p. 76). These aspects all stem from the broad moral principles of society in which people are regarded as "ends in themselves". Among other things, these principles afford some guarantee that "humane standards", even when they are *technically* unnecessary, will be maintained in handling inmates, but, beyond that, the status, the relationships, and the civil rights of inmates have to be taken into account by the staff who deal with them. And there are occasions when

staff are reminded by their obligations in these matters of

standards and rights not only by their own internal superordinates but also by various watchdog agencies in the wider society and often by the kin of inmates. . . . This forces upon the staff some of the classic dilemmas that must be faced by those who govern men.

(p. 77)

Nevertheless, any conflict between obligation about "humane" standards and technical or administrative efficiency is liable to be resolved often enough in favour of efficiency. So, cleanliness is ensured by collecting all dirty clothing and issuing clean replacements indiscriminately; lousy heads of hair are shaved; "biters" have their teeth pulled out; chronic fighters get lobotomies performed on them.

While the special requirements of people-work establish the day's job for the staff, the job itself is carried out in a special moral climate. For while the staff sees itself as having to meet with the hostility and demands of the inmates, all that staff can legitimately do has to be within the limits of the rationale espoused by the institution. This rationale prescribes a set of official goals, or mandates, which, given the frame of reference of psychiatric treatment, say, or of "security", 'seem admirably suited to provide a key to meaning – a language of explanation that the staff, and sometimes the inmates, can bring to every crevice of action in the institution' (p. 83). Set within the rationale of the institution, every official goal 'lets loose a doctrine, and within institutions there seems no natural check on the licence of easy interpretation that results' (p. 84).

Of course, the very fact of entry into a total institution, as previous researchers had found, means that 'normality' is redefined for the inmate:

> Normality is never recognised by the attendant in a milieu where abnormality is the normal expectancy. Desires and requests, no matter how reasonable, how calmly expressed, or how politely stated, are regarded as evidence of mental disorder. . . . Even though most of these behavioural manifestations are reported to the doctors, they, in most cases, merely support the judgments of the attendants. In this way, the doctors themselves perpetuate the notion that the essential feature of dealing with mental patients is in their control.[8]

In other words the staff confer a kind of all-embracing identity on the inmates that will make it possible to control them and at the same time defend their own actions and the institution in the name of its avowed aims.

For this reason, ambiguity of purpose is built into the institutions set up by "normalising" regimes as receptacles for those who fail at their testing limit. In pursuit of their officially declared aims, administration and staff are pushed into a form of tyranny, turning 'the exercise of authority . . . into a witch hunt'. The actions which the staff in prisons justify in the name of "security" are a clear instance. While mental hospitals are officially dedicated to the remedy, or at least the care, of those deemed not responsible for their conduct, staff in them nevertheless demand of inmates that they assume moral responsibility for their conduct. And although the abnormal conduct which delivered the inmates into the hands of mental hospital staff is no more than what must be expected of them, and thus is normal, in one generally accepted sense, inmates must submit to penalties for offenses against the rules. For

> inmates must be caused to 'self-direct' themselves in a manageable way . . . both desired and undesired conduct must be defined as springing from the personal will and character of the inmate himself, and something he can himself do something about. In short, each institutional perspective contains a personal morality, and in each total institution we can see in miniature the development of something akin to a functionalist version of moral life.
>
> (p. 87)

The ambiguity of purpose embodied in total institutions leads to an expansion of the authority vested in the staff of total institutions into something approaching complete domination.

Power, in this sense (or in any sense, in fact) is understandable only within a given context. While the *kind* of authority and the *extent* of control are critically important in any command or administrative system, they are especially so in total institutions; authority and control are manifestly different in ships and monasteries, orphanages and concentration camps. In all cases, however, the authority by which members of staff exercise control derives ultimately from society at large, expressed or made explicit through the medium of law and the institutions of government. But that authority has to be translated into the kind, and the severity, of the sanctions which may be used to compel obedience – in short, into power over the lives of inmates. The intensity and the extent of power, in the case of establishments of the kind we are considering, may be amplified into tyranny simply by invoking the principles ('control' or 'security') on which the authority and control of the staff rest.

VI

Goffman's picture of the pressures exerted not only by total institutions but by work organisations generally on the behaviour and self-conception of the people who belong to them amounts, as I have already suggested, to a small-scale version of that presented by Michel Foucault some years later. It is almost as if Foucault had taken up Goffman's interpretation of the process by which organisations impose an appropriate identity on their members and expanded it into a much wider thesis about how political power is exerted in modern society. The connection is all the more striking because neither of them, as far as one can judge, was aware of the other's writings.

Foucault's notion of normalisation as power is best seen in the context of a debate, or discussion, about the nature of power which has been in increasingly active progress since the 1950s. The beginning of the debate is even earlier, if one included Gramsci, as most people probably would (except that his prison writings were hardly available before then) and earlier still, if one takes Nietzsche as the point of origin, as he is (or is claimed to be) for most of those who figure in the debate. The debate has become virtually the central issue for students of politics – at least in those countries in which "sciences pol." is not the training ground for turning lawyers and economists into civil servants – and many sociologists regard the different forms, and meanings, of power as the primary concern of their discipline, too.

One has to begin by noting that power is an amorphous, or rather, a protean, concept. This at least is common ground for the authorities on the matter who are probably the most cited: Max Weber by academic writers and Hannah Arendt by non-academic writers. Rather surprisingly, there is also some agreement between them on one other feature. For Arendt, power (and she obviously has political power in mind, perhaps as the prototypical, or ultimate, form of power) belongs with the members of a society which they act together out of an understanding they have in common to attain objectives they have in common. Power "corresponds to the human ability not just to act but to act in concert".[9]

Admittedly, the idea that (political) power has to be thought of as essentially communal does not seem much of an advance. It is, after all, some two hundred years since Hume made what seemed to him the obvious point that power in society belonged with the governed rather than with any government, simply because there were so many more of them. It also happens that "communal", in these days of pervasive individualistic thinking, is not a particularly cogent or meaningful term in this connection. In fact, "communal violence" was, until 1989, a phrase far more commonly used than "community power"; so far as contemporary Europe is concerned, only in the autumn of that year and the first months of 1990 has Hume's "obvious" point been validated in successful political action.

The problem remains of how it is that when people "act in concert" it is usually at the behest or in support of people who are deemed powerful simply because of the support the people give them. In Arendt's terms, power is turned into violence. And violence (Arendt's main concern in this essay) she regards as essentially instrumental. Political leaders are somehow able, for purposes of their own, to make *instrumental* use of the power inherent in "the human ability not just to act but to act in concert".

In the other corner of the ring we have Max Weber, who also thought the word too vague to be of any use for analytical purposes, and expelled it (*Macht*) from his glossary of terms on that account[10] (or, rather, gave that impression, but brings it back in when he finds it convenient). What he did, however, was to settle on "domination" (*Herrschaft*) as the preferable term. Power is still *evinced* in concerted action, but this time the human ability to act in concert is a consequence of the authority exercised over people by an accepted leader.

Weber's formulation, still the most widely accepted, is the clearest statement of what has been the traditional formula of the Western world since the seventeenth century. It centres on legitimate authority, but is founded on the notion of sovereignty, both in its original, monarchic, sense and in its reconstruction in the contractual form given it since the eighteenth century. In both its traditional and its reconstructed meaning, the notion treats power as a kind of property possessed by some, who exercise it over others. And it is just this notion which has been under attack as out of date, or too limited, or both.

Ideology, in the Marxist sense widely adopted in the twentieth century, seemed to point to a solution of the problem of popular support. It suggests, too, that there are other sorts of power than the exercise of "domination". The role of ideology was, however, played down by Marx and most of his followers, who relegated it to the status of epiphenomenon, an adjunct of the control of "true" power, which was military, political, or as now, economic. It was left for Gramsci to show how this obscured the patently obvious fact that it was popular support which maintained most forms of government most of the time, whatever other power base they may have, or have had. It was especially democratic parliamentary regimes which had become adept at combining consensus and force, each complementing and balancing the other, with force *appearing* to be supported by the agreement of the majority.[11]

The other criticism of Weber's "jural" sovereignty is that it ignores the practicalities of politics. Even under so-called "absolute" monarchy, it has been argued, rival groups competed for dominance in the royal councils. Nor was it a matter simply of sovereign power consisting in the monopoly control of the armed strength necessary to suppress opposition; the resources of opposition were just as varied as the political interests it defended. In the parliamentary democracies which emerged in the eighteenth and nineteenth centuries, supreme power was something contended for by rival political parties, themselves ad hoc coalitions of contending interest groups. The level of stability necessary for any kind of complex civil society to survive was ensured by "consent", a kind of tacit contractual understanding arrived at by all parties to keep rivalry and contention within bounds. This second formulation emerged during the nineteenth century, but is nowadays more easily recognisable as that of the David Easton-Gabriel Almond school of political scientists of the 1950s. It is a way of looking at the nature of governmental power not far removed from conceiving of it as founded on a relatively stable equilibrium sustained by competing interest groups – rather in the manner predicated of a national economy in classical economics.

Governmental power (sc. "the modern state") could equally well be said to be founded on the repression of conflict. And this is in fact how Foucault sees it. The argument is that, at certain determinate and historically specified moments, contention between classes or interest groups has broken out into open conflict, leading to a period of turbulence in which the pre-existing balance of political forces has been destabilised and then disestablished. The superior force – armed or unarmed – seized by or available to one or more of the groups at some point is then used to freeze open conflict between political groups into the particular imbalance prevailing at that point. What is achieved is in fact a stabilising of whatever balance of power existed at the time between contending classes and social groups, however unequal or inequitable their relative situations were. This has happened in the most obvious, "revolutionary", sense a number of times in England during the seventeenth century and more frequently in France since 1789, but it has happened also in plenty of other countries, whether or not the change has been accomplished by revolution. Once the new constitutional form is established, power again reverts to those "on top".

The pluralism ("conflict-repression") of American political scientists, like the contractualism of earlier political philosophers and the classic, "rational-legal", theory of Weber, takes power "to be a right, which one is able to possess like a commodity, and which one can in consequence transfer or alienate, either wholly or partially, through a legal act or through some act that establishes a right, such as takes place through cession or contract".[12] Marxist interpretations have adopted the same pattern, with property rights (ownership of the means of production) seen as the legitimating principle behind political domination in either form.

In either case, the result has been the same. It is one in which power is exercised "perpetually to reinscribe" whatever *disequilibrium* had been established after some critical episode in the history of a country "in social institutions, economic inequalities, in language, in the bodies of each and every one of us".[13]

Foucault conceives of power, in its "normalising" guise, as working from the bottom up, not from the top (jural sovereignty, supremacy after struggle) down. He locates power "at its extremities, in its ultimate destinations, with those points where it becomes capillary, that is, in its more regional and local forms, in its institutions". The "paramount concern, in fact, should be with the point where power surmounts the rules of right . . . and extends itself beyond them, invests itself in institutions, becomes embodied in techniques, and equips itself with instruments and even violent means of material intervention."[14] And he follows this up by referring to his own studies of the history of prisons and of the treatment of the insane. Power looked at in this way is seen as the disciplining of men, much as technology is envisaged as the disciplining of nature. The disciplines are essentially social; "they are the disciplines of the barracks, the hospital, the school, the factory".[15]

They are also (and Foucault did add them in his later writings) the disciplines of the family, of the neighbourhood, and of the social encounters of everyday. For the "disciplining" is, in the first place, a matter of the internalising of the normative codes of behaviour prevailing in society, through the socialising agencies of family and school. Second, a "privilege and penalty system" of the kind Goffman saw at work in total institutions imposes itself throughout society. Inducements are offered for conformity and penalties exacted for misconduct by socially – sometimes legally – accredited agents of the normative disciplines. What it amounts to is that in modern society, the power and authority of a regime's establishment (sc. the "State") has come to "colonise" (Foucault's word) the social controls we recognise as existing to preserve social order.[16] "Normalisation" (the undertone which the word's use in East European regimes for the suppression of riots, strikes and dissident movements is relevant) is a complex form of organisation in which we are all agents of power, all involved in the exercise of power. With the normalising agency of social control serving to complement traditional instruments of power and authority, state and civil society become indistinguishable.

It is in some ways a very Durkheimian formulation. Indeed, it could in some ways be regarded as a tribute to the influence exerted by Durkheim, who has been portrayed as a principal ideologue of the Third Republic and may on that account be regarded as one of the instrumental agents of the transformation.

There are of course limits to normalising power, just as there are to sovereignty, jural or contractual, and to systems of rule which are established out of conflict situations. What Foucault and Goffman (for here Goffman's sociology is in step with Foucault's history) have attempted is to construct a framework within which it might be possible to identify, observe and record the exercise of power in terms of its third version as hegemony designed for "normalisation". Both have done so by concentrating on dissidence and the way it is dealt with.

Naturally, it is at the limits that the validity of all three versions of power is tested, and their nature made apparent. The power of central authorities is put to the question, resisted, and even challenged, through a number of almost institutionalised procedures: public appeals, protest demonstrations, riots, rebellion, conspiracy, and revolution. The equilibrium, at first so precarious, which is eventually established out of a period of turbulent change by "conflict-resolution" (sc. "conflict-repression") regimes, is recurrently threatened by movements for constitutional reform and extra-parliamentary activists, with subversion and "destabilisation" a constant danger, real or imagined. These are the commonplaces of "current affairs" journalists and newspaper reporters, tightly framed within the perspective of "political" history.

The material evidence in the case of normalising power is also commonplace, but this time in the sense of being too commonplace to be recognised for what it is. Modern families have their "incompatible" spouses of their "refractory" children. The industrial relations problems of factories have a history all their own. The public education system was created in the nineteenth century in large part quite explicitly to "gentle the masses",[17] to serve, in Foucault's terms, as an apparatus for normalisation. Social institutions of all kinds have either to cope with a stream of unregenerate deviants, criminals, and misfits or to 'extrude' them (Goffman's word) into the prisons and mental hospitals which are the designated institutions for handling refractory members of society who are not merely troublesome but, in actually challenging 'normalising' power, potentially disruptive.

If we construe the pressure to conform to social norms as normalisation, in Foucault's terms, the essays on total institutions and on the "moral career" of the mental patient can be seen as investigations into what happens to people who test the forces of normalisation beyond their limits of tolerance.

This bleak vision of the human condition in contemporary Western society has to command attention because it is based on exceptionally intensive and comprehensive empirical observation in Goffman's case, and historical research in Foucault's. There are, I should add, other connections between their ideas. Goffman's analysis of an organisation's relationship to its members (which will be outlined in the next chapter) amounts to a small-scale model of how Foucault's normalisation process works out in "complex organisations" – a major social sector that Foucault barely mentions.

The coincidence of the two views is all the more striking because neither of them, so far as one can judge, was aware of the other's writings. It adds significance. Nevertheless, there are problems about accepting the picture they draw. The inducements which Goffman mentions which are offered by organisations so as to, in effect, turn their members into "organisation men" – bonus payments, amenities, promotion prospects, and so forth – are really the small change of labour-market bargaining, and are seen as such by negotiators on both sides. The mechanisms by which organisations induce their members to identify with organisation goals and values are more occult, and more compelling, than Goffman realised. In Foucault's case, the techniques employed in the normalising process are hardly as miscellaneous in origin, piecemeal in their incidence, and uniform (or random) in their effect as he seems to make out.

This is a theme which will be resumed in the final chapter. For the time being, it has to be borne in mind that while Foucault's concern was to point to the existence of such limits by examining the sanctions which are applied when they are exceeded, and so to demonstrate the nature, purpose, and extent of normalising power, Goffman, in *Asylums*, took the investigation much further in empirical terms. And in *Stigma* he gives an account of the way in which normalisation operates *within* the limits of tolerance.

NOTES AND REFERENCES

1. J. Habermas, *Legitimation Crisis* (1973), Heinemann, 1976, p. 18.
2. C. Lévi-Strauss, *La Voie de Masques*, vol. 2, Skira, 1976, p. 118.
3. By far the best account of the several meanings attached to the word "bureaucracy", and the debate over them, is to be found in Martin Albrow, *Bureaucracy*, Macmillan, 1970.
4. See Maxwell Jones, *Social Psychiatry: A Study of Therapeutic Communities*, Tavistock, 1952.
5. C. T. W. Curle and E. Trist, "Transitional communities and social reconnection: a follow-up study of the civil resettlement of British prisoners of war", *Human Relations*, vol. 1, 1947, pp. 42-68. and 240-88.
6. See T. Burns and G. M. Stalker, *The Management of Innovation*, Tavistock, 1961, ch. 5.
7. See *Asylums*, p. 74, and M. Foucault, *Power/Knowledge* (ed. C. Gordon), Harvester Press, 1980, p. 88.
8. The quotation (*A*, 85) is from J. Bateman and H. Dunham, "The State Mental Hospital as a specialised community experience", *American Journal of Psychiatry*, vol. 105, 1948-9.
9. H. Arendt, *On Violence*, Harcourt Brace Jovanovich, 1970, p. 44.
10. M. Weber, *Economy and Society*, Bedminster Press edn, 1968, p. 53.
11. See J. Joll, *Gramsci*, Fontana, 1977, p. 99 (quoting *Prison Notebooks*, p. 1638).

12. M. Foucault, "Two lectures", in *Power/Knowledge* (ed. C. Gordon), Harvester Press, 1980, p. 88.
13. M. Foucault, "Two lectures", in *Power/Knowledge* (ed. C. Gordon), Harvester Press, 1980, p. 90.
14. M. Foucault, "Two lectures", in *Power/Knowledge* (ed. C. Gordon), Harvester Press, 1980, p. 97.
15. C. Taylor, "Foucault on freedom and truth", *Political Theory*, vol. 12, 1984, p. 159.
16. M. Foucault, "Two lectures", in *Power/Knowledge* (ed. C. Gordon), Harvester Press, 1980, p. 107.
17. See, especially, D. V. Glass, "Education and social change in modern England", in *Law and Opinion in the Twentieth Century*, (ed. M. Ginsberg), Stevens, 1959.

7

"ABNORMALISATION"

Three organising ideas run through the essays on mental patients and their treatment. One I have taken as reflecting – or best pictured as – Foucault's notion of "normalisation" as *the* characteristic medium of power and authority in modern society, with the assessment and treatment of individuals as mad serving as one of the more potent instruments of the disciplinary powers assumed by the modern state and modern society to ensure conformity with prescribed normality. This is not to say that the apparatus of power devised by the monarchic, oligarchic, contractual, or other systems formerly dominant has disappeared; the longevity of legal systems alone ensures the survival of many of its principal elements. But legal systems, and the jural principles invoked when it comes to new legislation, it is argued, tend more and more to work through institutions and agencies directly engaged in normalisation. Those judged (by due process) to be too recalcitrant for ordinary normalising forces to work on are consigned to repositories specially designed for their safe-keeping and for their reform, or reconstitution, or re-education, into normal members of society. Prisons and mental hospitals are the most numerous and prominent of these institutions. In the case of prisons, safe-keeping is the primary purpose, and the reformation of their inmates, while part of their formal rationale, is a secondary consideration; with mental hospitals the two purposes are, at least officially, in reverse order.

The second of these organising ideas is of mental illness as a specifically social phenomenon. The central question raised is about the interpretation as mental illness of behaviour which everyone, more or less, has come across, and all have perhaps themselves displayed. But there is another, more fundamental, way in which mental illness is properly to be regarded as a social construct. Behaving in the way the mentally ill do sometimes behave is what would be taken in a normal person to be an abnegation of personal responsibility, a dereliction of moral duty. Hence, the attitude adopted by the psychiatrist to the patient is entirely different from that of the medical physician or surgeon – even though psychiatrists, as members of the same profession, tend to see it as much the same.

The treatment and management of physically ill or injured patients is seen by doctors typically as a matter of repairing a damaged part, correcting some malfunction, or expelling some organic invasion. This "service-relationship", as Goffman labels it, is reflected not only in the physician's approach but in the patient's attitude too; the illness, the injured part, or the malfunction tends to be referred to as extrinsic to the inner, the real, self. Patient and doctor can, in the ordinary way, discuss it in a fairly detached, "objective" manner. But in the case of the mental patient, it is a matter of restoring the "inner" self – the carrier of personal identity – to something approximating to a responsible and effective member of organised society. Anything a patient has done, said, thought, felt, or believed at any time in the past or the present is open to scrutiny and analysis, and liable to evaluation in normative terms.

The third organising idea relates to the dual aspect that "hospitalisation" wears for mental patients. The significance of their fate lies as much in their exclusion from their familiar world as their incarceration in a mental hospital. Here Goffman somehow captures the numbing quality of bereavement and betrayal that was associated with banishment and exile in earlier times. The word he uses is "extrusion"; the mental patient (like the convict) is extruded from normal society, and almost all the relationships and rights formerly enjoyed are now lost. Extrusion from the wider society also means inclusion in a stable community composed of "abnormals". The patient has therefore to associate with individuals who are in most respects as dissimilar as those on the outside, and very nearly as varied in the variety and degree of aberrant behaviour they display. What they have in common is now less a matter of conduct or character than of the common fate they share with him, a fate, moreover, which is determined by a handful of people, not by his own intentions and decisions, or by the opportunities, involvements and casual chances to which he could attribute his former course in life.

It is, moreover, a peculiarly all-encompassing fate, with its own impregnable defence against protest or any other efforts the patient may make to influence it. For, now that he is stigmatised as mentally ill,

> the individual's persistence in manifesting symptoms after entering hospital . . . can now no longer serve him as an expression of disaffection. From the patient's point of view, to decline to exchange a word with staff or fellow patients may be ample evidence of rejecting the institution's view of what and who he is; yet higher management may construe this alienative expression as just the sort of symptomatology the institution was established to deal with. . . . In short, the mental hospital outmanoeuvres the patient, tending to rob him of the common expressions through which people hold off the embrace of organisations – insolence, silence, sotto voce remarks . . . these signs of disaffiliation are now read as signs of their maker's proper affiliation.
>
> (p. 306)

I

Goffman's titles demand attention. There is an oracular air about them. This is especially so in the case of the essays built around his mental hospital research; the first and last essays in the *Asylums* are prime examples. But he can overdo it a little. The word "moral" in the title of the second essay, "The Moral Career of the Mental Patient", adds nothing to it apart from a little confusion; the connotation the word carries is not Durkheimian this time, but that which "morale" has in English. Again, the word "career" has been adopted because, he tells us, it has a "two-sided" meaning – something which hardly seems worthy of mention and is, in any case, an underestimate; it turns out that there are at least three sides, or aspects, to the mental patient's career. One relates to self-image, 'felt identity', and other 'internal matters held dearly and closely'; a second to the 'publicly accessible' complex of official position and legal status; a third to the 'meaningful social world' that mental patients compose out of their situation.

The deterioration in the situation of the mental patient does not manifest itself as a steady decline; there are several distinct stages. Much of the first essay in *Asylums*, as well as the second, is taken up with tracking these successive stages and their effect on the patient's morale. Admission to a mental hospital is in itself a traumatic experience, especially for those committed by a combination of associates, legal and medical authorities and their own family, all of whom, they feel, have ganged up against them. Subsequent experience of the kind recounted in "The Moral Career" essay, worsens their situation, and, in terms of any larger social reality, "adjustment" to their situation of the kind described in the third essay, "The Underlife of a Public Institution", has to be seen in most cases as an ultimate stage of deterioration – morally, as well as in morale.

But a patient's 'moral career' begins before he enters a mental hospital; indeed, in many cases, "commitment" – voluntary or involuntary – may not occur at all. This becomes increasingly the case after 1960 or thereabouts, when the notion took hold that it was often more salutary, more in the patient's interests (and certainly cheaper) for the mentally ill to stay at home, in "community care" – i.e. to contrive a kind of niche for him out of his familiar social setting, occasional visits to a psychiatric clinic, and psychiatric counsel made available to his family and perhaps to others with whom he is in frequent contact. It is this situation, and the way in which it highlights the specifically social configuration which Goffman gives to mental illness and its manifestations, that form the subject of a later essay, "The Insanity of Place".

As in the *Asylums* essays and the discussion of the behaviour of the mentally ill in *Behavior in Public Places*, mental illness is defined as a specifically social phenomenon: 'The conduct regarded as pathological is what is seen as "inappropriate to the situation"' (*RP*, 355). The words "regarded" and "what is seen as" in that sentence are, of course, of paramount importance. They raise questions about the ways in which behaviour qualifies as "abnormal", and, from this, why a diagnosis of mental illness is arrived at. An alternative conceptual context (rather than framework) for clinical description and diagnosis is proposed, in line with the interpretation of social relationships in terms of the "social ethology" developed throughout *Relations in Public*. What diagnosis should be concerned with, the argument runs, is not the "deviant" or "abnormal" behaviour of someone who is mentally ill but his disruption of relationships, of social organisation, in his family, his neighbourhood, or his workplace. He does this by acting in ways which demonstrate that his assumptions about himself are utterly incompatible with his place in that organisation. One of the consequences – and aggravations – of this disruption is that the patient's family, companions, and colleagues tend to form, along with the psychiatrist, another relationship, this time a surreptitious, collusive, alliance formed for protective and defensive purposes.

So, before examining what is "pathological" about inappropriate behaviour, there is first a fundamental point to be established concerning social norms, social control, and social deviation (*RP*, 346-51). In conventional sociological terms, people conform with social norms because of the operation of social controls of different kinds and at different levels. First, there is personal control, by which the individual acts 'as his own policeman', taking it upon himself to admit his offence and offer reparation – not (or not especially), it is to be noted, to soothe the damage or wounded feelings others have suffered, but so as to 'reestablish the norms and himself as a man respectful of them'.

Personal control of this kind may be backed, if the need for it appears, by "informal social control", which is a matter of rebuffs or rebukes delivered by companions, bystanders, or those who feel they have cause to take offence. The offender is made aware of having offended, and is persuaded to act thereafter so as to reaffirm 'common approved understandings'. The third kind of social control consists of "formal" social sanctions administered by police and other designated agents authorised to maintain public order. In the end, of course, both the second, informal, and the third, formal, kind of social controls depend for their effectiveness on the first, personal, kind – on the individual's own awareness that he has erred, and that he needs to take corrective action. Pleas of innocence, too, may also be taken as an affirmation of knowledge and support of the rules of social order.

So much for the orthodox sociological account of social control. It is, one should note, a very rudimentary, beginner's level, account, that had long been deserted by students of crime and deviant behaviour. As Goffman hardly needs point out, it gives a 'very narrow picture of the relation between social norms and social deviations'. Where the orthodox account goes wrong, Goffman contends, is in treating social norms as applicable to individual conduct and social control to the individual's *attitude* to his conduct. For one thing it is the expediential calculus of an individual – his assessment of what he stands to lose or gain – which is affected by social control, not his moral sensitivity, which is presumed to act independently of the views and actions of others, even if it is consonant with them. Nor are offences unfailingly followed by sanctions; and when they are applied, they do not necessarily diminish the frequency of offences. Giving offence may lead the offender simply to avoid future encounters with those he has offended. In the case of the formal social controls exercisable by resort to the law, the cost, uncertainty, publicity, possibility of reprisal, and other contingencies may make it inadvisable. And there are other possible outcomes which show the whole apparatus of social control to even less advantage. Offenders may win out, and make others toe the new line they have drawn (children are pastmasters at this). School rebellions, prison riots, ghetto riots 'illustrate the same theme', with the labour movement and the suffragette movement cited as further examples.

He goes on to suggest that the orthodox account also goes wrong in another way. So far as everyday social interaction is concerned, an offender may well avoid not only any untoward consequences for himself, but any disruption for others, too, provided he is sufficiently tactful, circumspect, or secret in his violation. He goes so far as to suggest (putting the injunction, "Thou shalt not be found out", on an equal footing with the main commandments) that not to be seen as offending is *precisely* the same as not offending. Here he pursues the contemporary students of deviant behaviour to the point at which they part company with more than traditional attitudes and belief, for, although the parallel is dropped rather swiftly, support for this line of argument is sought in the attitude of the law to intentionality, ignorance, competence, and so forth. This, says Goffman, suggests that it is not conformity with the law that is at issue 'but rather in what relationship he stands to the rule which ought to have governed him' (*RP*, 350).

However, Goffman's main concern is that social control of everyday behaviour and interaction with others is satisfied by a show of conformity with social norms. What matters most is what other people make of an individual's conduct. If any particular infringement of a social rule does not amount to openly flouting its applicability or denying its propriety ('sanctity'), it does not call for social control. Further, following the argument of earlier essays in *Relations in Public*, even if offence is given, what the "normal" offender does is not so much to offer reparation but to demonstrate that the offence does not represent his true attitude to the social norm.

In any case, inappropriate behaviour, being part and parcel of the whole business of remedial interchanges, bulks large in the kinds of social interaction which occurs in public places. Children tend to be excused automatically, although the threshold between excusable and inexcusable behaviour rises with age. And mistakes are very easy to make; the man at the kerbside in a crowded street who is gesticulating and grimacing wildly may, after all, be trying to attract the attention of an acquaintance across the road. All of this is widely understood and accepted. So the inappropriateness of any behaviour is not enough for it to be identified as a sign of mental illness. A good deal of latitude is ordinarily allowed. What does matter is when the inappropriate or offensive behaviour is seen as being wilfully and pointedly directed at others, without being licensed by a previous request, or accounted or apologised for afterwards.

What matters still more – and this is where Goffman points his argument in a new direction – is that the signs and symptoms of mental illness contravene the very substance of social obligations. Social norms are not designed for the systematic control of the individual *per se* but of the relationships in which his membership of organisations and communities involve him. An individual, by acting in an offensive way, and in the absence of any remedial work or subsequent show of repentance, seems to 'proclaim to others that he must have assumptions about himself which the relevant bit of social organisation' (e.g. family, social gathering, workplace) 'can neither allow him *nor do much about*' (*RP*, 356; emphasis added).

II

The use of the term "social organisation" has a rather special significance, for with it a new frame of reference makes its presence felt. (The indefiniteness of this form of words – "makes its presence felt" – comes from the fact that its adoption is at no point clearly articulated.) Briefly, "social organisation" denotes a social structure built out of relationships in the family, a neighbourhood, a place of work, etc. (In "The Underlife of a Public Institution", in fact, Goffman uses the term "social structure" in preference.)

"Organisation", then, becomes the term used for the network of relationships between individuals, as against interaction between them, which is a matter of social order. The analysis of social interaction, which formed the theme of the *Interaction Ritual* essays and their companion pieces, is a matter of identifying the grammatical rules governing the way people behave in each other's company; the analysis of social organisation concerns the significance for their relationship with others which individuals may, and do, read into such behaviour. Thus,

> The treatment an individual gets from others expresses or assumes a definition of him, as does the immediate social scene in which the treatment occurs. It is a 'virtual' definition, based on the ways of understanding of the community and available to any member. . . . The ultimate reference here is a tacit coding discoverable by competently reading conduct, and not conceptions or images that persons actually have in their minds.
>
> (*RP*, 340)

Summarily put, as he is socialised into living as a member of an organised group like a family, a set of friends, etc., the individual comes to make assumptions about himself, assumptions which 'are delineated in terms of his approved relationship with other members of the group and in terms of the collective enterprise – his rightful contribution to it and his rightful share in it' (*RP*, 343). In other words, organisation, even at this level, provides for a division of social labour, distributing the entirety of the activities which define its existence as an organisation among the members and coordinating them according to acknowledged rules. 'Thus, many of the obligations and expectations of the individual pertain to, and ensure the maintenance of, the activities of a social organisation that incorporates him'.

Character and self are seen as belonging to an individual in virtue of his conduct in the particular *place* he occupies in an organisation – a family household, at work, a group of friends, a neighbourhood, and so forth. The actions of each member of a family are expressive of what he knows his social place to be in it – 'and that he is sticking to it' (*RP*, 362-3). In complementary fashion, 'the self is the code that makes sense out of almost all the individual's activities and provides a basis for organising them' (*RP*, 366).

Wittgenstein, whose name crops up a number of times in later writings, gets no mention in this essay, but the idea Goffman is trying to convey is much like Wittgenstein's notion of definitions deriving from rule-governed behaviour: a chess piece, for example is what it is, not because of its shape or size but because of the rules of the game, including those which govern its potential moves. In fact, Goffman's treatment actually enhances the basic Wittgensteinian thesis by remarking that an individual can only be removed from his "place" in any socially organised entity – a family, say – by shifting to another "place" in some equally "real" organisation, such as the organisation he works for, or a group of familiar companions, i.e. among people with whom he has also established himself in a "real" place, but where a different sort of game is being played, with different rules. "Keeping his place" means cooperating in the common activities, supporting and developing relationships, and helping to maintain the organisation.

If, without the warrant of an "authorised" move to another organisation in which he also has an accepted place, one member of an organisation begins to demonstrate through his behaviour that he is wilfully refusing to keep his place, it must be seen as a threat to the well-being of the other members, individually and collectively. Since an individual encodes through his actions and expressive behaviour the *workable* definition of himself accorded to him by others closely involved in the same organisation, open disregard of the need to keep his place makes him the source of continual frustration and threat. 'The selves that had been the reciprocals of his are undermined' (*RP*, 366). More – he is striking at the very 'syntax of conduct' (*RP*, 367).

Rather surprisingly, Goffman sees the response of those closest to this individual who has turned into an agent of disorganisation as one of helplessness. This may turn out eventually to be the case, but only when all else fails. And "all else" comprises a formidable battery of strategies, all of them to do with the capacity for collusive action possessed by a circle of family, relatives, colleagues, or even dependents or subordinates. Families, neighbours, companions, colleagues often seem able to avail themselves readily – sometimes too readily – of all kinds of cooperative – or conspiratorial – strategies designed to limit the damage threatened by an individual who grows increasingly fractious, demanding, overbearing, unpredictable or simply unable to cope with his part in joint activity.

This is clearest of all – and so common as to be familiar to most people who have worked in organisations, as well as students of them – in the case of people who are at the head of established concerns. The response of managing directors to the social isolation which goes with being "the man at the top" varies. He tries either to exploit his position or to escape from it; in either case, he may do so legitimately (i.e. in accordance with ideas prevailing in the concern about what a man in his position can do) or illegitimately. And among these four possible strategies, exploiting his role is rather more common than escaping from it, and over-playing more than under-playing. In which case, his social isolation is almost invariably increased:

A sudden change of policy, the upsetting of promotion prospects by his importing a senior manager without consultation, wayward changes of intention during a meeting, outbursts of temper, dismissals or promotions on what appear to subordinates as insubstantial grounds . . . prompt the same, equable, non-committal responses and comments or even the same compliance or applause that more acceptable or even successful strokes in the past have won. The perpetual encounter, universally within the concern, with responses which are either fabricated or blank, sets an increasing distance between the man at the top and his subordinates. His situation can, in fact, approximate to that of the known psychopath who is confronted with an unending and unbroken series of interactions in which his opposites are playing him false, withholding normal reaction to his conduct, and substituting any convenient response which will soothe or placate him and allow them to escape.[1]

Behaviour by anyone, in any organised setting, which comes to be seen as 'out of place', in Goffman's terms (i.e. "out of character", too demanding, undependable, etc.), forces those around him, especially those who bear the full brunt, into reshaping the social organisation which his conduct threatens to disrupt. And this usually entails the "extrusion" of the offender from the ordinary traffic of social interaction. There is, as I have said, a sizeable range of possible ways in which this can happen, or be made to happen; they vary in severity, in comprehensiveness, and in their ultimate consequences for those concerned, particularly the "disorganisation man" himself, of course, but not exclusively.

In the end, of course, if such spontaneously reactive strategies fail, the helplessness Goffman mentions does supervene. When it is acknowledged, this helplessness in the face of disruption provokes the thought of mental illness; for acknowledgement signifies both that it is entirely appropriate to feel helpless, and that it is entirely appropriate to seek help. Interpretation is all.

Pragmatically speaking, mental illness is first of all a frame of reference, a conceptual framework, a perspective that can be applied to social offences as a means of understanding them. The offence, in itself, is not enough; it must be perceived and defined in terms of the imagery of mental illness.

(*RP*, 354)

Having to resort to outside help in the face of some crisis – disaster, accident, malfunctioning, danger, threatened litigation, or incapacity or disorder in someone close – is a familiar contingency in ordinary people's lives. However, one of the characteristic features of modern society is the substantial organisational apparatus holding itself in readiness to provide support. What one does is to call up the relevant section of that apparatus. And in order to do so effectively, the kind of "perspective" or "imagery" presenting itself may vary enormously in precision. What is to be done is usually something decided by a number of individuals – relatives, acquaintances at work, policemen, priests. In the kind of contingency under discussion, what is of the first importance at the very outset is finding the right perspective, imagery, or even a name for what is wrong – and the search for it has become the professional preserve of the medically qualified. For the family and for others close to the individual, the decision to be reached is whether or not to call in the family doctor – or that of the firm, school, etc.

III

The entry of the doctor, and eventually the psychiatrist, brings with it a revolutionary change to the organisational framework of the individual now defined as mentally ill. He is now to be regarded, and to regard himself, as having abdicated from all his placements in the organisations in which he had his being, lived his life, and carried out his part of the total activity of the several organisations. There is a new organisational set-up and a new frame of reference. There are now, he finds, two all-important relationships: one he has with the psychiatrist, and the other he has, or is treated as having, with himself. Both are modelled on those implicit in the psychiatric model of the doctor-patient relationship and of the ineluctably "undivided" nature of the patient's self.

Goffman allows that psychiatrists 'more or less' accept that the behaviour of mentally ill persons is, on the face of it, a matter of deviating from the social norms which govern conduct. But psychiatry is a branch of medicine. The medical frame of reference treats the signs and symptoms of medical disorders as pathological departures from the 'biological norms maintained by the homeostatic functioning of the human machine' (*RP*, 345). Psychiatrists, too, use the selfsame "medical" frame of reference (or assume that they are doing so,

Goffman claims) when they interpret behavioural deviance as 'abnormal'. Yet 'biological norms and social norms are quite different things, and . . . ways of analysing deviations from one cannot easily be employed in examining deviations from the other' (p. 346).

There is a crucial difference between mental illness on the one hand, and physical illness or injury on the other. The argument not only of "The Insanity of Place" but also of "The Medical Model and Mental Hospitalization", the last essay in *Asylums*, hinges on this difference. People suffering from physical illness or injury treat it, and the part of their bodies affected, as something apart from their "true" selves. This ability of hospital patients to dissociate their "true" selves from their illness and from the part or aspect of themselves affected, and to cooperate with others in dealing with these things quite objectively is simply one instance of an almost universal propensity or capacity. We are accustomed to treat parts of ourselves – our bodies, behaviour, even thoughts and feelings – in a detached way as another part of the self, something separable from the inmost part: that which is "really me". It is a kind of psychological trick which all of us – those brought up in the cultural traditions of the West, at least – customarily perform on ourselves. We all know how easy it is, at times, for us to "objectify" our bodies, and our mental capacities too, so as to devote ourselves to training and improving their performance in a carefully objective and impersonal way, quite as if their musculature, nervous system, mental grasp or intellectual skills led separate, though dependent, lives from our "selves".

It is this capacity which is not only allowed for but exploited in the medical mode. Injury, malfunction, disease, even pain or disfigurement is seen as something apart, something which the patient, as well as the doctor, should be able to consider, and to talk about, in a detached, objective manner. It is explored in both essays, but at even greater length, and with some stylistic flourish, in the later one: 'With certain exceptions' (infants, and patients either comatose or completely helpless) 'persons have the capacity to expressively dissociate their medical illness from their responsible conduct (and hence their true selves), and typically the will to do so' (*RP*, 353). And again,

> The interesting thing about medical symptoms is how utterly nice, how utterly plucky the patient can be in managing them. . . . And more than an air is involved. However demanding the sick person's illness is, almost always there will be some consideration his keepers will *not* have to give. There will be

some physical cooperation that can be counted on. . . . Proper
sick-room etiquette . . . may only be a front, a gloss, a way of
styling behaviour. But it says, 'Whatever my medical condition
demands, the enduring me is to be dissociated from these
needs. . . .'

(*RP*, 351-2)

This distinction serves as foundation for the comprehensive criticism
Goffman directs, in the fourth *Asylums* essay, against the principles of
the hospital treatment of mental patients, as well as the practice. The
criticism is not directed against any explicit claim by hospital
authorities in general and hospital psychiatrists in particular to expert
knowledge or professional competence. What he is contesting is the
implicit claim that the relationship of the psychiatrist to his patient is
organised around, and in terms of, the model of personal servicing
performed by experts, as manifested in what he calls 'the classic repair
cycle', and which is closely followed by general practitioners.

This "repair cycle" is spelled out in detail. It is interesting enough
in itself to make it worth recounting in brief, but there are also a
number of debatable points. Goffman breaks the cycle down into six
phases, beginning with *accidental* damage to a personal possession
(one's car, vacuum cleaner, or foot) and a period during which the
damage does not right itself automatically or by anything the owner
does.

So far, he says, no blame attaches to whatever caused the damage;
it is only if the owner does nothing, or fails to seek or follow expert
advice that a moral issue may be made out of it. But he is surely
wrong to ascribe moral neutrality to causing damage. What is
commonly called 'accidental' damage is very often caused by
carelessness, negligence (sometimes criminal negligence), or mistakes,
and even quite remote possibilities of this kind of cause call for
apologies, accounts, or reparation. Blame *is* laid, moral stands *are*
taken.

At the third phase, in which a "server" becomes involved, the whole
possession, damaged parts included, is placed *voluntarily* at the server's
disposal, for him to repair. ('It is remarkable', Goffman notes
parenthetically, on page 331, 'how at this juncture a lab coat of some
kind appears, symbolising not merely the scientific character of the
server's work but also the spiritual poise of a disinterested intent.' It
is remarkable, too, how often white coats seem to turn into red rags
for Goffman.) Repair work has its own sequence of observation,

diagnosis, prescription, and treatment. When this is finished, there may be a period of convalescence, or attentiveness, or cautious use, but, finally, the stage is reached 'when the possession is pronounced "as good as new"' (A, 332).

What becomes obvious as the essay continues is that the cards are being stacked against the mental hospital's claim to provide "expert service" (along the lines Goffman defines) long before it has appeared on the scene. The charge laid against the mental hospital, when it comes, is that, 'compared to a medical hospital or a garage, a mental hospital is ill-equipped to be a place where the classic repair cycle occurs' (A, 360). This general charge is supported by a number of specific ones:

1. The first of these relates to the distinction between the affected "inner" part or sector of the patient undergoing treatment, and an unaffected "outer" part which obtains for the way his expert service model works out in 'medical' (sc. "general") hospitals. Doctors, nurses, and others are said to treat the unaffected parts of the patient as the residence of the patient's true self, look to him for cooperation, and interact with him in a commonplace, everyday, manner. The same distinction, he suggests, could just as well be observed in mental hospitals with at least some of the patients suffering from disorders identified as "organic" in origin. This does not happen, he says. The diagnosis may be "medical", but the mental patient's care and management, seemingly, must accord with the living conditions available for mental patients with functional ailments in the same general category of behavioural disorder.

2. There is little attempt at continuity in the clinical management of patients. Again, this is in contrast to what happens in general hospitals, where the *management* of a patient is the responsibility of one consultant who of course has assistants of varying degrees of seniority and experience who work under his overall direction, and who may also consult other consultants. In a mental hospital, what dictates the handing over of a patient from one doctor to another is not some referral system, or a need for consultation, but the roster of shifts worked by staff psychiatrists and the ward system, by which patients are assigned to residential accommodation according to the merits of their overall conduct.

3. When it comes to "functional" cases, there is no sense in which their ward life is a technically appropriate response to their condition, as resting in bed is for medical hospital patients. Despite this, it is

argued by mental hospital staff that 'the life conditions of the patient are both an expression of his capabilities and personal organisation at the moment and a medical response to them' (A, 360).

4. Since all patients' living arrangements are prescribed by a psychiatrist, and may be modified by him on psychiatric grounds, the power exercised over mental patients in the name of "expert service" is uniquely extensive and diffuse.

5. While this power over the lives of inmates is officially in the hands of the psychiatrist, it is the ward attendant who holds the key, since it is up to him to observe and record patients' behaviour. And he is in principle able to do this continuously throughout the day, as against the occasional "therapeutic hour" in the presence of a psychiatrist. Yet, while he has a great deal of influence over the treatment accorded patients, the ward attendant is often too busy to do more than observe and record transgressions of the rules. In practice, Goffman remarks, the ward seems the worst place for the observations which are of such importance in prescribing correct treatment.

6. Nevertheless, the much closer and more continuous relationship assistants have with patients puts them in a much better position than psychiatrists to correct the kind of behaviour patterns which are taken to be the signs and symptoms of disorder. Also, since the ability to monitor and conduct this kind of "therapeutic learning" is, though important, hardly a specialised technique, it is not something that can be allocated an appropriate place in the status and skill hierarchy of the establishment. So, the continuous training in behaviour, good or bad, afforded by an attendant is likely to be far more effective than intermittent instruction or coaching by a psychiatrist. This also goes for those (Goffman calls them "menials") who prepare patients to see the psychiatrist. Presumably, they practice just as much "psychiatric intervention" as anyone, psychiatrists included.

All Goffman's criticisms seem to spring from one underlying feature, which is that the division usual in general hospitals between "patient management" (the province of the clinician responsible) and "patient care" (the nurse's responsibility) is regarded as impracticable, or is glossed over or simply disregarded in mental hospitals. And this, in turn, springs from the actual, but unacknowledged, custodial function of the mental hospital, and, as consequence, the regimentation to which all patients are subjected. Both the custodial function and regimentation require the diffuse spread to all members of hospital staff, assistants, "menials", guards, and others, as well as doctors and nurses, of authority over and supervision of the "entire patient".

Goffman's account is not in terms of explanatory causes, of course, but of the interpretation of meaning. The first kind of account would identify certain deficiencies which independent study might presume to be thwarting, hindering or distorting the efficient, satisfying and effective fulfilment of the mental hospital's purpose, which is the care and, if possible, cure of the mentally ill. These malfunctions would be matched against certain features of the organisational structure (administrative, clinical, domestic-service, maintenance, etc.), the methods and technical performance, or the functions and operating practices of the hospital which are identifiable as inappropriate, inefficient, or ineffective. Both sides of this picture would be explicitly (or, more commonly, implicitly) held up against some normative model of organisational, technical, and operational efficiency, satisfactoriness, and effectiveness.

What Goffman offers instead is again a normative model. But it is a model of one kind of relationship which people form so as to approach and to deal with each other. This particular relationship is that of service – between the one who serves and the one who is served – and the implication is that it is as primordial as kinship or command. Like all relationships, it constitutes a framework for establishing social identity and for prescribing proper conduct; it can also bind people together or set them against each other. Clearly, then, the framework implicit in relationships of these kinds contains a set of assumptions that – rather like a theoretical model – interlock with and support each other.

From this starting point in the very first paragraph of the last *Asylums* essay, Goffman works down through divisions and subdivisions of his service model to that particular variant represented by the relationship of doctor to patient and of psychiatrist to mental patient. Additional qualifications to the basic service model are added at each new point of branching, so that the broad scope of the original specification is particularised and the range of items in the category reduced, either on the servers' side (specialised as against non-specialised practitioners – trained experts as against specialised but non-expert occupations, etc.) or on the recipients' side (individual clients rather than crowds, audiences, or a succession of customers, etc.).

At all levels, though, what is being presented is clearly recognisable as instances of ordinary contractual relationships agreed between individuals. On the way through the sequence, however, one comes across mutant forms, produced by the insertion of extraneous features, as well as the variants which result from simple division. Thus the service performed is specified as repair work, which introduces a third element, and the dyadic relationship becomes a triad: expert – valuable possession – client. And the service performed is also split between 'mechanical, handwork operations' on the client's valued possession and verbal exchanges with the client which are technical, contractual, and sociable.

Up to this point, Goffman's model could be interpreted, not inaccurately, as an attempt to combine two well-established and widely recognised socioeconomic relationship models, namely economic exchange (of the kind commonly governed by the law of contract) and professional service performed for a fee, with all the connotations of professionalism that implies.

The argument is entertainingly constructed, and is plausible and persuasive enough for his purposes. But there is another shift, this time of a developmental or evolutionary kind, which comes with 'the move away from peddler carts and home visits and the development of the workshop complex'. A good deal of importance is attached to this last shift: 'From the point of view of this paper, the most relevant strain in the application of the service model to medicine resides in the workshop complex' (A, 346). Goffman does mention some of the problems that this brings into his expert service model, but he treats them as largely incidental or of marginal importance. The examples he gives are: some hospitals are run for profit; training programmes or research may also be part of the hospital's functions. 'Non-service' functions like these, he says, may introduce considerations other than patients' needs into decisions about treatment.

But problems, or complications, are also introduced into his model by the "workshop complex", and the consequent shift of the server-served relationship to one between a hospital, and hospital doctors, and their patients, that he does not mention, at least at this particular point. The first is that the "workshop complex" is in this case not simply a large stationary establishment with which the server replaces his home visits or tinker's cart but an organisation created, funded, maintained and, to some extent, administered by individuals other than the "expert server". The expert server is himself an agent of the establishment, and the resources, instruments, buildings, he makes use of in performing his services are the establishment's property, not his.

A more important complication is that the relationship between individuals is replaced by one between an organisation and a population of patients. This is in fact remarked on towards the end of the essay, but only in the context of the extra rights and entitlements which their employment by an organisation gives *doctors*. First, the "legal mandate" they have confers on mental hospital doctors "automatically" the kind of authority over what their staff do and over what happens to their patients or clients which other professionals have to be accorded voluntarily ("in interaction"). Second, their position gives hospital doctors a peculiar advantage in coping with the ethical or career difficulties posed by their hospital roles, namely, the ability to leave the hospital, 'a typical reason being in order to go where "it will really be possible to practise psychiatry"' (p. 371). Third, there is the custodial function performed by the mental hospital, which is a "public service" over and above – and, as he insists, at odds with – the classic repair cycle he proposes as model for the psychiatrist-mental patient relationship.

Apart from the complications already mentioned, the establishment and maintenance of hospitals brings in considerations of "public goods", involving interests and relationships between organisations and society at large quite different from those affecting individual servers and their individual clients. This broaches a number of intractable problems within the field of public welfare and welfare economics which I am not competent to discuss, and which in any case are hardly matters that can be pursued here. But it seems evident that the requirements of a model to fit the relationship he is discussing are perhaps rather more numerous, exacting, and complicated than Goffman seemed to think.

What is special about mental illness, Goffman argues, is that no dissociation of the "ill" part of a patient from the "well" part is allowed for, still less the capacity of an unaffected self to exist separately from an affected body. Other people – including the doctor – discount completely the patient's capacity to distinguish an inner "me" from "what is wrong with me". The therapist is authorised to find out and make use, for purposes of diagnosis and treatment, of everything a patient does, or feels, or thinks at any time. 'None of a patient's business is none of the psychiatrist's business' (*A*, 358).

This is not the only thing that is special about mental patients. Most of them find themselves in hospital not because they have sought help in "servicing" their disability but because others have put them there – sometimes, in fact, against their will. Even some voluntary patients, too, may come to feel that they have been "railroaded" into hospital with the help, or at least the consent, of their nearest and dearest. Coupled with the resentment such feelings inspire, this renders them unlikely to conform to the role, normal to the "expert service" relationship, of a client seeking expert assistance.

IV

It is apparent from what has already been discussed that being admitted as a mental hospital patient is a consequence of an assortment of contingencies. It is not the foregone conclusion of clinical assessment according to an authoritative or universally accepted set of criteria. Even the feeling that one is 'losing one's mind is based on culturally derived and socially engrained stereotypes'. In many cases, even the most spectacular and convincing symptoms, like 'hearing voices, losing temporal and spatial orientation, and sensing that one is being followed' (A, 132), are fairly common; however frightening at the time, in psychiatric terms, they could mean no more than an emotional upset arising out of a stressful situation.

A more important consideration, in any event, is that the number of prepatients who do believe they are losing control and enter a mental hospital voluntarily is relatively small. Willing or unwilling, however, inmates of mental hospitals have been "extruded" from society, and although the kinds of behavioural offences which lead to admission or commitment to mental hospitals are different from those which have other extrusory consequences and lead to imprisonment, divorce, or dismissal, 'little is known about the difference, and alternative outcomes frequently seem possible'. What is more, there seems in psychiatric terms little to choose between those offences that end up with commitment to a mental hospital and the much larger number that never do. And Goffman quotes E. and J. Cummings to the effect that while mental illness seems to be a condition which afflicts people who have to go into a mental institution, "until they go almost anything they do is normal".[2]

In practice, a great deal seems to hang on contingencies such as socioeconomic status, the visibility of the offence, or even on there being a mental hospital nearby, whose connection with psychiatric assessment seems fairly remote. There are other contingencies, too, connected with the circle of people and agencies involved rather than the mental condition of the person centrally concerned. They have to do with the potency, individual and combined, of the agents (or agencies) who are or come to be concerned in the patient's destiny. Goffman assigns these to three categories: *next-of-kin*, or whoever it is that the patient first turns to when he is troubled (because he believes that person to be the last to believe him insane, and one who will do everything possible to save him from incarceration); *complainant* (i.e. instigator), being the person who initiates the process which ends with incarceration (and who, as one ascends the social scale, is the more likely to be also next-of-kin); and *mediator*. Mediators are the clinicians, clergy, social workers, teachers, police, lawyers, and so on, to whom the patient is referred. Mediators are professional specialists, with experience in handling difficult people and the ability to distance themselves from troublesome behaviour and proceedings which comes from professional training. Referral usually involves a succession of mediators, and somewhere among them there will be one who turns out to have the authority to order commitment, and will do so.

So far as the patient's later moral career is concerned, what counts is the prominence of the part each of these three kinds of agent plays. Typically, it will be the next-of-kin who sets up interviews, persuades the patient to attend, provides the mediator with information, and, eventually becomes "the responsible person" who represents "the patient's interests". However circumspect or crude the process, when the patient comes to look back on it, the experience of being present and witnessing it is likely to induce the feeling of having been betrayed, as having been third party to what he may come to regard as a kind of 'alienative coalition' (p. 138).

There are other aspects of his progress towards the mental hospital that contribute to a mounting sense of betrayal. The agents who confront him at each stage tend to keep up the pretence that nothing more will occur to diminish his status or freedom. At each encounter, he is encouraged to join in a flow of small talk that skirts around the actualities of his situation and his likely destiny. 'The spouse would rather not have to cry to get him to visit a psychiatrist; psychiatrists would rather not have a scene.' If he complies with all such implicit demands 'and is reasonably decent about the whole thing, he can travel the whole circuit from home to hospital without forcing anyone to look directly at what is happening or to deal with the raw emotion that his situation might well cause him to express' (pp. 140-1). The stages are marked by a progressive stripping of more and more of the rights, liberties, and satisfactions he once had.

Goffman's comment on the whole process is that it is a tribute to the power of social forces. So is the outcome. There are, among those who come to be patients in mental hospitals, wide variations in the nature and severity either of the illness which psychiatric diagnosis might suggest or of the behavioural and other peculiarities which people around them might observe and comment on. Nevertheless, once they have begun the process, they meet with much the same set of circumstances, and tend to respond to them in much the same way. 'Since these similarities do not come from mental illness, they would seem to occur in spite of it' (p. 129).

The prepatient starts out on his career with relationships and rights, 'and ends up, at the beginning of his hospital stay, with hardly any of either. The moral aspects of his career, then,' (as inmate) 'typically begin with the experience of abandonment, disloyalty, and embitterment' (p. 133).

V

Admission is an especially traumatic experience for "involuntary" patients who make up the majority of patients. The new inmate's reaction to the situation he finds himself in – and to the new light this sheds on those who were closest to him, and who, he feels, got him into it – tends to follow certain regular patterns. One common pattern, which comes from a strong desire simply not to acknowledge being the kind of person who could possibly be reduced to this situation, is not to admit to any sense of loss or betrayal. He may avoid talking to anyone, stay by himself, even be "out of contact" or "manic", so as to avoid any interaction that presses a politely interactive role upon him and 'opens him up to what he has become in the eyes of others' (p. 146). Rejecting next-of-kin on visits by staying mute, or refusing to enter the visiting room, then, may be regarded not simply as a response to betrayal (which it may well be) but evidence that 'the patient still clings to a remnant of relatedness to those who made up his past, and is protecting this remnant from the final destructiveness of dealing *with the new people that they have become*' (emphasis added).

The posture of total withdrawal, which amounts to a declaration of nonentity – of their social and personal identity as not present, though their bodies may be – is usually given up after a time, and the trappings of social and personal identity resumed. Attendants call it "settling down". With the start of the inpatient phase of his 'moral career', every inmate, willing or unwilling, is exposed to the routine abasements, degradations, humiliations and profanations described in the first essay in *Asylums*. Thereafter,

> the main outlines of his fate tend to follow those of a whole class of segregated establishments – jails, concentration camps . . . – in which the inmate spends the whole round of life in the grounds, marching through his regimented day along with a group of fellows of his own institutional status.

> (pp. 147-8)

It is a regimen which represents an endeavour "not merely to enforce conformity but to compel acceptance of a self-conception which incorporates the values and standards which the organisation sees itself existing to uphold and to impose" (above p. 155). While these values and standards are not identical with those normative for society as a whole, observance of them holds out the promise of a return to the world outside. In other words, while the regime is designed to act as a process of "normalisation", the norms that inmates are to observe are those which the institution deems appropriate for them, who are, by the very fact of their presence, "abnormal" (above, p. 158). Conformity and acceptance leads, in fact, to what is commonly known as the "institutionalisation" of the patient, by which, in successfully adapting himself to the world inside, and accepting its rules, standards, and values, he renders himself unfit for the outside world.

The events which led up to his admission now sort themselves out retrospectively as an important part of an endeavour to reconcile himself with his fate. Not unnaturally, the individual patient's response to his present predicament may lead him to insinuate 'that he is not "sick", that the "little trouble" he did get into was somebody else's fault, that his past life had some honour and rectitude, and that therefore the hospital is unjust in forcing the status of mental patient upon him' (p. 150). Goffman is at pains to point out that none of this signifies any great departure from ordinary, indeed "normal", behaviour. Anyone reaching a particular stage in his career will be inclined to compose a picture of his past, present and future 'which selects, abstracts, and distorts in such a way as to provide him with a view of himself that he can usefully expound in current situations'. In the case of the mental patient, the setting and the authority to which he is subjected are constant reminders that he is one of those who have suffered some kind of social collapse on the outside – have failed in some overall way. So, what was essentially a fairly commonplace line of exculpatory talk may be, and frequently is, expanded into a kind of apologia which he can use to restore some semblance of normality, and show himself as someone who is in accord with, and reflects, basic social values. Glowing accounts of a successful occupational career, and minatory stories of how he was pushed, rather than fell, from grace, can lend verisimilitude.

Furthermore, a diversity of social roles and informal networks in the patient community may be built and maintained on the basis of reciprocally sustained fictions. For it is one of the classic functions of informal networks of equals to serve as mutual audiences for reminiscences, anecdotes, and allusions which tend to validate self-images and virtual social identities. Tales are spun which are 'somewhat more solid than pure fantasy and somewhat thinner than the facts' (p. 153).

It is precisely this situation that becomes a constantly recurring trap for the inmate. For there exists, in the psychiatric work-up of his past provided by his case-history, an official version of his past, with its own rationale, to set against his own recollection. Junior hospital staff are well aware that the custodial job which is their main responsibility is made easier by the ability they possess to discredit patients' stories about themselves and expose the falsity of any claims they make about their past. What is even more daunting, a patient may find himself confronted by those in authority who tell him that 'his past has been a failure, and that the cause of this has been within himself' (p. 154).

So the patient finds himself exposed to the constant threat of an abrupt dislocation of the normal machinery of social intercourse, which allows 'virtual' social identities the customary protection of tact and the avoidance or the cloaking of embarrassing episodes, and faced, instead, with mechanistic, pre-interpreted responses to the 'normative expectations' and 'righteously presented demands' of ordinary social intercourse. Each time the staff deflates the patient's claims, his sense of what a person ought to be and the rules of peer-group social intercourse press him to reconstruct his stories; and each time he does this, the custodial and psychiatric interests of the staff may lead them to discredit these tales again. His conduct is coded, and the key to it is accessible to others but not to him.

A patient's record often reports the false line taken by a patient in answering embarrassing questions; and even when there are no facts known to the recorder which contradict his account, the possibility that they might nevertheless exist is left an ostentatiously open question. 'The events recorded in the case history are, then, just the sort that a layman would consider scandalous, defamatory, and discrediting' (p. 159). Mental hospitals systematically provide for circulation about each patient the kind of information that the patient is likely to try to hide. And in various degrees of detail this information is used daily to puncture his claims. Not that Goffman questions the desirability of keeping records or staff's motives in keeping them. The point is, rather, that, even though these facts about him are true, the patient is still driven, by pressures which derive from his whole cultural upbringing and background, to conceal them; yet, knowing that they are neatly available, and that he has no control over who gets to learn them, he inevitably feels all the more threatened.

The effectiveness of the system is strengthened by the exchange of information between staff supervising different areas of patient activities, and by the conferences attended by all levels of staff. Finally, gossip at coffee-time and lunch breaks often turns on the latest doings of this or that patient, the assumption being that everything about him is in some way the proper business of the hospital employee. So, instead of the variety of figures that any one person usually cuts in the eyes of different acquaintances, the inmate is confronted with a unitary conception of him and a unified approach, sustained by a kind of collusion which he will inevitably regard as directed against him, even though the staff may genuinely believe they are acting in his best interests.

A quite lengthy section of the essay is given over to what amounts to an indictment of this particular aspect of the hospital system. Quite apart from the standards of confidentiality and personal rights generally held to be universally applicable, employing such means to induce docility, submissiveness, and diligent cooperation in the pursuit of normalisation is hardly in accordance with the moral neutrality claimed for medical pronouncements and psychiatric diagnosis. And while the information, or most of it, gathered in case records may well be true, 'it might also seem to be true that almost anyone's life course could yield up enough denigrating facts to provide grounds for the record's justification of commitment' (p. 159). And again: 'Apparently it is felt that the more power possessed by medically qualified administrators and therapists, the better the interests of the patients will be served. Patients, to my knowledge, have not been polled on this matter' (p. 156, n. 35).

VI

The "settling down" period is followed by instruction in the system of privileges and penalties (which consist largely of the removal of privileges). In the process, he is also made aware of the way in which the "ward system" operates, since rewards and privileges themselves lie mostly in the relative comfort or rigour of the ward in which he is placed. The "ward system" signifies much more than the dormitories in which patients are lodged. It consists in fact of a series of graded living arrangements built around wards, administrative units called services, and parole statuses. Any infringement of the "house rules" which cover virtually all aspects of inmates' activities may be penalised by a move to a lower grade ward, which amounts to loss of privileges. A period of law-abiding obedience means, in turn, that a patient may eventually regain privileges, i.e. 'reacquire some of the minor satisfactions he took for granted on the outside' (p. 148).

There are two kinds of forces brought to bear on the mental patient, which can be thought of as "inner" and "outer". The first, "inner" kind, which Goffman labels 'moral', are the mental, cultural, and emotional pressures. The "outer" kind are both legal and physical: the authorities which empower the hospital administration and the walls (and, if need be, physical constraints) which keep him inside. The dividing-line between two kinds is straddled by both the privileges and penalties system and the "ward system", the rank order of living accommodation in which the first system is embodied.

He is told, for example, not to look on his placement in the ward system in terms of reward or punishment, but as an index of his general level of social functioning, his status as a person. 'The ward system, then, is an extreme instance of how the physical facts of an establishment can be explicitly employed to frame the conception a person takes of himself' (p. 149).

This account of the social significance of settings marks an advance on what Goffman had to say about them in *The Presentation of Self* (above, pp. 117-18). The different relationships between self and setting which come from the degree of control exercised over it by organisation on the one hand and the individual on the other are now spelled out at length – with mental hospitals representing the organisation-dominated extreme. It is at the extreme not only because of the 'uniquely degraded living level' but also because of the 'unique way in which significance for self is made explicit to the patient, piercingly, persistently, and thoroughly' (p. 149).

Shifts up and down the privilege-penalty system make for much movement between wards, especially in the first year. Each move brings with it some drastic change in relative comfort or discomfort, and so makes for a rather fast-moving system of social mobility. And all of it is visible as a consequence of the doctrine which institutional psychiatry has made its own. In making use of the variations and fluctuations in living standards represented in the ward system, it actually speeds them up. The ward system comes to be regarded as 'a kind of social hothouse in which patients start as social infants and end up as resocialised adults'. It is a view which contributes much to the importance that staff can attach to their work, and to the pride they take in it. But it also demands that psychiatrists and administrators turn a blind eye to the way the ward system works as a punishment and reward system useful for disciplining patients. There are in fact plenty of reasons why inmates make trouble, or get into it, for dogged refusal to follow the rules, and for "dumb insolence". But all of them find their official interpretation in terms of psychiatric relapse, or moral backsliding, thus protecting the view of the hospital as an agency of resocialisation. The same goes for conduct regarded as deserving of promotion up the ward system.

The relative ineffectiveness of the mental hospital as an agency either of therapy or of patient care is, at least in part, owing to the nature of the privilege and the ward systems. This is first because it is, inevitably, sometimes brought into action in error; second because it is frequently resorted to for reasons other than therapeutic; and, third, because it is a *system*. For some patients, eventually, it is a system which, in learning, they can also learn how to beat, or how to work. For, when the worst and the best are known, and neither involves expulsion, undisciplined or hostile behaviour can lose the stigma meant to be attached to it. At the same time as he learns to be dismissive about what the staff see as hostility or deference, backsliding or self-reforming zeal, the mental patient also learns that the same indifference shows up among the staff and inmates, too. And he learns that he can construct a defensible picture of his self that is something outside of himself and which 'can be constructed, lost, and rebuilt all with great speed and with some equanimity' (p. 165). Out of his hard-won awareness, then, the patient may construct a social and personal identity, and roles to go with them, which could be as serviceable to him, here and now, as any proffered by the institution.

In other words, the patient can adopt the same attitude towards the "enforcement system" of constraining rules that is open to anyone who decides the game is not worth the candle, and, without opting out (which may be impossible,) turns the interactive game he is playing into one in which he contends with the system itself – a strategy Goffman analysed in more detail in *Strategic Interaction*. In the end, Goffman suggests, the whole disciplinary-cum-treatment system seems to generate a kind of sophisticated apathy.

> In this unserious yet oddly exaggerated moral context, building up a self or having it destroyed becomes something of a shameless game, and learning to view this process as a game seems to make for some demoralisation.
>
> (p. 165)

And again:

> In casting off the raiments of the old self – or having this cover torn away – the person need not seek a new robe and a new audience before which to cower. Instead he can learn, at least for a time, to practise before all groups the amoral arts of shamelessness.
>
> (p. 169)

VII

The third essay in *Asylums*, "The Underlife of a Public Institution", is devoted to the 'meaningful social worlds' composed out of a situation which, 'distasteful and barbarous' as it might be to those to whom it is unfamiliar or who keep their distance from it, becomes less so the more familiar it becomes. This is not to deny, he adds, that a minority of patients seem utterly incapable of following any rules of social organisation, or that the social order maintained by the majority of patients is at any rate partly the consequence of the measures of control that mental hospitals have somehow managed to institutionalise. But the issue with which Goffman wants to confront the reader is the relationship between deterioration in the morale of the mental patient and the abject condition to which confinement and the attentions of psychiatrists and hospital staff reduce him, and, following on this, the particular kind of 'meaningful social world' which the patient is disposed, and able, to build for himself.

In the opening pages of the essay, there is a rather convoluted discussion of the nature of individual involvement in "social entities" of all kinds, from groups, organised or unorganised, with shared beliefs (like a religious faith or an ideology) to "natural" groupings (like family, groups of friends, or nation), sociable occasions (a conversation, a party), and organisations. All such bonds of involvement imply obligations, which, if they are taken at a sufficiently abstruse and general (or, conversely, mundane and immediate) level, are of two kinds: 'some will be cold, entailing alternatives foregone, work to be done, service time to put in, or money paid; some will be warm, requiring him to feel belongingness, identification, and emotional attachment' (p. 173).

This two-dimensional character of social bonds, says Goffman, reflects the dual nature, explicit and implicit, of contractual agreement of any kind. 'Behind each contract there are non-contractual assumptions about the character of the participants. In agreeing about what they are and do not owe each other, the parties tacitly agree about the general validity of contractual rights and obligations' (p. 174). He does complicate things a little for himself here by invoking Durkheim as his authority ('As Durkheim taught us', etc.). However, while the second of the two sentences quoted is a fair enough rendering of Durkheim's line of argument, the first – concerning assumptions made about the character of the parties, is not.[3] In Durkheim's view, arrangements entered into between individuals of their own free will would in themselves be insufficient; the operation of self-interest would alone be enough to render such undertakings impossibly risky, and so reduce society to utter chaos. Formal contracts, like informal undertakings and agreements, were always, he argued, underwritten by the tacit acceptance on both sides of what has become an intrinsic part of the normative framework governing interpersonal behaviour in society, namely, belief in the fairness – the justness – of the contractual agreement (i.e. that it was not entered into under any form of duress or deceit) and in the justness of the price, or obligation, itself. Neither can exist without the concurrence of all other members of society, a concurrence which, if need be, may be ratified by appeal to courts of law. Assumptions about the character of other parties to the contract do not enter into it – apart, of course, from the very generalised idea of their being either trustworthy or sufficiently aware of the penalties attached to any default.

Pursuing his own interpretation of "what Durkheim taught us", Goffman goes on to assert that 'every bond implies a broad conception of the person tied by it' (p. 175). By the end, Durkheim's very generalised premise of a belief in the observance of fair dealing being common to both parties in any contractual undertaking becomes 'a definition of the participant's nature or social being' (p. 179). Every organisation is made up of contractual arrangements ('bonds') between its members and "the" organisation (sc. those legally authorised to act on its corporate behalf). "Organisation" in this context stands for any organisation – industrial plant, trade union, political party, or mental hospital, but Goffman has in mind particular kinds of organisation: the 'instrumental formal organisations' mentioned in the previous chapter (above, p. 155). Implicit in the purpose-built social arrangements of formal organisations, it may be remembered, there is a 'thoroughly embracing conception' of the people who belong to it as members – a conception of them as human beings, and not simply as members of the organisation.

Conceptions of this kind expand a contract simply to participate into a definition of the participant's nature or social being. It is not, incidentally, the same notion we find elsewhere in Goffman, of the individual as the creature of society; what we have now is an "ideal type" individual, constructed out of conventional notions, plus very rough trial-and-error experience, of what it takes to convert the individual into a human resource, biddable subject, or malleable material. Goffman's point is that this image is incompatible with other images of the individual as an autonomous human being (or, for that matter, of the individual as a patient for medical treatment). Implicit images of this kind are an important section of the values which every organisation sustains, regardless of the degree of its efficiency or impersonality.

He goes on to ask how the individual reacts to this definition of himself. The answers turn out to be not very different from those which used to be subsumed under the heading of "responses to alienation". At one extreme there is open default, defiance of any retributory action, and the rejection of whatever implications the bond has for his self-image. At the other, all the implications that involvement may have for himself and for his self-conception may be wholeheartedly embraced. And there are, of course, intervening stages, which are in practice encountered more often; an individual may fulfil some obligations and dodge others, put a good face on acceptance some of the time, but occasionally show some disaffection.

Organisations, especially working organisations, operate on the general assumption that, since the organisation is dependent on the active cooperation of its members, its members will in fact cooperate – that (in the terms Goffman has introduced) the individual member will 'identify himself with the organisation's goals and fate'. All the same, organisations are not ignorant of the different ways their members react to these general assumptions, and take steps to strengthen the bonds of identification and attachment which are supposed to go along with the contractual commitment itself. Such bonds are, in the first place, commonly fortified by specific inducements: pay, obviously, but also added incentives like bonus payments, additional comforts and conveniences, promotion, and so forth. Second, standards of accommodation, furnishing, building, food, and so forth are provided which are up to standards deemed appropriate to its purposes and membership by the organisation (i.e. its administrators and the public authorities or owners to whom they are responsible). Third, the threat of punishment and penalty may also serve as inducements towards cooperation.

Goffman adds the telling point that, implicit in the counter-measures devised by the "organisation" (i.e. its management or administration) is a knowledge of the various ways in which members react *and*, he adds, an understanding of some important aspects of members' character which the members (i.e. workers, prisoners, patients) are believed to share.

The question of whether the members of the organisation do, or do not, accept the view of their character implicit in these measures is of some importance. For they carry two implications for the identities and self-conceptions of members: first, that they *are not* fully committed to the organisation's goals or loyal to its regime and, second, that they *are* the kind of individuals who will respond to the inducements, positive and negative, they are being offered in order to get them to approximate more closely to the standards of commitment and loyalty the organisation requires. For an inmate to accept side-payments and privileges, or conform to prescribed behaviour under threat of punishment, is to accept 'a view of what will motivate him, and hence a view of his identity' (p. 180). 'Every organisation, then, involves a discipline of activity, but our interest here is that at some level every organisation also involves a discipline of being – an obligation to be of a given character and to dwell in a given world' (p. 188).

So, underneath the prescription of activities, of how members should conduct themselves, of where they should be at certain times, and so on, there is also prescribed a conception of the kind of persons they are. To fall in with the activities prescribed by the organisation is also (and this is Goffman's main concern) to accept the organisation's assumptions about one's identity, 'to accept being a particular kind of person who dwells in a particular kind of world' (p. 186).

On the other hand, not to engage in prescribed activities, or to engage in them for other reasons, or in ways other than those intended by the organisation, is to reject the self – and the world – designated by the organisation.

VIII

Acceptance or rejection of the organisational self designated by the organisation need be neither an absolute nor a permanent choice. Becoming an "organisation man" means contributing required activity in a cooperative fashion, according to the contractual undertaking presumed by membership reinforced by certain inducements of an institutionalised kind: welfare, incentive payments, privileges, and penalties. It also means, by implication, subscribing to the values inherent in the organisation and fitting into the world designated as appropriately his own. This kind of reaction Goffman entitles 'primary adjustment'. 'Ritual insubordination' stands at the opposite extreme; there is protest, total withdrawal into mute passivity, rejection of any appeal, and defiance of any threat or act of retribution. They are 'empty of intrinsic gain and function solely to express unauthorised distance – a self-preserving "rejection of one's rejectors"' (p. 315), and so quite distinct from ways of adjusting to hospital life.

What he is really interested in are 'secondary adjustments', out of which the "underlife" of the mental hospital is built. They, too, amount to ways in which patients try to place a barrier between themselves and the institution with which they are supposed to cooperate and identify. Secondary adjustments are ways in which individuals routinely use means or seek ends which are unauthorised, and so avoid, or dodge, not only what the organisation thinks they should be doing, and getting, but also what kind of persons the organisation thinks they should be. Of course, rejection may be partial, selective, intermittent, but – at least in the terms Goffman employs – it is not at all the same as open refusal to cooperate, or blatant violation of officially approved values, or defiant rejection of his officially designated 'self'.

The term "underlife" – which Goffman uses for the world built out of the wide assortment of 'secondary adjustments' which make up most of the empirical material which goes into "The Underlife of a Public Institution" essay – is taken from the more familiar "underworld". The word denotes habitat rather than actual area, comprehending both the public, or semi-public, haunts of petty, and not so petty, criminals, prostitutes, racketeers, and the like, and the places they live in. The quite explicit inference Goffman makes is that the underlife of a mental hospital bears the same relationship to the officially and formally prescribed ways of life of a mental hospital as does the underworld to the daily round, the business activities, and the social life of respectable citizens, and to the public administration of a town, a metropolitan area, or a country.

He also distinguishes secondary adjustments from other directions that patients may follow in an effort to distance themselves from their institutional selves. Some inmates of some total institutions (convicts, prisoners of war, mental patients) have for example managed to lose themselves, at least for a time, in "removal activities" like educational courses, specialised studies, learning a foreign language, religion, sports, gambling, or theatre productions. Goffman introduces a nice twist by suggesting that there are patients who manage to provide themselves with an escape world by an enthusiastic embracement of therapy; 'by actually receiving what the institution formally claims to offer, the patient can succeed in getting away from what the establishment actually provides'. And, in a final comment on "alternative" secondary adjustments, he notes that, 'Some illicit activities are pursued with a measure of spite, malice, glee, and triumph, and at a personal cost, that cannot be accounted for by the intrinsic pleasure of consuming the product' (p. 312). There is a sense of practices being employed simply because they are forbidden, and 'which seem to demonstrate – to the practitioner if no one else – that he has some selfhood and personal autonomy beyond the grasp of the organisation' (p. 314).

Of course, the organisation itself makes adjustments, too, of both primary and secondary kinds. In the first place, it is worth noting that the three kinds of inducements proffered by an organisation (i.e. pay, privileges, promotion prospects; welfare provision; punishment and penalties) are by way of being the "primary adjustments" of the organisation to the expectations and values of members. Melville Dalton,[4] whom Goffman quotes at length, provides a fairly comprehensive catalogue of unofficial rewards and penalties given out by organisations and their managers to their subordinates for contributions of special effort or skills outside contractual undertakings as ordinarily perceived. Again, systems of control over the behaviour of its individual members by groups of workers – control which extends to the amount and quality of work done – may well be known to management, but nevertheless winked at. What we have in industry, then, is virtually an openly acknowledged version of Schelling's "accommodation game": a system of accommodation of the kind familiar in politics, where a group formally in opposition to another not only maintains the appearance of good relations with its opponents but puts itself to some inconvenience on their behalf, sometimes makes positive efforts to help them out of difficulties, and allows them some share in rewards. This makes sense, not only because it makes life easy for themselves, naturally, but also fends off "outsiders" and any possible interlopers and so keeps the political system going.

Since both primary and secondary adjustments are ways by which an individual reconciles himself to or distances himself from the rules, purposes and values of an organisation (and vice versa), they manifest themselves over a wide range of possibilities. Being socially defined, they may well change their aspect at different times and places – as, of course, do the rules, purposes and values of an organisation.

> Organisations have a tendency to adapt to secondary adjustments not only by increasing discipline but also by selectively legitimating these practices, hoping in this way to regain control and sovereignty. Domestic establishments are not the only ones in which there is a regularisation through marriage of previous living in sin.

(pp. 196-7)

Essentially, primary and secondary adjustments are matters of social definition within any particular organisation at the time they occur. This can be carried to the point at which so little regard is paid to the officially approved standards of conduct that secondary adjustments have to be perceived and analysed in relation to the system which may be unauthorised but is nevertheless recognised practice.

Collectively, the secondary adjustments made by members of an organisation represent 'the *underlife* of an institution, being to a social establishment what an underworld is to a city' (p. 199).

The "underlife" with which the essay is concerned, for the most part, is that of patients. But, of course, the staff have their own secondary adjustments, and there is a staff "underlife", a half-surreptitious domain in which, as well as accommodating a few downright illicit activities, patients are made use of as baby-sitters, gardeners, and handymen, food is taken from patients' kitchen, and the hospital garage used for repairs on the family car; there is, in short, a black market in services. Goffman tends to dismiss these, both because they are 'minor' and because there was at the time a sizeable literature on secondary adjustments by the employees of business firms. He perhaps overlooks the part they play in presenting a model with which most patients become familiar, or as vindication or palliation of patients' own infringements.

Many secondary adjustments by patients were of necessity managed within prospect of the staff, and some with their conscious or unconscious connivance. There were also, of course, illicit activities which had to be kept out of sight or positively hidden from any possibility of surveillance. In addition, there were places kept under relatively loose surveillance either because staff tended to keep away or ignored any patients unobtrusively present. 'Free places' is the term Goffman uses for both these kinds, but he also applies it to lodgments in wards like window sills, the space nearest the nurses' station, or the entrance. To take advantage of free places required knowing not only where they were but also the tightness or looseness of supervision exercised over them and some skill in eluding or neutralising it.

'Licence, in short, had a geography' (p. 230), and a fairly complex one. There were a few places to which access was cornered by a group of patients, who assumed a sort of proprietary right to exclude others, and most patients sought to preserve territory they could feel was their own, even when it was the minimal shelter provided by a covering blanket. Beyond this, there was what Goffman calls 'the

201

vicarious consumption of free places' – 'one of the most poignant instances of make-do in the hospital' (p. 237). This would consist of standing by the window or the judas-hole of the ward door in a closed ward in order to watch people enjoying the relative freedom of the grounds or even of the space beyond the ward entrance.

IX

Part, at any rate, of Goffman's point in itemising and grading 'free places', places for storing possessions, legitimate as well as illegitimate, and methods of undercover communication in painfully meticulous detail, lies in the section in which he deals with the 'social structure' of underlife in the mental hospital. 'Social structure', in this connection, signifies relationships by which individuals make use of others – and it is made clear that this characterisation is meant to apply very widely, perhaps to all social relationships.[5] He groups the very considerable array of possibilities into five fairly general categories: coercion, economic exchange, "social exchange", private relationships ("buddies", cliques, homosexual couples, etc.), and clientage.

In ordinary social life there is a general principle of "first come, first served", and, when the alternative principle of the stronger taking whatever they want prevails, some attempt is made to disguise it. In the mental hospital, this only happened on the "good" wards; on "bad" wards, those patients who steadfastly kept silent, and withdrew from anything which might cause disturbance could always be dislodged, however bigger or stronger they were than the interloper, by the loud-voiced.

> Hence, on the bad wards, a special pecking order prevailed, with vocal patients in good contact taking chairs and benches from those not in contact. . . . The out-of-contact stance created a situation open to private coercion. Attendants sometimes joked about the 'svengali' role, pointing to a patient who specialised in the cold use of another.
>
> (p. 264)

Forms of exploitation included open expropriation, blackmail, and forced sexual submission.

In simple barter, trade, or sale, individuals are in fact making use of someone else. But it is commonly accepted that the exploitation is mutual, and so contributes to the welfare of both sides. On this, Goffman follows Durkheim rather more closely than he did earlier:

> The social conditions required for this kind of cooperation include some degree of mutual trust regarding the reality behind the appearance of what each offers, some consensus regarding what would be an unfairly high price, some mechanism for conveying and committing oneself to a bid and an offer, and a belief that it is all right to use persons and goods in this fashion.
>
> (pp. 264-5)

They are tacit conditions, but are essential elements of economic exchange in the ordinary way and may therefore be regarded as "expressed" in the satisfactory conclusion of a transaction. There are, he adds, additional considerations which modify the process of exchange, but, in the case of gambling, and the many other transactions in the mental hospital which were against regulations and made undercover, trust was a much more prominent factor than usual because of the possibility of entrapment by a member of staff, betrayal by an informer, or blatant failure or refusal to deliver.

There were a few things which patients might buy in their own canteen and from vending machines. Patients permitted an occasional excursion into town were able to buy things, some of which, illicit though they were, might be smuggled in. Inside, there were services available, too. However, cash purchases were in any case somewhat restricted, simply because they involved money. No regular pay was forthcoming for hospital work, and, although some could be smuggled in by visitors, most money came into circulation among patients from small handouts by patrons among the staff and from payment for the jobs performed unofficially for staff; car-washing, Goffman asserts, was the chief source. But cigarettes – inevitably – became an equally acceptable form of currency.

There are other transactions which, although they have the appearance of gifts, are in effect reciprocal exchanges of symbolic expressions of concern and regard. Here Goffman is following Marcel Mauss' best-known essay.[6] While what is proffered on each side may well be carefully gauged so as to amount to an equal exchange, a two-way transfer of this kind has to be distinguished from open economic exchange. He illustrates the distinction by citing the contrasting significance of money in either case. Staff *paid* for car-cleaning, but often *gave* a small sum to patients who worked under their

203

supervision, 'not as a reasonable market payment for any service but merely as an expression of appreciation'. Like a tip, it was 'meant to measure *appreciation* of a relationship, not *exchange value* of work done' (p. 277).

Relationships of varying degrees of intimacy are part of what may be called the "primary adjustments" of individuals in almost any establishment; but almost any establishment also has rules which forbid certain kinds of relationship – "office affairs" in firms, or "bug-house romances" in the mental hospital are cases in point, simply because they 'can absorb a great deal of the participants' time, filling out much of the world in which they live' (p. 277). In the present context, though, the significance of "buddy" and courting relationships, cliques, clientage, and the like lies in the part they played in the economic and "social" exchange systems. Patients with such relationships lent each other money, clothing, cigarettes, paperbacks, helped each other move from ward to ward, brought each other mildly contraband materials from outside, tried to smuggle comforts to anyone of them who had "messed up" and been put in a locked ward, gave each other advice on how to get privileges, and traded information – itself a critically important good.

The gifts and the forms of assistance which were the material content conveyed by this traffic, all carefully itemised in the text, were for the most part pathetically trivial, which goes to reinforce the point he wants to make. For in many cases, all that the kind of gift or form of help preferred, or the response which was forthcoming, amounted to supplies – 'ritual supplies' (p. 280) – which could be used to sustain private relationships. This was a consideration important enough for some secondary adjustments to be directed towards procuring goods or services which could be passed on to others.

The relationship between staff and patients could work (or "be worked") so as to contain a sizeable element of patron-client relationship. The place a patient occupied in the hospital organisation was defined by two principal coordinates: the "ward system" and the "assignment" system. Patients were assigned, officially, in accordance with their therapeutic needs rather than their wishes; because of this, and also because, in principle, the hospital provided patients with everything, there was no need to pay them for the work they did. All the same, staff in charge of work assignments 'did feel obliged to "show their appreciation" of "their" patients' (p. 287); and the obligation was recognised widely enough for staff who were less forthcoming to find themselves without patient helpers. Indeed, the patronage system could be said to have been incorporated into the official functioning of the hospital, since tobacco and cigarette papers were issued to staff in charge of patients' work. More important, and more general, than side-payments in tobacco were concessions which took the form of "time off" during working hours, visits to the canteen, and permission to attend the social occasions arranged in the recreation building. Some of the patients regarded as fairly steady would try to extend the patronage system still further, expecting their patrons to intercede on their behalf for better accommodation, a day off in town, or a reduced penalty for some infringement. Small indulgences could come to be treated as reasonable expectations, to the point at which a patient might 'work the man rather than the assignment' (p. 291) by trading on his relationship with a former patron to get extra tobacco or a little money.

X

How far the involvement of both staff and patients in this half-hidden, semi-official practice of clientage prompted, or condoned, the more widespread 'underlife' activities is impossible to guess. Many forms of secondary adjustment listed by Goffman are simple contrivances for inconspicuous survival ("getting by") or for covertly obtaining some minor advantage ("making out"), or, at best, using one's knowledge of the operating systems of the hospital to acquire some small benefit or gift without being entitled to it ("working the system"). The milieu and the official world of psychiatric doctrine, custodial authority, and restrictions on permitted movement and activity are special to the mental hospital, but the general character of secondary adjustments Goffman describes is much in line with what is by now common knowledge of the ways of life not only of the underworlds of cities, prisons, and concentration or PoW camps, but of the black ghettos of American cities, the West Indian and some Pakistani communities in Britain, and their counterparts in France and elsewhere – not to mention the locales inhabited by what Americans call the "underclass".

Existence tends to be 'cut to the bone' in any and all of these places, and people have to learn how to 'flesh out their lives' (p. 305). What counts is the maintenance of some kind of world in which life can go on in something approximating, or analogous to, the 'outside world,' from which patients (or convicts, or concentration camp inmates, or prisoners-of-war – or, for that matter, the poor, the destitute, the "down-and-out") see themselves exiled. And while it may be perfectly true that, just as 'rules create the possibility of infractions', so 'restrictions can create active desire, and active desire can lead one to create the means of satisfying it' (p. 284), materials are essential. These have to be created out of resources which are, *by definition*, inaccessible in any ordinary or legitimate way. And they can only be made available, or accessible, through the relaxation of surveillance exercised by custodial forces – police, guards, hospital staff. What is more, such relaxation has to be to some extent measurable and predictable. So, even in the case of the "underlife" community – or perhaps especially – some form of social control is essential.

This may be achieved in a number of ways, involving 'secondary adjustments of a very special class – a class of adjustments which underlie and stabilise a vast complex of other unofficial, undercover practices' (p. 299). Goffman follows up this pronouncement by citing the prison commonplaces of "accidents" arranged for members of staff, work slow-downs, mass rejection of certain kinds of food, sabotage, collective teasing, and 'ritual insubordination'. But he found no instances of any of these kinds of action in the mental hospital – something which he ascribes to 'weak informal organisation on the part of patients' (p. 302). For, 'instead of clinging together to uphold their patient status against the traditional world' (something which is not uncommon among convicts, PoWs, concentration camp prisoners, etc.), 'they sought in cliques and dyads to define themselves as normal and to define many of the other patients as crazy. Very few patients, in short, were or came to be proud of being patients' (p. 302).

One might add (although mention of it is conspicuously missing) that it is perhaps just possible that a lingering residue of the humane attitude towards patients in their care, by which nurses and attendants are supposedly guided, may account for prevalence of secondary adjustments involving patronage of patients by staff.

On the other hand, since secondary adjustments may be read as ways in which individuals make use of each other, then it is clearly possible to conceive of ways in which some secondary adjustments of relatively neutral or benign significance are themselves used as cover for ones which are essentially delinquent or malign. The physical restraints on movement outside and inside the hospital generated "make-do" devices, and a secret geography of "free places", the minimal supply of cash in circulation, and of commodities available, made for a private currency of cigarettes and a covert economic exchange system. In much the same way, the poverty of the means available to patients to furnish social exchanges with the material or behavioural content by which to convey dislike or contempt meant that basic ways of establishing relationships might be inverted, distorted, or combined, so as to conceal actual intentions.

For example, a patient who was trying for a "loan" or a couple of coins to make up enough for a purchase could so style his begging request as to imply that the attendant – or the other patient – he approached was so securely respectable – so "square" – as to be ludicrous, and thus become legitimate prey. The way of accomplishing the transaction, in short, could be used as 'a means of expressing distance from one's situation and of elevating one's dispossessed condition into an honourable one. Whatever its meaning, such begging was an instance of persuading others to show sympathy before they themselves seemed ready to do so' (p. 296).

For a few patients, 'the hospital provided a kind of game situation in which one could pit oneself against the authorities, and some of the relationships that flourished seemed to do so partly because the participants enjoyed the intrigue of sustaining them' (p. 285).

There was another side to the same coin. The licence assistants had for restraining a patient "for the patient's own good" provided a convenient cover for private coercion. Giving a cigarette butt was often done in ways designed to humiliate; and buying small services with a cigarette could be done in an "imperious" manner. Assistants would make a patient restricted to a back ward say 'pretty please' for sweets bought with patient's own funds.

XI

Goffman defined 'social structure', it will be remembered, as the set of relationships by which individuals make use of others (sc. are made use of by others). It is this definition which makes it possible for him to describe the "make-do" relationships and activities constructed out of the bits and pieces of the "real world" remaining to them as at least a semblance of social structure. He went on to give this rather special notion of social structure a far wider application.

The issue is that every sector of social life and, more specifically, every social establishment, provides the setting in which characteristic faces are placed on the arrangements by which use of another is possible, and characteristic combinations of these arrangements are sustained behind appearances.

And there is a final footnote on the same page (p. 298) urging the adoption of a single framework for the study of 'stable combinations of coercive, economic and social payments' which make for

> the similarities and differences between such payments as: prebends, titles, bribes, gratuities, tributes, favours, gifts, courtesies, honorariums, bounty, lagniappe, booty, bonuses, ransoms. It should be borne in mind that in most societies economic exchange is not the most important way in which monies, goods, and services are transferred.

In effect, we are being offered another of Goffman's two-way insights. In the first place, the inference is that the array of social relationships which make up the interpersonal bonds of society in general are of such fundamental importance for the maintenance of individual identity that even in the most straitened circumstances people will somehow recreate them – provided that those circumstances are stable enough to warrant their formation. Second, however, the fact that these very peculiarities nevertheless subtend a 'social structure' which, however distorted, still reflects the 'social structure' of everyday society makes it possible to look at things from the other side. The suggestion is that an examination of everyday social relationships would reveal that they too embody coercion, economic exchange, clientage, private relationships, and social exchange, often in combinations designed to give diplomatic cover to malign or hostile intent.

NOTES AND REFERENCES

1. T. Burns and G. M. Stalker, *The Management of Innovation*, Tavistock, 1961, p. 215.
2. E. and J. Cummings, *Closed Ranks*, Harvard Univ. Press, 1957, p. 102.
3. Durkheim's main concern, at the time the series of lectures from which Goffman draws his reference were first delivered, was to rebut the notion (which he attributed to Herbert Spencer) that society was essentially contractual in nature. The lectures were apparently given first at Bordeaux during the 1890s, and subsequently at the Sorbonne in 1904 and 1912. They were first published in 1950 under the title *Leçons de Sociologie Physique*

They were first published in 1950 under the title *Leçons de Sociologie Physique des Moeurs et du Droit,* and in translation (by C. Brookfield), as *Professional Ethics and Civil Morals* (Routledge and Kegan Paul) in 1957.

4. M. Dalton, *Men Who Manage,* Wiley, 1959.
5. Goffman seems to have caught some of the wash created by the appearance of several publications (by Thibaut and Kelley, George Homans, Peter Blau, and others) which took the notion of economic exchange as a very general model for human relationships of all kinds. The limitations on the thesis proposed by later critics do not, I think, affect Goffman's general position.
6. M. Mauss, *The Gift* (trans. I. Cunnison), Cohen & West, 1954.

8
GRADING AND DISCRIMINATION

The Old Testament spirit of wholesale denunciation which percolates through the *Asylums* essays spills over into *Stigma* and *Gender Advertisements*, each of which deals with aspects of the apparently irresistible and almost universal inclination to classify other people and to discriminate in our behaviour towards them in accordance with the social grading in which we have placed them. In effect, we turn degrees of approximation to some normative conception of physical attributes, religious beliefs, educational attainments, physiognomy, skin colour, and other endowments which come ordinarily or mostly from accident or parentage into badges of merit.

One can say with some certainty that some such grading system has always existed in the historical past of the societies we know. But it is also the grading system that, in Foucault's view, has been seized upon and assimilated into the normalisation processes of the modern nation state.

> Modern society . . . from the nineteenth century up to our own day has been characterised on the one hand by a legislation, a discourse, an organisation based on public right, whose principle of articulation is the social body and the delegative status of each citizen; and, on the other hand, by a closely linked grid of disciplinary coercions whose purpose is in fact to assure the cohesion of the same social body.[1]

So, although their subject-matter is at some remove from that of the *Asylums* essays, *Stigma* and *Gender Advertisements* can be seen as elaborations of the theme of normalisation as a form of power. Both examine the way the normative system of society operates on social interaction between people, but the focus of attention is on the way the differential grading imposed by society at large on individual persons shows up in interaction, not, as in the earlier essays, on the neutral rules governing social interaction by which social order is maintained.

I

On the first page of the first essay in *Asylums*, Goffman declared a 'chief concern' of his to be the development of a 'sociological version of the structure of the self'. The same concern shows up in all his published writings, which means that the account he gives of the self has to be made up from a series of passages dealing with differing aspects of the idea of the self (and of the person), with each formulation subject to some amendment, usually slight, in the next.

Since each renewed attack on the problem is essentially analytical, it tends to lead to a further partitioning of the original, molar, entity (the individual), without much regard to any overall synthesis of the whole, or indeed any reasonable coherence between the parts. In the process, the original entity of uncompromising selfhood one feels (perhaps for no good reason) one was born with seems to cede more and more of its uniqueness and significance to its dealings with others and with the physical, mental, and social situations in which it finds itself. In the concluding sentence of the essay on "The Underlife of a Public Institution", indeed, we find Goffman asserting (carried away, perhaps, and not for the first time, by a pleasing image and his own fluency) that all that is left of the individual self is what 'resides in the cracks . . . of the solid buildings' of the social world (p. 320). It is the kind of statement which is seized upon by critics[1] – and is also rather at odds with the kind of formulation one finds elsewhere in his writings.

There seems nowadays to be fairly general agreement on a distinction to be drawn between two conceptions of the self – of "I". On the one hand, there is the sense of enduring and unique subjectivity, which is irreducible and also utterly unknowable to others (except to God, as caution prompted Descartes to add). Since it is the perpetual subject, it has no attributes – is simply an indefinable presence. On the other hand, there is the subject-in-action. Everything that the subject does, thinks, intends, or wishes, besides being conscious, or accessible to consciousness, is communicable and knowable; it is the socially available self. As such, it is subject to change through experience, interaction and contention with others, physical and mental circumstance, and force, influence and persuasion.

There are passages in *Stigma* which refer quite unambiguously to the first of these – to 'what Erikson and others have called "ego" or "felt" identity' (*S*, 105), and to a sense of selfhood – the 'core' of a person's being, 'a general and central aspect of him, making him different through and through, not merely identifiably different' (p. 56). It is precisely the same notion that Mauss speaks of as "le *moi*" – the ineradicable awareness, universal in mankind, not only of one's body but of one's individuality, mental and physical.[2] But Goffman mentions it simply to make clear that he is *not* dealing with "ego" identity, but with other aspects of identity and the self. (And in this respect, too, he follows much the same line as Mauss did in his 1938 lecture.)

Goffman's term for the second denomination of self is "identity" (Mauss' "la personne"). This consists of social identity and personal identity. Together, they cover the several aspects of self which are socially "in play" with others, affecting them and affected by them. What Goffman is dealing with in discussing identity, social and personal, is the commonly accepted notion of a person's "nature" or "character", which can change with his experience, or be changed by it. If we envisage identity, social and personal, as those aspects of the self which are "in play" between the individual and society in his physical and social encounters with other people, then it is this conglomerate which is reflected in the self-image – the conception we have of ourselves – the aspects of which "I" am conscious and which G. H. Mead called "me". It also refers, of course, to the conception others have of us. Both self-image and the conceptions others have of an individual are essential elements in the whole conceptual configuration.

The distinction between 'social identity' and 'personal identity' met with in "Role Distance" and elsewhere (above, p. 133) still obtains, but 'social identity' now has two extensions built on to it: '*virtual* social identity' ('virtual' initiates the usage more fully exploited in *Relations in Public*), and '*actual* social identity'.

Social identity, as before, is socially endowed: a person is envisaged, on first showing, as equipped with a 'complement of attributes felt to be ordinary and natural' for him as a member of one or more socially established categories – age, gender, social standing, and the like; in other words, social identity resides in what others anticipate a person to be from first appearances. With strangers – e.g. passers-by, customers, or foreigners – their normative expectations regarding us are usually arrested here, at the point of stereotype pigeon-holing.

In a social encounter which is more than transient, however, we are able to 'lean on' other people's anticipations and transform them into normative expectations on our part. Such expectations amount to 'righteously presented demands', which are unconscious, as well as tacit. 'We do not become aware that we have made these demands until an active question arises as to whether or not they will be fulfilled. So the demands we make are best called demands "in effect" and the imputed character a *virtual social identity*' (S, 2). In other words, a stereotyped or non-specific social identity modulates into a virtual social identity which we regard as our due and which is, to some extent, subject to manipulation by us.

Virtual social identity looks as if it has something in common with "front", a term much used in *The Presentation of Self* and the earlier essays; but it could also stand for the "social self" implicit in those essays, the self more or less consciously portrayed in the various roles a person assumes. It is not, however, quite synonymous with either. The later term, "virtual social identity", has a much more ad hoc connotation. It signifies an un-selfconscious, almost automatic, response, aimed at intimating what *kind* of person we are rather than superimposing on this an image of the person we would like others to think us.

Actual social identity, on the other hand, is what a person 'could in fact' be proved to be. The implication is that actual social identity is based on objective evidence: 'While the stranger is present before us, evidence can arise of his possessing an attribute that makes him different from others in the category of persons available for him to be.' It may make him a less desirable kind of person (for that category), or a more desirable one; the point is that there may be some incongruity; a virtual social identity may therefore have to be corrected in order to form an actual social identity (S, 3).

Personal identity, no less of a social construct, also has two sides to it, although this time the distinction between the two is part of our common working knowledge of the society we live in. First, there is the visible or available information about a person, ranging from official certification (now depressingly familiar as "ID") and personal appearance to outline biography, which, in combination and refined by additional detail, can eventually distinguish one individual from all others. Second, the knowledge which people belonging to the same small, long-standing, social circle – family, group, team, etc. – have of one of their number implies much the same kind of unique identity. In both cases, of course, what counts is the specific dissimilarity which makes for difference between generically similar features. One could elaborate this further by introducing the factor of patterning, and pattern-recognition, but what counts is that this uniqueness is *ascribed*, or ascribable, and is something quite other than the felt uniqueness of ego-identity. 'Personal identity can and does play a structured, standardised, role in social organisation just because of its one-of-a-kind quality' (*S*, 57).

Since the *Asylums* essays and *Stigma* are concerned with assaults on the self, and with some of the ways in which it is defended, the 'sociological version' of the self presented in them is not so much of a 'structure', or even of a self undergoing the normal, expected, changes of the kind we recognise as continuous throughout adult life. It is a contested area – almost a battlefield. The self-image and the conception others have of the self, seen in this light, seem as if they were scorecards, recording the shifts, the gains and the losses sustained by the two sides.

The self that is under discussion in *Stigma*, as in *Asylums*, is anything but a small remnant that 'resides in the cracks . . . of the solid buildings' of the social world (*A*, 320). It is rather what might be entitled, if the term had not been pre-empted, the "social self". It is, at all events, the socially available self, the self that is "in play" with its physical, mental, and social experience and with its physical and social surroundings, and is thus subject to change. Goffman's notion of career applies to one aspect of the self's mutability.

This picture of the self seems rather distant from what one finds in *The Presentation of Self in Everyday Life*. There, the self capered about not only between its different manifestations but between the front it presented in each manifestation to an audience and what it was prepared to disclose to others engaged in the same performance – or even engaged in the same sort of performance. The self, in its interpretation of the roles available to it, seemed very much in command of its performances – even though the roles themselves were ready-made by "society". There are passages in the book in which the "self" seems even to hold up some presentation of itself which it hides behind. The self of *Asylums* and *Stigma* is even further removed from the psychological entrepreneur of "Role Distance" and the character gambler of "Where the Action Is". And when we come to *Frame*

Analysis, there is another Russian doll model to encounter, one in which the self as speaker divides into three or four "sub-entities" – 'principal', 'animator', and different 'figures'; the same capacity for multiplying the self in this way presumably holds good in non-verbal interaction, too.

II

The descriptions, analysis, and discussions which *Stigma* contains are all founded on the premise that 'Society establishes the means of categorizing persons and the complement of attributes felt to be ordinary and natural for members of each of these categories' (*S*, 2). This categorisation system itself is not explored or described at any length in *Stigma*. (Some aspects of it are given more careful scrutiny in *Gender Advertisements*.) Its details, as well as its existence, are taken to be self-evident. It is simply a matrix for identifying other members of society ('conferring a social identity on them'). The system is necessarily rather complicated, with gender, age, colour, and social status in the forefront, but closely attended by other characteristics like demeanour, speech, nationality, and ethnic origin, but it is familiar to everyone and incorporates values which are seemingly identical for everyone.

At the outset, then, we are presented with a "categorisation system" by which we place people on first acquaintance according to the characteristic expectations we have of individuals in this or that generic class of persons ordinarily met with in society. The "first appearances" we pick on are, by definition, patently visible.

So far what we have is essentially a sorting system of a fairly neutral kind. "Normality", too, hardly enters into discussion to begin with. All we have is a footnote on page 7 suggesting that the notion of a 'normal human being' may originate in the medical or the 'bureaucratic' attitude. But it turns out, on page 128 of *Stigma*, that the system is for *grading* people, not just for sorting them into categories. Some norms, like being able to see, to hear, to walk, to read, and so forth, may be sustained by most people, but along with the sorting process goes an appraisal of the "goodness of fit" of an individual's displayed characteristics and those of the category he seems to belong to. What is also important is his grading according to quite general standards of mental and physical accomplishment, educational level, etc., including what Goffman calls "comeliness".

Some of these are akin to ideal standards, measured against which most people must fail at some period in their lives, and some with standards which are completely beyond attainment for almost everyone:

> For example, in an important sense, there is only one complete unblushing male in America; a young, married, white, urban, northern heterosexual Protestant father of college education, fully employed, of good complexion, weight and height, and a recent record in sports.
>
> (S, 128)

One wonders why he left out possession of an income in the top five per cent range. One wonders still more when he adds that '*Every* American male tends to look out upon the world *from* this perspective . . .' (emphasis added).

Evidently, Goffman's grading system comprehends a number of quite different criteria, as of course it must if it is to be all-inclusive. It encompasses acquired characteristics, both physical (permanent injury and trained capacity) and mental or cultural (different degrees and sorts of care or neglect in upbringing and educational opportunity, etc.) as well as congenital. There are structural elements involved, too, which may again be either inherited or acquired, having to do with differences in power, prestige, and esteem.

We confer a 'social identity' on an individual on first acquaintance. We assign him, on the evidence immediately available – principally his appearance, the social setting and nature of the encounter – to one category or another. The individual is, so to speak, credited with a set of anticipated characteristics 'ordinary and natural' to the social category in which he seems at first sight to belong; in addition, freedom from physical, mental or moral defects not immediately apparent is taken for granted.

This being the case, the categorisation system must exist prior to, and independently of, social encounters. Goffman, by implication, says as much when he says (S, 2) that it is "Society" that establishes 'the means of categorizing persons and the complement of attributes felt to be ordinary and natural for members of each of these categories', and, a few lines below, that we apply the system unconsciously.

While, to begin with, the individual may present, in Goffman's terms, a 'virtual social identity', over time, actuality forces its way in. In the ordinary way, his 'actual' social identity amplifies, adjusts, or adds to the virtual social identity he first proffered. But if that virtual social identity is found by others to contain features distinctly less approved than first appearances seemed to suggest, then he has to be displaced categorically from the social identity first ascribed to him and put in a less desirable one. 'He is thus reduced in our minds from a whole and usual person to a tainted, discounted, one. Such an attribute is a stigma' (p. 3).

Goffman then complicates matters rather pointlessly by inserting the suggestion that, while stigma attaches to some discrediting attribute, it is the substantive difference between someone's presumed, or assumed (i.e. virtual), identity and the actual identity eventually revealed that is important. 'It constitutes . . . a social relationship between attribute and stereotype' (S, 4). Translating the signs which stigmatise an individual into a discrepancy between virtual and social identity is merely to repeat the notion of grading inherent in the categorisation system that Goffman started with. It is also at odds with the major distinction he wants to draw later between the "discredited" (people whose stigmatising characteristics are self-evident or even know beforehand, as is often the case), and the "discreditable", where the discrepancy, while unknown or invisible, is open to eventual discovery and thus remains a constant or intermittent threat.

The way in which normalisation exercises the power it does is revealed in the way the stigmatised are judged. Grading someone means positioning him on one scale – the degree to which he approximates to full "humanness" – and another – his social standing. His life chances are defined and, to some degree, determined by that scale. Since someone with a stigma is 'not fully human', the way is clear for the exercise of discriminatory practices of various kinds; and it is by these means that his life chances are 'effectively, if often unthinkingly', reduced. And people construct a 'stigma-theory' to provide an ideological explanation of his inferiority (S, 5).

The use of words like cripple, bastard, and moron in the metaphors and images of casual everyday discourse shows how deep and how pervasive the notion of non-acceptability reaches, and also the extent to which judgments which relegate individuals to an inferior category of human beings are essentially moral judgments. What is more, such judgments share the same inescapable character as that which seals the fate of mental patients, in that any defensive response on his part to his situation is interpreted as additional evidence of his deficiency.

Alienation from normal society may of course act as an insulation, as moral protection. There are also circumstances in which, or categories for which, stigmatisation can be mutual, and still others in which it can be neutralised. Mennonites, gypsies, shameless scoundrels, and orthodox Jews (the examples Goffman cites) have the kind of belief in their own identity which goes with the feeling of being a fully paid-up member of the human race, and a corresponding feeling that it is the rest of us who are not quite human. (Foreign visitors, and this includes tourists, sometimes encounter and experience much the same kind of reaction.)

Typically, though – and this is of central importance – the stigmatised individual shares the beliefs about identity – and normality – of the normal beings he encounters. Those who carry their stigma from birth learn about their disadvantaged situation at the same time as they learn the standards which define it as such, and through the same socialisation process. For others – those left handicapped later in life by illness or injury and those who learn late in life that they bear a congenital stigma – the two processes of social learning occur as separate phases.

In either case, the same "stigma trap" awaits him, ready for the onset of awareness. He learns the identity beliefs prevailing in society at large (which means actually acquiring or adopting them); at the same time, he acquires some broad idea, however vague, of what it would be like to possess a particular stigma; finally, he learns that he has a particular stigma and, this time in full detail, what it is like to have it. Fully aware of the complement of rights, entitlements, and recognition which are the birthright of membership of the society he was born into, the stigmatic is confronted by the perpetually recurring possibility of ordinary, normal, members of society rejecting his claim to be one of them.

The stigmatic is, in this respect, the archetypal "marginal man", much more so, in fact, that the immigrant, the Jew emerging from the ghetto, the person of mixed race (the "mixed blood" of former usage) to whom the label was first applied by Robert Park. Park used it to define the situation of the cultural transient or cultural hybrid. Later, Everett Hughes extended it to include people faced with what he called a "status dilemma" – typically, negroes in America.[2]

Stigma, in Goffman's essay, covers a far wider range of predicaments than these. Indeed, the net is cast so wide as to be unconvincing, at first sight. The catch he counts through at the beginning of the book includes the blind, the deaf, the crippled, the maimed, deformed, disfigured, diseased, prostitutes, and the mentally ill; also blacks, Jews, 'ethnics', lower class persons, homosexuals, illiterates, on to people with colostomies, mastectomies, to diabetics, stutterers, etc., and winding up with the old, along with ex-convicts and ex-mental patients.

But he has an ulterior purpose in mind beyond that of compiling a catalogue of abnormal roles and status positions. In the end, as we discover towards the end of the essay, all members of society are players in the stigma game; everybody, he says, has some stigma of his own; the only question is about the kinds of stigma he has personally experienced.

III

The most elementary differentiation of stigmata is into three "objective" types, one relating to physical deformities, one to defects of character, and a third to race, nationality, religion (and in Britain, Goffman adds, social class). Cutting across these patent differences, however, there is another distinction, this time of a more "subjective" kind. It has to do with acceptance, which is a matter of overwhelming importance for the stigmatised person.

There are, in any encounter, several ways of responding to the situation open to him. But his choice depends on whether he assumes that his stigmatising characteristics are known beforehand, or are immediately recognisable (*the discredited*), or that they are neither known nor immediately perceptible (*the discreditable*). The distinction is important for Goffman's analytical treatment of the different kinds of response made by the stigmatised, even though any one stigmatised individual may well have experienced both situations.

Since they relate to the many specific and immediately perceptible stigmas, responses which are available to (or at least, observably used by) the 'discredited' are fairly numerous. 'Direct' responses range from the removal of defects by plastic surgery to remedial education for illiteracy or speech defects (including the "wrong" accent). 'Indirect' responses are more varied. The most publicised are those which lead to the mastery of activities from which they might be thought barred by their defect: swimming, playing tennis or hockey, skiing, and the like. But the stigmatic, anticipating non-acceptance and defying it, may also choose to brave it out by ostentatious display, or by clowning. And Goffman springs another of his shock insights when he points out that all such responses are 'temperamentally' different but 'substantively' the same as those which are believed to *increase* awareness of others' problems and character defects and so to act as compensation for isolation, pain, or incapacity.

Responses of this kind, whether direct or indirect, take time to work out, though, and Goffman's concern is with more spontaneous occasions of contact between stigmatics and normals. The mere fact that the anticipation of such occasions often leads both kinds to avoid them demonstrates, and underlines, their significance. And their significance likes in the embarrassment experienced on *both* sides of the encounter. On the stigmatic's side, this consists in not knowing what the others *really* think of him, an embarrassment which may reach the point of his "hunting" between the extremes of bravado and withdrawal. Others ("us") are embarrassed by his embarrassment. What can all too easily happen is a build-up of mutual awareness of the kind mentioned earlier (p. 45) which conventions and the like are designed specifically to avoid or overcome. What is involved, notes Goffman, is an infinite regress. 'Each potential source of discomfort for him when we are with him can become something we sense he is aware of, aware that we are aware of, and even aware of our state of awareness about his awareness' (p. 18).

There are, of course, available institutionalised escape hatches, offered by conventions, from the dithering irresolution which this piling up of mutual awareness threatens (above, pp. 44-5). Goffman makes no mention of this, although it lies close to his social interaction interests. The institutional forms which apply to the conduct of social interaction feature prominently among the phenomena analytically independent of individuals that Durkheim called "social facts".

The kind of regression which mutual awareness makes possible happens rarely in everyday encounters because of the possibility of resorting to routines, conventions, or understandings which can, so to speak, depersonalise an otherwise embarrassing mutual consciousness. But the problem typically facing stigmatics is that, since the routines and conventions to which people can resort in social interaction are founded on the mutual deference proffered by equals, they cannot cover encounters between individuals who are unequal in striking and important ways. There simply are no widely observed conventions for encounters between stigmatics and normals; centuries ago, we are told, such conventions were observed between co-religionists, Christian,

Jewish, Moslem and other, but these, if they existed, are now lost. In the absence of an adequate system of conventions, the stigmatised individual may find repeatedly 'that he feels unsure of how we normals will identify him and receive him' (p. 13).

So, most of the time, stigmatics make their social way by means of what I have called "understandings" (above, p. 45). Each family or small group of companions which has one or more members with a stigma usually creates its own understanding. Those whose stigma is immediately perceivable (i.e. "the discredited") can best look, outside these small social circles, to establish understandings among those who share his affliction – the sympathetic others whom Goffman labels 'The Own'.

This has its drawbacks – although outside Alcoholics Anonymous and similar groups convened in homes and centres for the disabled by welfare workers and well-meaning volunteers, one is unlikely to find that interchanges are limited to the boring exchanges of tales with other fellow-sufferers that Goffman says form their currency. But in the nature of things, the social grouping of stigmatics is almost bound to be restrictive. Residential establishments and "centres" cater for those with a specific stigma; then there are, he says, 'the huddle-together self-help clubs formed by the divorced, the aged, the obese, the physically handicapped, the ileostomied and the colostomied . . .' (p. 22). The implication is that the formally or informally organised associations he goes on to list, which are formed by or for homo-sexuals, ex-convicts, ex-addicts and the like, all share the same drawback: the reasons for their coming together are precisely those which lay the tripwires that make encounters with normal people difficult – or sometimes impossible. This hardly applies, however, to his final category: ethnic, racial, and religious ghettos. Here the family, not the individual, is the basic unit.

Another set with whom stigmatics form understandings are 'the "wise", persons who are normal but whose special situation has made them intimately privy to the secret life of the stigmatized individual and sympathetic with it' (p. 28). It is made up in the first place of relatives, naturally, but also of those employed in centres for the treatment, care, service, and supervision of disabled or stigmatised persons – and this includes barmen and policemen as well as doctors and nurses. Relatives and other close connections who choose, or are obliged, to stay by some kinds of stigmatised individual – 'the loyal spouse of the mental patient, the daughter of the ex-con, the parent of the cripple, the friend of the blind . . .', are likely to find that they have to share some of his discredit, Goffman remarks, somewhat obscurely; he presumably would allow some distinction to be made between the "moral blame" attached to the stigmatic and the desire to avoid awkward or embarrassing encounters. The point he wants to make is that their presence on the social boundary between stigma and normality provides 'a model of "normalisation"',* by which he means, he says, treating the stigmatic as if he was not one – although there is the danger, he adds, that this 'stigmatophilic response of the wise', while serving to counter 'the stigmatophobic response of normals . . . may confront everybody with too much morality . . .' (p. 31).

Most groups and categories have their representatives, professional or amateur, 'native' stigmatics or outside sympathisers, whose job it is to act as spokesmen for grievances, attract sympathy and support, and voice the opinions, feelings, and interests they have in common. Publications serve the same purpose, but, beyond this, build up a fund of exemplary stories for consolation, admonition and reproof, promote political action, and formulate what Goffman calls an "ideology" for a group or category of stigmatics.

Organised groups and associations, journals, spokesmen, lobbyists, as well as loyal relatives and sympathetic friends all present the stigmatic with the dilemma of how far to go in identifying himself with those who share the same stigma. It is directly related to the ambivalence which is the endowment conferred on him by his upbringing as a member of his society (and thus fully acquainted with normative requirements and expectations) and his awareness of stigma, with its perpetual threat of non-acceptance among normal people. This ambivalence shows itself typically in an oscillation between identifying with his "own" in general, or with those less obtrusively stigmatised and thus relatively "normal". Alliances may be formed with "insiders" and with "outsiders". He may be outraged or shamed by those who "minstrelise" their stigmatised social position by acting it out in flamboyantly extravagant or comic fashion, yet feel

---

*The meaning (a slightly odd one) which Goffman gives to "normalisation" will not, I hope, be confused with the meaning I have taken from Foucault. He also uses "normification" (a word of his own coinage) to stand for 'the effort made by a stigmatized person to present himself as an ordinary person, although not necessarily making a secret of his failing' (p. 31).

psychologically at one with them and steer clear of the attempt, at the opposite extreme, to lay claim to normality or to cover up his abnormal characteristics. 'In brief, he can neither embrace his group nor let it go' (p. 108), and this continuing self-doubt, occasionally veering towards self-alienation, is reflected precisely in much of the writing, talk, drama, and humour produced by those who, either in spite of their stigma or because of it, have become public figures, and represent the "political arm" of their group or category. So, even though 'these philosophies of life, these recipes of being' – the jokes, the insightful remarks, the defiant proclamations, the assertions of common humanity, and the like – are all uttered from what is clearly the standpoint of one individual speaking his own mind, they derive in fact from the existence of the group, or category, of people in the same fundamentally ambiguous situation.

'This' says Goffman, taking an uncompromising stand on what he clearly believes has to be his own "philosophy of being" as a sociologist, 'is only to be expected, since what an individual is, or could be, derives from the place of his kind in the social structure' (p. 112).

It is a pronouncement which puts him, and sociology, at odds with the most deeply felt beliefs of the Western – Jewish, Hellenic, Christian – tradition. They are beliefs, which, in the present context, are best attested by the words Primio Levi used when writing to a German correspondent about his feelings towards the German people:

> I cannot understand, I cannot tolerate the fact that a man should
> be judged not for what he is but because of the group to which
> he happens to belong.[3]

Of course Goffman is right; common knowledge and the daily newspaper bear him out. Of course we agree with Primo Levi; we would be less than human if we did not – which makes Goffman's truth only a half-truth at best, and Levi's declaration of faith a principle which we all too often fail to uphold.

IV

The profound ambiguity of the stigmatic's situation is in fact to be found in the statements which claim to speak for the individual's "real" – and discrediting – fellows. 'If he turns to his group, he is loyal and authentic; if he turns away, he is craven and a fool. Here, surely', Goffman announces, waving his sociological flag, 'is a clear illustration of a basic sociological theme: the nature of an individual, as he himself and we impute it to him, is generated by the nature of his group affiliation' (p. 113). And it is the nature of the stigmatic's group affiliation, he suggests, which lands him in an inescapable predicament – one most clearly exemplified in the familiar problem of militancy. If the objective is to purge his 'differentness' of the stigma which attaches to it, his stand will make the assimilation he seeks more difficult for himself, whatever benefit it may bring to later generations. If separateness is what he wants, then he must reflect, even adopt, the words and attitudes of those who want to ostracise him and his like.

So, in the long run, the militant simply magnifies for himself the dilemma of the ordinary stigmatic.

The pleas he presents, the plight he reviews, the strategies he advocates, are all part of an idiom of expression and feelings that belongs to the whole society. His disdain for a society that rejects him can be understood only in terms of that society's conception of pride, dignity, and independence.

(p. 114)

Thus, in stressing his distance from what his society takes as normality, he has to insist on his cultural affinity with it.

It is all very convincing, but there is a major qualification which has to be inserted – and, in point of fact, Goffman makes a glancing reference to it. There is a 'stigma trap' into which the militant dissenter must inevitably fall 'unless', he adds, 'there is some alien culture to fall back on'. But there are always alternative, if not alien, cultural propositions "to fall back on", unless we make the impossible assumption that all members of a modern society share the same uniform, homogeneous, self-consistent cultural values and beliefs.

The lapse is not unsurprising, although this time it is hardly his habitual Durkheimian stance which is responsible; rather it is his tendency, in his preoccupation with "microsociology", to distance himself from the consideration of social structure and cultural systems and treat them as somehow "given", and therefore imponderable. The same tendency shows up later, in *Gender Advertisements*, although the implication is reversed, for, in that essay, structural factors are given far too little weight.

The aspects of ambiguity so far dealt with refer to the relationship of spokesmen – advocates and militants alike – with the group itself.

Offsetting this aspect of his situation is the manner in which a different sort of advocacy – one which concerns the mental adjustment of the stigmatic to his predicament – relates to the wider society of "normals" outside the group. This relationship is couched in terms of mental hygiene, indeed of psychiatry, rather than politics, and the usual kind of homily directed at the stigmatised urges him to make a "good adjustment". He is (a) "to make the best of things", to see himself as much a human being as anyone, save for his exclusion from some aspects, or some areas, of social life; but (b) cautioned against going beyond what can be achieved through self-control, determination, training, and other paths of virtue and to stop short 'when the issue of normification arises, that is, where his efforts might give the impression that he is trying to deny his differentness' (p. 115). And, since normals have their own troubles, he should not feel resentful or self-pitying. 'A cheerful, outgoing manner should be cultivated.' The implication is clear: 'The skills that the stigmatized individual acquires in dealing with a mixed social situation should be used to help the others in it' (p. 116).

So, by an extraordinary reversal of the objective situation the evidence points to, the exemplary quality demanded of the stigmatised in dealing with normals is tact. They are under obligation to protect the normal from the consequences of the treatment accorded by them and their fellows to the stigmatised. A "good adjustment" means first that the stigmatised ensure at all times that they stay their side of the line which divides them from normals, and, second, that normals may rest assured that the unfair penalties exacted by their behaviour towards stigmantics will be concealed from them.

And the concluding irony is 'not that the stigmatized individual is being asked to be patiently for others what they decline to let him be for them, but that this appropriation of his response may well be the best return he can get on his money'. He ends up as 'a resident alien, a voice of the group that speaks for and through him' (pp. 122-3).

Goffman rounds off his argument by, as it were, thrusting its tail into its mouth. All of us know well enough that, at certain times and in certain places, acceptance is more or less conditional, subject to provisos of which we are not fully aware. All of us have, at times, felt enough of an outsider to try harder to conceal our awkwardness and convince others that we too possess a 'standard subjective self', while knowing at the same time that the more we try, the stronger the demand that we represent a model of freedom from awkwardness. All of us can remember occasions when acting the 'resident alien' was all one could hope for. Beginning school, or beginning our first job, we are all marginal individuals, we all bear the outsider's stigma. And all of us can remember less momentous occasions when we were "not sure of ourselves", when we were confronted by the possibility of having our claim to be one of them rejected by those around us whom we believed to be fully accredited members.

It is at this point that Goffman introduces his "ideal American male" as the norm against which (American) men measure others – and themselves (above, p. 216). And, for all that this ideal American male is also something of a figure of fun, Goffman is right. For we know, too, that there are situations in which, if only we were more like him, we could keep countenance instead of blushing for our presence, remain self-assured, and, indeed, *defy comparison*, for that is what it amounts to. And there are other sets of attributes which the setting, or company, could well impute to us and thereby confer a 'social identity' which is essentially false but which we might unthinkingly assume as a 'virtual social identity'. It may be impossible at such times for someone to sustain the attributes imputed to him, however much he may wish to, and however free he might be of any stigma. For it is a matter of *being* the kind of person one appears at first to be, rather than *acting* in conformity with the normative expectations which apply to behaviour.

Stigma management, Goffman concludes, is a general feature of society, a process occurring wherever there are identity norms. The same features are involved, even when trivial differences distinguish the normal from the stigmatised, differences 'of which the shamed person is ashamed to be ashamed. One suspects that the roles of normal and stigmatic are cut from the same standard cloth' (p. 130).

"One suspects?" Surely the "cloth" is the categorisation system which he mapped out at the start of the book. What the "system" amounts to is a replica of the social structure, made manifest (or "operational") through the capacity and readiness of every adult member of society to arrive at an almost instantaneous assessment of the place in it of even the most transitory of new acquaintances. And the lack of self-confidence which new social situations sometimes arouse in us provides further evidence, this time through our unsureness about ramifications of the system (which must surely exist), wider than we had previously known.

Stigma is a superbly constructed essay, comprehensive in scope, imaginative and sensitive, ending with the "normal" reader confronted with a nicely contrived revelation of the implication of his own cherished normality in the "spoiled identity" created by the discriminatory system of which he is part, and which he operates. But the subtitle, "Notes on the Management of Spoiled Identity", carries with it a reference to the basic structural features of society from which both our social and personal identities derive, and which are virtually ignored after the opening pages.

V

As I have already suggested, Goffman's dedication to the micro-sociology he did so much to develop as a subject occasionally lays him open to criticism. This is even more apparent in *Gender Advertisements*.

The "categorisation system" mentioned at the beginning of *Stigma* is made up of a mixture of acquired and inherited characteristics; some of the latter, which are inescapable, also figure as stigmas. So some people stand to be stigmatised simply because they are black, "ethnic", or old. Women, of course, do not. But there is a passage in *Frame Analysis* in which, as I remarked earlier (above, p. 58), he canvasses the idea of femininity being regarded as in some ways a declension from an essentially masculine norm and therefore the mark of a lower grade of human being.

It arises from the question of how it is that relegation to some subordinate category of humankind seems to be accepted by most of those who are so classified. Only a minority show resentment, and fewer still openly protest. Most of the answer lies in what Goffman calls 'the stigma trap' (above, p. 218), but this still leaves unanswered some residual questions. These are touched on in the *Stigma* essay, but it is the later book that provides the beginnings of a possible answer. There is a passage in it which suggests that physical or mental incapacity gives a kind of licence to say or do what is ordinarily inadmissible. It is the existence of rewards of this kind, he presumes, that induces some people to pretend incapacity (childishness, physical incompetence or incapacity, boorishness), simply in order to obtain that kind of licence: the father in Dostoevsky's *Brothers Karamazov* is one representative – almost archetypal – figure. But if it is possible to *pretend* to be handicapped, the question arises of how far the appearance of incapacity depends on a recognisable *style* of behaviour.

This raises the further question about how far an insane person, for example, may be adopting the style he thinks appropriate for the insane; how far is it a matter of behaviour rather than mental derangement? 'Surely', he goes on,

> when members of a subordinated social group (such as American Indians) are seen as non-adult, as children not to be trusted, they are engaging in a strategic alignment, an exploitation of common stereotypes concerning irresponsibility and sometimes simply the playacting of irresponsibility for what can be gained thereby? And children themselves? How early in life could they cease to act childlike?
>
> Nor is the matter of conscious simulation the final issue. *Men often treat women as faulted actors with respect to 'normal' capacity for various forms of physical exertion. Women so treated often respond by affirming this assessment.* On both sides there may be unquestioning belief and a long-sustained capacity to act accordingly without guilt or self-consciousness. Nonetheless, cannot the question be put as to whether 'real' incapacities are involved or merely institutionally sustained belief?
>
> (FA, 196-7; emphasis added)

Gender Advertisements is an attempt to provide some sort of answer to this question. This time the evidence is provided in the form of photographic reproductions of the illustrations used in advertisements to show the various dimensions of the subordinate "placing" of women in relation to men in a number of different contexts. There is a good deal of the kind of sublety one would expect from Goffman in the arrangement and annotation of the photographs, but none of it counts as new information. How could it? For what advertisers and their photographers put into these illustrations is exactly what we are meant to read into them; and what is put in is extremely unsubtle – they are, after all, meant to be instantly comprehensible. The only question is whether we all read the same things, and here, as in the case of most of his writings, the appeal is to common interpretation based on community of experience. After all, this is also what advertisers must appeal to. (A note on page 74 warns that 'For the effective reading of his text, the writer depends upon effective viewing by his readers – words here serving to point, not specify.')

There are over five hundred illustrations, classified in six sections. The largest section, "Licensed Withdrawal", portrays people (children and a few men are included, but most are women) betrayed by some psychological involvement which compels them to withdraw from 'the social situation at large'. At its most extreme, this can amount to "flooding out" – abandoning control in tears, laughter, giggles, or hiding from onlookers behind one's hands, because of grief, fear, shyness, embarrassment, or anxiety. Milder forms of *displayed* withdrawal are accomplished by averting the head or the eyes, or, more subtly, by a rapt, "withdrawn", facial expression. And one can take refuge behind a door, a book, an object – or a man, if one is a woman, and a woman if one is a child – and so down to snuggling, nuzzling, and embracing. All portray a range of expressive relationship characteristics from seeking refuge down to trustfulness and dependency, but all also show that they are withdrawing *behind* a mother or a father in the cases of a child, or a husband – or simply a man – in the case of a woman. They are withdrawing from whatever or whoever else is present, behind the protective cover afforded by someone who more closely approximates to the fully-fledged norms of membership of society.

The other sections, in which the salient grading features are "relative size", "the feminine touch", "function ranking", "the family", and "the ritualization of subordination" are all fairly self-explanatory. One thing missing from the *catalogue raisonnée* is the overtone of sexual attraction that so many of the illustrations carry; but it could be said that this must be "taken as read", the supplementary gloss that advertisers regard as an obligatory element in advertisements which have, after all, to attract attention.

The illustrations are, it should be said, taken exclusively from newspaper and magazine advertisements. Posters, which announce, and television advertisements, which narrate, are entirely different kinds of confection. The illustrations themselves are, in consequence, "stills" – photographs or line drawings – accompanying the direct message (which may do no more than announce the name of the product, if that) of the advertisement. Which means that whatever message the illustrations convey may be, and usually is, indirect, suggestive, a matter of manner, of style, rather than literal meaning.

The message conveyed indirectly by most of the illustrations is not of "institutionally sustained beliefs" about the incapacities of women relative to men, but of *care* (a notion which ranges from "cherishing" and "carefulness" to "caring about") and dependency. The presumption is that advertisers think their readers will associate a display of people who are obviously "caring" (even if it is only about each other) with some product, or service, or association, which, since they care about it too, often in something like the same way, is therefore worth while in something like the same way.

What is portrayed in the illustration, therefore, is a specific kind of relationship, one which demonstrates involvement, regard, affection. And since the demonstration is confined to what can be contained in a still photograph, this can only be conveyed by the *pose* which they adopt. The relationship must be recognisable from the manner, the style, of the posture.

This is easy enough, because there is a wide range of indicative gestures, facial expressions, postures which display an individual's alignment to what is going on in any social situation, and his relationship to other participants. All behaviour in the company of others affords some information of this kind, however minimal, however briefly glimpsed. However, there has been developed, or been articulated, a range of conventionalised acts which proffer condensed, easily read, versions of the informative behaviours more important to themselves, personally and socially. Where importance and emphasis are looked for, some of these versions are elevated to the level of ceremonies ('situated social fusses', he calls them), to which people resort when they want to solemnise 'apparent junctures and turning points in life'. The requirements of mutual deference, acknowledging relationships, and the lubrication and punctuation generally of social interaction are met by more perfunctory ritual performances. More fleeting and more frequent still are the specialised routines by which people indicate at the commencement of any encounter, in the quickest and most easily recognised way, the alignment towards the others they will adopt.

VI

Having established that conventionalised acts of the kind represented in his advertisement stills are designed to convey information about alignment and intention, the argument of the text is then shunted sideways. Such acts are in fact, he argues, nothing more or less than the *displays* familiar to students of animal behaviour. Displays are, properly speaking, sequences of activity which are designed as communications, of a kind which is entirely utilitarian. They are not simply shorthand or emphatic versions of ordinary expressive behaviour, which conveys information about 'social identity, mood, intent, expectations', or about how the individual wants his relationship to others to be viewed. Instead of "displacing" a sequence of actions, the individual (or animal), sets out deliberately to provide an effective and easily interpreted expression of his situation and his intentions. Display often (though by no means always, as Goffman seems to suggest) takes the form of a "ritualisation" of some intended or threatened action, which allows, it is thought, for some response to the invitation or threat it conveys to be made by any witness of it, and, thereafter, for negotiation about it.

What goes on during these occasions of ritual expression is connected with social structures, but rather loosely. For one thing, displays tend to occur mostly at the start and at the finish of encounters. They are designed to bracket an individual's participation in its entirety, or particular interventions by him, and so are somewhat apart from the business in hand. Because of this, displays are employed and what is believed to be the appropriate context for them chosen quite consciously.

Furthermore, 'once a display becomes well established in a particular sequence of actions', it can be transformed – in the way exhaustively discussed in *Frame Analysis*, the publication immediately preceding this book. 'A section of the sequence can be lifted out of its original context, parenthesised, and used in a quotative way – a postural resource for mimicry, irony, mockery, teasing, etc.' This means that the process of styling a sequence of activity can itself be stylised – an unserious commentary delivered within the frame of the stylised act itself. 'What was ritual becomes itself ritualised, a transformation of what was already a transformation, a "hyper-ritualisation" (p. 3). And, as the illustrations testify, displays can be fabricated. So, a display is only a display – 'not a picture of the way things are but a passing exhortative guide to perception'.

We have by now travelled some distance from the ethological model Goffman started with. Needless to say, transformation, in Goffman's usage – "framing" – is as much part of the animal world as it is of human behaviour: Bateson got the idea from watching monkeys and otters. But it does not stretch as far as "hyper-ritualisation" – making (reflexively) a display out of the displays themselves. And the new elasticity conferred on the basic notion of display is not the first transformation. Animal display is, as he says, strictly utilitarian, but its utility is usually regarded as something provided for the species, not

231

the individual member of it. It is a genetic endowment (even if we allow for an intermediary "imprinting" process) rather than a cultural facility acquired by observation and learning.

The transformational interpretation of display is taken still further when it comes to gender. There are two stages of the argument. The first begins by granting that division into male and female gender is decided by visible biological difference. Nevertheless, it remains true that male behaviour and female behaviour – our conceptions of masculinity and femininity and the attitudes of individuals towards each other and towards themselves as male or female – are very largely culturally determined. Even to think of gender as an essential and central element in personal identity is of cultural rather than biological origin. The essence of human masculine and feminine nature 'is a capacity to learn to provide and read depictions of masculinity and femininity'. In doing so, people have to adhere to a programme – a regular code for interpreting what is depicted. But this is an ability they acquire as individual persons, not as male or female, as it is in the animal world. To *portray* gender is not a matter of one's identity as a male or a female; one has to learn a communication code.

The second stage of the argument directs attention to the main repositories of conventionalised performance and ritual displays of social and personal identity, alignment to others, and intended mode of participation available for social interaction which may call for gender displays. And these are European court life (especially as modified in later times for military practice) to begin with, and, second, parent-child relationships. The first is of minor significance, allowing for some parallel to be drawn between the manner of expressing the superior status of royalty, presidents (French and American), film celebrities, hotel guests, shop customers, husbands, and men in general, and the corresponding manifestations of deference and subordination by reception committees, aides, shop assistants, doormen, wives, and women in general. But it is the second cultural (or structural) configuration, the parent-child relationship, which is taken to be the main model for the expression of gender relationships. The main reason for this seems to be that it is a model of an unequal and non-reciprocal relationship which is universally available. ('Most people end up having been cared for as children and having cared for children.') It is also a model of an authority relationship which seems unique in that it lasts for a limited period and, it is claimed, is exerted "in the best interests" of subordinates.

Goffman makes no allowance for any causal interleaving between physical (biological) characteristics and manners of behaving, which are culturally prescribed, or, at least, belong to the cultural order of things. He also assumes that gender display, since it must be for the most part disengaged from any prescription of behaviour in terms of biological sex difference, must be a copy of ritual conventions. Nevertheless, ritual conventions may themselves be grounded in physical (biological) needs and constraints – or even, as Goffman's argument suggests, in family and authority relationships.

We are now, it seems, to presume that elements of social structure like these are a more fundamental factor in social behaviour than gender. Then comes another of what I have called his "finesses". We are told that both what children are allowed to do and what they must consent to being done on their behalf by parents (or by any other adult who happens to be handy) is said to *'pertain'* to the way in which adults manage themselves in social situations so as to demonstrate 'respectful orientation' to the situation and maintain 'guardedness' while it lasts. This could mean that the licence allowed and the constraint laid upon children is akin to the licence and constraint which his parents, as adults, allow themselves and submit to in the company of others. It could also mean that when children are present "in company", their behaviour has to be such as will allow their parents to sustain their own alignment to the situation. (There is a tacit analogy with the codes of behaviour expected of servants and waiters, subordinate officials in the presence of their superiors, and visiting strangers.) I see no way of deciding which of them is the 'key issue' that Goffman says "it" is. My guess is that it is the first, not because it is the more likely of the two, but because it makes better sense of what follows.

There are two sides to the basic pattern of the parent-child relationship (it being understood that it is the American "middle-class" family which is to be taken as the norm): 'orientation licence' and 'protective intercession'. The licence enjoyed by the child is grounded in the assumption that all his present needs (i.e. "basic" or "reasonable" needs) have been, and that any future needs and wants will be, catered for. Licensed withdrawal ('employing patently ineffective means' for escaping from a situation by burying his face, "flooding out", and so on) comes under the same heading. Protective intercession includes obtaining things for him which are too heavy, too dangerous, or out of his reach, mediating between him and other people, children or adults, and between him and "the outside world" in general.

The balance between the two aspects reflects two governing notions. The first is that 'a loving protector is standing by'; intercession extends beyond those matters in which a child is helpless and dependent to providing cover for his copping out from situations too awkward, too novel, or too complicated for him to handle. The second is that there is a price to be paid. He is subject at all times to commands, which may be reinforced by physical control; whatever he is doing may be interrupted without warning or ceremony, his time and territory being seen as expendable; he can be treated as a non-person, talked past and talked about as though he were absent; he may be teased, or brought into conversation and then treated as simply an object of attention. What is more, other adults present with his parents may claim much the same rights in these regards as they have. It is as if the presence of children were permitted simply so that they might serve as lay figures in scenes designed for parents to act out their parental roles.

The conclusion Goffman arrives at is not that the parent-child relationship is the *model* for relationships and alignments between men and women, but that it provides a large fund of ritualistic expressions for superior-subordinate interaction 'warmed by a touch of relatedness; in short, benign control'.

These ritualistic expressions, which are in the nature of things utterly familiar to virtually everybody, are used as a resource for defining the attitudes and alignments which are themselves the reflection of differences determined by social structure. They can be drawn on, Goffman goes on, in adult social gatherings which involve persons of different grades in terms of social status, organisational rank, age-grade, prestige – or gender. 'The superordinate gives something gratis out of supportive identification, and the subordinate responds with an outright display of gratitude, and, if not that, then at least an implied submission to the relationship and the definition of the situation it sustains.

> It turns out, then, that in our society whenever a male has dealings with a female or a subordinate male (especially a younger one), some mitigation of potential distance, coercion, and hostility is quite likely to be induced by application of the parent-child complex. Which implies that, *ritually speaking, females are*

equivalent to subordinate males and both are equivalent to children.

(*GA*, 5; my italics)

In the end, therefore, gender relationships (which include sex discrimination) are *structurally* determined. This is obvious enough, and is nowhere denied in the essay. What is denied is that the structural relationships, which in the most relevant regard are in fact power relationships, are rooted in biological difference.

The argument that discrimination is founded on differences in manual competence, in intelligence, and in vulnerability (and is therefore, it is assumed, justified) has lost what validity it ever had in the past. Nor are differences in physical strength now regarded as justification for blanket discrimination between all males and all females; the protective (military) role which is historically a male preserve is hardly relevant to the broad spectrum of life experience to which discrimination has applied, and still does. The role of breadwinner, or at least of principal economic provider, as counterpart to the child-bearing and child-rearing role of women, has lost its lifetime significance. And common knowledge, let alone the substantial correctives applied to it supplied by Philip Ariés and those who have followed him, admits that substantial changes have occurred to the *structural* relationships between men and women over the past two hundred years.

After one has paraded, and discarded, the usual simplistic arguments which see in biological differences sufficient explanation for sex-discrimination, there remain the structural arrangements themselves. Goffman ends his essay by arguing that it is not enough to attempt to redress the adverse balance of the relationship women have to sustain by direct assault on the structural arrangements themselves. While 'the analysis of sexism can start with obviously unjust discriminations against persons of the female sex-class, . . . it cannot stop there' (*GA*, 8). The essentially political concerns of sex discrimination are embedded in a vast welter of ritualised expressions which denote subordination.

Strategic Interaction began with the claim that the 'study of social interaction' is 'a naturally bounded, analytically coherent field – a sub-area of sociology'. The claim was reiterated, and made stronger, by his quoting Herbert Spencer in a prefatory note to *Relations in Public*. And in *Gender Advertisements* we find:

After all, it is in social situations [i.e. face-to-face encounters] that

235

individuals can communicate in the fullest sense of the term, and it is only in them that individuals can physically coerce one another, assault one another, importune one another gesturally, give physical comfort, and so forth. Moreover, it is in social situations that most of the world's work gets done.

(*GA*, 5-6)

This last sentence deserves to be met by one of his own phrases; for it is "true [to a limited extent] as it reads, but false as it is [meant to be] taken". Much of the "work" of social interaction, and most of the aspects of it which Goffman took as his field of study, is done in order to perform tasks which are preformulated. Much of it is undertaken so as to satisfy individual needs and wants. A great deal of the work of social interaction is also the product or outcome of what is "given" in social structure and in individual appetites. It is done to express or to alter structural relationships – of power, lineage and inheritance, ownership of resources, age grade, social status, organisational position, family place, and so on – and to create, build on, or compensate for the inequalities which derive from them.

For these reasons, the strategy Goffman ends by advocating seems to me to be wrong, and, what is more, contrary to the historical evidence. The partial emancipation gained by women's movements over the past century and a half is surely the result of the direct assault on "structural arrangements" which have in political terms denied women the vote, in jural terms relegated them to the status of their children and other "dependants", and in economic terms excluded them from professional occupations and directed them into the more servile and poorly paid "service industries". The advances registered in greater liberty, more social acceptance on an equal footing with men, more equitable division of labour in the family, and the rest, have all *followed* the gains registered in structural reforms.

VII

Is there some overall view which reconciles all Goffman's various notions of what he called the 'self', the 'individual' the 'person', and 'identity'?

The first thing to say is that he makes difficulties for the reader, and for himself, by treating the first two, or even three, terms ('self', 'individual', and 'person') as interchangeable. If one regards such strictly terminological problems as really quite minor, there seems to me no reason why Goffman, or anyone else, should not develop different models of the "person" when he comes to deal with the different analytical tasks he set himself. So long as any model developed in one of his books is not incompatible with that in any other, it seems sensible to develop each in a pragmatic, ad hoc, fashion.

But the incompatibilities are not merely terminological. The biggest problem arises from his failure to grasp one vital distinction that has to be made if the whole analytical enterprise is not to founder in the conceptual morass created by all the attempts made over some hundreds of years to find a rationally defensible answer to the question "What am I?" This is the distinction to be drawn between self-awareness and consciousness of self.

It is a distinction which lies behind, and determines, the distinction between the self and the person. Together, self and person constitute the "individual" (pace Goffman's dislike of using the word in this way). Self-awareness is best thought of as anterior to consciousness of self, a matter of feelings and emotions, of the senses and of desires, dispositions, intentions, as well as of knowledge. The self is the perpetual subject, has no attributes – is simply an indefinable presence. As Kant (I believe correctly) says, the self proper, as it exists in itself, is necessarily unknown to us (i.e. is an impossible object of knowledge).

Admittedly, it is all somewhat confusing. Self-awareness can itself become predicated, the object of knowing rather than the pervasive subject of knowing along with feeling, etc. It is possible to *talk* about self-awareness, for then it has become an object of consciousness, part of the "person", the subject-in-action, and, as such, communicable and knowable, socially available. If we take *self-consciousness* to signify the accessibility to consciousness of everything that the subject does, thinks, intends, or wishes, then awareness of the self enters into self-consciousness – the perception of oneself objectively as a person.

If, as I think is desirable, we reserve the word "self" for Mauss' ineradicable awareness (above, p. 109), and think of the object of consciousness of self as "person", a number of difficulties become avoidable; for example, Goffman confuses the "self" – the straightforward statement of the sense of selfhood as the core of personal being which he took from Erickson – with "person" by going on with the sentence and making the self not only 'a general and central aspect of him', but 'different (from others) through and through, not merely identifiably different' (p. 56). Difference implies comparison, and it is impossible to compare self-awareness.

It is his dismissal of the distinction which most moral and social philosophers have drawn between "self" and "person" (or *personnage*, etc.) – or his obliviousness to it – which led Goffman into his "demythologising" forays against what he at times seems to regard as a totally sentimental attachment to the idea of the self as an autonomous entity existing independently of others. In *Stigma*, Goffman articulates the idea of the *person* as a composite of social identity and personal identity which embodies the characteristically socially constructed aspect of the individual, and is at pains to separate this out from the idea of the self. But there are passages in other essays which present the self as if it were simply the instrument, or mirror, of rules which "govern" individual behaviour in social encounters. They are passages in which his vision of a rule-governed social order seems to demand a counterpart in the image of a socially constructed self, and the autonomous selfhood one thought one was born with surrenders its uniqueness and significance, manifesting itself in appropriate responses to the company it keeps and to the physical setting, the mental configuration, the emotional charge, of the social situation in which it finds itself.

NOTES AND REFERENCES

1. M. Foucault, *Power/Knowledge* (ed. C. Gordon), Harvester Press, 1980, p. 106.
2. See "Social change and status protest: an essay on the marginal man", and "Robert E. Park", in E. E. Hughes, *The Sociological Eye; Selected Papers*, Aldine-Atherton, 1971.
3. P. Levi, *The Drowned and the Saved*, Macdonald (Sphere Books edn), 1988, p. 143.

9
REALMS OF BEING

Frame Analysis is Goffman's longest and most ambitious book. It is about how we shape and compartmentalise our experience of life and of the world of objects and events around us, and about how the experiencing and acting self, too, can be compartmentalised into a series of part-selves, each a potential factor in the production of experience for ourselves and for others. Goffman also takes up the notion, which *The Presentation of Self in Everyday Life* seemed to have exhausted, of the essential theatricality of ordinary behaviour, but this time it is turned inside out and used not simply as a metaphor but as a paradigm for social conduct. Theatricality is now presented as the necessary consequence of the individual's capacity for partitioning the self into a multiplicity of part-selves. Several chapters are taken up with showing how closely plays replicate, as well as exploit, the capacity of the self to divide itself into a set of personalised ("personified") constituent parts. There are other, 'impure', forms of make-believe which have something of the same character, but the theatrical performances of plays is the true replica of the multiplicity of selves of which the individual disposes. The penultimate chapter extends the frame analysis of experience (sc. perception) and action to include conversation.

Besides being Goffman's longest book, *Frame Analysis* is also probably the most difficult for the reader to grasp. This is not at all because he ventures, for once, into high theory and even philosophy. References to phenomenology and citations of Husserl, William James, Alfred Schutz, Wittgenstein, Austin, and others were all becoming commonplace in sociological writing well before *Frame Analysis* was published; they are in any case passed over with a lightness of touch which I am sure owes nothing to caution. Some of the difficulty arises from his increasing disinclination to use one word where ten will do

– something which becomes very obvious from the first introductory chapter. But the main obstacle to understanding (which has led to certain misapprehensions about the nature and the aim of the book) comes, I think, partly from the nature of the task he set himself, partly from the kind of material he presents by way of circumstantial evidence, or illustration, but mostly from his virtually total exclusion of all elements of social behaviour and considerations of social structure other than the "microsociological" concerns which engaged his immediate attention. For most of its length, in fact, *Frame Analysis* is as much an essay in cognitive psychology (or psychological theory, perhaps) as in sociology or anthropology. Indeed, the origins of the phenomenological tradition to which Goffman claims to adhere lie in the interests of Brentano, Husserl, William James, whose names he cites, in psychology; the same goes for Wittgenstein, too, of course.

The overall theme of the book has two aspects. They are dealt with quite separately, and in sequence, although they overlap in Chapter 8. The first half concerns the different realms of being into which we divide the world we experience (or into which we assume it is divided), and the contrivances which we habitually employ in order to sort out the world we experience into these different realms. After the opening chapter, the next seven are taken up with the detailed exposition of the conceptual framework for describing the world of "lived experience" (a general notion which seems not very far removed from the *Lebenswelt* theme that Husserl was working on during his last years) and the different realms into which we organise it.

The second half of the book begins, in the same Chapter 8, with a discussion of the various ways in which the different realms of being are tethered to the continuing world of things and activities around us – the ordinary, everyday world from which we may often be partially or temporarily removed, but to which we always return. It goes on to examine our ability not only to discriminate between the different realms but also to juggle with them, with the analysis of the first half of the book employed almost as a set of theorems for developing a number of corollaries. Chapters 9-12 deal with how beset by vicissitudes and how subject to assault by illusion, fabrication, pretence and deception is our capacity to discriminate between the different realms and the border controls we try to impose between them. Alongside these accounts, however, there is also a mounting argument which goes beyond cataloguing the accidental impairment or deliberate manipulation of our capacity to frame our perception of the world around us. The very fact that such vicissitudes occur at all is turned around (by a now familiar Goffmanesque device) to cast what we regard as the real world and normal experience in a new light, and to show the world we take as real to be no more real than any of the unreal worlds we compose out of its elements.

I

In *Frame Analysis*, Goffman claims explicitly to be treading the same phenomenological path as Husserl and Schutz (and William James, who is nowadays frequently associated with the same tradition). The explicit claim is new, but his use of a phenomenological approach is not.

Goffman's earlier writings had dealt with how we perpetually ensure that the way we dress and behave are reasonably appropriate to the different places, occasions, persons, and circumstances in which, or among which, we find ourselves. This is something we are often self-conscious about, and it is not surprising, nor especially unacceptable, to have it pointed out that our ways of behaving in these regards – our manners – are culturally determined, or even "socially constructed". Goffman went beyond this to show how the way we talk with friends, eye strangers, walk along a crowded street, and much else that we regard as ordinary, taken-for-granted, indeed natural, are essentially social constructs, too. What is more, the same applies not only to institutions (which, again, we knew about, when we thought of it) but to the social identities we are assumed to have and to the personal identities we know we are. Constructs all, they are not even fabricated by ourselves, as we tend to think, but prefabricated by the society, the community, the social class, the occupation or organisation of which we are established or temporary members.

These writings were based largely on his own observation of how people behaved when, during the course of their ordinary daily lives, they were in the company of others; references to other social scientists' studies were confined for the most part to the supplementary evidence of a similar kind he found in their reports. It was the way Goffman used his material, however, that made his work distinctive. As I have suggested (above, p. 76) the kind of analytical approach he adopted departed from traditional practice among social scientists, approximating more and more closely to that characteristic of the study of animal behaviour. This is not simply a matter of meticulously close observation. What counts is the determined shedding of preconceived notions, especially those – like instincts, sexual and parental roles, emotions – which provide their own ready-made interpretations of behaviour. Allied to this is a readiness to reframe hypotheses and invent new ones in a search for a satisfactory account of "what is *really* going on here".

By the time he came to write *Frame Analysis*, even 'the question, "What is it that is going on here?"' has become, he says, 'considerably suspect' (p. 8). The question is one to which truthful answers of radically different kinds could perfectly well be given. At the most commonplace level, the answer one participant in a situation gives may differ radically from that of someone else; and a retrospective view – of a football match, say – which would incorporate assessments of it and comparison with other matches could well be distinctly different again. The point being made here is perhaps now best known as the "*Rashomon*" problem.

More seriously still, if one stresses the word 'it' in the question, matters are biased 'in the direction of unitary exposition and simplicity'. It is by raising this kind of question, rather than by references to James, Husserl, and Schutz, that Goffman comes close to what goes by the name of phenomenology. For, in claiming as its primary objective the examination and description of "things as they are in themselves", phenomenology seeks to penetrate, or circumvent, habitual patterns of thought. The special bias which the universal application (or misapplication, rather) of "Occam's razor" has given to rational thought is especially pertinent. For phenomenology tries above all to override the temptation to simplify, to reduce, which has given us the handy identities and judgments we commonly use. This is especially the case with the unitary self – "the postulate of a thinking 'I'" – which, for Nietzsche, was one of the "necessary falsehoods of the philosophers, inventions masquerading as discoveries, without which life would not be possible".[1] Traditional philosophy, empirical as well as idealist, nominalist as well as realist, has taken these "inventions" as its point of departure.

Since the only knowledge offered us of "things as they are in themselves" are appearances – phenomena – this requires, among other things, establishing the meaning they have for us rather than trying to discern the nature (the "reality") of things *in themselves*. It is, Husserl pointed out, a procedure which the natural sciences adopted long ago. Indeed, it could be, and has been, argued that the intellectual approach and the mode of procedure of phenomenology are really much older than its name, being deeply embedded in the tradition of scientific method and of European thought. It is a claim which establishes phenomenology firmly in the line of descent from Kant's critical philosophy (along with the hermeneutics of Dilthey, Heidegger, and Gadamer, to which Goffman's own approach in fact more closely approximates).

Interest in phenomenology, which had been a principal resource for a number of what were claimed to be "radical" approaches in the humanities and the social sciences, was past its peak by the time Goffman finished *Frame Analysis*. It had caught the attention of critics and humanists in the English-speaking world during the immediate post-war years, mostly by way of contemporary French writing; few social scientists responded to that kind of interest, but sociologists became more directly influenced through the new gloss that Alfred Schutz (who spent some time at the New School in New York) had put on Weber's methodology of *Verstehen*. For it was Weber who insisted that if sociology was to be a science devoted to the explanation of human behaviour in society, it had to engage with the interpretation of human behaviour which explanation presupposed, *as well as* (not rather than, *pace* Clifford Geertz) causal explanations of it.

It would be quite misleading to give the impression of there being a clearly defined phenomenological tradition or even "school". Phenomenology seems in fact to have been rather more fissiparous than other philosophical movements. Quite apart from the intricacies of its interaction with the hermeneutic tradition, there are major differences in the way phenomenology has developed in France, the United States, and Britain. Yet all three acknowledge the same German origins and also accord central importance in later years to Heidegger and Gadamer. And each country has its own divisions, too. Still, for the layman in general, and for the humanist and the social scientist in particular, the major focus of activity and interest since 1945 has been France. Sartre, Merleau-Ponty, Ricoeur, Deleuze, and Barthes are all familiar names, and although few, perhaps none, of them could properly have the label "phenomenologist" attached to them (or would accept it if it were), all do unquestionably take the phenomenology of Brentano and Husserl as a major point of departure, and return fairly often to it.

The approach Goffman adopts for much of *Frame Analysis* has a striking affinity with some of these later offshoots of phenomenology.

The most obvious is "deconstruction", the successor to the "structuralism" of the sixties, but there are resemblances to other developments, notably the prolonged attacks mounted by Foucault, Derrida, and others on "Kantian man", the conception of man as a privileged, autonomous subject, the transcendent, noumenal being whose representations of objects constitute reality. Yet there is no mention of structuralism, of deconstruction, or hermeneutics in the book. On the face of it, Goffman seems to have developed his approach independently, for, although he certainly knew something of concurrent trends in European philosophy and criticism, this particular development, which received a good deal of attention in the later seventies, may have been unknown to him at the time he wrote the book.

Deconstruction is Derrida's translation of Heidegger's *"Destruktion"*, a term which applied to philosophical discourse the kind of procedure used to reveal the special quality of poetic discourse. Simplifying to the point of crude oversimplification, the procedure could, at its most elementary level, be said to consist in the examination of what is lost when poetry is "paraphrased" in prose. (A "literal" translation into a foreign language would work in the same way.) It then becomes possible to discern more clearly what the poet has put into his poem by his choice of words and his arrangement of them. In other words, one way of finding out how a poem is constructed is by divesting it of the clothing in which the poet dressed it. It is not a matter of trying to develop some special insight into "the poetic experience" or into the poet's ideas, sentiments, perceptions, or feelings before they are articulated in a text; "deconstructing" a poem does not get us any closer to the poet's intended meaning, which includes all sorts of overtones and unsayable elements. The object is to isolate, and then examine, the strictly linguistic work which the poet did in "finding words", and to discover how he put to use his sensitivity to the potentialities and constraints of his native language.

At this elementary level, the method of deconstruction developed in "poetics" is simply the attempt to take out of a poetic utterance whatever it is that the words the poet chose to put into it. And this is precisely what Goffman says he is doing with the "human interest" stories that provide much of his evidential materials, and which he picked up from popular biographies and, especially, newspapers: anecdotes and reports of miscellaneous pathetic, funny, untoward, bizarre situations and goings-on: the *faits divers* of French newspapers.

As such, they are parodies of what is ordinarily regarded as usable evidence; for they have a dramatic coherence and unity, and make their point with a clarity and completeness which bears little resemblance to our everyday experience of happenings around us. Each story makes its single, exemplary point wrapped up in a little amusement or a little wonderment. But that, Goffman says, 'is their point'. For these stories are preconditioned by our own knowledge and experience of the world we live in.

> Their telling demonstrates the power of our conventional understandings to cope with the bizarre potentials of social life, the furthest reaches of experience. What appears, then, to be a threat to our way of making sense of the world turns out to be an ingeniously selected defence of it. We press these stories to the wind; they keep the world from unsettling us.

'What was put into these tales is thus', he concludes, 'what I would like to get out of them' (p. 15), which makes the "deconstructionist" point.

This leads to a further question (although Goffman does not raise it). Where does what is put into these tales – or these poems – come from? Since, in the case of poetry, it is a matter of choosing the "right" words and the "right" arrangement of them, the answer is fairly obvious; it comes from other poetry, other writings, other *texts*. But the same answer, according to Derrida (who, in this respect, is not alone) has to be given in the case of other kinds of writing; it is notably the case with philosophical texts. Concatenations of words can refer only to other strings of words; one cannot find some "truth" or "knowledge" which is independent of them. It is not possible to deconstruct a text and so reconstruct or recapture the esoteric singularity and truth it was thought to contain. The signs (words) in such texts refer only to other signs. And in general, our understanding of any piece of writing is anchored firmly in our experience of other writing.

I suppose that, nowadays most people, at some time in their youth, must have come across the idea of listening to broadcast news as if it were entirely enclosed in quotation marks, or had it suggested to them. (As a joke, it is at about the same level as watching a television talk-show with the sound turned off, speeding up a video track, and so on.) What it does is to transform "actuality" into unreality. Derrida suggests that if one were to treat any piece of writing, of even the most unambiguous kind, as wholly enclosed in quotation marks, it would be impossible to decide where the "truth" it "represented" lay. All writing (including his own) should be treated in this way, and so cast adrift from any anchor which might attach it to a unified, real, world.

Goffman, although he does not go nearly as far as Derrida, seems to be aiming in much the same direction. His notion of all experience and perception as organised in terms of frames bears some resemblance to the quotation marks Derrida uses as a prop for his argument in *Eperons*, his essay on Nietzsche. However many degrees of complexity – of layerings – Goffman's transformed frames may have, there is always a "rim", by which the framed experience is "anchored" in the "real world" of ongoing events. But, as we shall see, the anchor often turns out to be lightweight, or easily displaced, and the reality of the world it is supposed to be anchored in is a matter of belief rather than unassailable fact.

So the deconstruction of "human interest" stories stands as a simple and readily accessible instance of the treatment Goffman wants to give to human experience in its entirety – or rather, to the world around us as we experience it. In *Frame Analysis*, he sets out to challenge universal and deeply entrenched beliefs about the nature of our experience of the world – or the nature of the world we experience: 'My concern', he says at one point, 'is to learn about the way we take it that our world hangs together' (p. 440). The key phrase here is, of course, 'the way we take it' – our ordinary, taken-for-granted view of how we experience the world around us and the events and activities which we initiate, take part in, and watch. His way of going about this is not to try to discover a meaning *underneath* what appears to be the case. What he does instead is to examine the different ways in which experience of the world comes to us, the different ways in which the world seems to "hang together" – and, as an aid to this, the ways in which it comes, or can be made to come, apart.

II

Most of the introductory chapter of *Frame Analysis* is taken up with Goffman's marking out his point of departure in phenomenology. He does so in traditional fashion, even to the point of finding fault with preceding attempts to redefine what we take to be the "reality" we experience and then informing the reader that the book is yet another analysis of what we take to be social reality.

Instead of seeking an answer to the question of *what* we experience and know ("What is *really* real?"), Goffman, following the track from metaphysics to epistemology increasingly preferred by Western philosophers since Kant, turns to the different, and 'much more manageable' question raised by William James: "Under what circumstances do we think things are real?" in which importance attaches to our feeling that some things are real and other things, somehow or other, are not. James himself tended to emphasise factors like selective attention, intimate involvement, and non-contradiction, but what was more important from Goffman's point of view is that he went on to make a stab at differentiating the several different "worlds that our attention and interest can make real for us". In other words, supplied by Aron Gurwitsch, James raised the possibility of there being a number of "orders of existence". Each order of existence, or "world" – scientific objects, abstract philosophical truths, myth – can have its proper being (or, perhaps, have a proper being conferred on it). "Each world, *whilst it is attended to*, is real after its own fashion; only the reality lapses with the attention."

At this point, Goffman accuses James of "copping out" in that, even though each world is "real" while it is attended to, "the world of the senses" is nevertheless accorded priority as that which 'retains our liveliest belief, the one before which other worlds must give way . . . James' crucial device', he says, 'was a rather scandalous play on the word "world" (or "reality").' Alfred Schutz, like James, gave priority to one particular realm – the "working world" this time. This is not good enough for Goffman. 'James and Schutz', he concludes, 'are unconvincing about how many different "worlds" there are and whether everyday, wideawake life can actually be seen as but one rule-produced plane of being, if so seen at all.' One is left, therefore, with the notion of there being a number of different worlds, from the everyday world to those of illusion or make-believe which we experience as in some way real *and* which are structurally similar, but with no way of using this structural similarity so as to throw more light on what we take to be everyday reality.

The primacy allotted to the ordinary and everyday by James and Schutz is admissible only as an 'operating fiction'. We take the "everyday" or "working" world as real because they are both comprehended within what he calls primary frameworks.

Goffman's own exposition begins in the second chapter, "Framing".

247

He gives no very clear definition of "frame", however. What we get is brief, to the point of being dismissively curt:

> Of course much use will be made of Bateson's use of the term 'frame'. I assume that definitions of a situation are built up in accordance with principles of organisation which govern events – at least social ones – and our subjective involvement in them; frame is the word I use to refer to such of these basic elements as I am able to identify. That is my definition of frame.
>
> (pp.10-11)

We are offered a few more scraps much later in the book. On page 345 we learn that frames organise involvement as well as meaning: any frame imparts not only 'a sense of what is going on' but also 'expectations of a normative kind as to how deeply and fully the individual is to be carried into the activity organised by the frame.'

Enlightenment does grow as one reads through the book, but I am not sure that it is ever complete. Most of the first four chapters, which contain the conceptual exposition, are taken up with further elaboration of the basic idea of framing. So we have perforce to go back to Bateson on framing. Goffman traces his concern with how experience is organised back to William James, Husserl, and Schutz. Bateson composed his own lineage for what he had to say about frames – a lineage which included Whitehead, Russell, Wittgenstein, Carnap, and Whorf. The last name is significant, for Bateson's own conceptual framework relates to communication, which is one action-level removed from the level of knowledge and experience to which Goffman's ideas refer. Bateson was building on ideas of communication, set theory and cybernetics which were "in the air" at the time (1952) when he began his researches on the behaviour of monkeys, otters and, eventually, dolphins; Goffman's, as I have mentioned, followed the wave of interest in both linguistic philosophy and phenomenology which affected social science and critical studies during the sixties and seventies.

Bateson says that his ideas about "frame" were sparked off by watching monkeys at the San Francisco zoo. He had gone there in order to determine whether or not animals were able to recognise the symbolic nature of the signs that they gave and received. "What I encountered at the zoo was a phenomenon well known to everybody: I saw two young monkeys *playing*, i.e., engaged in an interactive sequence of which the unit actions or signals were similar to but not the same as combat."[2] More to the point this must have been at least as evident to the monkeys as to their human observer. The only explanation, Bateson thought, must be that the monkeys were capable of exchanging signals which meant "this is play".

Combat can also be transposed in similar fashion into threat, in which a snarl, a clenched fist, or a step forward is aggressive in that it represents possible future aggression, but is not itself an attack. Bateson goes on to mention play-acting ("histrionics"), and ritual as further modes of transposing what is otherwise to be "taken for real". Each mode requires some sign to be communicated to some, if not all, others for it to be "taken for" the mode of action intended. When it comes to deception, however, things become complicated. And there are other "not to be taken for real" acts which also involve more subtle, even paradoxical, messages – acts ranging from "a playful nip" (which hurts as well as standing for the aggressive act which it fictionalises) to Hollywood films (in which we take what we see on the screen as both "for real" and fabricated).

Which brings Bateson to the discussion of frames and contexts. He uses the word itself to denote a signal message which, he says, is "metacommunicative". By this is meant either an explicit message or one implicit in what is happening which instructs the receiver or helps him to understand the messages (intentions) within the frame. Examples range from the punctuation marks which frame a parenthesis or a quotation on the printed page to "such complex metacommunicative messages as the psychiatrist's definition of his own curative role in terms of which his contributions to the whole mass of messages in psychotherapy are to be understood."[3]

Later, Goffman came round to adopting the word "metacommunication" himself, to refer to specific signs which tell the receiver how the message itself is to be taken, in terms of "frame" or "footing" (below, pp. 324-5) or how it relates to what is there, or happening, outside the "frame". Employing the conceptual apparatus – the discourse – developed or appropriated for the analysis of communication does lead to difficulties, though, as Goffman suspected. The trouble is that any ambiguity he thought he was avoiding returns when it comes to the frame analysis of talk. Hence the introduction of "footing" to indicate the understanding shared by speaker and hearers about the current frame in which interaction is occurring; a change in footing goes along with a change in frame (FT, 128).

Unfortunately, the whole topic is awash with ambiguity. One kind of metacommunicative signal, obviously, is designed to avoid any paradoxical messages, or doubts about their meaning; but another kind – and Bateson instances signals which denote "this is play" – may positively inject paradox or ambiguity into a sequence of acts, or provoke it. And what kind of message, "metacommunicative" or any other kind, is transmitted from sender to receiver in the case of a child playing on his own – or in the daydreams, role-distance gambits, and character-building exploits of grown-ups?

There are other complications, and deeper paradoxes. Gombrich, too, has discussed the significance of frames, and has remarked on the modes of transposition which translate one manifest reality into another. A broomstick, given a crudely carved head, with reins attached, can "become" a horse. It is not an image, a portrayal, or a specimen of a horse; all that is needed to translate the stick into a riding-horse is, "first, that its form [makes] it just possible to ride on it; secondly – and perhaps decisively – that riding matter[s]".[4] Gombrich's essay, "Meditations on a Hobby Horse", is itself a "play" on Swift's "Meditation on a Broomstick" which adopts Swift's model of vapid rumination but turns it to distinctly un-vapid ends. We have become accustomed to see a painted, framed, canvas as a window on a reality outside of itself. Yet

> The paradox of the situation is that, once the whole picture is regarded as the representation of a slice of reality, a new context is created in which the conceptual image plays a different part. . . . For that strange precinct we call "art" is like a hall of mirrors or a whispering gallery. Each form conjures up a thousand memories and after-images. No sooner is an image presented as art than, by this very act, a new frame of reference is created which it cannot escape. It becomes part of an institution as surely as does the toy in the nursery.[5]

Goffman, while elaborating the concept of frame well beyond what was comprehended within Bateson's own papers, did not depart very far from the original notion. He did drop the communicative aspects and the context of communication theory adopted by Bateson in favour of something closer to the "institution" Gombrich suggests, but a good deal of Bateson's "psychologism" remains. Goffman's "frame" incorporates much of what psychologists mean by "mental set" – the anticipatory response of an individual which is directed towards interpreting and assessing the situation so as to guide his own actions.

To regard perception as the active probing and testing-out of the environment is axiomatic for both "frame" and "mental set". Generalised schemata and prototypes composed out of previous experience are summoned as first approximations, then refined or amended as more information is added. On this basis, perception amounts to a series of reiterated endeavours to *recognise* what "it" is that is there or going on. The individual does so in terms of an elementary ordering of what he perceives or experiences which will, somehow, impart meaning to it.

III

As usual, Goffman seems to find the task of working out and defining (with copiously illustrated examples) the branches and subdivisions into which his interpretative schema is articulated much more to his liking than that of arguing out its rationale. Perhaps we are to take it that Bateson's essay provides authenticating authority not only for the basic notion but also for the way Goffman chooses to elaborate it. In any case, the detailed account of primary frameworks, keys and transformations, rekeyings, laminations, rims, brackets, and the different types of falsification takes up over a hundred pages of the book.

"Primary framework" is Goffman's term for the organising principle by which the world of "everyday reality" is, in Schutz's account, sustained by intersubjective understanding. There are two kinds of primary framework – natural and social. Natural frameworks are determined by the physical world, which is organised and, ultimately, vouched for by the interpretations given it by the natural sciences. This still makes it, of course, a human, mental, and therefore, eventually, social, construct, although Goffman does not say so. Neither does he say that the natural framework has some priority over the social, although it seems to be presumed in subsequent passages. Social frameworks, on the other hand, are best construed as background understandings which are basic to our reading of other people's motives and intentions. Social frameworks are the mental contexts in which events are interpreted as products of the 'controlling effort of an intelligence, a live agency, the chief one being the human being'. Imputing a specific motive and intention goes into selecting which of several social frameworks is applicable, and also brings in appraisal of actions in terms of their 'honesty, economy, safety, elegance, tactfulness, good taste, and so forth' (p. 22).

We apply notions of causality to both classes of primary framework, but, despite the primacy accorded to natural frameworks, the understanding which social frameworks allow for also includes 'patent manipulation of the natural world in accordance with its special constraints' (p. 23) as well as the variety of special personal and social worlds in which the actor can become involved.

Both primary frameworks, we are told, are to some extent integrated so as to form a 'framework of frameworks', and so constitute an element of central cultural importance to the social order in that it furnishes a common framework for the organisation of perception and experience. This might be construed as a concession to the idea that primary frameworks are somehow anchored in an intersubjective consciousness shared by members of the same cultural community, which would be a major concession to the Schutzian interpretation. And the remarks which conclude this section do nothing to recognise or to reconcile the different approaches: 'We tend to perceive events', he says (p. 24), 'in terms of primary frameworks, and the type of framework we employ provides a way of describing the event to which it is applied' – which gets us nowhere except into a tautological loop. (The issue is eventually resolved, but the reader has to wait for several hundred pages.)

Widely shared as they may be, and important to the safe conduct of our lives as they are, primary frameworks are yet susceptible to challenge and subversion. There are events, from miracles to feats of juggling, which lead spectators to doubt their own senses and suspect their overall approach to events to be profoundly flawed. Other events involve momentary loss of control of one's limbs or speech, and one's 'social framework', in which individual guidance and control are what makes sense of what is happening, is supplanted by a 'natural' one, with events totally conditioned by natural forces; Goffman calls them 'muffings', 'goofs', and 'gaffes'. And accident, good fortune, bad luck, or "sheer coincidence" are credited with producing significant events which ordinarily only occur through planning and organisation. In fact, Goffman suggests, 'muffings' and fortuitous occurrences are interpretations of the untoward, the unexpected, or the inexplicable that serve to preserve our belief that every event can be safely lodged in one or other category of primary framework.

Experiencing what exists and what is happening around us in a number of different ways amounts to saying that there are several different worlds of experience. There is, to begin with, the natural world of physical objects (including our own bodies and other people's) and of events and activities (including our own and other people's), and we tend to regard this as the real world – the *really* real world. But there are others which we experience as part of, or at least closely attached or geared to, the same world of natural events and social "goings-on" while treating them as worlds of a different kind. We accord no less "objective reality" to theatre, films, and television, although they make up what we treat as a make-believe world, or sub-world – a "realm" – of its own. Other realms of make-believe extend from children's play and playing the fool to elaborate, though innocuous, deception and day-dreaming. Sporting contests and games make up another realm; so do ceremonies. Again, there exists a whole range of activities which are not themselves regarded as "really real", but which reproduce activities which are: rehearsals, practice runs, demonstrations or exhibitions, and the like. All these realms are accorded a sort of experiential actuality, but the particular guise worn by actuality in each of them is different; it is sustained by our involvement in it for the time being, and our detachment, for the time being, from involvement in the world of natural objects and social goings-on to which we accord priority.

All of which hardly counts as news. We are all aware of how we can "lose ourselves" in a film, in day-dreams, in a game, in watching sports or a street fight, even – as Canetti pointed out some time ago – in simply being one of a crowd. While we do attach prior, or primordial, reality to the natural world and to the social life going on around us, and for the most part independently of us, we know that we can and do experience not only this "real" world but others at one, two, or several "removes" from reality. In each case we experience a distinctive sense of reality or unreality, each with a character of its own, and – importantly – with its own capacity to involve us in what is going on in it.

Mostly, however, we perceive the world around us, and what is going on in it, in terms of "primary frameworks": the "real worlds" of physical objects and of human action and happenings ("goings-on"). This is so insistently the case that, even when we find we are wrong – have been misled, are out of touch, or making false assumptions – we, and any others who may be involved, find it quite acceptable that it was, in a way, correct to assume what we did. After all, everybody tends to believe his own eyes – i.e. assumes that on the whole perception is isomorphic with what is perceived, as Goffman puts it – although he again dodges past the essential element of intersubjective cognition that has to be taken on board here. For his assumption of "isomorphism" is bound up with its ratification by 'any others who may be involved'.

Goffman, taking this as given, goes on to point to the other parallels and similarities – isomorphisms – we assume to exist between what we take to be the real world and the various less real, or unreal, worlds. He then moves on from the details of the character of these different worlds to the ability we have not merely to inaugurate and sustain them ("framing"), but to switch from one realm to another. We are also capable of transforming the activities we are experiencing in one realm into another with an altogether different mode, or "key" – using camouflage or mimicry to turn an innocuous sequence into one full of menace or combat into play, for instance. To organise what we are experiencing in terms of a distinct realm of being, or lived experience, segregated from other realms, ties in with the ability we also possess, knowing just what is involved, to create them for ourselves, and also to fabricate them, or to subvert their credibility, for others. This ability he calls 'keying'.

In Bateson's account of monkeys at play, real fighting clearly serve as a model, but actions stopped short of true aggression ("bitinglike behaviour occurs, but no one is seriously bitten"). When we come to consider what it is that distinguishes fighting from play, and how it is that all the participants engaged in play seem fully aware of the distinction, we have to assume some kind of transformation taking place by which activity becomes charged with the sense of "this is meant to be play" instead of "this is meant to be serious". There are in fact markers which show that the activity is being, and is taken to be, transformed in this way: the stronger participants forego their superior strength and competence; the expressiveness of some acts is exaggerated; there is a good deal of repetition, stoping and starting, and inconsequential activity.

There may be signs in addition to mark the beginning and end of playfulness (or any other kind of framed activity) for the benefit of others. These signalled limits Goffman calls 'brackets'. These are not always supplied, however; play is often a solitary and spontaneous performance, although others who turn up may be free to join in.

As Goffman points out, our ability to make similar transformations in speech is well known to linguists and, following Wittgenstein and

J. L. Austin, to philosophers. "Code" is the term most frequently used to identify the special ways of displacing utterances from their lodgment in everyday discourse. "Register", a linguistic term less popular now than it was, perhaps comes closest, referring as it does to 'the linguistic requirements of a particular kind of social occasion'. Goffman, however, wants a term that will apply the notion of displacement to all social behaviour, and chooses "key" – presumably to exclude any connection with linguistic and other meanings and references. "Key" he defines as 'the set of conventions by which a given activity, already meaningful in terms of some primary framework, is transformed into something patterned on it but is seen by participants as something quite else' (pp. 43-4). This definition is enlarged upon later, but not significantly added to, or amended. He admits that the word is not entirely apt, and a term with so specific and wide a use in a specialised context does, I think, become awkward, if not positively misleading, as he uses it. Changes of key hardly effect the fundamental changes in musical manner or content that he is looking for; modulation is, for example, actually integral to a Bach fugue.

Frames other than those comprised within primary frameworks apply to 'realms' rather than 'worlds' of experience. There are five major categories of such realms, most of them with several subcategories:

1. *Make-believe*, for example, includes day-dreaming and 'dramatic scriptings', as well as the playfulness which is central to this category. The term 'dramatic scriptings' itself covers not only theatre, TV, and radio, but books, newspapers, and magazines.
2. *Contest* features in most sports and games, which suggests that the model from which they derive is fighting, with rules and other limitations restraining both the degree and the mode of permitted aggressiveness.
3. *Ceremonies* (weddings, funerals, and other ritualised performances) are 'dramatic scriptings', too, but prearranged behaviour in these restricts the core activities to a single 'doing, to be stripped from the usual texture of events and choreographed to fill out a whole occasion. In brief, a play keys life, a ceremony keys an event' (p. 58).
4. *Technical redoings* are 'strips of what could have been ordinary activity . . . performed out of their usual context, for utilitarian purposes openly different from those of the usual performance';

255

subclasses include trial sessions, runthroughs and rehearsals. These are all directed towards improving "actual" performance; but there are also demonstrations or exhibitions, recordings, experiments, and role-playing sessions of the kind employed by some psychotherapists.

5. *Regroundings* apply to activities which upset some of the basic assumptions which ordinarily go to sustain any particular frame. They are activities in which the intentions or motives of one or more participants may be quite different from what is supposed to obtain ordinarily, as with gentry (or indeed royalty) acting as sales assistants at "charity bazaars", the well-to-do performing hard physical labour "for exercise", test-cases in law, and shills in fairgrounds and casinos.

All such "keyings" (i.e. situations, activities, and experiences at one or more removes from the primary frameworks of actuality) tend to be limited by their appropriateness, by standards of "good taste", and so on. The use of records of actual events in newspapers, film, sound recordings is limited by the rights – legal, political, moral – of the person or persons concerned.

With all the distinctions we now have between the realms of experience which are transposed by such "keys" and the actuality of the worlds of experience which belong to the primary frameworks themselves, it seems as if Goffman has deserted, or forgotten about, the stand he made against giving any priority to the "everyday" or "workaday" world we experience through primary frameworks. This is not the case, however.

Although all realms may generate involvement – indeed, must do so if they are not to seem entirely pointless – there is a suggestion that the absence of keying breeds a special awareness of primary frameworks. We are advised 'to be careful' and withhold judgment on this central issue on page 47: 'perhaps the terms "real", "actual", and "literal" ought merely to be taken to imply that the activity under consideration is no more transformed than is felt to be usual and typical for such doings'. But this only thickens the fog. We have in fact to wait until the end of the book before these ambiguities are finally resolved and the initial denial of priority to any "real" or "everyday" world is uncompromisingly reaffirmed.

Frameworks are comprehensive categories of experience and perception; the term is reserved mostly for primary frameworks. Frames are definitions of the situation by which we organise our knowledge and perception of "goings-on" around us, activities which are "guided", i.e. social, but include the physical objects present. Such goings-on are normally divided into more or less distinct strips of activity, but frame, and frameworks, may change even within the same strip, as with "We waited till the rain stopped and then started the game again" (p. 25), where there is a shift from a natural to a social primary framework.

Furthermore, 'a key can translate only what is meaningful in terms of a primary framework' (p. 81). Also,

> keyings seem to vary according to the degree of transformation they produce. When a novel is made into a play, the transformation can be said to vary all the way from loose (or distant) to faithful (or close), depending on how much liberty has been taken with the original text.
>
> (p. 78)

Keyings are themselves vulnerable to rekeying. A rekeying does its work not simply on something defined in terms of a primary framework but rather on a keying of those definitions (p. 81). The primary framework must still be there, else there would be no content to the rekeying, but it is the keying of that framework that is transposed.

When the idea of framing is expanded so as to include rekeyings as well as keyings we end up with a picture of successive transformations (keyings) laid on top of each other, with the original model, which is locked into one or other primary framework, at the base. The whole construction bears a close resemblance to Ryle's "pyramid" of increasingly sophisticated actions with each higher layer made feasible only because of all the layers of cognitive experience which have preceded it.

This impression is confirmed when Goffman goes on to say that it is the 'outermost layer' (the 'rim') which ties the whole activity to 'the real world'. In Ryle's account, what is actually happening (sc. "in the real world") is inherent in, and can only be understood as, what the actor means – his intentions.

It would all be clear enough, I believe, but for the example which Goffman gives – the rehearsal of a play – which seems to me to confuse things. The play, he suggests, could itself contain the rehearsal of a play as part of its text (as when Falstaff and Prince Henry rehearse the Prince's forthcoming interview with the King). Here, says Goffman, the rehearsal by the actors engaged for the play, and engrossed in what they are trying to achieve, represents the innermost core, and performing the play itself is the outermost lamination, the rim – which, I think, is the reverse of what one would look for from his analysis.

IV

Up to now, *Frame Analysis* has been concerned almost exclusively with setting out the basic assumptions and analytical procedures of what, once again, looks like an elaborate taxonomic enterprise. There has been little indication of what will be the point of it all beyond the claim that the phenomenological approach Goffman is adopting will reveal that how we perceive and experience the world around us is largely a matter of how our perceptions and experiences are organised. With Chapter 4, "Designs and Fabrications", there is a distinct change of gear. We find ourselves back in a world in which he has by now an established mastery – the world of pretence, false fronts, illusion, deception, and lifemanship. And what goes on in this world, as we have learned from his early essay "On Cooling the Mark Out" onwards, will be used as evidence to demonstrate how often our own everyday lives, experiences, and perceptions are compounded – necessarily and unavoidably, though mostly without conscious thought – of pretence, falsity, deceit, and so on. This is by no means the end of the account rendered in *Frame Analysis*, though. The whole book is an exercise in the deconstruction not only of lived experience – of the ways in which we grasp what is going on around us – but of subjectivity and the individual self.

Keying, by itself, shows that activity is open to transformation into quite another kind of felt, or perceived, experience. It now turns out that transformation includes fabrications: ways of inducing false beliefs in others about what is happening. In keying, all those present or participating share the same view of what is going on. When it comes to hoaxes, satire, "sending-up", camouflage, mimicry, illusions, "frame-ups", and a host of other kinds of fabrications, there is necessarily a distinction between those who are "in the know" and those who are not; the latter are 'contained' by the fabrication. The rim constructed for the frame is visible only to those who know of its construction, so that when the falsification is revealed to those contained by it, what seemed "real" is now wholly discredited.

Fabrications may be classified according to the numbers of people, the kind of things, and the time involved; here they are classed according to whether they are intended to be benign or exploitative. 'Benign fabrications' are those claimed, at least by their perpetrators, to be on behalf of the interests of the persons they are practised on, or at least not to be against them. They have a sort of social insurance cover in the understanding, first, that the victim will soon be let in on the joke and, second, that he can be relied on to take it "in good spirit" or "like a sport".

"Leg-pulls", practical jokes, and surprise parties come under the heading of benign fabrications. But so do the standard deceptions practised on terminally or dangerously ill patients by physicians and psychiatrists, and the same kind of excuse is often employed to defend the sometimes brutal hoaxes traditionally practised on new recruits in the army and the navy, and on apprentices in some trades. An even more dubious subclass are those deceptions performed in what are said to be the best interests of the individuals they are aimed at (or of society at large), but to which they might strenuously object if they had foreknowledge of what was really happening. One subcategory includes the kind of experiment routinely performed by academic psychologists on students and the public; Goffman himself clearly regards a large proportion of these as distasteful and hardly legitimate, even if legal, and they scarcely count as "benign", even on his reckoning. Withholding news or evidence from another that might distress him may count as ordinary tact, and even as a necessary precaution when practised by ships' masters or airline pilots on passengers, but all too often security personnel adopt the same kind of measures in dealing with the relatives of victims or suspects as well as with the public. (So do governments, one might add, in dealing with virtually anybody.)

Most of these cases do seem to stretch any prescription of what counts as "benign" to extravagant lengths. Many, if not most, of them raise questions about any assumption that their effect on the victim's interests is benign, or nul. It is an assumption which is certainly not valid in the case of "vital tests", the deceptions practised on unsuspecting individuals in order to test their loyalty and character, much used in spying circles – and by commercial organisations. 'What seems special about complex organisations is not that they employ vital tests, but that they can often manage to legitimate such activity' (p. 99).

One is on firmer ground when it comes to exploitative fabrications. But by now Goffman's interest lies in a further distinction which is more pertinent to the development of his analytical framework. This is the difference between direct and indirect fabrication.

There are, in principle, two parties in a direct fabrication: a fabricator and a dupe. There are some direct fabrications which attract prosecution or civil action at law: confidence tricks, false advertising, mislabelling, cheating at cards. Other practices – like the false official-looking letters employed in tracing runaways, absconding debtors, or husbands defaulting on maintenance claims – employ deceptions which hardly count as benign, but are legal, and even, as in the deceptions practised by big business and government, claimed as morally defensible.

Indirect fabrications are those which

engineer a definition of a second party in order to dupe a third party into certain false beliefs concerning the second. The second party – the victim – need not be taken in and indeed is unlikely to be. What is required is that the person who has been misrepresented be unable for some reason to convince the third party of the facts.

(p. 107)

The very possibility of indirect fabrication suggests that the notion of containment bears not so much on the fact of deception as on the relationship of the people involved. The classic example is the "frame-up" – creating a situation which provides an irresistible lure to engage in discreditable conduct – false witness, planting evidence, and other forms of entrapment. And false facts as well as true ones can allow their knower to blackmail a victim.

There are two points of interest in what he says by way of conclusion to this section. First: 'I have dwelt at length on indirect fabrications', he observes, 'because they provide a bridge from the houses of cards erected by con men to the lives of ordinary people.' His unceasing interest in the ways of criminals comes in here not so much to mirror the ways of everyday social behaviour in the rather sardonic manner of his earliest writings (although there is still a trace of that) but to bring out the identical nature of social practices on both sides of the curtain of morality and legality. It also underlines the critically important part played by the intentions of actors – although he tends to obscure this by referring to 'relationships'.

Second, there is an early hint of his ultimate definition of man as essentially *homo fabricator*.

> The reason why the individual can confidently continue to assume that others will feel that he is playing matters straight is not that he is – even if he is – but that no one has been motivated to organise information in order to render him discreditable.
>
> (p. 111)

This, too, has further implications; there is a subterranean link with the idea of mutual understanding which runs through the "Strategic Interaction" essay (though it was Schelling who made more of it). The mutual understanding so essential to all relationships – even adversarial ones – is not something which has to be actively created, promoted, and sustained for each and every occasion, in ad hoc fashion, but exists as a basic assumption of normal social intercourse.

What are called "understandable errors" stand apart from fabrications. We make allowances for being "betrayed by our senses" occasionally, while believing, at the same time, that this arises from special circumstances (dreaming while asleep, for example) and that more information (or simply waking up) will soon set things right. But there are self-deceptions for which allowances are not made, such as a propensity to lapse into what are labelled "dissociated states" and psychotic fabrications, where the individual presumably deludes himself not within a dream but within the world sustained by other persons. 'Since one of the upsetting things "psychotics" do is to treat literally what ordinarily is treated as a metaphor', psychotic tendencies of this kind may be seen, from the point of view of frame analysis, as situating him 'in the world of social frameworks and the real-life doings performed within these frames, but . . . in radically disqualifying terms' (p. 115).

This, in turn, brings up the question of how fabrications of any kind relate to the 'ongoing stream of wider social activity in which it occurs' (p. 116)? Bystanders who "happen to be present", including workmen and others with a right to be where they are, may of course know "what is really going on", but do not themselves have to become involved, even vicariously. Even those involved have a good deal of latitude in the degree of involvement they have in what is going on: 'There is hardly an encounter in which one participant doesn't exercise momentary tact in his treatment of the other, acting, in fact, as if he more approved of the other than is the case' (p. 117).

This is not an early-warning reference to a topic dealt with at length in Chapter 8 ("The Anchoring of Activity"), but a somewhat belated nod in the direction of there being rather more latitude and flexibility in social situations and social controls than he allowed for in his earlier writings.

To take Goffman's own example, although the 'sociable smile' offered by the manager of a shop to his customers 'can conceal some unsmiling concerns' (about shoplifting, among other things), 'it seems [nevertheless] that legitimate shoppers get used to this sort of thing . . . and accept the arrangement as not discrediting their relationships to management' (p. 119). In fact, such acceptance might well stem from a kind of watchfulness which affects everyday social interaction. There are two sources of this watchfulness. First, deceptions of all kinds often have strips of "straight" activity incorporated in them so as to lend greater verisimilitude. Second, caution is generated by our knowledge or experience of past deceptions, knowledge which is brought to bear on other activities – past, present, and future – having some resemblance to those which have been discredited.

No mention of this kind of watchfulness occurs (although it featured largely in *Relations in Public*). Attention is given, though, to suspicion and doubt, which are the two ways in which watchfulness surfaces in specific, conscious, terms. Suspicion 'is what a person feels who begins, rightly or not, to think that the strip of activity he is involved in has been constructed beyond his ken, and that he has not been allowed a sustainable view of what frames him'. Doubt is 'generated not by concern about being contained but concern about the framework or key that applies, these being elements that ordinarily function innocently in activity' (p. 122).

V

The one place in which we are relieved of suspicions and doubts about what it is that is going on is the theatre. It is not a difference in meaning, consequentiality, role performance, or even mode of presentation which distinguishes theatrical performances from ordinary everyday activity. What counts is the difference in frame. The keying of action from its primary framework of "real life" into the theatrical frame demands of the audience that they exclude any other possible frame than that of watching "a performance". This is what Coleridge's "willing suspension of disbelief" really amounts to. Any quandary which the actor's dual identity might pose for the audience is solved, not by immemorial convention which playgoers have to learn, but because, from childhood on, mimicry has familiarised us with the distinction between stage performer *propria persona* and the character he plays. (See below, p. 275.)

Chapter 5, in which the theme of theatrical performance is first broached, begins by counting up the differences between stage performance and other kinds of action. What is critically important is the discarding of that 'visual respect' which forbids us to stare at others or to examine their behaviour in all particulars. When they are stage performers, individuals become objects 'that can be looked at in the round and at length without offence' (p. 124). It is as if performers and audience existed in different realms of being – which they do, of course, in frame terms. The distinction between the two is reinforced by the licence the audience has to respond to what is happening on stage by laughter, applause, and even, in some cases, cries of encouragement or disapproval. Such responses are by convention treated not as interruptions or even interjections calling for any response by the stage performers but as simply not occurring at all (although at certain junctures audience applause may receive some acknowledgement). In the second place, the area within which the "players" perform is barred, physically and by social injunction, to people who make up the audience. And third, there are clear, firm, brackets to mark beginnings and endings, with final applause and curtain calls wiping the make-believe away.

While the theatre provides the normative frame, there are other kinds of staged performances to which, to some extent or other, the same frame applies. Goffman suggests a number of declensions from what he calls the 'purity' of staged and scripted performance, 'purity' standing for the degree to which the watchers' claim on the activity they watch excludes the claims of any other possible frame: 'No audience, no performance.' 'Pure' performances may be taken to include variety acts, personal appearances of various sorts, the ballet, and much of orchestral music. Other kinds of performance, to which later sections of the book refer, are, in descending order of "purity":

1. Contests or matches when presented for viewing. Here the degree of "impurity" relates to the extent to which the contestants act as if it were the outcome of the contest that drives them, not the social occasion or the ticket money. "Purity" in these cases (i.e. those features which are independent of the performance aspects) is

bolstered by the paraphernalia of leagues and rankings, prizes, and the like.

2. Private ceremonies, like weddings and funerals, which 'tend to provide a ritual ratification of something that is itself defined as part of the serious world'.

3. Lectures and talks – a more heterogeneous class, in that instruction, and entertainment are present in varying mixes.

4. "Work performances" are, he says, the most "impure" of all, in that arrangements are made for spectators in specially prepared places on some construction sites, or on "conducted tours" of factories or prisons by employers or authorities who are third-party to performers and audience. Perhaps the archetypal case is that of the "invisible menders" who used to do their work on show in the display windows of shops.

The first and critically important difference between theatrical performance and the ordinary goings-on of "real" life lies in the fact that the action portrayed by a stage play is planned beforehand. Actors, director, playwright, and all backstage contributors and participants share the same fund of information – about 'why events have happened as they have, what the current forces are, what the properties and interests of the relevant persons are, and what the outcome is likely to be' (pp. 133-4). This is in contrast to the everyday world of real events, where an individual may be able to predict some natural events with a fair amount of certainty, but interpersonal outcomes are necessarily more problematic – even more so where his own future is concerned. But with a stage play it is the audience which is contained; all those who are party to the staging of the performance have some opportunity to "play the world backwards". (See above, p. 101.)

On the other hand, while their information about what is going on is more nearly complete that in real life, the players must, for the action on stage to make sense, act as if they had different and less complete information states. 'In brief, each character at each moment is accorded an orientation, a temporal perspective, a "horizon"' (p. 134). Moreover, within the frame of the play, 'the performers can be seen to be playing at containing each other' (p. 135), so that the fabrication itself (the play) becomes keyed by each of the players. Second, there is the fact that audience, too, is allotted a particular information state by the playwright which is different from his and from that acted out by the players. The oddity is that this holds good even when the play is one well known to the audience, for 'being part of the audience in a theatre obliges us to act as if our own knowledge, as well as that of some of the players, is partial. . . . We actively collaborate in sustaining this unknowingness' (p. 136) at the same time as knowing perfectly well that what is going on before us is not real life.

Clearly, the complexities of the theatrical frame go well beyond what is involved in simple keyings or straightforward fabrications. There is a sizeable 'corps of transcription practices' required to transform 'a strip of offstage, real activity into a strip of staged being' (p. 138). Goffman lists a few of the more familiar conventions of the picture stage theatre of the nineteenth and early twentieth centuries:

1. a clearly marked arbitrary boundary for the world of the play, with the front of the stage constituting an imaginary "fourth wall";
2. players positioning themselves so as to face the audience as well as – or in preference to – each other;
3. speaking in turn, without breaking into one another's lines, although scripted and rehearsed parts of the action may include "interruptions", "confused talk", "uproar", and the like;
4. giving the audience all the information it needs to follow the action, but incidentally, or covertly, so that 'the fiction can be sustained that it has indeed entered into a world not its own' (p. 142);
5. "heightened" speech (carefully articulated and projected); interaction on stage "fraught" with significance, 'on the assumption that nothing that occurs will be unpretentious or insignificant' (p. 143).

This last convention has some special interest, for conversation on stage, however "fraught", has to be conducted nevertheless in the manner of actual face-to-face conversation, in which much, if not most, or all, the content is of little consequence as information bearing on relationships or future action. What the audience is to attend to is pre-selected.

However, when Goffman says that 'the theatrical frame is something less than a benign construction and something more than a simple keying' (p. 138), he is either missing his own point or being deliberately misleading. For what we have been presented with so far is something completely different from either. Theatrical performances are a sort of make-believe which is foisted on, *and* fostered by, their audience. *Foisting* the make-believe of a play on an audience is accomplished by a remarkable synthesis of practised deceptions, the surreptitious conveyance of significant (and the suppression of insignificant) information, and a set of assumptions contained in the conventions observed by both players and audience. On the other hand, the make-believe and all that goes to sustain it is *fostered* by the remarkable capacity audiences have for becoming engrossed in a 'transcription that differs radically and systematically from an imaginable original' (p. 145). One might also observe that all this applies, *a fortiori*, to painting, which Goffman does not mention. It applies to a lesser degree to radio drama and novels, which he does.

The foundations of the conceptual structure Goffman is building are really complete by the end of Chapter 4; the next chapter, "The Theatrical Frame", lays the foundations for later excursions into the more complex varieties of framing and fabrication, for much of which dramatic writings and performances provide the most handy illustration and evidence, because they are either published or familiar to most readers.

The real complications begin with Chapter 6. What we have by way of conceptual foundation is, at its simplest, the two primary frameworks: *natural* and *social* (or 'guided'); and the two types of transformation: *keyings* (replications of a model in a different key, but with everybody concerned knowing about it), and *fabrications* (replications of an 'actuality' when some are and some are not aware of the transformation which the current 'actuality' has undergone). Fabrications are commonly, but not always, deceptions practised by the knowing on the unknowing, who are thereby 'contained' by the fabrication.

With this as the conceptual baseline, we are now to consider the fact that what has been transformed in terms of key or fabrication may be transformed again – and again and again. What is more, what has been keyed may be fabricated, and what was fabricated may be keyed. Goffman's examples may help:

> The sawing of a log in two is an untransformed instrumental act; the doing of this to a woman before an audience is a fabrication of the event; the magician, alone, trying out his new equipment, is keying a construction [fabrication], as he who provides direction for the trick in a book of magic, as I am in discussing the matter in terms of frame analysis. An Avis girl serving a customer generates a simple bit of social reality; when a company agent is sent around incognito to see if service standards are being maintained (if indeed this spying happens), a vital test

occurs, a transformation of what others contribute to her straight activity into a fabrication.

(p. 157)

Further, when all this is conveyed to us by a full-page Avis advertisement, 'we are looking at a keying of a fabrication'.

Each successive transformation, keying or fabrication, counts as a layer, or lamination, with some untransformed reality lying at the core, and the outermost layer (which establishes the reality status of the whole activity) as the rim of the frame. Goffman lists three types of forms of 'recontainment', i.e. of transformations which involve several layers, *two* of them being fabrications.

The first type includes many which are, officially or unofficially, standard practice in contemporary society, notably spying on welfare claimants, the secret monitoring of gamblers in casinos, wiretapping. The premise is that the person under surveillance is secretly engaging in some malpractice, which covert monitoring will uncover, and the subject at least discredited and possibly penalised or prosecuted. In fact, Goffman points out, it is a basic premise of social life that secret monitoring constitutes a violation of personal integrity. This, it is worth while remarking, also goes for people of unchallenged rectitude – those whose life is "an open book". We all, in fact, take such precautions as we can afford to ensure privacy; the "open book" is available only to licensed borrowers.

A second type, popularly attributed to political, criminal, and industrial intrigue, is by no means confined to it. Organisations, governments, criminal networks and law-enforcement agencies may be betrayed by an "undercover" spy introduced into them as a member or someone with the right credentials. Journalists sometimes practise the same sort of penetration – as do some social scientists engaged in "participant observation". This is not the end of it, however, for in everyday life gossip, and the disclosure of matters thought by the family, organisation, or group to be private to them may be read as betrayal.

Enticing potential offenders into committing an offence (entrapment) constitutes the third type. Like the others, it is regarded as a device especially favoured by law-enforcement officers of all kinds, although, again, it is also said to be practised by journalists.

While recontainment techniques are often treated as acceptable and even commendable when their use is backed by government departments and directed towards the unmasking of the more obnoxious kinds of criminal behaviour, they remain questionable in ethical terms – if only because, without the licence claimed, or assumed, to exist in the ultimate objective of enforcing the law, some agents' own actions would be illegal and all of them treacherous.

The legal and moral licence claimed for "recontainment" practices, Goffman points out, derives from the conventions of framing; the presumption is that, rather as a game, or "play" does, 'it insulates a misrepresenter from the immorality of misrepresentation' (p. 175). But recontainment by these devices, if discovered by the intended dupe, may itself be recontained, and quite simply. All that the target individual or group need do then is to carry on as though unsuspecting, and, by leading their monitor, infiltrator, or entrapper astray, turn the tables and reverse the frame. 'Such containing of recontainment is something more layered than the Big Con' (p. 178).

The vulnerability of recontainment strategies to further recontainment and frame reversal can lead to mutual and sequential containments of the intricate kind which are the stuff of popular spy fiction. But the question does arise of how many laminations a strip of activity may sustain. Obviously, an end is reached when no one involved is able to trust anyone else, and the mutual understanding essential to any kind of relationship or negotiation is lost. In other cases, of transformations in which the outermost layer – the rim – is keying or merely a harmless fabrication, the layering may go to extravagant lengths. Goffman cites the "play within a play" in *Hamlet* as a case in point, but Tom Stoppard's *Rosenkrantz and Guildenstern Are Dead*, with its own added fabrication of the play's action occurring in the interstices of the original *Hamlet*, is the true showpiece of this particular genre.

There seems in fact virtually no limit to the number of laminations which can be added before it all ends in confusion or stalemate. The number is irrelevant, though. What matters is whether all participants can count on producing the effects, and the responses from others, that they intend by their actions. And this is precisely what happens when everybody – performers and audience alike – is educated, in Ryle's sense (see p. 44), to the requisite level of sophistication, a level which by definition comprehends all the previous levels of learned competence and knowledge, and is intent on maintaining the structure of the fabrication.

The 'great lesson' lies first of all in the speed and facility with which 'the audience can follow along and read off what is happening by attending to the relevant framing cues' (p. 186) and, in the second place, in the unquestioning assumption by the playwright and the whole theatrical ensemble that the audience can and will do so.

NOTES AND REFERENCES

1. J. P. Stern, *A Study of Nietzsche*, Cambridge Univ. Press, 1979, p. 65.
2. G. Bateson, "A theory of play and fantasy" (1954), in *Steps to an Ecology of Mind*, Paladin Books, 1973, p. 152.
3. G. Bateson, "A theory of play and fantasy" (1954), in *Steps to an Ecology of Mind*, Paladin Books, 1973, p. 161.
4. E. Gombrich, *Meditations on a Hobby Horse*, Phaidon Press, 1963, p. 7.
5. E. Gombrich, *Meditations on a Hobby Horse*, Phaidon Press, 1963, pp. 10-11.

10
THROUGH THE
LOOKING-GLASS

The seventh chapter ("Out-of-Frame Activities") of *Frame Analysis*, leads into a second principal concern of the book, which is to reveal theatrical performance as originating in the management of the self, not the reverse, as *The Presentation of Self* made out. This is a radical change. We are no longer dealing with theatrical performance as a metaphor for individual behaviour; it is simply a heightened version of it. Staged performance, now, is worth close examination precisely because, since it is consciously planned, written out, and projected into a special objectivity of its own, it provides easy access to the study of the intrinsic character of individual activity and experience.

There is another side to the coin. In the final chapter of the book, we are told that the everyday activity we think of as "real life" and the world of common experiences we take to be "reality" are best construed as social constructs. It is as if the world of being we take to be the world of everyday reality were itself contrived to "act natural" and "be natural", and as such best regarded in the same terms as those realms of being we see as make-believe or fabricated.

Frame analysis serves both to connect the "theatricalised" experience of the self with the surrender by the everyday world of objects and activity of the primacy which we tend to accord to it and to explain why it is that belief in a "real world" has to be surrendered. We are able to see this because of the many mistakes in framing that occur. Many of these may be, and usually are, passed over as transitory or insignificant errors, but when those concerned happen to be more than ordinarily involved in what is happening, they can be disconcerting or bewildering. The immediate consequence of bewilderment about what is going on – when our experience, as Goffman puts it, seems to have been "negated" – is an abrupt increase in involvement; the need to know what is *really* going on becomes acute.

It is precisely this increase in involvement which is aimed at in the theatre and in staged performances of different kinds. It is a purpose which becomes even more obvious in a variety of theatrical devices, some of which go back to classical drama, although Pirandello is usually acknowledged to be the master-hand. Yet, as we well know, negative experiences are not confined to the theatre. Doubts and suspicions about what is happening can arise in any number of circumstances, especially when the information on which we base our understanding of them is minimal, or deliberately restricted, or regarded as a valuable commodity in itself, or, as can happen, fabricated.

Framing – the cardinal principles on which we organise our experience – is inherently fragile and vulnerable. Even what we take to be guarantees of the validity of our experience, or the "connectives" in normal use by way of verification can be converted into instruments for playing them false.

Finally, we are returned to William James' question, of just how it is that we take what is around us as "real", with Goffman supplying a very different answer.

I

We begin, then, with the relationship of activity which is framed to what lies outside it. Ordinarily, there is plenty of unframed action which is concomitant with, and sometimes contributory to, what is going on inside the frame. This clearly applies to staged performances too, even though they make demands on performers which compel them to suppress all side-involvements, ignore distracting noises or movements, and conceal inadvertent body movements and noises. While such "disattend" tracks are many and varied, some of them are extremely consequential in regard to the various components and phases of activity in frame, 'regulating, bounding, articulating, and qualifying it' (p. 210). Here Goffman incorporates what Bateson has to say about "metacommunication", although for the time being he prefers to speak of 'directional tracks' and 'back channels', Bateson's term not becoming acceptable Goffmanese until *Forms of Talk*. The central element consists of 'paralinguistic and kinesic cues' which provide two-way channel qualifiers, markers, and the like in conversation. Gestures can make the same contribution, and cues like nods, head-shakes, and murmurs 'which tell a speaker that he is or isn't being listened to', warn him that the listener wants to take his turn in talk, and so forth.

Still, there are limits – a kind of 'evidential boundary' – to what any participant is able to observe of what is going on in the vicinity. This opens up the possibility of a 'concealment track'. It has an obvious affinity within the 'backstage' of *The Presentation of Self*, but concealment now applies also to what is going on *inside* the actor. His outside serves as a screen for activities he wants to conceal, just as his body may conceal what is happening on the other side of him. Clearly, the concealment track is of major importance in exploitative fabrications, and in "behind the scenes" activities of all kinds, but it has to be employed whenever an individual feels obliged to conceal his "real" thoughts and feelings, or his "real" intentions – whenever, for example, tact is called for in social interaction.

The secondary structure of subordinate channels is, like everything else that enters into framing, capable of itself being transformed. Channels – subordinate tracks – ostensibly for dealing with one kind of activity, once they are established, may be exploited for other purposes. For example, the minor adjustments to comfort which good manners permit can, and often do, serve as subtle directional cues which the actor can draw upon to establish an alignment to the situation that he can disclaim if necessary, and which an audience, or his companions, can ignore. There are other forms of feedback: 'the "takes", "burns", "fishy looks", glowerings, and various expressions of sympathy and agreement' (p. 221). And, third, there is the whole battery of half-empty, behind-the-back, gestures reviewed in "The Underlife of a Public Institution" (above, p. 153), by which losers of all kinds – children, underlings, inmates – try to save face.

Again, there are occasions when "actual" activity is recorded, or filmed, or overheard, and so made the subject of instantaneous transformation. Such occasions, in creating the special status of onlooker for people present but not directly involved in the action, turn an accident, a quarrel, a chase, into a performance. It is the presence and the participation of an audience which is the essential ingredient. It is the same kind of transformation which happens with games, where, once again, activity pursued for its own sake becomes a *spectacle* for outsiders to watch.

Theatrical performances proper afford spectators a larger role, since the activities on stage are geared to audience response, and designed to facilitate its perception. Once again, however, this kind of transformation caters for some manipulations of the facilities which it affords. There are 'editorialising functions' for mediating between players and audience: prologues and epilogues, a chorus, soliloquies, a character offering informative comments in asides, explanations to other actors ('a footnote that talks'). The argument is that re-created material, especially dramatic scriptings, allows subordinate channels of interaction themselves to be staged – i.e. incorporated in the performance. Parallel conventions exist for the printed work.

Chapter 8 contains a recital of the ways in which the very connectedness of framed experience to any environing "reality" can mislead. Activities, however subject to transformation, have to take place in the world of natural objects and ongoing social activity. 'Fanciful words can speak about make-believe places, but these words can only be spoken *in* the real world.'

We are brought back to the book's starting-point, with Goffman reintroducing William James' question of "Under what circumstances do we think things are real?" Having dismissed James' answer as 'inadequate', Goffman's own answer is, quite simply, that we do not know. James' "principles of convincingness" (or 'whatever it is that generates sureness') are 'precisely what will be employed by those who want to mislead us' (p. 251). There are plenty of circumstances in which it is possible to *think* things are real, but none in which we can know *for certain* that they are. In framing a strip of reality, we have, at the same time, to anchor the strip to what went before, what comes next, and whatever may be going on around us.

Consistency between all these elements is built into the framing of experience. So the fact that they are all consistent with each other is no guarantee of their "reality". The process of framing incorporates whatever of the environing world we need in order to organise, and understand, what is going on in that part of the world we have reserved for our special attention; it has, Goffman says, a 'recursive' character.

We have therefore to look more closely at the ways in which the activity which is "in frame" is connected with ('anchored in') ongoing activity around it. All are suspect.

In any activity (Goffman instances a game of chess, but one can think of a job interview, a journey by air, a fight), the persons directly involved and any bystanders, companions, or others present but not directly involved have some common understanding of where the claims of the ongoing world leave off and where the claims of the activity take over. This understanding is both part of what the persons directly involved bring to the activity from the outside world, and a necessary constituent of that activity. It is almost complementary to the concept of involvement developed in "Fun in Games", where onlookers and bystanders as well as players are all affected, although the game may amount to no more than a side-involvement for some.

Even with a game of chess, to take Goffman's own example, there are resources, like lights, room space, and time needed, other people's rights, for example to stand by and watch, or, in certain circumstances to interrupt, or to ask the players to postpone or shift, perhaps to inform others of their whereabouts, and so on. The very points at which activity inside the frame leaves off and the external activity takes over – the rim of the frame itself – becomes, for the participant, 'classed with other "comparable" activities and taken into his framework of interpretation, thus becoming, recursively, an additional part of the frame' (p. 249).

Of course, very many framed activities, especially the more routine or significant of them, are carried on amidst the enormous complex of resources and services, both material and institutional, which contemporary society holds ready and available for use. This means that connections between any framed activity and the ongoing world of events outside it can be made instantly and without our giving much thought to them. It is only on rare occasions that we become aware of any transition beyond the rim of framed activity to the ongoing world of objects and events outside. On the other hand, there are certain conventional markers which are used to designate beginnings and endings of strips of activity designed for specific frames, there are certain understandings used to preserve a sense of connectedness even when disconnectedness seems manifest and, ultimately, there is the sense of continuity which is ensured (we think) by the presence of the same self in everything we do, every role we assume, and every relationship we sustain.

Goffman distinguishes five different kinds of connection, or of basis for connection, between activity frame and the environing world of things and events. He calls them 'episoding conventions'; 'appearance formulas'; 'resource continuity'; 'unconnectedness'; and 'the human being'.

1. *Episoding conventions* are (metacommunicative) boundary markets which distinguish activities framed in a certain way – particularly those requiring some sort of planning and organisation by a group

or agency – from the flow of events around them. They are both temporal and spatial: the frame of a picture, the tuning up of an orchestra, the handshake at the commencement of a bout in boxing, the vestibule of a theatre just before a performance. The bracketing of a play, or sporting contest, lecture, etc., within the frame of the occasion as a whole enables the inner frame – for the events which endow the occasion with its significance – to generate 'a realm that is more narrowly organised' (more definitely and securely framed) 'than that represented by everyday life' (p. 262).

2. *Appearance formulas* refer to the sort of conventions by which a distinction – and also a connection – is held to exist between an individual person, actor, or player and the particular part, role or function he is currently adopting. There is a general understanding that 'a given individual can perform different roles in different settings without much embarrassment about its being the same individual', an understanding that covers even getting different roles entangled with each other (as when a salesman is faced with a relative, or some notable person, as a customer). For, when he assumes a role, an individual does not take on a different identity, with a different biographical past, or a new character, but simply a *social* identity, 'a bit of social categorisation' (p. 286). There are also what Goffman calls 'out-of-role rights' (p. 275). Apart from the calls of other roles which an individual might bring into play – of the kind featured in "Role Distance" – these 'out-of-role rights' are brought to bear on the situation when someone overacts or guys the part he is playing. One can also point to the growing fashion for "informality", in which the conventional attributes of a role are shed in favour of those of personal identity, or "character".

3. *Resource continuity* refers to *belief* in the 'permanent residual character' of the world around us. It rests on the fact that whatever goes to make up an interpreted and organised stream of activity must somehow go back into the outside world from which it came. Times when it may be impossible to prove that something has occurred are profoundly upsetting – a circumstance of which fiction-writers have made much use.

4. This belief in the continuity and permanence of the environing world is backed up by a kind of fail-safe belief – an all-in insurance cover. "*Unconnectedness*" stands for a residual understanding that there are elements in the immediate environment which are unconnected and irrelevant to the matter in hand. When this

assumption about "unconnectness" breaks down, and what was thought unconnected proves relevant, perhaps especially so, words like luck, accident, negligence, coincidence, happenstance, are brought into use.

5. Lastly, the "*Self*" – the ultimate guarantee that what people do, and what events befall them, are anchored to the world around us. The self, we believe, is an abiding presence behind any role that may be assumed.

Warned by an ironic 'three cheers for the self' (p. 294), the reader is presented with testimony which challenges such confidence. The first item – once again drawn from theatrical, or para-theatrical, performance – is one attested by audience familiarity with films and television series in which the "personality" of an actor is discernible behind all the different roles he sustains. The discrepancy between the two is something which, supposedly, generates in the viewer an appreciation of the performer as a "character" in his own right, so to speak. With growing sophistication, however, audiences come to be well aware that this self, this apparently more personal character, is itself assumed for the purposes of performance. Much the same kind of thing can happen between readers and writers.

These observations apply, strictly speaking, only to the world of theatre and published writings. But the same sort of discrimination manifests itself between the individual as a person with an enduring identity and the role he happens to be playing at the moment, even in ordinary face-to-face interaction between people. This is not a matter of duplicity, or of "showing-off" or even of "presenting" oneself in the sense intended by the earlier book. There is 'a sense of the person behind the role' (p. 298), and of a difference between the two – of the kind discussed in "Role Distance" (*E*, 152) – which can only be produced by what is happening in the immediate situation. What we have to remember is that when a stage actor builds up in his audience a sense of the part he is playing as a character, with all the qualities a genuine individual might possess, he does so with no more resources at his disposal than we have; the materials he has for creating his "genuine" self are in fact precisely the same as we have when we create our "natural" one.

But this is only one of the many deceptions other people can practise on us. The subject of the chapter is the reliance that we place on the self for the continuity of the world around us.

II

Having examined the way in which our framed experiences are anchored to the ongoing world around those experiences – and having also established that the anchors are fairly insecure – Goffman turns to those circumstances in which, even though he is not the victim of deception, an individual's perception of what is happening may be dislodged from his assumption that he knows just what it is. "Misframings" of different kinds make up a special category of situations which are innocent of deception and are yet liable to be discredited.

1. *Ambiguities* relate simply to the puzzlement that sometimes arises in an encounter about just how the situation should be defined. Puzzlement may be either of the "what in the world is going on?" kind, which involves ambiguities about primary frameworks, such as "being deceived by one's senses", for example. Or, more simply, it may come from uncertainty as to which of two possible definitions really applies, whether some fabrication is involved, and an accident which seemed fortuitous was not intentional.

2. *Errors in framing* are of different kinds. "Framing errors" involving primary frameworks are the most serious – i.e. tend to have the more awkward or embarrassing sequels. The difficulty can become acute 'in circumstances where we feel a natural framework alone ought perhaps to override social ones', when what we thought dead is really alive (or ground we though safe becomes alive with danger). "Mistaken identity" errors are of much the same kind, except that they are about individual physical components (persons as well as objects) of a scene.

   "Keying errors" come in two forms' "downkeying" (a passer-by who misreads a street scene of police pursuing thieves performed as part of a film and joins in all too successfully), and "upkeying" (someone taking a direful or threatening event as a joke).

   "Tracking errors", lastly, are those framing errors which have to do with the organisation of activity into main and subsidiary tracks. Thus, the "disattend" track may be misused, and events or actions (such as a cry for help) treated as out-of-frame when they are very much part of it; mistaken assumptions (by a television or radio performer, for example) about private comments and gestures being confined to a "concealment" track may lead to their becoming embarrassingly public.

3. *Frame disputes* are those arguments, or contests, which arise over what framework or transformation ought to be applied or what, if any, misframing was involved. Some are comparatively easy to settle because one side admits to having made a mistake. Others may be settled eventually because one of the versions counts as the "official" one ("vandalism" v. "innocent horseplay", "shoplifting" v. "absent-mindedness", for example). Still others, however, arise from frame failures which have to do with misconceptions dealt with earlier: "muffings", and the life, chance connectedness, suspicions of being deceived, ambiguity and error. In all such cases, frame failures cut the individual off – if only momentarily – from confirmation from what is going on around him that he is correctly involved with it.

Mistakes may be admitted, but it often happens that they are admitted on both sides, the first by way of excusing himself, the other in mitigation of the other's error. 'So again a frame debate may ensue, the parties now agreeing as to how matters ought to have been perceived, differing only in their views as to why they weren't' (p. 323).

Our perceptions and experience are anchored – or we believe them to be anchored – in the reality of ongoing things and events. There are, it seems, three kinds of grounds on which our confidence is founded. First, along with all the complexities and niceties of framing goes a finely tuned capacity for discriminating among them. Next, we are surrounded by other individuals who, ordinarily, go along with our perceptions of what is happening and whose behaviour, if there is a discrepancy, serves to warn us of it. Lastly, while the overall framework of the framing arrangements common to all of us seems to be as unquestioned as our shared cosmological beliefs, it does in fact have a sizeable institutional backup – and what we take to be an ultimate court of appeal. This, says Goffman, scepticism held (ominously) in abeyance for once, is the established authority of science and of the generally accepted world-view, together with the host of intermediaries who act as guardians of the educational system, organised religion, and public opinion.

Nevertheless, while it is exceptional to find ourselves in the wrong, it is always possible for our *framing* of events to lead to ambiguity, error, and frame disputes. Framing is susceptible to a number of vicissitudes; one can be mistaken about the appropriateness of a frame, find ambiguities about it, or have its appropriateness disputed. All these 'ordinary troubles', as Goffman calls them, are encountered incidentally, and dealt with briefly and immediately or, in the case of disputes, resolved by informal agreement or formal adjudication. But there are other frame disturbances which cannot be disposed of quite so easily and may therefore give rise to some consternation. They may be caused either by accident or by intention, but the bewilderment or annoyance which they arouse comes from the fact that any framed activity is one in which an individual is also psychologically involved.

For the individual, the meaning to be accorded to an activity is established by its frame, be it "accurate" (i.e. with a primary framework shared by all other individuals present or somehow related to what is going on), or fabricated (produced by deception, delusion, or illusion). But involvement also comes into it, although it is something of which the individual is usually unconscious, at least in part. (To attempt to focus one's feelings and attention intentionally would require one to shift one's involvement on to the effort to do so.)

The degree of involvement varies widely. It carries with it an interlocking (intersubjective) obligation, so that in all cases there is some socially prescribed degree of involvement, or upper and lower limits to it, supported by the normative expectations of other participants. Any lapse affects others.

It follows that 'breaking frame' – any occurrence out of frame which disturbs the balance of participant involvement and cannot be ignored, controlled, or handled in some agreed fashion – may well lead to bewilderment and annoyance.

1. *Accidental disengagement.* This is best identified from occasions in theatrical and broadcast performances, which are by definition planned to ensure that the character being performed is acting compatibly with the setting and the rest of the action. A misread cue, a "sound effects" failure, or any other of a dozen possible mishaps may make it impossible for the scene or the script to sustain the frame of the show. Of course, scripted performances can override frame breaks in unruffled fashion – just as, in real life, we can sometimes "carry things off ".

2. *Flooding out.* Once again pressed back into service, "flooding out" stands for the kind of disengagement manifested by, in some cases, running away from some happening 'in panic and terror', and in others 'by dissolving into laughter or tears or anger' (p. 350). But there are recognisably standard circumstances which provoke flooding out short of these two extremes: children or youngsters having to adopt a role (in a classroom play, or as participant in a

formal ceremony) in which they feel intrinsically not themselves. There is a common reaction to physical self-restraint demanded for a portrait, a fitting, or an inspection parade, which is to turn the occasion into a joke, and so make laughing or giggling permissible. Once again, faced with the impossibility of maintaining a staged role, or "stagey" behaviour, an individual finds it preferable to project a wholly fictional self and to guy *that* rather than to perform a role before an audience all too well aware of the limitations of one's resources in presenting a role and sustaining a "personal" character behind it (above, p. 275). Finally, there are those occasions – first hearing himself on a tape recording or seeing himself on film – when an individual is confronted with a duplicate self. In all these instances, Goffman is arguing, flooding out occurs as a (rather desperate) escape from a situation which has become unmanageable because it is, or has become, outside the limits of the frame, or of the personal identity sustaining it.

3. *Flooding in.* By extension, a similar construction can be put on occasions when someone seemingly outside an activity in progress is suddenly revealed as an unsuspected participant. It is the reaction to such occurrences which is labelled 'flooding in'.

4. *Dislodgment.* Of course, flooding out or flooding in are not the only possible ways of responding. "Downkeying" occurs when a performer gets "carried away" by his part, when a children's game gets "out of hand", or – something once familiar in the nineteenth-century theatre or the early days of cinema, now commonplace at football matches – when members of the audience try to take an active part in the performance. "Upkeying", in the same context, can occur in gambling sessions which 'degenerate', with bigger and bigger bets being placed on worse and worse odds, 'to the accompaniment of increasing laughter' (p. 366), and in theatres and cinemas when the audience breaks into laughter at the more "serious" episodes of a play or a film. In both kinds of instance, the individuals concerned stay within the organisation of the role adopted for the activity but the key shifts. It is not that the downkeying or upkeying that occurs is intentional. What happens is that they become dislodged from commitment to the beliefs and feelings of those employing the frame and who are presumed to have prescribed its limits and organised the level of commitment to them. Once dislodged in this way, the same individuals have to find a new organising frame by adding more transformation layers or subtracting them.

Scripted presentations of stage, film, and television, and the unscripted but programmed presentations of sporting contests seem more vulnerable to flooding out and key shifting than any other kind of social activity. It may well be that this is because their frame structure is so much more complex. Looking at individuals as performers is a very different matter from looking at them "in real life" – i.e. when situated in a primary framework. They are located in a different realm. 'Amateur and professional sports share the interesting feature that they can be looked at', so long as the looking is done on ski slopes, golf courses, and other locales which have been appropriated and equipped for that particular purpose. For 'if the same person were sitting in a park, reading, he would be protected from being stared at – at least in this way' (p. 373).

III

The chapters on "Ordinary Troubles" and "Breaking Frame" dealt with the accidental errors and misconstructions to which the organisation of perception and experience is liable. With Chapter 11, "The Manufacture of Negative Experience", and Chapter 12, "The Vulnerabilities of Experience", we move on to the ways in which this liability to error and misconstruction may be exploited.

Once again, the reader is bombarded with instances of fabrication and deception, and it is hardly surprising that critics have latched on to this and have treated *Frame Analysis* as merely a further exploration of the world of theatricality, confidence tricks, false credentials, pretentiousness, and spies they found in *The Presentation of Self* and other writings. But, as Goffman insists (rather desperately, perhaps) near the beginning of Chapter 12, his concern is not to show how the world around us is filled with lies and falsity, and must therefore be constantly regarded with doubt and suspicion, but 'to learn about the way we take it that our world hangs together' (p. 440). Exploring the ways in which the world does *not* hang together is one way of informing ourselves of how, in the ordinary way, it does.

Each chapter deals with one of the two aspects of experience: psychological involvement in what is going on (Chapter 11), and cognitive awareness of it (Chapter 12). In the nature of things, evidence of the testable, verifiable kind we regard as "scientific" is simply not available. What we have instead are two kinds of illustrative material.

The first consists in recounting some of the elementary features of sporting contests and games. There are formalistic accounts of how stage, film, and television presentations are organised, transcripts of newspaper items, and a few re-told anecdotes about the behaviour of players and spectators. None of this material is in the least problematic; whatever truths they contain are self-evident – as indeed they have to be. If Goffman is so much more lavish with his illustrative material than most, this is because the theses he wants them to support are fairly novel. The multiplicity of illustrative instances gives them the mutual reinforcement he feels necessary *not* to increase their validity but to provide a broader grounding for the ideas he wants to propound, to sharpen the reader's sensitivity to the implications he wants to evoke. The same kind of explanation holds good for the sizeable proportion of grotesque, unseemly, distressingly pathetic or absurd, pretentious, and vulgarly comic incidents and actions among the accounts, anecdotes, and reports. Their purpose is to prod the reader still further by setting before him illustrative material of strongly disparate provenance. The nice, the funny, and the nasty are juxtaposed, provoking a "double-take", either mild or severe. The point of it is to activate and to keep at its most alert what sense the reader possesses of the fallibility of our capacity to organise our perceptions and experience.

The second resource is also made up of familiar material: theatrical performance (together with television programmes and films) and extracts from the published texts of well-known plays. Again, it is the reader's familiarity with this sort of activity that counts, for it, too, is intended to call up responses in the reader from his own knowledge of the awful – or funny, or embarrassing, or shocking – things that can happen. These are what plays, films, television documentaries, and drama are made out of – whatever moral lessons, warnings, or intimations of mortality, and whatever kind of amusement, fantasy, speculations, or shudders they are designed to provoke in their audience. But there is an added purpose in the use of this material in the present book. All "scripted" material of this kind is framed as fabrication; it can therefore be exploited for dramatic purposes in quite special ways, ways which have directly to do with the analytical scheme Goffman is presenting.

Involvement – that essential accompaniment of framed experience – is variable. Depending of course on the activity, it can verge on boredom at one extreme and almost complete absorption at the other.

But it is never, in the ordinary way, complete. There are almost always some side-involvements to be sustained alongside the main involvement (see Chapter 3, pp. 50, 52-4). Correspondingly, there is some marginal awareness of things and activities outside the rim of the frame; it is this which allows for attention to be given to "directional" tracks, to "overlays", and to the "concealment" tracks available to oneself (above, p. 277). In a sense, this less than total involvement is the necessary correlative of retaining control over what one is doing and what one is looking at. There is always some 'affective reserve', and, along with it, 'a measure of cognitive reserve also, a wisp of doubt concerning framework and transformation, a slight readiness to accept the possible need to reframe what is occurring, and this reserve, as well as the emotional kind, varies' (p. 378).

But all this can change, and involvement become total, or virtually so. It does so, notably, when the individual suddenly becomes, or is made, aware of a frame break, and is therefore wholly preoccupied with his lapse from appropriate behaviour or trustworthy perception and with the task of grappling with his predicament. At this point, he loses whatever conscious control he had over what was happening. Experience – 'the meld of what the current scene brings to him and what he brings to it' and which constitutes current reality – loses whatever form it had. It is, in Goffman's terms, "negated".

'Negative experience' is characterised by the *absence* of 'organised and organisationally affirmed response'. While such lapses seem more frequent in face-to-face interaction, there is one other sizeable category of activity which shows the same sort of vulnerability. This is made up of 'the strips of depicted social situations presented commercially in movies, TV, and print; but these make-believes are social, too, merely once removed from the viewer, who may, of course, be solitarily viewing' (p. 379).

It is this second, fabricated, category with which Goffman is mainly concerned. This is partly for the reason given above, but also because of other features of negative experience, which make that particular reason more substantial and more appropriate. The first point is that the disorganisation wrought by negative experience may itself be organised (i.e. framed) so as to encompass a broader range of goings-on. For example, someone who has "flooded out" and is overwhelmed with embarrassment has lost control, temporarily, over his situation, stopping short only of bringing the developing situation to a standstill also 'shows himself as having been bested – that things were too much for him'. His "defeat" may count as "victory" for anyone who can claim responsibility for it, and, in its way, a triumph for the onlookers who have not succumbed.

Schadenfreude, in other words, is not necessarily, or always, provoked by accidental circumstances. It may be incidental, or even planned. The endeavour to organise an occasion so that everyone participating will feel intensely involved may well succeed to the point of "over-involving" a few, who get carried away – a not unfamiliar occurrence at rock concerts and with that predictable handful of people at fairs who are "dared" into roller-coaster rides and the like which prove too much for them.

The whole issue turns on the blend of the privileged status accorded to onlookers (who are able to keep the whole sequence of events in frame), the concern they may feel for those directly affected ('affective sympathy'), and thankfulness at being spared (either by providence, or by competence, wariness, or intelligence of a superior order). And part of their own continuing strip of framed action will carry with it just as much involvement as for those for whom it may collapse. The whole television genre of quiz shows is founded on the vicarious involvement of an audience in the actual involvement of contestants.

The frame break organised out of a deception which is cleared up in the end, to the amazement, embarrassment, or discomfiture of the dupes, is of course the stuff of drama – as the phrase, "dramatic change" testifies. It has the effect of reformulating the way onlookers understood the sequence of events up to the break. The basic pattern is for one set of characters to be "in the know", and the other excluded, with all being revealed at some point; a frame break sizeable enough to count as a dramatic change will ordinarily also break up previous involvements and some remembered experience, duly stored as having been lived through in terms of the appropriate frame. Since enhanced involvement comes with the revelatory frame breaks that induce negative experience, it is no surprise to find that staged performance is a supremely favourable locale for the study of negative experience. Involvement – indeed, engrossment – is precisely what professional performers purvey, and what their audiences expect.

Using frame breaks to "negate" experience (and so manufacture involvement and capture attention) is not always a matter of some sudden change of physical circumstance, or revelation of some fabrication concealed from some participants. There are some commonly practised ways of inducing negative experience in face-to-face encounters. The most familiar, perhaps, is teasing or taunting someone until he loses control. Second, there are forms of 'stressful persuasion' which have entered into the routine practice of police interrogation, psychotherapy, and small-group political indoctrination, where the conventional mode of seeking information in conversational exchange may itself be set up as a fabrication, a staged performance.

Such "reflexive" devices are also much used in staged performances. Goffman identifies four kinds, each of them representing an attack on one or more elements of the frame sustaining the action – the make-believe transformation of theatrical performance. Pirandello, the master of theatrical devices for inducing negative experience, makes use of all of them. The point, in every case, is that the frame break is written into the script as part of the staged performance. And the purpose, in every case, is to jolt the audience into deeper involvement than they are prepared for.

The first consists in treating as non-existent the brackets which set the staged performance proper firmly and clearly off from the rest of the occasion (raising the curtain, darkening the auditorium, etc.). Next comes the device of trespassing the line dividing performers (with their carefully defined status as exhibits) from their audience (with their privileged status as onlookers only of the action) by one or other performer who addresses the audience directly. The most common form it takes is for the performer to turn aside from his character he is portraying and to comment on himself, his role, or his fellow-actors – a device stereotyped in earlier drama in the character of the fool, but still employed by comedians as a way of "sending-up" pretentiousness in themselves, or others, or even the audience. The trick, which amounts to positively violating the frame bracketing the staged performance from the occasion, is as old as Aristophanes, but was still usable by Groucho Marx in films, as well as being exploited by night-club entertainers and circus clowns.

There is, lastly, the possibility of using an occasion to examine the assumptions underlying the enactment of the activity which is, or was to be, the purpose (therapy, teaching, etc.) which brought participants together.

All these various "reflexive" devices still keep the theatrical frame in place, even while it is manipulated to the point of violating it altogether. All is still theatre. During the 1960s, indeed, a number of productions in the "legitimate" theatre relied heavily on what Goffman calls 'the theatre of frames' (p. 420). And since that time there seems to have been a trend towards pushing the limits of the theatrical frame further and further apart; witness the exploitation of insult and embarrassment by comics and the scenes of sexual intercourse and violence displayed in films, all taken to ever greater extremes. (The arrival of "snuff flicks" in the market for pornographic films is further testimony.)

Sporting contests seem to reflect the same tendency, with the all-too-familiar exploitation of the mechanics of staging them, histrionic enactment of their roles by the contestants and (a further refinement) manipulating the dividing lines between framed activity and "real, live" action on which the very existence of scripted activities and spectator sports depends. All come under the now fashionable label of "hype".

The questions that then remain are: who profits?, whose purpose is served?, who is in charge? – to which, of course, there is only one answer. The negative experiences generated in audiences in order to maximise their involvement are the work of those who either organise the proceedings or figure as the chief performer.

It is nevertheless feasible for those not "in charge" to create negative experiences for those presumed to be in control. This is most obviously true of children, who can become adept at testing out the presumptive limits of the control to which they are subject, but adult heckling or "barracking" is directed towards much the same end. However, as always the case with framing, this too can be keyed, and shows are produced which admit of intervention by the audience.

In recent years, television news cameras have given increasing opportunities and scope first for "confrontation" – the frontal attack on 'the ground rules of a social occasion . . . followed by a pointed refusal to accept the authority of those who attempt to restore order' (p. 428), and, subsequently, to the planned or opportunistic framing of such events as an assault on "law and order". Such manoeuvres, practised for somewhat vague political ends during the 1960s, became known as "social sabotage", but variants of the same tactics were later taken over by the political establishment (and so achieved a kind of respectability) in the "dirty tricks" carried out in election campaigns.

IV

The inherent fragility of the framing process means that the sense of what is going on is liable to be falsified, and our involvement in it subject to sudden and radical alteration. Since we are – however infrequently – aware of this as a hazard, we are occasionally led to doubt, or to suspect that we are being, or have been, misled. The vulnerabilities of experience in this sense are not of course quite the same as the material hazards to which we may be exposed. Losing a job, suffering a serious illness, being involved in a traffic accident, or being falsely convicted of a crime are all possibilities we may encounter, but not because of errors in our assessment of what is happening.

What is at issue here is strictly the matter of false assumptions and incorrect interpretations. The elementary fact is that whereas mistakes of this kind are quite frequently made, most of them are corrected almost instantaneously simply by locating the object, or incident, or utterance in the ongoing context of natural objects, events, and talk. 'The context', he remarks, in a passage that is a virtual repetition of his account of how activities "in frame" are "anchored" in whatever is going on around them (above, pp. 273-6), 'rules out our wrong interpretation and rules in the right one' (p. 441). Even beyond this, there is still the feeling that truth will out: 'The unexplained is not the inexplicable.'

Hence, it is unwarrantable to regard all realms of being and everything that happens in them with the same sceptical eye. To do so, moreover, is to run the risk of overlooking the vulnerabilities that do exist, and the conditions which make for them. There are in fact several ways in which verification is either built into our perception and experience or is made instantly available. This is most apparent in speech and writing. The different meanings that a word may have on its own are ordinarily reduced to one by what we know of individual participants' involvement in current actions and in previous ones and by their behaviour, as well as by the verbal and physical context. This is even more true in the case of writing. Clearing what is ambiguous out of what we write is intrinsic to the lengthy process by which we learn to master our native language – although it confronts us in conscious form when we learn a foreign language.

Yet this same mastery of language makes it possible for a speaker or writer to subvert the built-in, spontaneous, means we have of verifying what we take to be actuality and ridding ourselves of ambiguities. He can produce puns, riddles, and stories with trick endings, and, by reframing a statement made without thought to any possible transformation, turn his reply into a witticism. (Once again we find Goffman veering towards Gilbert Ryle's notion of a pyramid of levels of competence and sophistication in our interpretation of meaning and intention – but never quite matching it.) Plays on words have somehow to be composed beforehand, and therefore say more about the safety to be found in words than the hazards. The same applies to the mix-ups of words and of objects familiar in nonsense verse, *Alice in Wonderland*, *The Goon Show*, and in newspaper and film cartoons; they are made possible, first, by the contextual standards that ordinarily obtain and, second, by the reframings that previous juggling with ambiguities have made familiar enough to be readable immediately.

Having staked out large areas of worlds and realms of being which are either sufficiently guaranteed free from doubt and suspicion or are clearly signposted as their natural habitat, Goffman proceeds to identify the kinds of occasion when we encounter framing ambiguities or errors, and we are led to suspect the role of the individuals within our frame. There are, in addition, occasions when we discover that we have been deceived, or deluded, and that what we took for reality was fabricated. Trivial occasions of this kind abound: people arrange beforehand to arrive "by chance" at a place where they are likely to come across someone they want to see, bait their talk so as to provoke opinions they want to counter or questions for which they have prepared answers.

More generally, the existence of "guarantees" and means of verifying our understanding is known to would-be fabricators as well as to ourselves, and serves as 'a detailed recipe for those inclined to cook up reality'. In other words, we may not live in an exclusively Hobbesian world, but its denizens may at any time invade ours. And even if the world is peopled with fewer fabricators than Goffman often seems to suggest, there are plenty of specific sources of vulnerability which are themselves part and parcel of the familiar world, assured and verifiable though it may be. Some are inherent in certain forms of power, especially the normalising power incorporated in the machinery of many organisations and social institutions.

The instances cited by Goffman are those he has made familiar in *Asylums*: a wrong assessment of someone's overall competence or mental capacity, of what he was doing on a particular occasion, of his attitude to others' behaviour, may consign him to a home for the mentally defective, a prison, or a lunatic asylum for years. But the same kind of power is exercised by the educational system and by any other organisation with the authority to sort or grade individuals and, in so doing, to determine their life situation or life chances.

At work, I think, is the possibility that every definition of the situation, every continued application of a wonted frame, seems to presuppose and bank on an array of motivational forces, and . . . any such balance seems to be disruptible. To be able to alter this balance sharply at will is to exert power; that is one meaning of the term.

(p. 447)

The third 'detailed recipe for those inclined to cook up reality' is systems of belief. Religious beliefs are the exemplary case. They are extremely durable; they are reinforced by established organisations and institutions able to exercise power in the specific sense of the term mentioned: and they affect the widest possible variety of ways of perceiving and experiencing things. Although Goffman makes no mention of them, ideological beliefs fall into the same category; Gramsci's notion of hegemony is especially relevant.

With these three "sources of vulnerability" out of the way (minor "doctorings" of the world, the exercise of a certain kind of power, belief systems), Goffman settles down for the rest of Chapter 12 (pp. 448-95) to describing the different kinds of favourable conditions for deception, delusion, and illusion. There are two main groups of situations which make it easy for us to fall prey to misconceptions about what is happening. The first relates to the *information* available for us to reach an understanding, the second to the *frame* we employ.

It has been argued that recognising what is going on depends much on interconnections with preceding and concurrent activities and on what we understand of its context. It follows that activities whose nature must be determined on minimal information are particularly liable to be wrongly framed. Framing our experience on insufficient information arises, in Goffman's catalogue, in nine different ways. The first two – isolated noises and information from the distant past – are obvious and familiar. Equally, information available only from a single person is notoriously liable to lead to misconstruction – so much so that it is usually regarded at law as insufficient.

Information *relayed* by a single individual, the fourth category, has the same dubious character. So has privileged access to past events, which can also be used in interpreting how an individual or an organisation has developed the way he or it has. Audio and visual recordings represented as repeating the whole sequence of events are even more suspect. They must certainly have been prearranged, the equipment made available, and so on, and may also have been "edited". It so happens, then, that precisely those artefacts – photographs, tape-recordings, film – which have come to be relied on as "documentary" evidence are just what may be especially suspect.

Information always has a cost (if only an opportunity cost, or one which may be treated as trivial), and often also has a market value. Information costs, and value, enter into activities like gambling and contests, the outcome of which is either dependent on random events or on performances which are relatively unpredictable or dependent on chance. "Fixing" transforms the whole activity into a fabrication.

Goffman ignores the question of cost, although it is implicit in much of what he says, but goes on to consider marketable information. Another source of vulnerability opens up when those who are charged with sustaining frames in which information is set seek to monopolise any proceeds from the information in their keeping. Government departments, business enterprises, political activists, research establishments, armed forces, police, and criminals all have an interest in guarding access to information they see as vital to success. The purpose of concealment, of course, is to have their own activities wrongly framed by outsiders. The opportunities which this provides for reframing through leaks, spying, and authorised investigations on the one hand, and contrived "leaks", "kite-flying", "disinformation", and so forth on the other have all become the familiar material of fiction – and newspapers.

To end this catalogue of informational vulnerability, we come to the doubts and suspicions that people may have about the sincerity of the feelings one individual may express, or even display, towards another. The accounts, fictional or non-fictional, of the micropolitics of cabinets, boardrooms, universities, and business organisations have familiarised us with the vulnerability which attaches to the relationships built up between people on the basis of their expressions of feelings about one another. But (a fortiori, Goffman suggests), the intimate relationship which two people can build up between them, a relationship in which they tend to develop increasing isolation from the ongoing world around them, is particularly susceptible to 'the doubts and suspicions and misframings to which isolated single events are subject' (p. 457). Assuming, first, that the relationship will be a significant part of the world for at least one of them, and, second, that it is possible for the other to counterfeit involvement, then doubts and suspicions may well be entertained by one of them – not necessarily the former. This is not infrequently the case between people who are merely formally related to each other as colleagues or acquaintances. Uncertainty and suspicion are not usually long-lasting in such cases because other sources of information are available, and other matters supervene, but with two individuals who are intimately related it becomes understandable that each 'can spend a considerable amount of time in private thought trying to piece out what the other really "meant" by doing a particular thing and what the implications of this meaning are for the relationship'. (p. 459) Vulnerabilities of this kind have provided the theme of countless novels.

The same dubious quality, Goffman argues, attaches to all the utterances, actions, postures, etc, which we take to be direct evidence of feelings, attitudes, character, and relationships. It could be said that all that exists, properly speaking, are beliefs, or 'doctrines regarding expression, gestural equipment for providing displays, and stable motives for encouraging certain imputations'. If this be granted, then it is manifestly difficult to distinguish counterfeit expressions from the real thing.

It is perhaps worth while pointing out, yet again, that the central issue in Goffman's recital is not the manifold ways in which tricks can be played on people's sense of what is happening. What he has in mind is to demonstrate how far what we experience of what goes on around us is the product of the means we have of organising our perception of what goes on around us. He is, in short, trying to show how experience is organised by using much the same kind of approach as that, say, employed by Gombrich when he instances various kinds of visual illusion to instruct us about the way we see paintings. Just as Gombrich is really concerned with art, not simply with illusion only, so is Goffman really concerned with experience, not deception.

The second set of possibilities for individuals to become liable to falsified experience concerns deceptions and illusions generated directly by misframing.

Resolving ambiguity, correcting error, and allaying suspicion are all likely to involve attempts to obtain additional evidence which will either confirm or banish suspicion. Hence, because of the almost inexhaustible supply of methods of re-framing or tampering with frames, there comes into being a variety of devices expressly designed to fake such back-up evidence: arranging for "independent" witnesses; for seemingly trivial events and objects to be "discovered" by careful searchers; for faked evidence to be scattered so as to provide support "in depth" for the wrong interpretation; for "vital tests" to be faked; for "cover" to be supplied in advance, i.e. seemingly good reasons for being somewhere or for doing something. Fake newspapers and broadcasts have been used for the same sort of purposes.

Next, since so much social activity is defined by being bracketed out of the world of ongoing events, it becomes possible that outside such bracketed episodes, during which special attention is being given to specific sorts of eventuality, people are – especially beforehand, but also afterwards – to some extent "out of role", and so off their guard. With letter bombs and terrorist attacks and in other ways, politics, especially international politics, has become (Goffman remarks, writing in 1970) 'unpleasantly creative'. Conjurors, mind-readers, and other entertainers work on bracketed episodes in much the same, though comparatively harmless, ways.

Other frame elements liable to be used – or misused – include the "disattend", "directional", and "concealment" tracks or channels for activities which are marginal or subordinate to the goings-on of the framed activity proper. The possibility of using them to deceive derives from the assumption that such out-of-frame elements will be ignored. Goffman calls this disposition *'informant's folly'*. Inevitably, remarks proffered as "off-the-record" often receive more attention than those who utter them think is due – as some politicians and celebrities, and their spokesmen, have discovered.

'Insider's folly', Goffman's title for the next class of vulnerabilities, refers to the tendency to give unreserved credence to the state of affairs revealed after a frame is cleared and a fabrication discredited. Onlookers and others who now find themselves possessed of "inside information", as well as those who collaborated in sustaining the fabrication, seem to regard this as the firmest possible basis for belief in what is going on. Playwrights from Sophocles to Pirandello have put this means of inducing belief – and, with it, audience involvement – to good use. 'In being eased out of belief in the play within the play', which is the archetypal form, the audience is 'automatically eased into belief in the play that contains the play' (p. 475).

A number of established ploys, some of them classic, testify to the effectiveness of the use of 'insider's folly' as a way of inducing belief and involvement. Con games depend for their success on the mark's being led to believe that he is himself a participant in moves aimed at swindling someone else; the versions of the con game used by the *agents provocateurs* from the police, government departments, newspapers, and political organisations are now an established part of the folk lore of radical political groups as well as of criminals and drug addicts. A 'well-plotted flooding out' induces not only involvement but also 'belief that the person who has broken frame is no longer in a position to dissimulate'. It is precisely the same 'insider's folly' that awards much more credence to what is said "informally" on a formal occasion than to the content of prepared statements.

In both the 1968 and 1972 American presidential election campaigns, it seems, the two parties issued invitations to rallies (presumably by the other side) that had not been planned, drove people who had not been invited to fund-raising dinners, and indulged in a whole array of similar "pranks", as Goffman calls them. They included the use of forged signatures, stolen letterheads, and faked press releases so as to cause trouble in the opposing party. All are subsumed under the label of 'false connectives'. Their inclusion arises from the fundamental assumption that 'deeds and words come to us connected to their source, and that ordinarily this connection is something we can take for granted, something that the context of action will always provide, something that ensures the anchoring of activity' (p. 479).

A final category, "frame traps", looks like the converse of "false connectives". Ordinarily, when someone's actions or words are misunderstood, he takes steps to provide a more accurate account. But there are circumstances in which, once an (adverse) assessment of someone's character has been arrived at, any countervailing claims or remonstrances he may make are usually discounted automatically as '"what can only be expected" of someone of that character' (p. 482). Much of what is read as prejudice works in this way, but it is also often at work in the diagnosis of insanity, 'transforming remonstrances into symptoms', and disagreement with a therapist's interpretation into "resistance".

By way of commentary on this rather formidable catalogue, Goffman offers four observations on their implications for ordinary living. The first concerns the opportunistic character of the fabrications and transformations of experience practised on us by playwrights, novelists, and artists, by journalists, advertisers, entertainers, television and radio producers, by pretenders, impostors and criminals, and yet again by friends in fun and by opponents and rivals in earnest. All are inherent, by its very nature, in framing. The repertoire of tricks that can be played with framing lies ready for use, as purpose and opportunity present themselves. What the catalogue of types of vulnerabilities points to, therefore, is not the multiplicity of ways in which people may be hoodwinked but to the sheer fragility of our grasp of reality.

Interestingly, we are most, or mostly, conscious of how easily experience becomes tainted when uncertainty is evinced by others. Fleeting expressions make us concerned. 'We give weight to an individual's signs of guilt or signs of being barely able to suppress laughter or signs of embarrassment and furtiveness, and not merely because of the impropriety of these expressions themselves. For these signs are evidence that someone in our world is insecurely in it, perhaps because he is in another or fears that we are' (p. 487). So to "act natural" (to revert to a theme discussed in *Relations in Public*) is to behave so as to reassure others that what seems to be the frame of what is happening really is. This, also, is what is meant by sincerity; what we call sincerity comes from behavioural competence.

Third, if it is possible to hint at the existence of a "truth" which lies behind the facts being presented or to imply that they have a "double meaning", then it is also possible to 'read double meanings when only one exists' (p. 488), or to "read between the lines" when there is nothing there. This, notoriously, is the kind of trap which awaits mental patients, but, although they may be the worst sufferers, they are not the only ones.

And, finally, there are those individuals and groups whose experience appears to them as the totally managed fabrication of some outside, transcendent, force or power. The exemplary case cited by Goffman is Festinger's study of an end-of-the-world cult. The repeated failure of the prophesied end to materialise meant for the members simply that they were to regard the expected day as deferred. Their faith was not subverted but, in fact, renewed. The Festinger report is often read as a downgraded version of the expectations of a second coming or hope of a Messiah which have been part of Christian and Jewish belief in the past. But it can also be read as an upside-down version of the conspiracy theories which have nourished conviction and fortified action not only for revolutionaries but for whole nations.

V

So, how do we get to know what an object is, or what is going on around us? And why do we accept some experience as "real", and other experience as not?

Goffman opens the final chapter of the book with yet another assurance that he takes 'ordinary, literal activity' as the bedrock reality of experience – the model on which, and out of which, transformations of all kinds are built up. This is not much of a concession, however. How different, he asks, is the actuality of everyday actions of ordinary, real, people from all the make-believe and fabricated realms we create out of it? Apart from the quickly changing frames in which it is contained, everyday activity itself can include sports, games, ritual, experiments, practising, deceptions, which are not particularly fanciful and yet depart a good deal from anything that might be called "real", "actual", or "literal" in the primordial sense in which we regard painting a wall, or gardening, or driving a car, or shopping, and all the other things which "have to be done".

Even at the level of the primary social framework – everyday actuality – the most commonplace sequence of the most commonplace activities will incorporate a number of kaleidoscopic changes of role, of bodily movements requiring different kinds of competence, of organisational and institutional context. And the behaviour which serves as the model of everyday activity is itself designed in conformity with cultural standards, the appropriate enactment of different roles, and an inexhaustible fund of 'associated lore, itself drawn from the moral traditions of the community as found in folk tales, characters in novels, advertisements, myth, movie stars and their famous roles, the Bible, and other sources of exemplary representation' (p. 562). What is more, the organisation of behaviour in this way mirrors, and is mirrored in, countless anecdotes, jokes, news stories, fashionable one-liners, and repartee which go to confirm people's views of how the ongoing world around them operates.

'Realms of being', Goffman concludes, 'are the proper objects here for study, and here, the everyday is not a special domain to be placed in contrast to the others but merely another realm' (p. 564). And while the nature, the structure, and the organisation of everyday behaviour must be the first object of social science, it should not be taken for granted that it is distinctive, categorically different from other realms of being.

By the end of *Frame Analysis*, we are presented not only with a self which exists only as a set of distinct parts, each "socially constructed", but a self existing in a world which also exists only as a series of "framed" constructs, none of which has any claim to reality other than that with which the self endows it. We have seemingly lost any grip on what philosophers like to call an "Archimedean point" – a fundamental axiom of intuitive knowledge or irrefutable belief of the kind that Descartes or Kant used as a starting point.

True, it is conceded that what we think of as the ongoing world of reality is more firmly anchored than most by the guarantees provided by the physical sciences; we are allowed to think of it as a few steps closer to what we like to think of as real life and a real world. But it should not escape notice that the natural sciences, too, have taken on board the notion of experience and perception as "constructions". Nobody now believes that we are born into a world in which all the objects are sorted out, distinguishable, and already labelled before we come on the scene.

There is a final complication. It looks very much as if the speculations of *Frame Analysis* have been overreached by natural scientists. To end with, here are three passages from the opening pages of Gerald Edelman's *Neural Darwinism*:[1]

> Perception may be provisionally defined as the discrimination of an object or an event through one or more sensory modalities, separating them from the background or from other objects or events. . . . One of the fundamental tasks of the nervous system is to carry on adaptive perceptual categorization in an "unlabelled" world – one in which the macroscopic order and arrangement of objects and events (and even their definition or discrimination) cannot be prefigured for an organism, despite the fact that such objects and events obey the laws of physics. . . .
>
> Given our provisional definition of perception, and in the absence of prior immutable categories of things, how in fact do we know what an object is . . .? [T]he environment or niche to which an organism must adapt is not arranged according to logic, nor does it have absolute values assigned to its possible orderings. This position does not deny that the material order in such a niche obeys the laws of quantum physics; rather, it asserts that at the time of an organism's *first* confrontation with its world, most macroscopic things and events do not, in general, come in well-arranged categories. . . .
>
> When we consider the world, there is no given semantic order;

an animal must not only identify and classify things but also decide what to do in the absence of prior detailed descriptive programs, with the exception, of course, of certain fixed programs handed down by evolution. This point deserves emphasis, because it is central to all other considerations; in some sense, the problem of perception is initially a problem of taxonomy in which the individual animal must "classify" the things of its world. Whatever solutions to this problem are adopted by an individual organism, they must be framed within that organism's ecological niche and for its own adaptive advantage. In other words, the internal taxonomy of perception is adaptive but is not necessarily veridical in the sense that it is concordant with the descriptions of physics.

NOTE AND REFERENCE

1. Gerald M. Edelman, *Neural Darwinism*, Basic Books, 1987, pp. 7, 26, and 24.

11

TOWARDS A RHETORIC
OF TALK

Chapter 13 of *Frame Analysis* brings a change in emphasis and direction, although this is not really apparent until one looks back on it from the perspective of the essays which make up *Forms of Talk*. This, Goffman's last book, is about talk as performance. While we use speech to inform, to order, to warn, and so forth, what we are doing in ordinary everyday conversation, which is the most frequent, if not fundamental mode of using speech, is above all to involve our listeners in our experience – to persuade them into accordance with our own views and into sympathetic regard for our experience. The conceptual schema of frame analysis is still very much there in *Forms of Talk*, but as one proceeds through the essays it is revealed as the foundation for a new methodology for the study of an ancient subject-matter: rhetoric.

It was, admittedly, Kenneth Burke's adoption of "rhetoric" for the title of his *Rhetoric of Motives*, the analysis of the way we interpret human action which is the sequel to *A Grammar of Motives*, that prompted my choice of the term for Goffman's undertaking. For in Goffman's case, too, exploration of the nature of human experience and of the fundamental purposes of speech came as a sequel to the study of the rules of social interaction – which he more than once referred to as a "grammar".

But what aptness there might be in the inclusion of "rhetoric" in the title of this chapter is quite independent of any superficial connection between Goffman's last book and the writings that touched most closely on his first. The term applies directly to the place Goffman's last writings occupy in the constellation of empirical and theoretical studies for which the study of language in its modern guise has been the seedbed.

Modern linguistics is usually reckoned to have begun with the lectures given in Paris before the First World War by the Swiss scholar Ferdinand de Saussure – or rather, with the posthumous publication in 1915 of his *Cours de linguistique générale*,[1] as reconstructed by his students. But its development and expansion, especially in Britain and America, was the outcome of the re-animation of interest in language which went with four quite separate developments which occurred simultaneously or in quick succession during the years after the Second World War. The first came with the technological development of electronically controlled servo-mechanisms and, along with them, the invention of computers, which gave new meaning to the notion of communication and of language. The second, virtually concurrent with the first, was the rise to dominance of a school of philosophy dedicated to the analysis of ordinary speech as the instrument or at least the repository of our understanding of the world and of other people. The third wave of interest and speculation came in the mid-1950s, with the appearance of a new school of linguistics, with Noam Chomsky as a central figure, whose interest focused on the "creation" of language, the apparently universal ability of human beings to construct and to understand any number of sentences in the language native to them, including sentences they have never heard before, and to do so quite naturally and unreflectingly, without any conscious reference to grammatical rules. Finally, there is what might be called the re-birth (with Lévi-Strauss as midwife) of Saussurian linguistics in "structuralism".

The last thirty years have seen not only the spread and establishment of the study of "general" linguistics in its own right as a distinct academic discipline but also a certain cross-pollination of psycholinguistics and sociolinguistics and an increased interest in semantics, as well as fresh approaches to literary criticism.

What is perhaps more pertinent is the more specialised and intensive interest in the philosophy of language that has accompanied these developments. This has attracted much more attention in France and North America than it has in England – although even here few people would follow A. J. Ayer in dismissing it as the last embers of the "Oxford" school of natural language philosophy.[2] At the hands of philosophers like H. P. Grice, J. R. Searle and J. Bennett, such studies seem not very distant from the Aristotelian conception of rhetoric as the use of language in such a way as to produce a desired impression.

Rhetoric was defined by I. A. Richards as "a philosophic discipline aiming at mastery of the fundamental laws of the *use* of language" (emphasis added),[3] which is not far off what Goffman was trying to do.

When one takes Aristotle's own methodology into account, Goffman's writings in *Frame Analysis* and *Forms of Talk* approximate even more closely to the classical idea of rhetoric. Aristotle's *Rhetoric* was an emphatically empirical work: he says he set out to deduce how speakers had been able to persuade and to move the feelings of their audiences from the store of recorded speeches (and speech) which had been accumulated by his time. Given the different scope of Goffman's linguistic material, this is also what he, too, was up to.

I

One might look for the point of departure of Goffman's approach to "natural" language (i.e. utterances by speakers in their native language) in Wittgenstein's injunction: "Don't look for the meaning of a word, look for its use", expanded and reinforced by J. L. Austin's analysis of talk as "speech acts".

Wittgenstein's intention was not merely to divorce meaning from its traditional identity with signifying, but to cancel the equally traditional separation of speech from the "ideas" for which it supposedly acted as vehicle. Austin, for his part, was concerned with dismantling the assumption (made by philosophers and others) that "the business of a 'statement' can only be to 'describe' some state of affairs, or to 'state some fact', which it must do either truly or falsely"[4] – apart, that is from those statements which express questions, commands, wishes, exclamations, and so on. People did lots of other things with words.

Nevertheless, whatever impetus or influence Goffman received from his reading of Wittgenstein and Austin, the line he took was in a different direction. He, too, aimed at dismantling some of the assumptions we have about the nature of talk. But they are different assumptions.

The essays in *Forms of Talk* are professedly expositions of the application of frame analysis to speech, which presumably means that one has to look for their theoretical basis in *Frame Analysis* as a whole. While this may be so in the larger sense, the basics for *Forms of Talk* are contained in Chapter 13 of that book.

Much of the material which has gone into showing how frame analysis works, and most of the accounts of strips of action which have been used for the examples and illustrations for each particular phase of Goffman's presentation, have either embodied transcripts of utterances or consisted of excerpts from plays, snatches of conversation, and the like. It is a little surprising, then, to find that the penultimate chapter of *Frame Analysis* opens with an elaborate presentation of what has been assumed throughout, namely, that 'spoken statements provide examples of most of the framings so far considered: fabrications, keyings, frame breaks, and, of course, frame disputes' (pp. 497-8). Nevertheless, the reader is taken by the hand and led through several pages concerning resemblances it had not occurred to him to question and, at the end of it, confronted with a difference.

The difference, of course, as Wittgenstein and Austin had insisted, lies in the fact that talking is not experiencing, or perceiving, the objects and happenings around us, but doing. Talk is performance, a form of acting on and interacting with what is, and with what is going on around us. Also, it is a form of activity that is peculiarly human, and social in character. This gives it central importance as subject-matter for the kind of sociological analysis Goffman took as his special concern.

However, we do a number of quite different things with talk. And Chapter 13 of *Frame Analysis*, "The Frame Analysis of Talk", is best read as the first of a series of essays in the frame analysis of different kinds of talk, a series which was contained in *Forms of Talk*. Altogether, we arrive at five kinds of talk. The differences between them are institutional: i.e. patterns of conduct recognised as feasible modes of social interaction by members of a particular society who may be assumed to share knowledge of (if not adherence to) the same values and norms.

There are of course other ways of classifying talk into different forms. One, which Goffman makes much of in *Forms of Talk*, is according to whether it consists of reading aloud from a prepared text, or (which may amount to much the same thing) uttering words which have been committed to memory for delivering on the occasion, and, third, 'fresh talk', talk typically uttered in the course of conversation, and so, to all appearances, unrehearsed and spontaneous. 'Fresh talk', of the kind considered normal for conversation, is the approved model for 'aloud reading' and 'memorised' utterances, even when they are manifestly nothing of the kind.

It is, however, the different institutional features which decide the distinctive theme of each essay. Two of them ("Replies and Responses" and "Footing") are concerned with ordinary conversation ('natural' talk), and these are discussed in the present chapter, along with Chapter 13 of *Frame Analysis*. The other three essays concern modes of talk which are (institutionally) quite different from conversation. One, "Response Cries", deals with utterances which are seemingly (but only seemingly) addressed to oneself or to nobody in particular, and the last two essays in the book with solo performances addressed to an audience which is not called upon or expected to reply (as in the case of a public lecture) or is unable to do so (as with radio listeners and television viewers).

These widely different institutional set-ups prescribe different modes of talk. Yet the social rules attaching to the various occasions do not affect certain fundamental characteristics common to all utterances. All forms of talk partake of the general character given to talk by their origin in conversation – in talk between, or among, individuals engaged in social interaction of some kind. There are no exceptions, Goffman argues, even in the case of self-talk, or of the exclamations and objurgations people often utter when entirely alone.

II

The simplest way to begin seems to be with what must nowadays be the common experience of first hearing one's own tape-recorded voice issuing from a speaker independently of oneself. Almost everyone is taken aback, some to the point of disbelief. Eventually one comes to accept the fact that there must be a large discrepancy between what we believe we sound like, and what we ("really") sound like to others. A next stage comes when we are able to (or have to) listen repeatedly to a recorded conversation between ourselves and others; we then discover, typically, that what we had thought was a series of relatively lucid, well-connected, well-formed utterances contains a number – an unexpectedly high number – of slips of speech, hesitations, self-corrections, and other departures from what we regard as an acceptable norm *and*, what is more, from what we thought characteristic of our own way of speaking.

Goffman's own starting point is from a further stage of discrepancy. We derive our standards of ordinary conversation, he claims, from the scripted dialogue of plays and novels. But while the latter may serve as an exemplary standard, it is one which very few people can meet. In the first place, a great deal of talk is 'unserious', and only very loosely tied in to the activities that are immediately proximate to it.

'Unserious', in this connection, simply means that someone engaged in talk need not do more than demonstrate that, when silent, he is giving some minimal attention to what is going on. Some perceptible response is essential; anything below the threshold of a detectable response is liable to bring conversation to a faltering halt.

For all that, the degree of responsiveness typical of natural talk corresponds to levels of involvement well below what most of us believe is called for. In general, speech utterances are connected with the world around by ties which are quite loose, and weak, even when they are not "bracketed out". Ordinary conversation is even more loosely tied. This makes talk more "vulnerable" than most activity to 'keying and fabrication, . . . for this looseness is precisely what transformations require' (*FA*, 502).

Keying and fabrication are intrinsic to most casual conversation: 'Licence abounds'. There is, for example, no special obligation for a person to be very consistent in what he says about his beliefs, opinions, or intentions, for anything he professes about these inner states can be neither proved nor disproved. Not that much time is ever spent in expressing feelings or any other kind of inner state, or, for that matter, in giving or accepting commands, decisions, promises, and the like. While it is true that utterances often are "performative", and convey commitment to action, or promises, or assent, dissent, caution, and much else, a good deal of the talk in which performative utterances are conveyed is only indirectly connected with the performative content; indeed, this may be a minor feature.

> What the individual spends most of his spoken moments doing is
> providing evidence for the fairness or unfairness of his current
> situation and other grounds for sympathy, approval, exoneration,
> understanding, or amusement. And what his listeners are obliged
> to do is to show some kind of audience appreciation.
>
> (*FA*, 503)

In the end, Goffman claims, what most speakers are doing most of the time is to recount what happened to them, what they saw, or how they managed to do this or that.

> For what a speaker does usually is to present for his listeners a
> version of what happened to him. In an important sense, even if
> his purpose is to present the cold facts as he sees them, the
> means he employs may be intrinsically theatrical, not because he
> exaggerates or follows a script, but because he may have to

engage in something that is a dramatisation – the use of such arts
as he has to reproduce a scene, to *replay* it.

(p. 504)

It is an attempt to induce some kind of involvement, an invitation to
the listener to participate vicariously in his experience. The narrative
form commonly used draws the listener into an empathetic re-living
of what took place, the speaker taking off in his replaying of what
happened from a situation approximate to what he guesses his
listener's present information state to be.

If so much of ordinary talk is made up of "replayings", it means
that anyone listening to it is put in the position of member of a
theatre audience. He too must "suspend disbelief" and 'be led through
the discovery of outcomes by those who, in some sense or other, must
already have discovered them' (p. 507). What it amounts to, in the
end, is that talk, much of the time, is not a matter of communicating
information but re-enacting dramatic episodes before an audience. 'We
spend most of our time not in giving information but in giving shows.
And this theatricality is not based on mere displays of feelings or
faked exhibitions of spontaneity . . . The parallel between stage and
conversation is much deeper than that' (p. 508). For talk, too, is based
on the foreknowledge possessed by the speaker and the ignorance
(which is often assumed rather than real) of his audience. His
complete knowledge about what he will be saying differentiates talk
from actual experience – not from staged performance.

So, whereas a few pages earlier it was said that the standard level
of involvement manifested by participants in the scripted dialogue of
plays and novels is one which very few people can meet when they
engage in ordinary conversation, we now find sociable talk assimilated
to scripted performance. Of course, there are differences. Plays and
similar make-believe replayings can shuffle fact and fiction together
in a lengthy preformulated sequence, with each performer's utterance
given maximum effect by cues worked out well in advance. Replayings
in social conversation are often doled out in parcels, each needing
the encouragement of requests, questions, or a display of interest. But
the differences are not categorical. Quoted remarks are hardly ever
truly word-perfect; events are reconstructed for greater effect; and
while it is impolitic, or at least impolite, to push one's respondents
repeatedly into appropriate responses in order to set the stage for
one's next utterance (to do so smacks of interrogation rather than
conversation), it is not uncommon for this to be done for a single

304

exchange: 'we fish for compliments, "steer" a conversation, introduce a topic likely to lead in a usable direction . . .' (p. 510).

In other words, there *is* a correspondence between the fabricated dialogue of stage performers who are acting out characters not their own and the organisation of ordinary talk. For a moment, it seems, we are back in the dramaturgy business. Previous chapters have mentioned ways in which what is going on inside someone's mind – attitudes, suspicions, intentions, critical reflections, and much else – may be conveyed intentionally or revealed involuntarily to others without being committed to spoken words. It makes for a collusive relationship which people excluded from it are able to perceive – are often, indeed, meant to perceive. But the intentional exposure of inner thoughts which makes for collusion between a speaker and someone else can be played out by the individual on his own. Irony, banter, sarcasm, innuendo, and false modesty all allow of 'the controlled, systematic use of the multiple meanings of words and phrases' (p. 515). Making fun of someone – "taking the micky", "kidding", and so on – involves modes of collusion and self-collusion which are just as complicated, the butt knowing quite well that he is being made a fool of, and that the others know that he knows; so does putting on a show of anger or bewilderment, and for much the same ends.

What all this points to, Goffman argues, is that the person to whom this kind of talk is addressed is supposed to treat the speaker as if he were one part of a dual character, one half being unaware of what is being insinuated about him by the other – the front performer. It is, incidentally, only if we make that kind of presumption that we can comprehend how innuendo, sarcasm, and other kinds of double-talk make their effect.

III

Evidently, it is not enough to credit the individual with a number of social roles; further subdivision, this time into analytical 'sub-entities', is necessary before one can grasp just what it is that is going on in ordinary conversation. The strategy for determining this lies in what has already been said about the capacity an individual has of splitting himself into two so as to make statements which seem to carry the implication of there being two distinct persons inside the one speaker. Organising our experience meaningfully requires, at the very outset, that actions be connected with their source, utterances with their speaker, and so on. This is simple enough in the ordinary way, although there are familiar classroom and night-time instances when people do fail to connect an utterance with an utterer. The selfsame instances also demonstrate that, sometimes, a conscious effort has to be made to attribute some action to its source. Hence, it could be argued, there exists the possibility of someone other than the "emitter" of a statement being regarded as the person responsible for it – "the originator" or "principal". A frame analysis approach allows for further possibilities. When, for example, someone answers the telephone and passes the question asked by the caller to a third person, he might well "act out" in a way that indicates who the caller is, or suggest to the caller how welcome, or unwelcome, the call is to the third person. So we now have one other sub-entity, an "animator", apart from the principal, or originator.

It seems, then, that "source" is divisible into two; there are, at any rate, two functions involved and, as the business of the telephone call suggests, each function could be performed by a different individual. So far as concerns the analytical requirements, the animator is simply the medium – ink on a page, a telephone handset, someone who repeats the utterance he has heard to its intended recipient. And, of course, the animator could also be the originator, the principal – as for the most part he is. In the case of reported speech, however, the difference between principal and animator comes to the surface. Furthermore, there are differences between the "I" referred to in such sentences as "I feel a chill", "I will take responsibility", and "I was born on a Tuesday". The I's mentioned in each sentence refer to different parts, or aspects, of the whole entity.

Thus, having skirted around J. L. Austin a few pages earlier, Goffman now takes a quick dive into Wittgenstein's debate with himself over the nature of identity, centred in the assertion that "there is a great variety of criteria for personal *'identity'*".[5] Goffman is preoccupied with the construction of a substantive case about the multiple nature of personal identity, so the illustrative material he uses is much more extensive, elaborate, and circumstantial than Wittgenstein's. It is also notably less dependent on introspection, which, as Wittgenstein himself says, in one instance, is "not unlike that from which William James got the idea that the 'self' consisted mainly of 'peculiar motions in the head and between the head and throat'".[6]

The two "sub-entities", principal (originator) and animator (emitter), are only the beginning. Once again, plays and performers provide the best sources for showing off these self-multiplying devices in all their variety. An actor who takes a part in a play animates a make-believe character, but can also animate other characters – dead, ghostly, animal, or robot-like – "through" the role he takes in the play. These are as much the creatures of the actor as are puppets and dummies the creatures of the puppeteer or the ventriloquist who animates them. All such entities may be labelled "figures", a third entity to add to the other two (principal and animator) which enter into the composite personal identity Goffman has now arrived at. Figures are dealt with in some detail. There are five kinds, each with its appropriate connectives, i.e. formula-like devices for letting an audience know who is supposed to be making this particular utterance or acting in this particular way.

"Natural Figures" are actual people (or, sometimes, animals) with an enduring personal identity of their own. They can, of course, also be identically the same as their current originator and animator, but there are also "Staged Figures", fictional or actual personages, past or present, that performers represent. They have much the same naturalness as the first kind, and serve as both principal and animator of speech and action – not entirely, though, since they and their actions are incorporated into a sequence of strips of activity which is make-believe, and often, as in stage plays and broadcast performances, the work of many individuals. There is also mimicry to be reckoned with, speaking with an assumed accent or tone of voice, and so on, all of which are designed to separate originator from figure. "Printed Figures" are equivalent to staged figures except that they exist in the world of print – fiction, biography, and some history – in which the writer reveals to his readers the thoughts and feelings of the figures he invents or reconstructs. Printed figures are sustained by a whole paraphernalia of connectives – capital letters, quotation marks, and so on – which are in conventional use.

Natural figures are able to talk about what they, or others, have done, are doing, and will or may possibly do. So, in a way, can staged or printed figures, of course. And, at a little further remove, we endow "Cited Figures" – the persons to whom we refer, whose actions or utterances we cite – with the same ability. There are presumably limits to how far this sort of embedding can go, but these limits must be different for different frames. The facility amounts to an embedding procedure comparable, as Goffman points out, to the elaborate bracketing used by logicians and, to a lesser extent, mathematicians.

Yet the kind of sophistication required for carrying out or interpreting such embedding in speech is not the exclusive property of people of higher educational or social standing. More to the point, whereas it may seem improper or inappropriate for the cited figure to refer to the process by which he is brought to light and life, this is precisely what does very often happen; it is one of the classic methods by which negative experience is generated.

Lastly, there are "Mockeries and Say-fors", in which someone acts out someone else (who may or may not be present). It is a familiar routine of entertainers (a mannered voice is fairly typical), but youngsters (and others) often enough resort to it as a device for "sending up" or "putting down". On the other hand, it is sometimes encountered among people who put words (more often, "baby-talk") into the mouths of babies – or pets. Its central feature is 'the process of projecting an image of someone not oneself while preventing viewers from forgetting even for a moment that an alien animator is at work' (p. 534).

Mimicry involves some juggling with connectives if they are to do their work, which is to show who or what, among the component elements of principal, animator, strategist, and figure, we are to suppose is saying or doing whatever is being said, or done. The speaker assumes some licence to take on some of the expressiveness which it is presumed would go with the words. A mannered voice may be used, though this is infrequent, but there is usually some alteration in the way the quoted strip of words is expressed, as well as a verbal connective. Vulgarisms and obscenities, or feelings and opinions and the like, from which the speaker may want to insulate himself, tend to be censored; if not elided altogether, they may be uttered with some altered expression.

One final sub-entity remains: the strategic role taken over by a lawyer or any other expert specialist who acts as spokesman for an individual, "standing in" for him when it comes to assessing a particular situation, taking appropriate action, and so forth.

The remarkable speed and facility with which, as Goffman notes, we latch on to the varied and complicated connections between figures and action must come, I think, from a propensity to connect up not only human action but natural events with some human or animal agency which, if not perceptible or overt, must operate behind the scenes. It is this same propensity which seems to be at work in the beliefs about witchcraft and sorcery described by Evans-Pritchard; it is also at work in the mind-body dualism attacked by Gilbert Ryle ("the dogma of the Ghost in the Machine") and in the even more obstinately persistent notion of the self as a kind of homunculus, seated in the innermost part of the individual, as the recipient of all perception and the author of all action.

What I am suggesting (and it is only a suggestion) is that one fundamental feature (or "category", if you prefer) of human thinking is to think of causation *in all regards* as the operation of human agency which is essentially covert. In the first place, as Robin Horton says, at its most general or primitive level, our idea of causation "draws its inspiration" "from the realms of human action on the non-human environment".[7] But even beyond that, overt human action itself is seen as "caused" by some inner individual essence, be it will, thought or intention, which is hidden from us. It comes naturally – as it did to Locke – to think of language as the product of ideas composed in the mind, with speech as its vehicle. It comes equally naturally, I suggest, to distinguish between individuals and the various "sub-entities" they may (or may be thought to) interpose between that inner "self" and what they are doing or saying.

If this is so, it is, incidentally, a feature of human processes of thought which is fundamental (and logically prior) to what Goffman calls the primary framework of *guided* action.

IV

By now, enough preparatory work has been put in for us to be returned to the central preoccupation of the chapter, which is face-to-face conversation. At any one time, the individual who is speaking may be said to "command" the audience which is made up of the others. With so small an audience for any one speaker, it is especially incumbent on each one of them to make it clear that he has heard what has been said, understands it, finds nothing to quarrel with in what is said, or how it is delivered, *and*, above all, to show some appreciation of the speaker and the occasion.

The parallel Goffman has drawn between stage performance and conversational talk is now carried still further.

During a stage play, the onlookers are radically cut off from the statements and actions made at any point by a character. Unlike the characters on the stage, onlookers can only respond through the back channel, disattendably expressing in a modulated way that they have been stirred by what is being unfolded before them – stirred in spite of the fact that they know the same thing will be given tomorrow for another audience.

So during actual conversation. 'It is not the shout of responsive action that talk mostly needs and seeks to get but murmurings – the clucks and tsks and aspirated breaths, the goshes and gollies and wows – which testify that the listener has been stirred' (p. 541). And we are reminded that what they are responding to is essentially as much a *replaying* as what is presented to a theatre audience (see above, p. 304).

If one turns now from the parallels between the utterances ("replayings") of stage performers and those made in conversation to the differences between them, some new light is shed on the limits and licences that framing rules offer to those involved in a social occasion. In performing a stage character, very little allowance is made for lapses in performance – missing cues, muffing lines, tripping up, and so on. Where such lapses are written into the part, of course (and the derivation of the word "malapropism" is evidence enough), there is all the licence which mimicry allows to an animator to distance himself from the figure he animates. In conversation, however, where animator and figure are one and the same, the licence is that which is ordinarily allowed an individual to forgo responsibility for his own actions; in this case, it is more a matter of how he deals with mistakes and any other of the contingencies of self-projection.

There are all kinds of distractions, errors, side-involvements, and so on. They are of different degrees of seriousness, ranging from flooding out in laughter or in angry vituperation, or taking time out to read a letter, down to taking a sip from a drink or lighting a cigarette. But their degree of seriousness is also calibrated on a scale determined by the seriousness of the occasion. What could be disturbing on a formal public occasion, to the point of reducing the level of audience appreciation or even destroying it, might be passed off in conversation.

How a speaker deals with these contingencies demonstrates the looseness which obtains between the individual and the role he sustains at the time. 'The individual is likely to take minor liberties' when he is performing a role, 'ducking out for a moment to stretch or apologise'. This looseness is in fact an assertion of the individual's right to have, and be seen to have, 'a right to a wider being than any current role allows' (p. 544).

In fact, of course (and nobody knew this better than Goffman), roles "allow" a great deal of scope in their performance; the *specification* of a role is no more than a stereotype, a lowest common multiple of expectations. It is in the margin between the performance of a role and its typification that individuals may deploy all those attributes celebrated in Goffman's earlier writings: "character", "style", "poise", "savoir-faire".

There is also looseness, albeit of a different kind, between utterances and meaning, a looseness explored fairly thoroughly by H. P. Grice in the distinction he draws between the "natural" or "timeless" meaning of an utterance (i.e. when heard or read independently of any other specific social connection between utterer and recipient), and the "non-natural" meaning it bears when it is directed to specific others on a specific occasion.[8] The margin is filled with the intentions of the utterer and also with the recognition of them by the recipient, such recognition being part of the intentions of the utterer.

This looseness, and the margin between "natural" and "non-natural" meanings is assimilated by Goffman to frame analysis. 'Talk appears as a rapidly shifting stream of differently framed strips, including short-run fabrications (typically benign) and keys of various sorts' (p. 544). Although he goes on to say that transformation cues indicate when, and how, utterances are meant to be taken as departing from the typical (Grice's "natural" meaning), this is not always the case. "Non-natural" utterances often mean no more than a vague *something*, a something which is not contained altogether in the words but requires recognition of the utterer's intention.

V

Modern linguistics has brought us to see that the rules of sentence formation which we follow in speaking our native language are somehow taken in as we learn to speak. They remain implicit, taken for granted – and forgotten about, except when grammatical mistakes occur. All the ways of behaving when we talk, and which we detect in the behaviour of others when they make public speeches, give lectures, divert people at a party, or are simply engaged in casual talk, are taken for granted in much the same way. The difference is that rules of this kind are more complicated than grammar, and rather nearer the surface of consciousness. For it is the selfsame paraphernalia of stage tricks, "framing" devices, "transformations", and so on that playwrights, novelists, and others have picked up and used for their own purposes in creating make-believe characters and presenting them equipped with the attributes of authentic individuals.[9] Item by item, they have all been used and made familiar for centuries past.

What Goffman is attempting is to bring it all together in orderly fashion and expose in some detail the extraordinary elaboration of the machinery we bring to perception and experience and speech to make it the organised world it is. In regard to everyday, casual, conversation, for example:

> No group in our society seems unable to produce such choppy, streaming lines of change in frame; and no competent person seems to be incapable of easily picking up the frame-relevant cues and ordering his experiencing of another's behaviour by means of them. And if a participant in a conversation did not constantly apply adjustments for frame, he would find himself listening in on a meaningless jumble of words and, with every word he injected, increasing the babble.
>
> (p. 546)

With the constantly reasserted distinction between the "I" of the speaker (animator) and the self he presents, or rather, represents (figure), and the constant recourse to narrative accounts, it looks as if, when face-to-face with other individuals, there is a perpetual effort to distance ourselves as animators from ourselves as figures, from selves on whom we can unload ultimate responsibility for what we have said and done. 'Whatever the reason, the life of talk consists principally of reliving' (pp. 546-7), and what individuals are up to when they are engaged with familiar companions in talk seems to be to frame themselves out of the way, and 'present a one-man show. He animates. That much is his own, his doing of the moment' (p. 547).

The margin between self as animator and self as figure is replicated in the latitude available for listeners to distance themselves from the actions or words which would serve as direct, mechanical ("natural") response. It is a latitude which overlays the rapidly shifting keys of the speaker with his own 'lattice of frame changes'. The 'choppy, streaming lines of change in frame everybody seems able to command' (p. 546) is in fact a device for distancing ourselves from the harshness of actuality. The facility with which we can pick up frame-relevant cues and construe them is a product of the perpetual effort we make to put a protective, comforting, shield between ourselves and the direct impact of the ongoing world on us, between consequentiality and what we say and do.

For supporting evidence, Goffman points to the increasing reliance of television generally on "documentaries" and of television news or films made "on the spot". Television news reporters specialise in interviews with people only beginning to clear themselves of total involvement in the experiences they have just been through, and therefore are 'able, merely by answering questions, to exude the reality of their concern. ("Were your mother's clothes still burning when you saw her trying to get out of the building?")' (*FA*, 550). This is followed up by a quick glance at the familiar arguments for (the better informing of the public), and against (the replaying of tragic events for viewers to experience vicariously). The end result of dramatising the world by live coverage (and, it is darkly suspected, its true aim) seems to be that real events can be smothered, and we can be 'inoculated' against reading their true significance.

Goffman is not concerned with either attacking or defending the "social responsibility" argument. Instead, he questions whether turning the happenings of the world around us into a show, something we can sit back and enjoy passively as a vicarious, second-hand, experience, is something altogether new.

> I believe we were ready for the enthrallment all the time. . . .
> For there is one thing that is similar to the warm hours we spend wrapped in television. It is the time we are prepared to spend recounting our own experiences or waiting an imminent turn to do so. True, we seem to have foregone some of this personal activity in favour of the work of the professionals. But what we have given up is not the world but a more traditional way of incorporating its incorporation of us.
>
> (p. 550)

The end to which Goffman has been driving the argument of this chapter is now in sight. It is, in a way, a reversal of the *theatrum mundi* image around which he constructed *The Presentation of Self*. We talk as if we saw life as theatre, but life, as it is represented when we talk about it, *is* theatre. The 'deep-seated similarities between the frame structure of the theatre and the frame structure of talk, especially the "informal" kind' (p. 550), are more fundamental than their differences.

So *Frame Analysis* as a whole, as well as the chapters in it devoted to the analysis of staged and scripted performance, is in a separate world of discourse – something more than a new conceptual framework – from that of *The Presentation of Self*. The distinction between the two books is put quite bluntly. 'All the world is not, of course, a stage', he says in *The Presentation of Self* (page 72). On page 124 of *Frame Analysis*, on the other hand, we have, 'All the world is like a stage . . .'.

We know of course that they are different. Life is real, whereas theatre (sc. theatre-like performances of all kinds) is not. 'It's make-believe. It really doesn't happen. And of course, in the sense meant, it doesn't. . . . Even ceremonials have greater actual consequence.'

But how real is the life the ordinary individual experiences, or talks about? The immediate answer is that it is both real *and* make-believe. Any individual's experience is made up of a great deal of action that he is engaged in, or intends, and of other people's action which involves him. All of this is real enough. 'On the other hand, it is known although perhaps not sufficiently appreciated, that the individual spends a considerable amount of time bathing his wounds in fantasy, imagining the worst things that might befall him, daydreaming about matters sexual, monetary, and so forth. He also rehearses what he will say when the time comes. . . .' And the time comes very frequently. A great deal of the day is, after all, spent in talk.

Does talk qualify as "real world" activity? In fact, says Goffman, 'it turns out to be just as much removed from actual worlds as is the stage' (p. 551). Cliques of colleagues and workmates, networks of friends and associates, families, and the other groupings in the complex infrastructure on which social organisation rests exist as theatres for the replayings which make up most conversation. And, Goffman suggests, there is some truth in the assertion that one of the functions of this social infrastructure is 'to provide each of us with sympathisers who will stand by when we recycle remains of our old experience' (p. 552).

There is however, it could be argued, one sizeable difference between real life and staged performance. It lies in the "dramatic" quality of make-believe theatrical performance. A simulacrum of the goings-on that fill everyday life would hardly do, except as an experiment, or a put-on, succeeding only because its perverse *un*-theatricality was being used to theatrical effect. Yet the replication of the most trivial everyday activities can go into the content of plays. The true difference lies in what is bracketed out of plays. Brief occurrences, trivial or serious, can be represented. Most of those which are too serious, or offensive, or costly, can easily be faked or represented in some symbolic fashion. Others can be reported as having occurred off stage. Other events, which are, like wars or revolutionary movements, too lengthy, or too large in scale, to be accommodated in the time and space available, may be represented by indirect means. There is an extensive repertoire of methods for indicating the occurrence of events which are too awkward for direct presentation. Clearly, however, it is preferable to have events directly presented, so that they can be seen and heard with something approaching their full impact in real life. For the true question is, 'what sort of material do onlookers find interesting and involving?' (p. 554).

The answer Goffman comes up with picks up the main theme of "Fun in Games" and "Where the Action Is". The rationale of games, the key to their very existence, lies in our involvement in them. That is how they came to be invented. So it is with drama. 'The dramatist provides a gamelike activity for the audience to get caught up in' (p. 555).

In a game, the players act and interact through emblems which serve as figures to them as animators (cards, chessmen, different kinds of ball) in arenas of different kinds (card table, chessboard, football pitch, billiards table, golf course, tennis court). The events are loaded with consequentiality, perhaps fatefulness. The game itself in its arena is screened off from the irrelevancies of the outside world, sometimes by its location, or by being housed in a purpose-built casino or hall, or merely by tacit understanding between players and onlookers or bystanders, but always by the 'rules of irrelevance' which involvement in the game prescribes.

The 'gamelike activity' that a playwright provides is a good deal more complicated. The characters do not act on and interact with each other at one remove, through emblematic figures like playing cards or chessmen, but directly; they are their own figures. The moves they make (the cards they play) are themselves fraught with significance, which may be deferred, or dependent on the moves and the plays made by other characters, but culminate in an ending to which the whole game-play has been moving – an ending which is the direct, culminating, consequence of what has been acted out, and which is manifest to all, performers and audience alike.

It is the 'fateful eventfulness' with which plays are filled that makes them "unreal": the concealments, disclosures, critical choices, sudden encounters and quick reverses, all of them with their specific effect on the lives of the characters. And the suspense generated by the fatefulness of the events and actions in a play is just what character-ises games: the feeling that one must 'look to the moment to find out what is going to happen' (p. 556). What happens in a play holds the same quality of eventfulness as a contest, which is itself a transforma-tion of a fight; but in plays the contention concerns the life situations of individuals.

These very same fateful events are what are momentous in our own lives: 'We feel that loss of a job, the going of a husband, the disclosure of a tainted past, and so forth are the sorts of things which do provide structuring to life, a key to the individual's "situation"' (p. 557). The point is critically important to Goffman's argument. It refers back to the argument concerning the content of conversational talk. To repeat: what most speakers are doing most of the time is to recount what happened to them, what they saw, or did, how they managed this or that eventuality. What a speaker does usually is to present for his listeners a version of what happened to him. In an important sense, even if his purpose is to present the cold facts as he sees them, the means he employs amount to an invitation to the listener to participate vicariously in his experience. The narrative form commonly used draws the listener into an empathetic re-living of what took place, taking off in his replaying of what happened from a situation approximate to what he guesses his listener's present information state to be. This means that 'listeners must in some way be ignorant of what is to be unfolded and desire to know the ending'.

This is precisely the case with the playwright. The suggestion is not that ordinary talk imitates drama but that drama is built out of the universal propensity for composing the offerings and responses that make up conversation in terms of narrative accounts of experience.

One could, in fact, argue that popularly recognised life-course themes do not merely make scripted presentation possible but are conceived of in order to make these entertainments possible. Human nature and life crises are what we need to make these entertainments possible. How else account for how well-adapted life appears to be for theatrical presentation?

(p. 557)

316

Plays, films, novels, stories, and also documentary reports, news items, interviews, and so on are all modelled on the dramatic narrative forms which make up the currency of most conversation. We know that ordinary talk is fragmentary; much of it is ill-expressed; sequences are not dovetailed together very neatly; most of it relates to events which are of quite minor significance for others, and their entertainment value is pretty small. Yet individual experience is full of random happenings and non-events; any attempt to organise has to accommodate itself to the larger organised environment of large-scale institutions, traffic, and prearranged events and activities. Compared with this, experiences replayed in conversation are highly structured. Sequences follow a certain logic, and events and action move from an initial situation reported in adequate terms towards their ordained ending and resolution. Moreover, when commonplace talk about experiences is elevated into a report, an autobiographical sketch, or a statement concerning events which have attracted public interest – when, in short, talk is addressed to a wider audience, there is a comparable shift towards a dramatised structure.

The individual's view of the experiences, whether they are his own or other people's, that he replays in his account

> would seem to be just as dramatic, just as biased in the direction of the eventful, just as much a response to our cultural stereotypes about the mainsprings of our motivation, as are those conceptions which are presented on the stage, or, of course, in any other of the channels for commercial vicarious experience.
>
> (p. 558)

VI

All five essays in *Forms of Talk* are meant to show how all forms of talk are analysable in much the same way, and reveal the same compartmentalised self as does everyday conversation and, of course, stage-acting. This is because all forms of speech behaviour, *including* theatrical performance, originate in ordinary speech – or rather the exchange of speech in talk – and are inherent in it.

The third essay, "Footing", supplements the discussion of everyday conversation in Chapter 13 of *Frame Analysis*, concentrating on changes in the situational grounds on which talk occurs. But in the first essay, "Response Cries", Goffman brings off a conjuring trick – turning the oddity of talk addressed to oneself to account as reinforcement for his thesis concerning social interaction as the structural foundation for all forms of talk.

Goffman makes his first move to the distinctive position he wants to take up by quarrelling with what he says is the traditional approach of linguistics to the analysis of conversation, which is to treat it as constructed according to a dialogic form: question and answer, statement and reply, and so forth.

Admittedly, there are forms of talk which seem indisputably to belong to the dialogue form. Even when elliptical answers are offered in reply to questions, it is usually perfectly possible (and standard linguistic practice) to "recover" a properly constructed sentence from it, and the same is true of interrupted sentences, ungrammatical turns of speech, and so on. But how does one handle non-verbal answers linguistically? or account for recapitulations and requests for them? or for muttered asides and interchanges between people present but not directly addressed? All such circumstances and contingencies (and Goffman is not sparing with his examples) bespeak an interaction between speaker and listener(s) which is much more complex and much more imprecise than a dialogic kind of structure allows for.

Also admittedly, there are features of conversation which relate to the correct transmission and reception of messages, features with which a communication engineer's approach would engage. Features of this kind, in which conversation might be defined as 'a two-way capacity for transceiving acoustically adequate and readily interpretable messages' (which could come from a training manual for telephone engineers) permit conversation to be mapped out as a system.

But, according to Goffman, so does a feature specified as 'Norms obliging respondents to reply honestly with whatever they know that is relevant and no more' (*FT*, 14-15). This comes straight from H. P. Grice's celebrated "conversational maxims", which derive from the fact that a conversation is not normally "a succession of disconnected remarks" but is characteristically a cooperative effort, at least to some extent.

Grice delivered his account of how conversation is constructed in a William James Lecture at Harvard in 1967.[10] It is an attempt to show that the implications often conveyed when we are talking and listening in conversation are assimilable to the rules of logic. What he in fact did was to elaborate his thesis about "non-natural" language uses (see above, p. 43) into an account of the varieties of what he called "implicature", and their uses. Out of this "cooperative principle", Grice derives a number of conversational maxims (and some "supermaxims"), grouped into four categories: quantity, quality, relation, and manner. In one rather limited sense, therefore, Grice's "conversational maxims" could be said to compose a system, but hardly in an engineering sense; the term, after all, could be applied in the same loose sense to Goffman's own analytical account of talk. So perhaps Goffman is a little over-eager in distancing himself from Grice's analysis; he certainly goes too far in representing Grice's distinction between "conventional" and "non-conventional" *implicatures* as one between 'conventional *maxims* and conversational ones, the latter presumably special to talk' (*FT*, 37 n.21; emphasis added).

Talk, like action of any other kind, has to "conform" to certain "social rules", such as taking turns to speak, responsiveness to the setting, and some deferential attention to the speaker. These tie it into the ongoing situation. So does the fact that talk interlocks with physical action by responding, promising, threatening, or describing. It is also, of course, a sort of action. But, although there is a border-land of movements, gestures, facial expressions, and the like, which may accompany, illustrate or modify what is being said, or substitute for it – even contradict it – talk is a very special sort of action, and quite unlike direct, physical, action. For one thing, talk involves the sub-entities discussed in the first part of this chapter. They go to make up what Goffman calls the "production format" of talk. There are other differences, too, in that participation in talk (as listener as well as speaker) may extend well beyond mere co-presence.

Keeping in mind the fact that the presentation of replayed experience, discussed in Chapter 13 of *Frame Analysis*, has to be tied into the information state of onlookers, listeners or audience by the competent use of appropriate connectives, it is evident that the audience, so far left out of the account, plays an essential part in the composite entirety. But its location in the analytical framework tends to shift. In a lecture, for example, the speaker's words are addressed unmistakably to the whole of the assembled gathering. Stage actors, however, address themselves to the other performers; the audience is there to listen in to what is being said – to overhear it, so to speak – and to appreciate it, but not to respond either in speech or action. Audience appreciation also extends, properly speaking, beyond the words being uttered by the actors to the decor, the production as a whole, and the occasion. In the case of ordinary conversation, there are often bystanders who may overhear what is being said (or sometimes eavesdrop), and so become unofficial ('unratified' is Goffman's term) participant members of the audience.

Speeches and performances of all kinds, from comic routines to the reciting of epic poems, point to the existence of a variety of participation frameworks – established institutional forms which allow of non-participating listeners and witnesses of orators, preachers, and actors. Similarly, it is just as unexceptionable for talk to include reported utterances of others distant in time and place. It is such fully institutionalised traditions, one might add, that provide experiential grounding for the virtually total segregation from each other of speakers and audiences in films, and in radio and television broadcasting, and for the seclusion of both from any kind of enveloping framework of action.

VII

Yet, while 'straightforward question-answer adjacency pairs do occur, and correspond completely to system requirements', one more often encounters interchanges which are 'not quite so naked'. These include, for example, the 'remedial interchanges' discussed in *Relations in Public*. Here the structure is more that of social ritual, involving constraints 'regarding how each individual ought to handle himself with respect to each of the others, so that he may not discredit his own tacit claim to good character or the tacit claim of the others that they are persons of social worth whose various forms of territoriality are to be respected' (*FT*, 16).

While ritual constraints, like system constraints – and the constraints of grammar – condition how talk is managed, the explanatory model they provide still falls short when it comes to the analysis of three-part interchanges, talking to oneself, and the like. Nor is there any way such a model may address the situation when the sets of conditions are at variance, or indeed in conflict, with each other. To take the more obvious examples, ritual constraints which apply to talk are different when differences in rank are involved, or some cultural variation, and system constraints are broken when misheard utterances are nevertheless met with signs of comprehension.

With all the easily discoverable qualifications and exceptions that exist when dialogue is taken to represent the fundamental structure of conversation, its acceptance as a conventional model is something of a puzzle. Goffman finds the rationale for the convention in the attention usually given to making sure that hearer and speaker agree about what was said and heard; agreement about what it means is seemingly of less consequence. In any case,

> Commonly a speaker cannot explicate with any precision what he meant to get across, and on those occasions if hearers think they know precisely, they will likely be at least a little off. . . . One routinely presumes on a mutual understanding that doesn't quite exist. What one obtains is a working agreement, an agreement 'for all practical purposes'.
>
> (FT, 11)

It is only when certain limits are unintentionally – or purposely – exceeded that ambiguities and doubts are aired; and there is a whole range of verbal and non-verbal devices used by hearers to inform speakers whether or not they were both audible and "making sense".

> Given these very fundamental requirements of talk as a communicative system, we have the essential rationale for the . . . organisation of talk into two-part exchanges. We have ,an understanding of why any next utterance after a question is examined for how it might be an answer.
>
> (FT, 12)

There are other difficulties which beset a less exacting interpretation of talk, this time as verbal interchanges between speaker and listener(s). Much of our understanding of what goes on in talk comes from our learning about it from printed texts, which lay out talk in terms of reasonably well-formed sentences, questions and answers, statements and replies, utterances and responses. And to reproduce a conversation in the printed text of a play or novel or in a newspaper report satisfies the condition of any body of print, namely, that *everything* readers might not already know and that is required for understanding be alluded to, if not detailed, *in print*. The unspoken elements of an interaction which are embedded in the physical and interpersonal setting and serve as cues for guiding interpretation are incorporated and handled so as to sustain a single realm of relevant material, namely, words in print.

To draw on these materials as sources in the analysis of talk is thus to use material that has already been systematically rendered into one kind of thing – words in print. It is only natural, therefore, to find support from sources in print for the belief that the material of conversation consists fundamentally of uttered words.

(FT, 32)

Pointing, gesturing, the omissions and "speaking" silences, and all the other bits of by-play that occur in a conversation mean that an unvarnished transcript of it can be impenetrably mystifying. Very often, though, it is possible to make out an intended meaning from the response to it.

In the same way the respondent's special background knowledge of the events at hand can become available to us through his words. Indeed, the more obscure the speaker's statement for his original auditors, the more pains his respondent is likely to have taken to display its sense through his own reply, and the more need we who come later will have for this help.

(p. 34)

A good deal of what Goffman is trying to get at here is encapsulated in the opening lines of *Hamlet*:

Bernardo: Who's there?
Francisco: Nay, answer me. Stand and unfold yourself.

– Francisco being the man actually on guard duty. The implication of a world turned upside down which runs through the greater part of the play is set out forcefully not in the challenge and response but in the paradox of the turns the new arrival and the man on guard take at speaking. Readers of the text (as against audiences) may have to have this pointed out to them in a footnote.

Again, some forms of face-to-face interaction are programmed for non-verbal responses. In fact, 'no face-to-face talk, however intimate, informal, dyadic, "purely conversational", or whatever, precludes nonlinguistic responses or the inducing of such responses' *(FT, 40)*; and talk very often fails to make sense without them.

Responses, non-verbal as well as verbal, have a much longer, and more flexible "reach" than replies; they can refer to happenings, actions, utterances, and so on extending back over much more than what had just been said. So,

although a *reply* is addressed to meaningful elements of whole statements, *responses* can break frame and reflexively address aspects of a statement which would ordinarily be 'out of frame', part of transmission, not content – for example, the statement's duration, tactfulness, style, origin, accent, vocabulary, and so forth.

(p. 43)

By now, Goffman has argued through the pre-existing formulations to the point at which he can assimilate the complications he has revealed in ordinary talk to those already established for social interaction. Instead of the one-by-one sequence of dialogue – question and answer, statement and reply, utterance and response – we now have an admixture of expressions, verbal and non-verbal, which may – and often do – *reach back* beyond the semantic meaning of what the previous speaker has just said to what he was saying it about. One has to look beyond the utterance to which the immediate response was made to whatever the response encompassed within its reach. And to grasp this, any listener has to wait for the speaker to disclose what he is referring to; he has no other way of discovering for sure what it will be: 'Our basic conversational unit then becomes reference-response' (*FT*, 50).

On the other hand, anticipation also enters in, as he made out in *Relations in Public* when he ran through "set-ups", "cut-offs", "one-liners", and other complexities of verbal back-chat (pp. 87-8, above): 'An important possibility in the analysis of talk is to uncover the consequence of a particular move for the anticipated sequence; for that is the way to study the move's functioning' (*FT*, 57).

Formalistic analysis according to dialogue form, or the requirements of effective communication, or the demands of ritualistic behaviour, or a combination of all three, is by no means dismissed as entirely inapplicable. It does apply, all too obviously, to the verbal exchanges found in plays, novels, records, and other places where words are used to represent what is happening. 'Natural conversation, however, is not subject to this recording bias – in a word, not subject to transformation into words. What is basic to natural talk may not be a conversational unit at all, but an interactional one' (*FT*, 48). What Goffman is arguing for is provision for the analysis of the sequences of interaction which occur 'at a higher level' than that of statement and reply. One has to look for the choices made about "reach", and how individuals construe what is reached for.

What finally emerges is an analytical model of talk which sees it as a series of response moves, each 'incorporating a variable balance of function in regard to statement-reply properties'. The image of talk Goffman has in mind is more of a dance, he says, than a game: a sequence of responses, or "response-moves", each capable of referring backwards (or, sometimes, forwards) in the sequence, each with a reach capable of well beyond the current framework and setting. Each response-move, too, is capable of manipulating the intersubjective mental world (or arena) created by and for talk by transformations into metaphorical, irony, bantering, mocking and any number of other readily available constructions.

'Such a formulation', he claims, 'would finally allow us to give proper credit to the flexibility of talk – a property distinguishing talk, for example, from the interaction of moves occurring in formal games and to see why so much interrupting, nonanswering, restarting, and overlapping occurs in it' (p. 52).

> What, then, is talk viewed interactionally? It is an example of that arrangement by which individuals come together and sustain matters having a ratified, joint, current, and running claim upon attention, a claim which lodges them in some sort of intersubjective mental world. Games provide another example – so does a sudden 'striking' event. . . . But no resource is more effective as a basis for joint involvement than speakings. Words are the great device for fetching speaker and hearer into the same focus of attention and into the same interpretation schema that applies to what is thus attended. But that words are the best means to this end does not mean that words are the only one or that the resulting social organisation is intrinsically verbal in character.
>
> (pp. 70-1)

VIII

The multiplicity of elements which may compose the social role of speaker ('production format') plus the shifting and somewhat elastic numbers constituting the potential audience ('participation framework') mean that the alignment of speaker to audience may change quite frequently and, consequently, has to be repeatedly defined and redefined. This alignment Goffman calls 'footing'. It is best envisaged as a second dimension of the posture assumed in speaking, "frame" being the stance a speaker adopts to what he is saying, "footing" signifying his stance to whomsoever is able to hear him (himself, of course, included):

> A change in footing implies a change in the alignment we take up to ourselves and the others present as expressed in the way we manage the production or reception of an utterance. A change in our footing is another way of talking about a change in our frame for events.
>
> (*FT*, 128)

Such changes are a perpetually recurring feature of natural talk – as when a teacher switches from instructing a class to admonishing them for inattention, or members of a committee switch to small talk after the conclusion of business. Goffman supplies a number of empirical instances from sociolinguists' researches, but these (since they are in print) give an inevitably incomplete account. Although changes of footing are typically indicated by changes in tone or accent, they may well be indicated by changes in bodily posture, or demeanour, or gesture, and may well occur without being marked by a vocal or any other kind of signifier.

Since what counts is speaker-audience alignment, much depends on the minutiae of the institutional arrangement within which any particular discourse occurs and on the intentions of speakers, the kind and degree of involvement displayed by audience, and the capacity of either side to manipulate the way talk is flowing. There are two sides of any interaction which involves talk, but the situation is a good deal more complex than what seems to be assumed in traditional linguistic analysis – of two individuals, a speaker and a listener. Among other things, such an assumption carries the implication that sound alone is what matters, whereas sight is obviously significant, too, as well as such elements in an encounter as changing the order of turns at talking, assessing the evidence provided by attentiveness, subordinate communications, and the like. And there are other amendments put forward to the linguists' paradigm – for instance, the fact that a conversation can include passages of silence, or of action other than talk, even though the whole episode is thought of as "a talk".

The more adequate definition of "a talk" he proposes is of 'a substantive, naturally bounded, stretch of interaction', with its start and closure typically marked by ritual brackets, and 'comprising all that relevantly goes on from the moment two (or more) individuals open such dealings between themselves and continuing until they finally close this activity out' (p. 130).

This satisfactorily brings talk within the scope of social interaction analysis. However, this may not of itself be appropriate for the actual talk that does occur during 'a state of talk'. This looks like a concession to linguistics, but is not, because the analysis even of 'moments of talk' requires a more elaborate conceptual apparatus than linguistics provides. So, at this point, there is a summary recapitulation of what is meant by 'participation framework', which includes adventitious bystanders in a position to eavesdrop or overhear by accident, as well as a variety of 'ratified participants' – i.e. more than one person to whom the speaker is addressing his talk.

Hence, 'an utterance does not divide the world up into two parts, recipients and non-recipients, but rather opens up an array of structurally differentiated possibilities, establishing the participation framework in which the speaker will be guiding his delivery' (p. 137) . . . 'Once the dyadic limits of talk are breached, and one admits bystanders and/or more than one ratified recipient to the scene, then "subordinate communication" becomes a recognisable possibility' (p. 133), something which includes by-play, collusion in concealed communication, innuendo, and so on. In other words, the unit of analysis becomes a gathering, as against an encounter (above, pp. 34-5).

IX

The principal, animator, and figure of the production format are not to be envisaged as social roles but as sub-entities required for the purposes of analysis. One way or another, a speaker is involved as one, two, or all three of them, whatever performative or other mode of utterance he makes. Time and place are directly involved in the same way, tacitly if not overtly. But a great number of utterances are composed with the speaker's self represented by a personal pronoun,

> typically 'I', and thus a *figure* – a figure in a statement – that serves as the agent, a protagonist in a *described* scene, a 'character' in an anecdote, someone who, after all, belongs to the world that is spoken about, not the world in which the speaking occurs. And once this format is employed, an astonishing flexibility is created.
> (p. 147)

When we use qualifications and disclaimers like ". . . I should think", or "I trust . . .", or "What I meant was . . .", 'we are projecting ourselves as animators into the talk. But this is a figure, nonetheless, and not the actual animator' (p. 148). Also, we can refer to things that we did, or thought, or happened to us some time ago, or somewhere else, when we were not the same persons as we are now – or at least were in some different social position. And again, if we refer back to something we once said, then 'two animators can be said to be involved: the one who is physically animating the sounds that are heard, and an embedded animator, a figure in a statement who is present only in a world that is being told about . . .' (p. 149).

It is in fact embedding – the frequent and varied and multiple framings to which we resort in talk – that makes it essential to resolve the primitive notion of speaker into production format. For what happens as utterances and part utterances are framed successively within each other, especially when they involve references to oneself, is that a pyramid of layerings is built up into thicker and thicker description. And each successive layer represents an extra degree of informational dependency on the situation represented by the previous layering. The multiplicity is a requisite of the multiplicity of different miniature "selves" standing for each level of experiential information.

A shift from one of these frame-levels to another means a change in footing: 'When we shift from saying something ourselves to reporting what someone else said, we are changing our footing' (p. 151). The counterpart differentiation of hearer into participation framework, with different hearers allocated to the status of participants in an encounter, audience members, or non-participant members of a gathering, is also needed so as to register the significance of changes of footing.

And, lastly, participation frameworks themselves may be subjected to transformation.

> We quite routinely ritualise participation frameworks [using 'ritualise' in the ethological sense]; that is, we self-consciously transplant the participation framework that is natural in one social situation into an interactional environment in which it isn't. . . . We not only embed utterances, we embed interaction arrangements.
>
> (p. 153)

These last passages become rather more easily comprehensible when they are set alongside the incident Goffman chose as principal illustration. The essay begins with a 1973 news bureau release about an episode involving President Nixon. The news report is quoted from the Philadelphia *Evening Bulletin* in full:

WASHINGTON [UPI] – President Nixon, a gentleman of the old school, teased a newspaper woman yesterday about wearing slacks in the White House and made it clear that he prefers dresses on women.

After a bill-signing session in the Oval Office, the President stood up from his desk and in a teasing voice said to UPI's Helen Thomas, "Helen, are you still wearing slacks? Do you prefer them actually? Every time I see girls in slacks it reminds me of China."

Miss Thomas, somewhat abashed, told the President that Chinese women were now moving toward Western dress.

"This is not said in an uncomplimentary way, but slacks can do something for some people, and some it can't." He hastened to add, "but I think you do very well. Turn around."

. . . Miss Thomas did a pirouette for the President. . . .

The fact that the report must have come from Miss Thomas' hand adds a little extra twist.

The kind of comment the incident immediately calls for has of course to do with 'gender politics', and Goffman provides an adequate supply of those. But the full force of the anecdote as illustration is in the reprise, which comes at the very end of the essay.

When Helen Thomas pirouetted for the president, she was parenthesising within her journalistic stance another stance, namely that of a woman receiving comments on her appearance. No doubt the forces at work are sexism and presidents, but the forces can work in this particular way because of our general capacity to embed the fleeting enactment of one role in the more extended performance of another.

When Helen Thomas pirouetted for the president, she was employing a form of behaviour indigenous to the environment of the ballet, a form that has come, by conventional reframing, to be a feature of female modelling in fashion shows, and she was enacting it – of all places – in a news conference. No one present apparently found this transplantation odd. *That* is how experience is laminated. . . .

NOTES AND REFERENCES

1. F. de Saussure, *Cours de linguistique générale*, Payot, 1916 (English trans. by W. Baskin, *Course in General Linguistics*, Philosophical Library, 1959).
2. A. J. Ayer, *More of my Life*, Collins, 1984, p. 188.
3. I. A. Richards, *The Philosophy of Rhetoric*, Oxford Univ. Press, 1936, p. 7.
4. J. L. Austin, *How to do Things with Words*, Oxford Univ. Press, 1962, p. 1.
5. L. Wittgenstein, *Philosophical Investigations*, Blackwell, 1958, para. 404.
6. L. Wittgenstein, *Philosophical Investigations*, Blackwell, 1958, para. 413.
7. R. Horton, "Material-object language and theoretical language: towards a Strawsonian sociology of thought", in *Philosophical Disputes in the Social Sciences* (ed. S. C. Brown), Harvester Press, 1979, p. 207.
8. H. P. Grice, "Meaning", *Philosophical Review*, 1957, pp. 377-88.
9. See Elizabeth Burns, *Theatricality*, Longman, 1972, Chapter 7, "Authenticating conventions".
10. H. P. Grice, "Logic and conversation", in *Speech Acts* (eds P. Cole and J. L. Morgan), volume 3 of *Syntax and Semantics*, Academic Press, 1975, p. 45.

12
TALK AND ITS
AUDIENCES

The three remaining essays of *Forms of Talk* – "Response Cries", "The Lecture", and "Radio Talk" – deal with talk uttered outside of conversation. All are directed towards establishing that talk of any kind, whatever its institutional character, is always a form of social interaction.

The reasoning behind the claim comes from frame analysis, with the modifications introduced by the essay on "Footing". Indeed, in that essay, Goffman suggests that talking to oneself provides the 'clearest evidence' in favour of his approach to the analysis of talk as embedded in the structure of specifically social situations (*FT*, 136). As for lecturing and radio announcing, the fact that changes of footing are all-important is justification for the claim that those forms of talk, too, may be properly regarded as forms of social interaction. In "Response Cries" he sets out to demonstrate that self-talk, as well as the imprecations and "half-word" utterances of the essay's title, although commonly taken to be unpremeditated, spontaneous, "involuntary", and addressed to nobody in particular, apart perhaps from oneself, are in fact specific modes of social interaction. Again, in the fourth essay, "The Lecture", it is the interactional aspects that are given most attention. "Radio Talk", the last essay, concentrates on the special circumstances of radio and television announcing which make for exemplary demonstration of the same conclusion: remedying errors by way of corrections and apologies calls for further talk addressed to oneself but meant to be overheard by an audience which is distant and unseen but very much within earshot.

I

Our time is divided between talking and keeping silent, but, most of the time, we stay silent. Silence is normal; talk, Goffman remarks towards the end of "Response Cries", has to be regarded as the exception. Furthermore, talk has to be *occasioned*, on the understanding that what we have to say will be of some interest or concern for others. .

When therefore, we come across someone who seems to be talking to himself, or not addressing anyone in particular, we are presented with something anomalous. Circumstances do exist, however, which make such utterances acceptable, or at least unexceptionable. "Response Cries" is about the three forms of talk which occur in this way: 'self-talk', exclamations (and imprecations), and 'response cries' (i.e. 'exclamatory interjections which are not full-fledged words) – and the situations in which they are taken to be warrantable.

These three kinds of utterance in fact make up the second of the two classes of 'roguish' (by which I take it he means "rogue") utterance that appear to violate the interdependence which is premised by talk. The first consists in talking to oneself (or rather, being *found* talking to oneself by someone). Both classes of "rogue" utterance form the subject-matter of the essay.

In considering self-talk, one has first to distinguish being "solitary", with no one in sight or within earshot, from being "on one's own", unaccompanied but in public, with other people around. A lot of talking to oneself does go on, so Goffman says, in both kinds of situation. This is certainly the case with small children, but it is also frequent among grown-ups, although it is only through self-monitoring, hearsay, and observation that one becomes aware of it. While much of it may be *sotto voce*, the manner of speech is not distinctive, or even unusual. What counts is that, while unexceptionable for children, and even though "a lot of it goes on", to talk to oneself is widely regarded as taboo for adults. It is at any rate taboo to *continue* to do so in public; any one of us may some time or another be caught talking to ourselves, but this is seemingly quite permissible, if we then stop doing so.

The reasons usually advanced for the taboo are that, although of itself not to be taken as a sign of disordered mind, it is childish, or betrays autistic tendencies. Goffman goes on to argue that this is to miss the point. Along with other forms of ignoring or disregarding others who are present, it not only shows disrespect towards those others but lack of self-regard too, in that we are publicly failing to sustain that alertness to what is happening around us and, especially, readiness to respond should we be spoken to, which are the marks of a fit and proper member of society.

Self-talk counts as an impropriety offered to anybody within sight or earshot (a 'situational' misdemeanour) rather than an offence committed in the company of people with whom we are conversing (a 'situated' one). Like other "mental symptoms", it constitutes a 'threat to intersubjectivity' (*FT*, 85).

To talk to oneself is to deter social interaction by mounting a semblance of being caught up in some other interaction. By not only staging the uttering of words but conjuring up the participation framework of true conversation and recreating in mimic form the context of interaction in which such words may be uttered, it excludes others who are present and who, in the ordinary way, would be "ratified" participants.

What we have also, according to Goffman, is another instance of the human capacity of ritualisation (in the ethological sense). However, the second wind which his discovery of the ethological usage of the term shows seems to be faltering. Ritualisation is now 'a crucial feature of human communication', but not only do we have behaviour which is 'ritualised – in something like the ethological sense', but *appearance* is ritualised, too. He does not explain how appearance can be ritualised, but we are offered a brief run-through of a number of 'processes' which he says are 'ethologically defined'. These are 'exaggeration, stereotyping, standardisation of intensity, loosening of contextual requirements, and so forth'.

Admittedly, people who talk to themselves do sometimes embellish their utterances with histrionic trappings, but these are surely minimal – *except* perhaps in the case of mental patients, and these, for once, are not mentioned. Gestural and expressive aids to speech are often standardised, even stereotyped, but this does not make them ritualistic. Encoding is not ritual.

Goffman is on firmer ground when he points to how behaving in this way may be regarded as 'a communicative arrangement', a means of realigning ourselves as regards any audience, be it companions or bystanders, and – importantly – in regard to ourselves. There are, after all, several quite common and socially acceptable ways in which the general rule – *No talking to oneself in public* – may be breached. Someone walking along a street by himself who trips and stumbles may, if he believes he was seen, engage in remedial work (see above, pp. 84-5) so as to correct any possible doubt about his competence at walking. He can do this with a little ritualised performance – a display – in which he can act out the special circumstances which make it a mishap, not the result of incapacity. But he might also help out by exclaiming at himself, uttering a 'cry of wonderment'. For it seems that 'verbalisations' quite in the absence of conversations can play much the same part as a choreographed bit of nonverbal behaviour' (p. 90).

Public speakers are sometimes inclined to deal with mishaps occurring to their text or in their speech in much the same way, expressing bewilderment or annoyance in utterances which are directed to themselves but audible to their audience. And there are, too, the well-publicised verbal antics of tennis-players and other sportsmen in similar predicaments; 'after all', Goffman comments, 'such clarity of intent is what sports are all about'.

Yet another kind of self-talk is "muttering" – 'the structural equivalent of what children do when they stick out their tongue or thumb their nose just as their admonisher turns away'. For the *sotto voce* is half-way between talk which is addressed to someone and self-talk which the someone is meant to overhear. Its transient nature is inherent; 'muttering is a time-limited communication, entering as a "last word", a post-terminal touch to a just-terminated encounter' (p. 93); it is innocent in formal terms, if one sticks to the letter of the law against talking to oneself in public.

Self-talk is, in such situations, best regarded as a protective device – something we hold in readiness for reacting to circumstances in which we think other people ought to know about our own reaction.

II

The "response cries" of the essay's title is Goffman's generic term for the second category of self-talk. This comprises all those objurgations, exclamations, and cries of distress or surprise by which we respond to some mishap, or to some unpleasant or unexpected happening, and which are called "meaningless" – i.e. have no indexical reference.

On the face of it, imprecations, which *are* blurted-out and, one would think, involuntary, seem far removed from self-talk. Nor can exclamatory utterances be taken as talk; they are not even accorded the status of proper words but regarded as 'a natural overflowing, a flooding up of previously contained feeling, a bursting of normal constraints, a case of being caught off guard' (p. 99).

Yet the curse or the obscenity uttered by someone when he trips up is not very far removed from the exculpatory utterance broadcast by someone on the same sort of occasion. An imprecation is just as likely, and, by expressing surprise or bewilderment, does much the same work of rectifying any false impression a momentary failing may have conveyed. There is further support for this interpretation of imprecations (and public toleration of them) in the otherwise odd fact that expletives are tailored to fit the susceptibilities of the likely audience; milder expletives are customary when there are women and children about, among strangers than among workmates, and so on.

Once again, Goffman invokes ritual: 'A response cry is (if anything is) a ritualised act in something like the ethological sense of that term' (p. 100). But the notion of ritual is not particularly useful in this kind of instance; what he wants to do is to eliminate a number of well-established distinctions applied to the meaning, or the intent, such expressions convey – a distinction between venting anger and expressing elation; between ritual display and displacement behaviour; between the cry of alarm (or disgust) and the shout of triumph; between intention and frustrated intention. "Meaning" is not especially relevant. The expressions are analytically equivalent in that they refer to experiences with which one expects others to feel sympathy.

This is best illustrated by the glossary he provides of the various standard cries, each with a painstakingly full account (much abbreviated below) of the significance to be attached to it.

Transition displays. Utterances like *Brr!*, *Ahh!*, and *Phew!* are for venting one's feelings about it's being too hot, too cold, or too uncomfortable in some way. One feature is that the expression refers to the kind of discomfort which, even if it is experienced by the one individual who utters the cry, is appreciable by others present.

The *spill cry* (*Oops!* and *Whoops!*) is a rather more complex matter. While it appears to publicise a loss of control, it really goes to minimise the accident, making clear one's awareness of what has happened. It may also serve as 'a warning to others that a piece of the world has gotten loose' and for them to take care. By using a cry specific to this kind of incident, we demonstrate that at least one part of us is functioning and, behind this, at least some presence of mind. A part of us proves to be organised, 'and standing watch over the part of us that apparently isn't watchful' (p. 102).

The *threat startle* (*Eek!* and *Yipe!*) once again makes a statement, this time about surprise and fear, but 'surprise and fear that are very much under control'. What seems to be involved is a kind of exaggerated mock-up of surprise and fear that deprecates any show of real concern – a 'warning*like* signal in dangerous*like* circumstances' (p. 104).

Revulsion sounds, such as *Eeuw!,* are responses to contact with something contaminating. Once again, uttering the cry seems of itself to minimise what damage there might be, for there is something unserious about such cries. There is, he says, 'a hint of hyperritualisation' about them, this being the term he brought into use in *Gender Advertisements* to denote a sophisticated ('recursive') play-acting of ritualistic behaviour when its employment becomes over-obvious.

All four response cries so far reviewed are those, says Goffman, which one finds uttered by individuals when others are present but not *with* them (in his special sense of "with"). The same kind of behaviour, though, occurs among people who are "with" each other, or engaged in an 'open state of talk'. Some distinction between the response cries appropriate to either situation seems to be implied, but is rather difficult to discern. Certainly, it is hard to think of any of the cries being the preserve of either the one situation or the other. However, most of the remaining response cries are almost self-explanatory; the *strain grunt,* where extreme exertion is guyed by being overplayed; the *pain cry,* often used to mean "I'm going to be hurt" rather than "I am hurt" (more often, Goffman says); and the *sexual moan,* 'strategically employed to delineate an ideal development in the marked absence of anything like the real thing' (p. 106).

The relevance of all this to the argument of the essay becomes apparent when we come to *"floor cues"*. This is his term for the muttered imprecation or exclamation which is designed to invite question or comment by a bystander or companion, and so open up an occasion for making some statement without being thought querulous or self-important. Typical examples arise when we make the sort of mistake we would like thought exceptional, or, more subtly, when we want to provoke some query which will give an opening for some shrewd or caustic comment on a newspaper item or passage in a book we have just come across. The list ends with *"audible glee"* – cries of *Oooo!, Wheee!,* and so on, which announce some triumph, or delight beyond expectation. These are a kind of reciprocal of "floor cries"; they call for admiring or envious attention rather than an opening for talk.

So, response cries, far from being "extracted" from us by some crisis, are now visible as 'standardised vocal comments' which are actually claims that, despite appearances, circumstances are not, or no longer, beyond our emotional and physical control. They may break into ongoing conversation as well as in gatherings, or when intermittent talk is part of some ongoing task or game. They may even be uttered in response to some verbal account of a situation which has been concluded or settled long beforehand and some distance away. 'Indeed, response cries are often employed thrice removed from the crisis to which they are supposed to be a blurted response.' For Goffman, they are ritualised expressions (in the anthropological sense, this time?); they also, perhaps, have some kinship with the connecting function performed by responses in ordinary conversation, although this is not suggested in the essay.

What is peculiar to all three kinds of extra-conversational utterance – talking to oneself, imprecations, and interjections – is that, formally speaking, they are conversational improprieties which reflect badly on whomsoever produces them. But what they also have in common is that they are produced in what are taken to be mitigating circumstances. This is easily seen in the case of imprecations; response cries function as a way of defending our composure, our ability to manage competently, our *amour-propre*, when we lapse from the standard of competence we believe we ordinarily maintain or are confronted with some untoward happening – just as when we are caught talking to ourselves.

The destination towards which Goffman has been herding his argument now becomes apparent. He points to the fact that there is one area in which we all constantly encounter difficulties in the face of untoward happenings, 'and that, interestingly enough, is in the management of talk itself' (p. 109). Thus, when people are momentarily at a loss for a word, or distracted, or have lost their place, the tendency is for them to fill in with some sound like *aah*, or *um*, to show that they have not stopped altogether, are trying to remedy what has gone wrong, and will continue; the sound is emitted so as to "hold the floor", repel interlopers, and advertise their intention to resume. These 'unblurted subvocalisations' (p. 109), although not precisely response cries, are of the same order. They are not directed at anyone in particular, even oneself. More particularly, they have a fairly standardised form, quite apart from the way they are rendered in writing. Self-corrections, with the corrected word or phrase usually uttered more rapidly and loudly, fall into the same category, fulfilling as they do much the same purpose, this time of showing that the speaker is really in full control.

Imprecations, for their part, are also best considered as a kind of response cry rather than self-talk. Unlexicalised cries are fairly conventionalised, amounting to what might be thought of as half-words – as the fact that every language seems to have its own special set of them goes to show. Imprecations have gone much further along the same lines, "ritualising" still further words which either religion counts as blasphemy or good manners and good taste as obscenity when used to express annoyance, revulsion, alarm, or some other reaction to unexpected or unwanted happenings. The point, once again, is that imprecations are quite carefully fashioned for the particular occasion of use; ordinarily, for example, it is in order to address imprecations to oneself but not to one's partner (or indeed, opponent) in games like tennis, bridge, or chess; words of applause or congratulation work in the reverse sense. In games of chance, the same balance is struck between those self-directed statements which invoke 'the fates, the dice, or some other ethereal recipient' in support, and those which are full-bodied imprecations following failure.

Response cries of all three kinds, which are not addressed to anyone else, or anyone in particular, but yet are meant to be heard, or rather overheard, constitute a kind of surreptitious communication. They can even occur in the course of conversation, amounting to what Goffman calls a 'structural ruse – . . . allowing witnesses a glimpse into the dealings we are having with ourselves' (p. 119).

III

The last two essays in *Forms of Talk*, "The Lecture" and "Radio Talk", deal with fully established institutions designed for, and around, occasions which afford opportunities for one speaker to address a much larger audience and for a much longer period than is customary for ordinary everyday talk, and to do so without interruption.

Although there are innumerable occasions when one person may speak at length to a number of people, the categorically different kinds of institutionalised arrangement which allow for this are rather few in number. Oral narration and reporting are among the oldest, although very much in decline until the advent of radio broadcasting. Forensic speeches constitute another category, one which includes presenting a case in a parliamentary assembly, to a committee, or to a private or public meeting as well as in a court of law. And there is the lecture, a means of instruction almost as old as the sermon, and obviously closely related to it but differing from it in that the style of language and delivery is nowadays typically rather impersonal, as well as serious.

"The Lecture", although the title is reminiscent of the kind of short film Robert Benchley used to make, is in fact the transcript of a lecture about lectures. It was delivered at the University of Michigan in 1976 at the invitation of the organisers of the Katz-Newcomb Memorial Lectures. The essay is therefore something of a *pièce d'occasion*. What Goffman has done is to make the *occasion* itself the topic of the *pièce*, using the lecture to convey, and also to illustrate, what he has to say about the lecture as one of the institutional frameworks in which talk occurs.

Again, it is the interactional aspects of this institutional arrangement for talk that are given most attention. There is some acknowledgement of the fact that structural features of society – relationships of power and status, and the values they embody – do have some bearing on the character of the institution itself, and even on the form social interaction takes within its confines, but Goffman concedes no more to the part they play than to remark that they are 'bled into these occasions' (p. 193).

His main concern is with public university lectures of the kind he is delivering, which are financed by special endowments – legacies by benefactors, gifts from commercial corporations or rich patrons, or subscriptions raised to commemorate former notable members – and administered by a specially appointed committee. And it is to such organisational (rather than structural) elements that Goffman turns first, after some deprecatory, almost demure, remarks about lecturing on lectures being perhaps 'a little special'.

Mention of the more innocuous features of the organisation behind the lecture, such as the committee's taking responsibility for success or failure, or being accorded it, is interlarded with one or two rather more sardonic references. One is to the dual function of the advertisements, the notices, and the press coverage of the event. These are of course designed to increase the size of the audience but also function as 'vanity presses', much as campus newspapers do for the administration. There are also some rather more dubious (and facile) ironies having to do with an 'obvious' link between formal organisations (universities, in this case) and the "star system".

> In a sense . . . an institution's advertising isn't done in response to the anticipated presence of a well-known figure, rather a well-known figure is useful in order to have something present that warrants wide advertising. So one might say that large halls aren't built to accommodate large audiences but rather to accommodate wide advertising.
>
> (p. 170)

The formal anatomy of the lecture begins after Goffman has made his way through his opening remarks. Visual aspects come first. The special style appropriate to lecturing is reflected in the characteristic layout, with speaker, along with a chairman, and perhaps one other person, to represent the sponsors and the responsible authority, on a platform, suitably equipped and furnished, at one end of an auditorium, and, seated in rows in front of them, a number of people prepared to listen. It is an alignment which conveys an inescapable sense of the speaker giving a performance in front of an audience. In contrast, then, to the alignment of speaker and listeners we are used to in ordinary conversation, where appraisal is mutual, there are tacit claims by the speaker to special abilities and skills, as well as command of specialist knowledge, and, on the part of the audience, to the right to pass judgment on the performance.

Like all performances – and games – the success or failure of a lecture depends on the extent to which the audience is involved to the point of engrossment in the 'special realm of being' it generates. And the central concern of Goffman's lecture-essay is how it is that, against all the apparent odds, public lectures do attract sizeable audiences and, often enough, do arouse and hold their attention – enough, at least, to measure up to the requirements of a successful performance. And the reasons for this, he argues, lie in the special qualities that make speaking as a live, or original, performance superior to any recording, broadcast, film, or printed version.

Of course, live performances of music are obviously superior to recordings or broadcasts which, however good they are, leave out some of the tonal values and distort balance. Colour prints of paintings are even worse, being at best poor mementoes of the originals. But considerations like these are reversed when it comes to lectures. In other modes of communicating knowledge (which now include linked computer facilities as well as the older forms of print, film, audio- and video-broadcasts and recordings available in 1976), errors in reading, speech defects, relative or occasional inaudibility, and other familiar ailments of lecturers and lecture halls can be eliminated. They are also often more economical, as well as more effective and more efficient.

Special lectures by visiting celebrities figure chiefly in what he has to say, but there are references to ordinary (university course) lectures. Although the latter differ in the way they fit into the structure of society and into university organisation, they nevertheless represent the norm, the "ideal type", in the Weberian sense, with the public lecture the "ideal", in the sense of being exemplary. In any case, it does not take much experience of lecture-going to know that success, measured in terms of Goffman's putative "involvement factor", can happen with the run-of-the-mill lecture, just as the public lecture can fail. Either way, the interactional elements with which Goffman is centrally concerned are much the same in both cases.

The arguments against the lecture simply as a means of imparting knowledge are now a commonplace among academics. The puzzle is why lecturing is still the mainstay of university teaching; and it is this puzzle that Goffman addresses.

First, to hark back to the comparison with live music performance and original paintings, their superiority does not altogether reside in their being exempt from the deficiencies of engineered transmission or colour printing. Being able to look at the musicians while a performance is in progress actually makes for more acute *listening*, as Stravinsky once said. Certainly, attentiveness – engrossment – is much easier at a concert than in one's living-room. As for paintings, "tactile values" do refer to something other than superior visual quality. In both cases, too, there seems to be an added value in being physically present with the actual production of music and the actual product of the artist.

Goffman does not refer to any such possible indicators or parallels, but he does have something to say about the special value attached to the privileged access to the author of what is being said which attendance at a lecture gives.

For while one might regard the lecture as one means of imparting knowledge, and not necessarily the most effective, people do in fact attend because something more than the transmission of a text is involved. Part of this "something more" lies in the fact that the delivery of the text is enclosed within a special, 'celebrative', occasion

– a "spectacle", to use the term he took over from Kenneth Pike (see above, p. 272). "Spectacles" in this special sense are those occasions which are marked off from what are seen as run-of-the-mill – an opening night as against an ordinary performance of a play, the office party as against a day at the office, a special lecture as against a course lecture. They involve the whole person, not a special role-playing segment of him such as might act out the performance of a role, or the animation of a lecture.

The celebrative character of spectacles applies in the case of public lectures, too. So, when it comes to formal frame analysis, the analytical division of "speaker" into animator, author, and principal is mentioned, only to be followed immediately by his asserting that 'it is characteristic of lectures . . . that animator, author, and principal are the same person'. Again, the intellectual authority accorded the speaker by virtues of his reputation, the organisational arrangements, the presence of authority figures from the institutional sponsors, and all the other ancillary effects which make the lecture an "occasion", add up to awarding the speaker a monopoly of the right to hold the floor for a prescribed period.

The business of reading a text aloud and so purveying information to an audience is meant to be central to the occasion, and so of course it is. Nevertheless, the self of the speaker makes itself evident to the audience in other ways. Indeed, the changes of footing the speaker contrives to make at the same time as delivering his text is of special analytical interest. The whole point of the different footings he adopts is the contrast they provide to what the text might convey by itself. He lists a number of feasible changes of footing, or 'distance-altering alignments', which act as a 'running counterpoint to the text'. 'A competent lecturer will be able to read a remark with a twinkle in his voice, or stand off from an utterance by slightly raising his vocal eyebrows'. There are also 'elaborative comments and gestures' (p. 174) and 'keyed' passages which depart from the footing established for the text into irony or quotation, or into bracketed or parenthetical remarks which point to the different stances adopted by others expert in the same field, and reflect on the judgment, enlightened or unenlightened, displayed thereby. There are any number of ways in which the lines a speaker delivers may be 'vocally tinted', and the knowledge that none of this could be conveyed by the printed word gives the audience a sense of 'preferential access to the mind of the author' (p. 175).

Keyed passages, bracketings, and parenthetical remarks call for different footings from that appropriate to delivering the main text. Another feature, also indissociable from live performance, is the management of those accidental and incidental extraneous happenings and sounds which are generically labelled "noise" by communication engineers. Communication is inevitably accompanied by noise. Of course, listeners may, and usually do, ignore all the minor distractions arising from noise generated by the physical setting, mechanical and electronic apparatus, human presence, and so on – and speakers follow suit. Distractions which arise from defects in the speech or oddities in the appearance of the speaker may be disattended to in the same way. But it is also possible for the speaker to break frame, and make some comment on the disturbance, to correct himself, or to offer accounts, excuses, or apologies. In all these, the speaker departs from his "whole person" presence, and comments, as principal, on the imperfections of the occasion ("spectacle") or, as author, on those of his performance as animator. 'What is noise from the perspective of the text as such can be the music of the interaction' (p. 186).

The vicissitudes encountered by a lecturer and, more especially, the way he handles them, can help substantially towards creating the degree of involvement in his audience which is the mark of success. This is largely because they reveal much more of him than any printed text, or even recording, could. In purveying his text to listeners who are there before him, a speaker 'exposes himself to the audience' and 'addresses the occasion. In both ways he gives himself to the occasion.'

And the *personal* access accorded to those present in the audience rides on the back of privileged access to the speaker 'as a significant figure in some relevant world or other'. The 'talk-circuit business' is really founded on making access of this kind available. And the reading of the text by its celebrated author as a live performance 'gives weight to the uniqueness, the here and now, once only' – the celebratory – 'character of the occasion' (p. 188). Which adds yet another layer of "ritual" significance.

Half way through his examination of how a lecturer manages himself as participant in a special kind of interaction, Goffman delivers a warning to his audience:

If, because of what I say, you focus your attention on this supportive animation; if, because of what I refer to, you attend to the process through which I make references, then something

342

is jeopardised that is structurally crucial in speech events: the partition between the inside and the outside of words, between the realm of being sustained through the meaning of a discourse and the mechanics of discoursing.

(p. 173)

Most of the lecture has in fact dealt with the "outside" of the words delivered in the kind of talk he has delivered. In so far as he has succeeded in involving his audience in what he has said, he has done so by involving them *along with himself*. 'The way he stands off from his topic and from its textual self' demonstrates that he has 'rendered both up to his audience' (p. 192). And, in so doing, he invites them to take the same stance and align themselves with him. Hence,

the individual who has prepared a lecture trumps up an audience-usable self to do the speaking. . . . And in exchange for this comic song-and-dance, this stage-limited performance of accessibility, this illusion of personal access – in exchange for this, he gets honour, attention, applause, and a fee. For which I thank you.

(p. 194)

This, however, is not the end. There is a kind of coda to the lecture based on a recapitulation of a theme which could have been recognisable only to those members of the audience familiar with *Frame Analysis*. It is a brief recapitulation of the "anti-realist" stance which he took up in his discussion of phenomenology at the start of the book and resumed more definitely towards the end.

For the "inside" of what he has been saying – 'the realm of being sustained through the meaning of a discourse' – has, he claims, a significance beyond any information or expert knowledge that may have been imparted. Any lecturer, whatever his subject, of whatever intellectual persuasion, invites his audience to share with him the assumption that 'organised talking can reflect, delineate, portray – if not come to grips with – the real world' – and to share also a belief that there is a real world out there to come to grips with:

It is in this sense that every lecturer, by presuming to lecture before an audience, is a functionary of the cognitive establishment, actively supporting the same position: that there is a structure to the world, that this structure can be perceived and reported. . . . Give some thought to the possibility that this

343

shared presupposition is only that, and that after a speech, the speaker and audience rightfully return to the flickering, cross-purposed, messy irresolution of their unknowable circumstances.

(p. 195)

IV

"Radio Talk", the last and longest essay in *Forms of Talk*, is also the least impressive. For all the peculiarity and unlikeliness of the subject-matter, the focus of interest is, once again, the understanding of what goes on in ordinary conversation. The essay begins with a synoptic account of the analytical framework so far developed – i.e. in previous essays as far back as *Relations in Public* – for talk of different kinds. It ends with the discussion of the implications for the microsociology of ordinary conversation of his analysis of linguistic errors and the ways in which they are handled by radio and television announcers.

Sandwiched in between is Goffman's analysis of, and commentary on, a large number of quotations from eight LP records and three volumes of "radio bloopers" collected by Kermit Shafer, of the kind made familiar in Britain by the series of television programmes presented by Denis Norden. The published material is supplemented by his own recordings and notes of the same kinds of mistakes and muddles, and of the remedies and excuses that they provoked, collected over a period of years, plus one interview with a "disc jockey".

The text abounds in illustrative quotations from these sources, some of them funny, most of them mildly amusing. Also in abundance are lists, the product of Goffman's familiar passion for taxonomy, now let loose unchecked. There are upwards of twenty catalogues, some of them several pages long, classifying the different kinds of possible speech faults, the standard techniques commonly used for producing a sense of spontaneity, the properties of human competence assumed to be common to everybody, and so on.

Admittedly, while linguistic errors are not necessarily to be dismissed as trivial, they are only part of what we, as speakers and listeners, have to take note of. Ordinarily, we are not specially concerned with how correctly people utter their words. We attend instead to the promises, commands, confessions, witticisms, stories, judgments, congratulations, and so forth which they convey. The interest lies in *what* is being said, and its import for us and for our future action. But first we have to speak, and to listen to, the words. "Ordinary language is *not* the last word: in principle it can everywhere be supplemented and improved upon and superseded. Only remember, it is the *first* word."[1]

Even so, and while Goffman does, in the end, make his point, there are some qualifications to be entered.

Competence in speech has so obviously its own unique importance that it is a little surprising to find Goffman listing it as one among the various qualifications for living in society, like seeing, hearing, walking, bodily manoeuvre, handling objects and, in contemporary Western society, literacy and numeracy. One mark of its special character is that speech has to be used to remedy or apologise for lapses from the expected level of competence in any of the other common human capacities (and not just for lapses in speech, which Goffman does point out).

There is also mention of another peculiarity, which is that there is a 'folk notion' that, in the ordinary way, speech is something people do faultlessly, effortlessly, and without a hitch; perfection is the norm. This may well be the case with seeing, hearing, walking, and other "qualifying competences", save for the kind of allowances made for those who are known to be, or manifestly are, unable to attain perfection. But the conception of "perfect" speech is notoriously different. There are well-known social, or regional, or even political elements which enter into the definition of perfect speech which are evinced in accent, vocabulary, pronunciation and even intonation. Departures from "perfection" in any one of these regards bring their own special retribution.

Considerations like these are not irrelevant. While allowances are made for deficiencies in speech, as Goffman points out, lisps, mispronunciations, verbosity, and so on are treated as "characteristic" (and sometimes as "uncharacteristic") lapses – i.e. they are seen as pertinent to the social or personal identity of the speaker. And Goffman is later at pains to report the comical verbal antics in which some radio announcers indulge and their (presumably local) audiences when tackling unfamiliar foreign names or phrases; certain lower-class, foreign, and regional accents may, on occasion, be safely guyed – none of which is acceptable when it comes to physical defects.

Goffman's statement, while leaving these qualifications aside, does carry the implication that in most people's minds there is a well-elaborated notion of what "perfect" speech amounts to in their native language. He is, I think, right, even though it has been fairly common knowledge ever since the first published transcripts of ordinary talk by phoneticians that the speech of ordinary conversation, no matter who is engaged in it, is imperfect, and sometimes very much so. Indeed, as many politicians now seem to know, faultlessly clear diction is so rare as to make its speaker slightly suspect. Of course, standards are applied, approval and disapproval being measured according to the level of competence a person displays. Such standards vary a good deal, however, according to the circumstances of the person, to what he is claiming or attempting to do, and the situation itself. Imperfections often go unnoticed, some by the speaker, some by his hearers, and some by both. A good deal of latitude is permitted in ordinary conversation. But it is a latitude which shrinks progressively in the case of debate, formal discussion, public speaking and lecturing, and in military, legal, and other settings in which a high premium is placed on precision and accuracy.

As ever with Goffman's methods, it is in the close study of errors and the way speakers try to remedy them that the special character of talk as an interactive process is revealed. In particular, it points to two relatively obscure but important aspects of talk. The first is that speaking is a matter not of culling appropriate words from the language the speaker has at his disposal and linking them in a linear sequence but of assembling a chain of ready-made expressions, phrases, and sayings from whatever repertoire he carries around with him – which ties in with some observations I made earlier (above, p. 124), with Goffman, this time, referring them to their source. In other words, speakers plan ahead – something which is also apparent from the fact that there appears to exist an array of standard techniques of circumlocution and ways of avoiding troublesome words and topics.

But the second consideration is more important; indeed, it comprehends the first. In terms of social interaction, the underlying structure of speech acts is a matter of what Goffman calls 'frame space', by which he means, largely, the degree of tolerance speakers require for the changes of frame and changes of footing they see as appropriate to the occasion, their self-conception, and the idea they have of their listeners. Speakers select their footing, changing it when necessary, and choosing the kind of expressions which they believe will sustain the frame they want for the event or the eventuality they anticipate having to deal with *and* which will substantiate the alignment they have adopted to their listeners. We are almost, it seems, back in the realm of *The Presentation of Self*.

The level of competence looked for among stage actors and broadcasting announcers and presenters is a good deal higher than it is in conversational talk, or even in lecturing. A high premium is put upon correctness and fluency in speech, not just because the organisations which employ them insist on it, as Goffman makes out, but because (as both the heads of those organisations and the announcers they employ are well aware) broadcasting news or conveying public announcements, warnings, and official instructions calls for exceptionally clear and unambiguous speech. Clarity of diction and an easy, firm, and constant control over speech production is the supreme occupational requirement.

Whatever the reason for the exigent standards called for, they make broadcast talk an especially favourable field in which to study speech errors and ways of coping with them. (The unembarrassed ease with which recordings can be made without prearrangement and even without the speaker's awareness are added advantages.) The same special circumstances afford exemplary demonstrations of the manifold occasions, *and* uses, of correcting errors and omissions by talk which is as if addressed to oneself but is meant to be overheard.

In ordinary conversation, objective criteria of speech error are largely irrelevant. Even the usual distinction drawn between those false starts, pauses, slips of speech, and so on where it is conceded that the speaker "knows better", and those errors in vocabulary or pronunciation where he evidently does not, is hardly objective. The degree of tolerance allowed is clearly socially defined – by setting, social occasion, and the social standing of speakers. Yet faulty speech is sufficiently common to have its own terminology in ordinary language; it is a glossary which linguists have refined, rather than supplemented, though not out of recognition. The difference between those faults that pass unnoticed and those that are perceived is not altogether a matter of training, lack of concern, or careful listening, however.

Lapses are more frequent when the speaker is excited, or over-anxious, or distracted by some extraneous happening. And once a fault has occurred, moreover, it can precipitate more, and worse, errors, even though a semblance of linguistic and grammatical form can persist through disjointed or mixed up utterances. Mistakes seem to arise in anticipation as well as execution, and speakers often seem to dodge dangers ahead by using circumlocutions and paraphrases. When all these are added together, it seems evident that speech errors for the most part arise from lapses in speech production rather than verbal incompetence.

Ordinary talk is faulty because there are more important considerations. However, the case of the radio announcer is different; he, almost uniquely, is supposed to be the perfect speech machine, and that alone; so far as his unseen but notionally (and, often enough, actually) hypercritical audience is concerned, he has to be word-perfect and his elocution faultless. What is more, there are all the things that can go wrong with a broadcast other than the announcer's faults in speech production. "Noise", in the communication engineer's sense, can interfere with what a listener can understand of what he hears as much as any mispronunciation or malapropism, and even in the case of what can be called speech errors, technically speaking, much can be blamed on transmission or management errors. Nevertheless, it is the announcer who has to apologise for whatever has gone wrong, make corrections, offer reassurances, cover up mishaps and join broken ends. Proficiency in these regards is as much part of the announcer's qualifications for his job as linguistic competence and fluency.

But "Radio Talk" is not exactly a handbook of instruction on elocution either for broadcasters or the general public. What is central to the essay is the interaction between the speaker and an audience which is unseen but assumed to be hypercritical. Broadcast talk, on the face of it, is an unpromising field for the study of linguistic errors, since in the nature of things they must occur less frequently than in almost any other set of circumstances. What, on the other hand, makes it an especially favourable field for Goffman to study is that there are all kinds of compelling reasons for the announcer to remedy any faults he commits and to apologise for them. More than that, he must somehow restore his utterance to what it was meant to be; and correction may be overdone, or misfire, and so compound the fault. This is not the end: he is obliged to explain, justify, gloss over, remedy or expiate faults which are none of his doing. Lurking in the text he is reading may be references which a minority of listeners might find tactless or objectionable, words which are susceptible to obscene meanings, pages out of order, gaps and imperfections in the text to be read. There are other contingencies, all carefully documented by Goffman, which have to do with the technical or organisational circumstances of a broadcast; familiarly, "noises off" may intrude themselves into what is broadcast, or – worse – microphones thought to be "dead" but are actually alive may broadcast to a suddenly alert audience utterances meant for any ears but theirs.

Three salient features emerge from this protracted recital of misdeeds, errors, and mishaps. First, the announcer, as the voice of the programme producer and of the broadcasting station itself, must find the necessary words for apologising for and remedying what went wrong. Second, he must do so in the absence of any audience response, which might inform him or provide him with cues for a suitable response. Third, whatever he says will draw attention to the error and so underline it, and may well also add to it.

All of which leads to the destination Goffman – fairly obviously, by this time – was aiming at. This, harking back to the concept of 'response moves' he introduced into the first essay (above, pp. 322-4) is to declare that the study of speech errors properly begins *a posteriori*, so to speak, with what ensues after they have been committed. Such a study has to comprehend 'any bit of speech behaviour to which the speaker applies a remedy, substantive and/or ritualistic' (*FT*, 224).

V

In order to get to grips with the analysis of errors in speech and their correction, Goffman takes the conceptual apparatus worked up in the frame analysis of talk a stage or two further. The splitting of the speaker's individuality into three 'features' (aspects) – animator, author, and principal – represents the "production format" of speech, it being understood that, in ordinary conversation, all three are congruent except for quotation, mimicry and other clearly bracketed episodes, which are accorded a distinctive frame. But, fundamental to the production format is what Goffman calls the 'production base'. By this he means the preparation and assembly of utterances according to whether they are recitations of a text which has been committed to memory, reading aloud from a prepared text, or 'fresh talk', i.e. utterances which are spontaneously composed on the spot.

Each basis of speech production matches one or other production format. Recitation and reading aloud call for some distinction between animator and the other aspects, whereas in fresh talk animator, author, and principal are one and the same. This congruence, or the appearance of it, may be replicated in memorised talk and reading aloud, but there are limits. But then, there are also limits to the freshness of fresh talk if, as was argued before (above, p. 346), what is taken to be spontaneous utterance has been composed immediately beforehand. The difference between the three formats makes itself felt mostly when it comes to speech errors, which can affect all three production bases. Losing grip of what one was about to say and so being "at a loss for words" is a different matter from losing one's way in a text which one is reading aloud or reciting from memory. Even so, an adroit speaker who can see ahead of what he is uttering at the moment can avoid trouble, thus providing himself with greater "production tolerance".

Then there is the splitting of the talk situation itself into "production format" and "participation framework", the latter comprehending all those within hearing of what is being said. "Frame" applies to the "production format" adopted by a speaker to what he is saying, and "footing" to the alignment of both speaker and audience to each other. Together, they compose his 'frame space' or so Goffman says – and here he loses track of his argument, to some extent, I believe. A speaker who is "in command" of what he is saying and has (therefore) established his acceptability among his hearers can, he says, claim wider tolerance ('larger frame space') on that account and so is able to avail himself of certain options while foregoing others. He is 'operating within a frame space, but with any moment's footing uses only some of this frame space. To speak acceptably is to speak within the frame space allowed one' (p. 230). But the frame space he is allowed is one accorded to the undivided individual – i.e. the speaker who is perceived by his audience as animator, principal, and author *in propria persona*, and any tolerance he assumes is available only as long as he remains so. Goffman says as much later, when he remarks on the case of an unpractised speaker who 'blurts out' a self-correction:

> Instead of maintaining the prior blend of animator, principal, and author, the speaker suddenly presents his plight as an animator into his discourse, speaking *for* himself as animator, this capacity typically becoming a character or figure in his statement, not merely the engine of its production.

(p. 231)

350

Radio announcers have to change footing fairly often, especially when it comes to the three-way discourse they have to maintain in talk shows and interviews. In a sense, they are acting as participants in a discussion or conversation which their audience overhears, as it would in a theatre. Sports commentators, too, being tied to the action they are reporting, have to mention interruptions and upsets, and frequently resort to a histrionic rendering of the player's tensions or mistakes or of spectators' responses. As for direct announcing, in which the announcer 'ostensibly' addresses himself to each individual listener as if he were the only one, to convey the effect of direct spontaneous speech carries with it the need to change footing frequently, as one would in ordinary conversation, so as to impart to what they are saying the conviction conveyed by fresh talk. The impression of fresh talk is fostered by their switching to a 'text-locked' voice when what they are saying is 'intended to be heard as aloud reading' (p. 239).

In a sense, what Goffman is arguing is that, since all talk derives ultimately from the "fresh talk" of conversation (which is how we learn to talk and the mode in which we most frequently do talk), announcers *naturally* resort to a simulation of fresh talk, '*as if* responsive others were before his eyes. So announcers must not only watch the birdie, they must talk to it' (p. 241). Indeed, an announcer can at times behave as if he were talking *with* his audience, and responding to what he imagines his audience made of what he had just said – "Or by switching voices he can reply to his own statement and then respond to the reply. In both cases the timing characteristics of dialogue are simulated.' (Which is hardly to be remarked on as either novel or peculiar to radio talk, since it is one of the more antique tricks of the music-hall comic's or street-corner speaker's trade.)

The professional competence of a radio announcer involves the assumption that everything will be in harmony between him and his text, his audience, and the broadcasting organisation. It is only when this harmony is flawed by speech error, technical fault, or unexpected event that the work he does to maintain it is exposed. What he has to do then is distance himself from what has happened – in Goffman's terms, amplify his frame space in order to accommodate an individuality (or an aspect of it) different from what he has already evoked. There are several kinds of manoeuvre which enlarge frame space beyond what is ordinarily prescribed, and so offer him means whereby he can cope with vicissitude, or avert it when it threatens.

Four kinds are listed. The first, and more straightforward, is the trick of enlarging on a text in extempore fashion (which can be simulated fairly easily), and employing a slightly different intonation or tempo to mark the transition from what is called the simple *use* of a word to *mention* of it.[2] This "alternative voice" is employed also in metacommunication, the second type, which has an extensive range of subtypes. An abrupt self-correction may be accompanied by a switch from the authoritative "voice" of the broadcasting organisation to a more direct one in which he speaks for himself; pronouncing foreign or "difficult" words may be marked by a switch from "use" to "mention"; unscripted disclaimers which separate the announcer from the pretentiousness or dubious authenticity of what he is reading; and reporting his own reaction to an interruption or a technical fault, and so allying himself with his audience rather than his colleagues.

This last manoeuvre, self-reporting, 'is not to be considered merely as a desperate measure in a crisis. During face-to-face talk its role is central.' It lays claim to a licence to 'tap in at will into (sic) what would ordinarily be his backstage thoughts concerning his current situation' (p. 295). What is implied is that in ordinary conversation (and, *a fortiori*, radio talk), there is for any speaker a tightly supervised borderline between disclosure of his own feelings, intentions, and so forth, and the requirements of what he sees as propriety, or formality. More obviously, it may be looked on as the line drawn according to the degree of closeness, warmth, or friendliness presumed to exist in the relationship between speaker and audience – and self-reporting of this kind can easily be overdone.

Subversion, the third category, relates more directly to the intentions and motives of speakers when they distance themselves from the words they utter. It amounts to betrayal by an announcer of the 'different interests and entities in whose name he ordinarily speaks'. Under this heading comes, among other devices, 'the overt collusive aside, an unscripted, frame-breaking editorial comment delivered *sotto voce* and rendered just before or after the derided script' (pp. 296-7).

Lastly, there is self-communication, in which self-monitoring is externalised, usually to administer a rebuke to himself, or to use a 'non-theatrical aside' to dissociate himself from his text or maybe take blame for some verbal blunder or indiscretion – while at the same time producing evidence of competent control over what is happening.

The upshot of these last sections of the essay is that apologies, remedies, self-reports, and the rest 'thrust the person making them upon us in a more rounded and intimate way – one that we hadn't bargained for – than the role that was meant to emerge for him. . . . He becomes fleshier than he was to have been' (p. 321).

In all these regards, it has to be remembered, it is not errors in speech that are at issue but the very considerable battery of remedies, precautions, self-depreciatory remarks, distancing moves, and the like. It is characteristic of ordinary informal talk that opening up in these ways is taken to be a mark not just of friendliness and intimacy between speaker and audience but also of assurance (self-assurance and reassurance, both). In so far as to talk in this fashion can stretch as far as chancing one's social identity, it could in some minimal way be taken as a mark of "character", in the sense Goffman gave the word in "Where the Action Is". This is not a point that Goffman makes, but what it comes to when someone feels morally obliged ("feels he owes to himself and his job") to thrust his whole individuality in front of the role-performing functionary he is officially paid to be, is that he is taking risks in order to "prove" himself. In their small way, announcers, like actors, are gamblers too, not with their lives, like racing-car drivers, or with their money, like casino players. Their stakes are their social and personal identities – and, of course, their jobs.

Goffman's own final pronouncement, however, is one which deflates even those small-time pretensions to characterful actions. Despite the licence of informality and improvisation which announcers are given (or assume), the appearance of fresh talk is accomplished by means of a limited range of stock expressions. On the other hand, 'what really counts is the frame space a speaker contrives to win for himself'. The standard utterances a speaker has at his disposal serve as a source of 'expressions through which he can exhibit an alignment he takes to the events in hand, a combination of production format and participation status' (p. 325).

VI

All Goffman's studies were designed to examine and to reveal how extraordinarily complex human action and social interaction are, even – perhaps especially – at the most commonplace level. It is true that the conceptual systems he devised often seem to match the complexity of the material he was working on, but it is also true that when he hit upon a device like dramatism to simplify his exposition by familiar analogy or metaphor, he ran into trouble with critics who thought he was seeking to trivialise human behaviour and expose it as self-inflating and conspiratorial and, therefore, as ultimately contemptible and vulgar. He tried to ease his task, when he came to write *Relations in Public*, by resorting to analytical concepts devised and made acceptable, if not familiar, by students of animal behaviour and then, in *Frame Analysis*, by latching on to the phenomenological approach which had become fashionable. Neither worked very well for him, though.

He baulked at the idea of fashioning a new theoretical system of his own – not a surprising decision, in view of the situation which prevailed in sociology, where theory-building and system-making had long outrun any conceivable demand. (Anthropologists cottoned on to this some decades ago.) When he came to *Forms of Talk*, though, the situation – or rather, his attitude towards it – seems to have changed. One can only guess at the reason for this, but one guess, which has some support from internal evidence in the book but more from what I remember of conversation and correspondence with him, is that he had by then absorbed all that he could of J. L. Austin's handful of published writings and had worked through the later Wittgenstein. It seems possible that the much more free-wheeling attitude he had begun to adopt towards his microsociological investigations was founded on their conception of doing philosophy as exploration, not system-building. He certainly did not "borrow" the idea from them as he had from others in his use of the terminology of dramatism, or ethology, or phenomenology, but he must have found in them some support for undertaking this new venture without benefit of a ready-made technical vocabulary or resort to the orthodox procedures of theory-building.

Let me offer two examples of what I am treating as evidence for this change of heart, or mind. Through much of *Frame Analysis* he presents the reader in chapter after chapter with the part which deception can play in ordinary experience and interaction. In *Forms of Talk*, though, we find that "deception" is much less prominent; the part it played is largely taken over by his notion of changes in "footing". Although he himself suggests that a 'change in footing is another way of talking about a change in our frame for events', it is better, as I suggested above (pp. 324-5), to regard it as a second dimension of the posture assumed in speaking, "frame" being the stance a speaker adopts to whatever he is talking about (a stance which can, and frequently does, change), and "footing" signifying his alignment towards his hearers (which can also change). For the most part, naturally, footings have to be recognised for what they are by the audience to whom the speaker's alignment is addressed for changes to be made and accepted. But the changes in footing registered in the President Nixon episode (see the last pages of Chapter 11), include not only "kidding", which is what prompted the rather sycophantic laughter, but also the manipulation of concealment tracks, and collusion. "Changes of Footing" also include, presumably, the mild deceptions by means of which Helen Thomas carried things off – in the interests of her eventual news item.

Footings are, I think, best seen as "understandings" – sets, or series, of local conventions entered into in ad hoc fashion by a limited number of persons engaged in talk (often fewer than those present) at a social gathering, and lasting no longer than the gathering itself. Their meaning (reference) is created by their use. In other words, they may be considered as constituents of a transitory "language game".

Second, there is in "The Lecture" some discussion of the way in which the business of correcting errors in speech or in the text can make for that closer intimacy between a speaker and his audience which makes even a formal lecture analysable as social interaction as well as an occasion for imparting information, publicising the sponsoring organisation, and so on. But the passage is merely prefatory to the last essay in the book, "Radio Talk". The mispronunciations, false starts, factual errors and so forth committed by announcers, lapses in transmission, revelations of organisational muddle, and all the other imperfections which can break into a broadcast, and the confessions, apologies, and excuses offered for them by announcers – all these trivia are recounted and analysed in the hope that doing so will enable him, and us, to penetrate what Austin called the "blinding veil of ease and obviousness that hides the mechanisms of the natural successful act" of speaking.

What Goffman was doing in "Radio Talk" (and in some of the other essays) was to find a "positively fresh start" to the study of language use in social interaction by looking closely at what happened when things went wrong. It is, I suggest, not far removed from what J. L. Austin was doing in "A Plea for Excuses", and in some of *his* other essays, which was to try to "get off . . . to a positively fresh start . . . in the philosophical study of conduct".[3]

NOTES AND REFERENCES

1. J. L. Austin, "A plea for excuses", *Philosophical Papers* (3rd edn), Oxford Univ. Press, 1979, p. 185.
2. See J. R. Searle, *Speech Acts*, Cambridge Univ. Press, 1970, pp. 73-6.
3. J. L. Austin, "A plea for excuses", *Philosophical Papers* (3rd edn), Oxford Univ. Press, 1979, p. 180.

13
LOOSE ENDS, AND
SOME CONNECTIONS

For reasons which I set out at the beginning (pp. 5-6),* the main purpose of this book has been expository rather than critical and analytical. Inevitably, some questionings and critical comments have cropped up, and exposition has turned into exegesis. But beyond this there is a sense in which Goffman's work strikes one as in some way inconclusive – or rather, perhaps, unfulfilled.

I do not mean by this that the picture of contemporary humankind one gets in *The Presentation of Self*, for example, and in some other essays, is too cynical and one-sided to be acceptable, as many critics seem to have found, or that it is incomplete. Whatever one makes of it, the picture is hardly incomplete. The same goes for *Asylums*. It presents a picture which is certainly complete in the sense of being a comprehensive indictment, but it could also be said to avoid any hint of the possibility of alternative arrangements for the treatment and institutional care of mental patients, and he certainly did know of some efforts in that direction which were well past the experimental stage (pp. 147-8). *Stigma*, again, is an essentially critical exercise; its one positive point is that for every one of us there are times when self-assurance fails, when we are afraid of failing to match the demands of a social occasion, when we feel alien or diminished, and in some way stigmatised. It could be argued that, in the main part of the book which leads up to this confrontation between normality and stigma, stigma is treated in a way which is at once too wholesale and too partial. By lumping all classes of stigma together, the animosities and unreasoning prejudices – racial, nationalistic, religious – which

---

*The page references in this chapter are to the passages in previous chapters which introduced the topics mentioned.

underlie so much of the propensity to stigmatise people who are unlike us are left out of account. And again, ways of redressing the unfair balance of disadvantage suffered by the stigmatised are either ignored or discounted, even to the point of demonstrating the hollowness of the attempts made on their behalf by spokesmen and sympathisers. By this time, the critical viewpoint maintained throughout all three books might well strike some as intolerably detached and altogether too Olympian – as indeed they seem to have done.

There is already a sufficiency of this kind of evaluation of Goffman's work, and I shall not attempt to add my own. This last chapter is in part an attempt reduce the exegetical observations arising out of particular passages in Goffman's writings to some kind of order, but I have thought it worth while going beyond this. The "loose ends" of the title of the chapter refer to questions that Goffman left unanswered, or suggestive leads that he failed, or at least neglected, to follow up. As for "connections", these are suggestions I have picked up from miscellaneous sources that seem to me to promise developments of Goffman's work along lines which lead to alternative readings to his own explicit but sometimes ambiguous inferences.

I

The deficiencies I have in mind are perhaps in part the consequence of Goffman's virtues as a researcher. The most notable feature of his work, that which brought him, though anything but a "pop" sociologist, a very large and international reading public, was the exploration and description of those "ultimate behavioural materials", the "glances, gestures, positionings, and verbal statements that people continuously feed into the situation". He brought to this work a quite exceptional talent for classifying his observations, which was one of his most valuable – and enviable – qualities as a researcher.

A flair for taxonomy is not the most spectacular of accomplishments. Indeed, it seems to have passed unnoticed by almost all Goffman's critics and commentators. Yet it underlay many of his more impressive achievements, which, as I suggested in connection with *The Presentation of Self* (pp. 113, 115), consisted as much as anything in the way he organised his subject matter so as to produce an array of instances immediately recognisable to his readers, for he saw his task as illustrating an interpretation rather than proving an argument. Inventories provide the foundations for all his essays, including the best of them, like the two which make up *Encounters*, the second and third essays in *Asylums*, and "Where the Action Is", although they are not so prominent a feature in them.

Of course, Goffman was by no means the first to treat the world of everyday conduct and face-to-face encounters (of "manners") as worthy of examination, analysis, and classification any more than Linnaeus was the first to attempt a taxonomy of the varieties of plant life. Even within the social sciences, the earliest anthropological writings (by missionaries, mostly, but also by government officials and army officers) had detailed the everyday "habits and customs" of the primitive, exotic, or otherwise strange peoples they encountered. Nor, as Goffman is at pains to emphasise, do his writings on these topics constitute anything like a full taxonomy of face-to-face encounters. What they do afford is exemplary demonstration of how to go about the dissection, analysis, identification, classification, and presentation of the elements of social interaction, observable by anyone who cared to look, in an organised and cumulative fashion.

Goffman's first aim, as I see it (p. 6), being discovery rather than the construction of general theory, his main endeavours were directed towards exploration and classification rather than the development of some theoretical explanation and the case he could argue for it. Nevertheless, some general theory has to underlie the way in which findings are presented, even if it is the wrappings of tradition, of what Burke called "ancient opinions and rules of life", or those of whatever social philosophy, or set of opinions, or ideology that has replaced them.

There is hardly any discussion in his writings of the way in which the traffic of social interaction, which is the stuff of social order, organises itself, or is organised, so as to constitute society, which we ordinarily conceive of as populated by organisations and social institutions, large and small – like Everett Hughes' warehouse of "going concerns" ranging from the US Congress to the corner shop (pp.142-3). What there is makes its appearance in fleeting references and asides. By the end, in his "Interaction Order" address (p. 28), it seems that while he believed that links between social interaction and social structure, social organisation, and social order itself must somehow exist, they have to be regarded as attenuated, extremely variable in duration, and difficult to determine.

While the connection between social interaction and the major institutions of society is in one sense self-evident, the question remains of whether it is in any way a causal connection, and, if so, of which way it operates. For Georg Simmel (who has some claim to be Goffman's *un*-acknowledged master), society is a dependency of social interaction, not its ruler. "The large systems and the superindividual organisations that customarily come to mind when we think of society, are nothing but immediate interactions that occur among men constantly, every minute, but that have become crystallised as permanent fields, as autonomous phenomena."[1] He goes on, in the next sentence, to acknowledge that, as social interaction "crystallises" into institutions and organisations, "they attain their own existence and their own laws, and may even confront or oppose spontaneous interaction itself".

Goffman, on the other hand, stood the quotation from Herbert Spencer (p. 22) at the front of *Relations in Public*, presumably because it was consonant with his own views. In any case, not only the essays in that book but most of his previous writings reflect a view of "ceremonial observances" as evidence of the "government" which society exercises over its members. The "formal organisations", "total institutions", and more intangible "crystallisations" like the social organisations which feature in "The Underlife of a Public Institution" (pp. 205-6) or the organised existences in which individuals are supposed to have their proper places ("The Insanity of Place") play a part much in accordance with Mandelbaum's thesis about the role of "societal facts" (p. 21). The structures and the organisation of society take a hand not only in writing the agenda for social action but in prescribing the responses individuals make to circumstances, events, and the actions of others.

The second, Spencerian, formulation is virtually the mirror image of Simmel's, reversing the significance attached to social interaction on the one hand and to organisations and the larger structural features of society on the other. Both naturally make allowance for the existence of the factors treated as having only an indirect bearing on the essentials of social existence, but the underlying presumption is that they can, or should, somehow be assimilated into what are presented as the fundamental realities. In Goffman's case, occasional glimpses are offered, especially in "Fun in Games" and *Stigma*, of larger presences – organisations, social institutions, and social structure – which from time to time impinge on the immediate concerns of social intercourse.

But there is a problem, which he eventually acknowledged in his "Interaction Order" essay (p. 26) of how to integrate his account of social interaction and the general theory of social order on which it rests, or at least to explain how they connect with each other. Certainly, clues to how this might be done are scattered about his writings, but for the most part the connections between his micro-sociology and the macrosociological concerns which dominate sociology are the most frayed of all the loose ends which lie about in Goffman's writings. They are of two kinds: first, what seem to be matters of conceptual haziness, or downright confusion, and second, suggestions and leads which he neglected to follow.

II

So, while his achievement certainly begins with his quite exceptional competence in organising his material as well as with the imaginative-ness and the special insightfulness he brought to the study of it, amassing descriptive data and putting it into some kind of order was merely the beginning. The main significance of Goffman's "micro-sociology", as with any other kind of social science, has to lie in its explanatory value.

There are any number of ways of explaining "what is really going on here". In recent years, however, most behavioural scientists have focused on two: interpretative and causal. And however direct or indirect, overt or subterranean his connection, Goffman was – as much as Bateson, Turner, Chomsky, Geertz, or Bruner – part of that influential 'tendency' which was moving into a new kind of interpreta-tive social science (p. 3). In interpretative explanation, meaning is irreducible, in any sense which could be labelled "objective", but resides in what it represents for other individuals. With Goffman, interpretation came first, at the descriptive, analytical, taxonomic stage of all his enterprises. This shows up clearly in his first book, as it does in the last. But causal explanation must enter in, if only by implication. For the most part, Goffman relied on Durkheim for the causal explanation of social order in general, as well as of the order maintained in social interaction. The bias – the Durkheimian bias – of the kind of causal explanation he found adequate to his needs also affected his interpretative explanation.

According to Goffman, social behaviour follows rules which govern the conduct of members of the same society when in each other's presence. All social behaviour is included, from the most rudimentary of anonymous encounters in public to conversation and the elaborate social acrobatics we sometimes feel called upon to attempt. The rules constitute what he calls a grammar and syntax (p. 24) of conduct, independent of the individual, as in the case of language. Each individual learns the grammatical rules of behaviour along with "learning how to behave", just as the case is with language.

In the case of social behaviour, as of speech, however, the term "grammar" is ambiguous. The grammar relevant to both is generative rather than traditional formal grammar (i.e. it consists of decision-rules, as in mathematics, by which the series of even numbers, for example, may be "generated" by using 2 as a base).[2]

So one has to premiss a 'generative grammar' of behaviour. The social world becomes, like language, not so much a construct (in the phenomenological, Schutzian, sense, in which individual actors live in a social reality which has been constructed "intersubjectively" for them) but perpetually under construction.

There is, however, a second fundamental distinction to be made when it comes to applying the notion of a generative function to social interaction as against linguistic utterances. Interaction with others is fraught with rivalry and conflict, which come from the overriding need we have to control – or at the very least survive – each and every one of the situations in which, or with which, we are landed. But "L'enfer, c'est les autres" is only half the truth of the matter. We need those selfsame others in order to survive at all, and still more if we are to be in control of our situation.

The very existence of this underlying opposition between competing and cooperating with others calls for some causal explanation of how it is that the processes of social interaction are ordinarily as well conducted as they are – which is a puzzle first propounded by Thomas Hobbes and to which no solution has since been found by philosophers, let alone sociologists. The explanation Georg Simmel offers, for example, is "sociability", something that goes with living together in society, is perhaps innate, but is in any case a prerequisite of social life. Which is at best only a half-answer to the problem, and at worst a tautology.

Rules

The answers Goffman came up with – "rules" and "ritual" – which he took over from Durkheim, are really not much better.

The word "rule" carries with it some of the connotations of law (so does "norm", nowadays, since legal theorists took to using it in preference to "rule", or as equivalent to it). In law, in order to count as acceptable, the fundamental test a rule must meet has no direct connection with its content (what it is about) but is a matter of its authoritative backing – its legitimacy. In other words, what counts is "Who says so?", "What is its pedigree?" by which is meant the manner in which it was developed or adopted.[3] Unfortunately, the question has no simple answer. This is hardly the place to pursue the matter further, even if I were competent to do so, but there are, I think, two good reasons for raising it.

The first is that the positive law tradition in jurisprudence, which dates from Austin and Bentham, follows Hobbes' own line, roughly speaking. The only valid pedigree of a rule of law is one that can be traced back to "the sovereign", which, in their case, presumably, means the legislature. In so far as Goffman provides an answer to the question, it seems to be "Society", which is really just as Hobbesian, and just as debatable.

The second reason for examining how it is that the rule of law acquires legitimacy – or did so acquire it in the first place – is much more important. If law is the most explicit of the normative systems by which social behaviour is controlled,[4] some interest attaches to its historical formation, since it may offer some collateral evidence about the origin and epigenesis of norms of conduct. The systems of law which exist now are the outcome of an unending process lasting centuries – and still in progress. One certain fact about them is that they originate in a patchwork of local jurisdictions, each with its own system of legal rules, a system rooted in tradition.

Tradition is commonly supposed (especially, it would seem, by social scientists) to have dominated medieval people's ideas and beliefs, medieval institutions of all kinds, and the way in which they organised themselves. Of course medieval European societies were 'traditional' – but so is our own. Many attitudes, modes of thought and patterns of behaviour towards others followed customary patterns, as did ascriptions of rights and duties, privileges, and obligations – as of course they do with us. It is, in fact, impossible to free oneself entirely from tradition. There is, after all, as Karl Popper has emphasised,[5] a scientific tradition which is extremely important but almost impossible to analyse, and therefore very difficult to start up or even to transplant from one society to another. But the true essence of the scientific tradition is that criticism of it – self-criticism, if one treats the community of scientists as a whole – is built into it. It is then a "living" tradition.

Perhaps the most telling illustration of the operation of living tradition (side by side, of course, with some that is "dead" or moribund) is the common law. Here is Professor Milsom on the early medieval origins of the common law in England:

> The starting point is in customs, not the customs of individuals but the customs of courts governing communities. These courts, in England essentially community meetings, had to make all kinds of decisions. What shall we do now? What do we usually do? Factually the human and sometimes supernatural pressures to do the same thing again may be quite strong. But if the body is sovereign in the matter and its decisions final, legal analysis can get no more out of this kind of customary law than those two questions. What matters is the present decision, the choice made now. That is guided or not by the past, but cannot be 'wrong' because of it. It is the past that must give way, and then the present will have refined or modified the custom.[6]

The last sentence of that quotation could be taken to memorialise much of human history as a whole, not just the history of law. For if the history of common law is the most telling illustration of what a living tradition means, and of how important it is to our present mode of existence, one can go to the other extreme and point to the history of Western art as the most vivid illustration of the same theme. Here, in parallel and in contrast to S. F. C. Milsom, is Ernst Gombrich on what artists make of tradition:

> There is an element in all art – certainly in all Western art – which might for brevity's sake be called the "cat's cradle" element. The young artist takes over the game from his predecessors and as he does so he introduces variations. In Western communities, at least, art has become a social game played among artists and the pattern that emerges with each move owes at least as much to the moves that have gone before as it owes to the ingenious variations introduced by the present player.[7]

Gombrich's "cat's cradle" is the kind of felicitous image which incites the reader to elaborate it still further. One could go on to say that making a cat's cradle is a two-sided affair, and in order to progress with its fabrication after a number of stages, what one person has made of it has to be handed over to the other. The social game of art also needs two sides: the artists' public (especially buyers, dealers, critics) as well as artists. And since the eighteenth century, if not long before, this public has taken an increasingly bolder hand in the introduction of new "ingenious variations".

The institutions of social life and social order have their cat's cradle processes, too. It is not enough to regard social order and institutions as the outcome of established routines, as Durkheim almost suggests at one point,[8] and others have argued (or assumed) since.[9] Like so much of what seemed plausible enough to take over and make part of the received wisdom of social theory in the past, the origin of the connection between routine behaviour and the structure of society seems to lie in nineteenth-century biology, in which theorists debated whether structure determined function or function determined structure. J. H. Woodger's pronouncement on this seems final: there is "no such antithesis in nature. The antithesis springs solely from our modes of apprehension and from the separation" (in our ordinary thinking) "of space and time".[10] What follows is strongly suggestive, *ante litteram*, of Gombrich's "cat's cradle", in that "temporal differentiation is just as obvious and important a characteristic of the living organism as is spatial differentiation". An organism is best conceived as "a spatio-*temporal* structure and . . . this spatio-temporal structure *is* the activity itself".[11]

Not that the innovative social (or biological) forms created in this way, it is as well to point out, are always particularly pleasing, or benign. Goffman's essays on mental patients and their treatment recount the fate of members of families and of other organisations who fail to meet the "normal" demands people in their position are expected to meet and also make demands on others which are felt to be intolerable (pp. 174-6). "Total institutions" are filled with such people, for whom things have "gone wrong" in a decisive way. Once inside, they are under compulsion to accept a self-conception of being "abnormal" as a necessary preliminary to restoration to "normality" (pp. 152-4). One response of mental patients to this is to construct a pseudo-self as a defence against the kind of self thrust on them (p. 194). Another is to create an 'underlife' out of the capacity people have, in almost any circumstances, to create a communal life of their own. What happens is that staff and inmates both discover, or invent, new forms of social action which are more or less autonomous (since they are not promulgated by any central source of formal authority) and more or less spontaneous (since they seem to be motivated as responses to what is seen as repression). The end result is a new structure of social order, new relationships, and new meanings, which may be either imposed on defaulters, or created by them (pp. 198-205).

Ritual

The idea of social interaction as rule-governed did tend to fade; it disappears almost entirely when we come to the last three or four of Goffman's books. However, he kept the concept of ritual in gainful employment for a much longer time, principally because his discovery of ethology enabled him to give it a new lease of life. But, not surprisingly, the term did become rather shopworn in the process. The student of animal behaviour who first saw the ritual practices of human societies as an analogy for certain patterns of behaviour among animals may have found it useful and striking. But the analogy does become suspect when it is re-transferred, and the anthropomorphic overtones of the first comparison are compounded by the animalism of the second.

It is tempting to take a leaf out of his own book and classify the different meanings Goffman gave to "ritual", but present purposes would be equally well and more economically served by considering some of the stages in what one might call the career of the concept.

In *Notes and Queries on Anthropology*, a handbook for students prepared by the Royal Anthropological Institute (with which Goffman must have been well acquainted in his Edinburgh days), ritual is identified without qualification as a religious practice:

> Ritual, *like etiquette*, is a formal mode of behaviour recognized as correct, but unlike the latter it implies the belief in the operation of supernatural forces. Religion is characterized by a belief in, and an emotional attitude towards, the supernatural being or beings, and a formal mode of approach – ritual – towards them. (Emphasis added).

This is entirely in accordance with Durkheim's usage in *The Elementary Forms of the Religious Life*.

Since then, anthropological usage has become more varied. Indeed, it does sometimes seem that anthropologists (regarded by other social scientists as having intellectual property rights over the concept of ritual) are prepared to serve up any old definition, so long as it suits their immediate purpose. Edmund Leach is not untypical. In the section he wrote for the UNESCO *Dictionary of the Social Sciences*, he defines ritual as "denoting those aspects of prescribed formal behaviour which have no technological significance. The 'prescription' is ordinarily provided by cultural tradition, but may in some cases be a spontaneous invention of the individual."[12] Ten years earlier, in the context of his interpretation of Kachin social structure, ritual is said "to express the individual's status in the structural system in which he finds himself for the time being".[13]

This is bad enough, but Goffman, having elided altogether the difference that anthropologists used to try to maintain between ritual and etiquette, went on to make free with ethological usage.

The term was first "borrowed" by Julian Huxley in 1914 to refer to the way in which social behaviour was coordinated between animals of the same species by means of signals which in effect symbolise one or other particular behaviour pattern. Since then, ethologists have treated rituals ("ritualised behaviour patterns") as concerned primarily with communication: "The first and oldest function is that of communication."[14] This serves as the basis for a number of other functions – e.g. channelling certain behaviour patterns, notably aggressive ones, into specific areas and the avoidance or prevention of interbreeding.

When Huxley first took over the word (in order to help explain the courtship habits of the great crested grebe, in fact) he was fairly obviously using it metaphorically, rather than treating it as an analogy. In doing so, he presumably shed what religious significance the word had. This secularisation was matched by the uses to which anthropologists put it later. Nevertheless, a distinction was retained. Ritual may have become recognised as *similar* to the routines of etiquette, but never as identical with them. Goffman ignores the distinction.

Moreover, when he came to write *Gender Advertisements*, he brings frame analysis into play. 'What was ritual becomes itself ritualised', and we have "hyper-ritualisation" (p. 23). It denotes a kind of recursive, or sophisticated, play-acting of ritualistic behaviour when ritual observances themselves risk being regarded as routine, and therefore perfunctory, or "empty". Such occasions present

367

opportunities for rising above the occasion, instead of to it. "Ritualised" performance or display behaviour is parodied, or so manipulated as to produce some response which is quite different from any which the ritual itself might evoke, but incorporates it; a kind of mock quotation is involved.

At this point, the way in which such "ritualised rituals" are to be interpreted depends all too obviously on the way in which the intentions of the individual are read. Which helps clarify the way in which intentionality features in the performance of ritual itself. The meaning of ritual depends on intention, which is indeed embodied in it. Indeed, one can go further, as Maynard Smith has, in a notable attempt to import ideas from the social sciences into biology, for once. He makes a plausible case for interpreting animal "ritual" performances as at least cognate with the kind of rational behaviour which is assumed to obtain in game-theory and which we take to be the perquisite of human beings: "One principle is common to human bargaining and animal conflict. It is necessary to give the appearance of being willing to hold out for the maximum, while in practice being willing to settle for less."[15] In other words, show fight until the last moment, when flight seems safer, and therefore more worth while.

III

It has to be said that, in practice, Goffman seemed to treat social rules, and rituals, as a *donnée* – as given. Nor did he show any interest in the question of 'how is society possible?' which is said to be so fundamental to sociology. It is not difficult to see why. Since Goffman's preferred method of proceeding was interpretative, he sought explanation "as a matter of connecting action to its sense rather than behaviour to its determinants", as Geertz put it. He appears to have regarded causal explanations for the phenomena he studied as something of a distraction, and not particularly interesting.

In any case, it was the problem before which Durkheim, his acknowledged master, had failed, according to most critics. Durkheim had in fact sought an answer to the question more than once. In his first book, he seemed to find one in his notion of the "mechanical" or "organic" solidarity on which societies, primitive and modern respectively, were grounded, arguing from the "retributive" and "restitutive" principles which he found characteristic of legal systems at different stages of their historical development (he unluckily got them back to front). Later, in *The Elementary Forms of the Religious Life*, it was religion and religious feeling which served as the social cement necessary to society – a conclusion which, unfortunately, as many critics have pointed out, is built into the definition of religion he starts out with.[16]

There is, however, a third possible interpretation of the connection between the "interaction order" and social order which may resolve the antimony set out in the two preceding paragraphs. It is a rendering which may be inferred from a number of observations scattered about in Goffman's writings and to which some ideas and reflections from other sources give further support. I do not suggest that Goffman lacked the perspicacity to work this out for himself. Simply, it was not the kind of thing that interested him.

Seeing social behaviour, including talk, as guided by the intentions of individuals rather than governed by the rules of society or patterned according to ritual codes opens the door to a reconsideration of the connections between the "ultimate behavioural materials" and Hughes' "going concerns", namely large organisations and social institutions.

What I am working towards is a picture of social order which is a credible alternative to that presented by Durkheim or by Hobbes and goes beyond that suggested by Locke – a glimpse of ways of construing behaviour and society other than those endlessly recycled since the publication of John Rawls' *Theory of Justice* by "liberal" moralists and their "communitarian" critics.[17] The order which people sustain in society is neither contractual nor imposed. It is so variegated in specificity, definition, articulate expression and, above all, sanctioning power, as to be impossible for anyone to grasp in its entirety. Yet, in the particular concrete situations it actually bears on, it works well enough, and often enough, to impart a sense of orderliness to social, economic, and even political life. This is because individuals (normally) allow their intentions to be read in their actions and their words, and (normally) believe they can read those of others. *But to be read they have to be readable*, which means that, in practice, the possibility of orderliness in social life is limited to occasions and gatherings in which it is possible for individuals to see, hear, and understand those others.

Towards the end of Chapter 2, I referred to H. P. Grice's distinction between the "natural" and "unnatural" meanings which could be imparted to utterances according to the intention of the speaker. From this I went on to suggest that social interaction related more to expressing and reading intentions in people's behaviour than obeying rules imposed by society.

Grice's ideas have proved to be extremely fertile (as well as contentious, of course) but they have to be seen as a feature of the growth of interest by philosophers, as well as by linguists and sociolinguists, in conversation (i.e. social interaction which is verbal, or largely so) in the years since Goffman's earlier books were published. In particular, the concept of rules has been subjected to some intensive critical scrutiny. D. K. Lewis, for example, having argued against the appropriateness of "rules" as applied to conversational interaction,[18] followed the lead provided by T. C. Schelling's variant of game-theory concerned with coordination problems rather than conflict, and proposed replacing it with "conventions". And Jonathan Bennett, later on, developed an account of conversational interaction along the lines of Grice's "seminal idea" of meaning as the understanding of intention.[19]

On top of this set of ideas (to which Bennett, in particular, has given a reasonable degree of consistency) one can add Ryle's. "Thick description", involves a "pyramid" of sophistication and competence built up, as he says, in socialisation – the process of education, training, and learning, involved in the formation of fully fledged members of society. The idea has an especial relevance to Goffman when one takes frame analysis into account. What Ryle is driving at with his concept of "thick description" in no way comprehends all that Goffman set out to convey in frame analysis, but it does make the fundamental notion a good deal more understandable, if only in that managing the complexities of framing devices is not some capacity the individual is born with, and competence in it virtually undifferentiated between individual members of a society (as Goffman sometimes seems to imply), but something that has to be learned through experience – through self-training.

Interaction order and social order

Amending Goffman's notion of social interaction as "rule-governed" in the way these writers suggest makes it possible, I believe, to see more clearly how the interaction order connects with social order. The form which Durkheim had given the notion in the first place, and which Goffman took over, was that the lives, feelings, and behaviour of individuals are not only, like language, an essentially social construct, but are subjected to the order imposed on them by the collective moral consciousness of society. Although Goffman tended to make less of this original conception, he never positively abandoned it, seeking instead to reconnect it with the phenomenological tradition.

I want to tie the ideas I have lifted from Grice and Ryle to a reading of Goffman's notion of social interaction as "rule-governed" which construes his rules as *decision*-rules by which a line of behaviour is *generated*. By reinterpreting that notion, they amend it in one critically important respect. I want also to go on, building on the arguments of all four – Grice, Ryle, Lewis, and Bennett – a conception of the coordinated behaviour on which social interaction depends as a matter of understandings, conventions and principles, the three terms sketched out briefly in Chapter 2 (p. 45). They denote successive stages of the coordinated understanding on which social interaction is based, from the quite localised reference of "understandings" to the quite general applicability of "principles".

But intention comes first. Speech, action, expressive behaviour, demeanour, and so on, *embody*, or *articulate* intention. And it is these expressive consequences which are rule-governed, in the sense that they articulate a line of behaviour which is generated according to decision-rules. Goffman's "rule-governed" social interaction then makes itself apparent as the instrument of individual wants, endeavours, emotions, and feelings rather than a consequence of normative controls exercised by society over its members.

As I have already said, the reinterpreted and amended account of social order and the interaction order it is rooted in draws on suggestions and implications in Goffman's own writings. The essays of central importance for such revision are "Strategic Interaction", "Fun in Games", and "Where the Action Is".

Relationships and collusion

To begin with, there are clues, and more than clues, to an alternative interpretation in his specification of the various social bonds assumed by or imposed on people who make up social occasions by their sheer presence at them. Social bonds of some kind establish themselves at the very outset of acquaintanceship, but may alter in scope, intensity, and gradient as occasions of meeting succeed each other. Conventions may become established as acquaintanceship is strengthened with successive renewals, and understandings may develop between particular individuals. On any one occasion, ties of some kind cover all those present, but may coexist with others between sets, subsets and pairs of people. They may be symmetrical or asymmetrical, and instituted mutually or one-sidedly, so far as the operating rank of people present is concerned, and may be so independently of what obtains on other occasions or in other settings.

The terms he uses in this connection – 'collusion' is a favourite – carry a suggestion of underhandedness, even conspiracy, which is slightly misleading. What can be said, though, is that in general, and among fully adult members of society, the social ties which underwrite appropriate conduct, demeanour and talk on any occasion depend for their validity – and indeed for their existence – on their being implicitly expressed rather than explicitly uttered.

While there is a multiplicity of different *kinds* of ties, all of them call for the conduct, utterances, comportment and expressiveness appropriate to each. Among persons who are presumed to be 'socialised' (i.e. competent adult members of society), the agreed basis for interaction – principles, conventions, understandings – has, in the ordinary way, to be agreed tacitly. It is tacit not merely in the sense of not needing explicit statement but because to make it so would be to destroy its applicability; the occasion could only continue in existence with a different set of ties and of principles – as Jane Austen's Elizabeth (p. 58) no doubt intended. 'Tact' and 'complicity', which also occur in his writings, likewise bespeak tacit understanding, unspoken acceptance, mute assent.

What we end up with is a very large, but finite, multiplicity of *local* social orders. The general pattern one can envisage is not unlike that which has been proposed by Saussure, with principles standing for his "language" (which represents the total resources available to a native speaker), and conventions equivalent to "parole" (the customary ranges of words and usages employed in everyday talk in different groups, classes, or milieux). The most localised, elementary, level of understanding may be taken as counterpart to cant, jargon, or the coded utterances of intimate companions.

Trust

Consider next the 'mosaic of ill-understood, varying practices' discussed in *Strategic Interaction*, along with Schelling's *Strategy of Conflict*, in which some kind of mutual assurance is called for between individuals who encounter each other as rivals, bargainers, opponents, or enemies, rather than as partners, colleagues, or friends. Schelling called such occasions "coordination games", for there is of necessity interdependence as well as conflict, partnership as well as competition. For Goffman, too, there are situations which call for mutual assurance; and this in turn has to be based, first, on a belief that the way a man behaves 'provides a window into his intent', and, second, on the knowledge that it is very often more rewarding *in the long run* to abide by one's word, even in the absence of any formal enforcement.

These references to trust are rather more substantial than the rather causal mention of Adam Smith's notion of "trust in the other". For "trust in the other" is not always essential to *all* forms of interaction. Distrust enters into social interaction as well as trust. A good deal of play is made with doubt and suspicion in *Frame Analysis*; in Goffman's treatment of them, they do not seem to amount to more than a response to uncertainty which consists of a reduction of trust to vanishing point. But distrust is not altogether a matter of the disappearance of trust. It can be a positive attitude to a situation, something quite other than simply lack of trust.

For the consideration of trust and distrust as a dichotomous pair of opposites, one has to turn to Niklas Luhmann. In situations of uncertainty – where trust enters in as a substitute for knowledge – there is a "threshold" at which distrust can supervene. Distrust, in fact, performs the same function as trust in that it removes uncertainty about the course of action to pursue. The function of trust is to reduce the complexity of situations which confront the individual, and thereby make it possible for him to act:

> Trust reduces social complexity, that is, simplifies life by the taking of a risk. If the readiness to trust is lacking or if trust is expressly denied in order to avoid the risks involved in the speedy swallowing up of insecurity, this by itself leaves the problem unsolved. . . . A surplus of complexity, however, places too many demands on the individual and makes him incapable of action. Anyone who does not trust must, therefore, turn to functionally equivalent strategies for the reduction of complexity in order to be able to define a practically meaningful situation at all. . . . Strategies of combat, of the mobilizing of reserves, or of renunciation make possible a conduct of existence based on distrust in a way which makes it possible to act within the circumscribed area.[20]

Trust and distrust are not in themselves rationales for action, but strategies for reducing the complexities of a situation to something we can handle, and so go ahead and act. "Handling", in this connection, signifies processes of selecting features we take to be more significant, recollecting and considering analogous situations, relating various courses of action to possible outcomes, and so on – processes which are specifically cognitive, in the way in which Schelling conceives the mutual appraisal which goes on in his coordination games.

Involvement

Involvement is a recurrent theme from *Encounters* to *Frame Analysis*. Hence the repeated references to games, which characteristically assume that participants will be whole-heartedly involved. Participation means 'adhering to rules of irrelevance', the players discarding their other preoccupations and interests for the time being, and so immersing themselves in the same little world of activity.

While "rules of irrelevance" may amount to no more than a repetition of the psychological commonplace that attention is essentially selective, the idea of 'realised resources' brings in a more distinctive feature. Special meaning attaches to particular actions and certain players acquire special identities. In the third place, there are 'transformation rules', according to which participants not only disregard much of what is going on around the central activity but discard many of their differences in status, rank, age, gender, and so on, while allowing other differences to play some recognised part in the proceedings. The properties of things, events, and persons which are valid for the world at large outside are transformed into attributes valid for the duration of the encounter. All three sets of rules – inhibitory, facilitating, and transformative – are related not only to the encounter but also to the "outside" world. It is, after all, in the structure of society and the larger world of events that such encounters are generated. 'Together, these rules represent one of the great themes of social organisation, being one basic way in which every encounter is embedded in society' (*E*, 33).

Focused gatherings of all kinds share the unique and significant properties of 'gaming encounters'. Psychological involvement is the centrally important property, in that perception and mind are almost wholly involved in the game, and anything else is ignored – almost, but not quite, totally. For, except on very special occasions, involvement must *not* be total. 'Whatever the main involvements, and whatever their approved intensity, . . . the individual is required to give visible evidence that he has not wholly given himself up to this main focus of attention' (*E*, 40). There is always some connection, tenuous but constant, and necessary, with the outside world in which the occasion had its origin.

Towards the end of the "Strategic Interaction" essay, the picture we have of normative control is one made of a miscellaneous and variable range of "enforcement systems", in some of which the constraints and the penalties for breaking with them are explicit and well-defined, in others more vague, more avoidable, but nevertheless supported by beliefs which are reasonably well founded.

What is important about these 'varied and skittish' workings of informal social control is not simply that such 'internalized standards constitute the chief enforcement system for communication in society', which Goffman calls the 'common-sense view'. They are, in effect, small-scale, "situated" (to use his word), *localised* systems of social order.

Local heroes

The same essentially small-scale element applies to the world of gambling, sport, and other activities, where individuals look for "action" and for the kind of prowess which exemplifies certain traits, Goffman suggests, which are useful to society and which reward them with the rich glow of "character".

We tend nowadays to look on an individual's actions as conduct – as an extension of the person. The essence of conduct is that it is mine or yours. Hence, conduct is said to be "characteristic". But this was not always the case; in the classical and indeed the medieval world, action could just as easily be regarded in quite objective fashion – as out there, an object for men to contemplate and to admire (or, on the other hand, to deplore and to execrate). While there is typical, or characteristic, conduct, in short, there is also what is regarded as characterful action. And it is precisely this guise that "action" takes on in the essay. It is a representation of behaviour which embodies values which are most highly prized in society (pp. 128-9).

While newspapers, and television and radio broadcasts, may reproduce the scene and events, the occasions on which such exemplary actions occur are essentially small-scale; even sporting occasions, when crowds of spectators are present, are localised, and the actual witnesses comparatively few. Readers, viewers, and listeners participate only vicariously. It is being physically present as witnesses that counts, it is in their astonishment and admiration that "characterful" action is celebrated, and it is the celebration which affirms the social value accorded the action.

What all this suggests is that social order is always, and essentially, locally produced. To try to work out the connections between social interaction and a social order which prevails throughout society is not only impossibly difficult, as it has so far appeared to be, but pointless. For the immediacies and restricted dimensions of everyday interaction and social encounters are neither the elementary constituents of the larger, remote "crystallisations" of social institutions, organisations, social structure, and the like that Simmel saw in them, nor the determinate outcomes of Mandelbaum's "societal facts" (p. 21). Instead, it might be that the social order and the social values which we think of as prevailing throughout society at large are not just abstractions ("crystallisations") but empty abstractions.

Mechanisms of social order and of normalisation

In Chapter 6 (p. 165), I suggested that account given in *Asylums* of the ordering of identities and work relationships by modern organisations amounts to a small-scale model of how Foucault's normalisation process works.

But it has also to be said that there are other points of resemblance which are rather less felicitous. The central point of both accounts is the ordering of the identities, conduct, and relationships of its citizens by modern government and of their employees and by modern organisation. But neither account made the kind of impact which was presumably intended. This is possibly because of the glut of premature autopsies of both the modern state and capitalist industrialism which the third quarter of this century produced, but, considering the attention which the rest of their work attracted, this is unlikely. There is a critical weakness in the case they present, a weakness which is attributable, in Foucault's case, to an uncharacteristic imprecision, and, with Goffman, in all probability, to a lack of first-hand knowledge of the ordinary run of work organisations.

Goffman's account of how a "formal organisation" relates its members to it is that it does so by defining – or rather, re-defining –

their personal as well as social identities. It turns them into "organisation men", to use a term which W. H. Whyte's book[21] made familiar at the time *Asylums* was being written. The means by which this conforming self is foisted on the members of an organisation are the proffering of inducements which, once accepted, are equivalent to tacit acceptance of a self tailored to fit organisational requirements. Yet, as I said earlier (pp. 165-6), the inducements he specifies – bonus payments, amenities, promotion prospects, and so forth – are really the small change of labour-market bargaining, and are seen as such by negotiators on both sides.

The mechanisms by which organisations induce their members to identify with organisation goals and values are really more hidden, more subtle, and much more compelling than Goffman seems to have realised. As for Foucault's account of how the normalisation process works, the techniques employed in the normalising process could hardly be as miscellaneous in origin, piecemeal in their incidence, and uniform (or random) in their effect as he makes out.

The social technology of organisation

The normalisation process is a much more purposeful affair than it appears to be from either Goffman's or Foucault's account, and in some ways a more conscious one. It originates in the fairly explicit, short-term, visible goals of those who benefit from it. And the principal beneficiaries are obviously the people who are at the head of large organisations – governmental, business, and service organisations.

It is not too easy to find something on which historians and social scientists are agreed, but a fair consensus has existed for some time on what constitutes the one central and distinguishing fact about contemporary society: namely, that it is a society of organisations. Kenneth Boulding and F. H. Hinsley, for example,[22] take as self-evident the extraordinary rapidity with which different forms of activity – from manufacturing industry to welfare and charity, from war to education, from government to entertainment – have become contained within organisations administered and controlled by managers and officials.

The broad picture to which Boulding and Hinsley point has been amplified, parcelled out and examined in detail, and the consequences for individual lives, for political systems, for economic welfare, and for the institutional life of society discussed in thousands of published writings. But what has become evident nowadays is that organisation, or the human propensity to organise for collective action of all kinds, did not begin suddenly to proliferate in all kinds of contexts just over a hundred years ago. Rather, a particular form of organisation began to overlay or replace other forms of organisation where they existed, and to be applied to more and more sorts of transactions and activities. This form was hierarchic in structure, followed a model already familiar in government offices and in armies, and offered the prospect of being able to utilise hitherto unprecedented accumulations of economic, political, or social resources for the acquisition of profit, power, or influence.

In order to build up these resources and to exploit them more fully, there has been an immense expansion in the technology of organisation. By this is meant, in the first place, the special skills and knowledge concerning business transactions, finance and accountancy, supervision and control, specification of tasks and arrangement of working relationships. Before industrialisation, it comprehended practical, experiential knowledge about the division of labour, awareness of when and where to make use of personal trust, loyalty, patronage, and how, when and where to resort to personal supervision, outworking, subcontracting, buying and selling, and the like. In modern society, they extend to the multiplicity of techniques available to bureaucratic and managerial organisations, from corporate planning, accountancy and management information systems to 'scientific management', 'human relations', and their successors.

All this is familiar enough, and I have no wish to depart from the central issue into discussing the peculiarities of the contemporary model of organisation, fascinating as it is, with its amalgam of Weber's modern bureaucracy superimposed on clientage, which is a form of organisation at least as old as civilisation. What in the present context is important about modern organisations, apart from their sheer numbers, is their sheer size. The expansion of governmental, industrial, service and other organisations to proportions comparable to those of national armies means that most people spend most of their lives working for organisations, making use of them, or holding themselves (or being held) at their disposal.

So much the better for them, of course. But what also matters is that social interaction has to occur for the most part in situations which are organisationally prescribed. The most consequential, even fateful, of our actions – those which call for involvement and are loaded with consequentiality and even fatefulness – take place within an organisational framework and in accordance with the ethos of the organisation in which they occur. More than that, values as well as utilities, goals as well as technical means, are conditioned, if not sometimes wholly determined, by what organisations make available.

In return, social interaction is conceived of as occurring within a primary social framework dominated by organisations. This indeed, is what gives them the substance of "societal facts". It is here, at the level of the "ultimate behavioural materials" of social interaction, that one finds the clearest demonstration of those propensities by which the social order is created and sustained – a demonstration rather more obvious and familiar, indeed, than what one can see on city pavements.

The last section of this chain of what are, at best, rather loose connections I have used to tie up Goffman's loose ends is a statement of the kind familiar enough in Goffman's work but taken from a quite different source:

> How could human behaviour be described? Surely only by sketching the actions of a variety of humans, as they are all mixed up together. What determines our judgment, our concepts and reactions, is not what *one* man is doing *now*, an individual action, but the whole hurly-burly of human actions, the background against which we see any action.

The quotation is from the fragmentary remarks, apparently cuttings from one or more fairly extensive typescripts, which Wittgenstein left behind him in a box file.[23]

What we do, what we perceive, and what we think and believe in, Wittgenstein argues (or rather, asserts), are the product of learning from others (or training by them) and a number of innate propensities (he called them "instincts"), most of which we share with animals. "We *inherit* our picture of the world."[24]

This inherited view of the world is also systematic; beliefs and knowledge make up a systemic whole, although the system is not so much a point of departure or a foundation for acting and communicating as "the element in which arguments have their life".[25] Wittgenstein's word for this systemic whole was "culture". It is perhaps more comprehensible these days as that for which the memory store of a computer is the analogue: the repository not only of "impressions" from the past but of the rules of all kinds of generative grammars and systems of decision-rules we acquire as we grow up, are educated, trained, and learn through experience.

Perhaps the closest analogy to the relationship between the interaction order and social order (and all that social order entails in the way of "going concerns" or "societal facts") is the relationship between what we say and our language – between the few hundred, perhaps thousands, of words we actually employ in everyday talk and the repository of all possible words we know, or can find in a dictionary of our native language. Language is in fact the archetypal system. Other parts of our cognitive equipment have the same character of usability *and* of a resource beyond any need of the moment but available to be called on. It is best thought of as a cultural inheritance, acquired by observation and instruction, and developed through training, imitation, and social experience.

In the end, social structure, social institutions, organisations are not factual entities, or causal processes, but concepts. And it is these which fashion social behaviour as it occurs at the generic level of social interaction, on the occasions and in the encounters when, our social identities being manifest to anonymous others or mere acquaintances, we are engaged in sustaining our *virtual* personal identities. For it is at this generic level, and through such occasions and encounters, that we need to draw on the conceptual "language", the cultural inheritance of notions out of which what Goffman calls the 'primary social framework' is constructed.

In other words social interaction is not simply the substructure of the "crystallisations" which make up Simmel's society, or an order detached from the social order made up of Goffman's 'solid buildings' in whose cracks 'the individual self resides' (p. 42). It is what endows those entities with the only kind of existence they have. Social interaction turns out to be not only where 'most of the world's work gets done', but where 'the solid buildings of the social world' are in fact constructed.

NOTES AND REFERENCES

1. G. Simmel, *The Sociology of Georg Simmel*, (trans. and ed. by K. H. Wolff), Free Press, 1950, p. 10.
2. See J. Lyons, *Introduction to Theoretical Linguistics*, Cambridge Univ. Press, 1968, pp. 156-7.

3. See R. Dworkin, *Taking Rights Seriously*, Duckworth, 1981, p. 12.
4. See H. L. A. Hart, *The Concept of Law*, Oxford Univ. Press, 1961, pp. 6-13 and *passim*.
5. K. R. Popper, "Towards a rational theory of tradition", *Rationalist Annual*, 1949, pp. 36-55.
6. S. F. C. Milsom, *Historical Foundations of the Common Law*, 2nd edn, Butterworth, 1981, p. 1.
7. E. Gombrich, *Reflections on the History of Art*, Phaidon Press, 1987, pp. 233-4.
8. E. Durkheim, *The Rules of Sociological Method*, Free Press, 1964, p. lvi.
9. See, for example, A. Giddens, *The Constitution of Society*, Polity Press, 1984.
10. J. H. Woodger, *Biological Principles*, Routledge, 1929, p. 329.
11. J. H. Woodger, *Biological Principles*, Routledge, 1929, p. 330.
12. E. R. Leach, "Ritual", in *Dictionary of the Social Sciences*, (eds J. Gould and W. L. Kolb), Tavistock, 1964.
13. E. R. Leach, *Political Systems of Highland Burma*, Bell, 1954, p. 10.
14. See K. Lorenz, *Behind the Mirror*, Methuen, 1977, pp. 207-14.
15. J. Maynard Smith, "Game theory and the evolution of fighting", in *On Evolution*, Edinburgh Univ. Press, 1974, pp. 22-3.
16. A summary account of criticisms is given in S. Lukes, *Emile Durkheim, His Life and Work*, Allen Lane, 1973, pp. 477-84.
17. See S. Mulhall, "The theoretical foundations of liberalism", *European Journal of Sociology*, vol. 28, 1987, pp. 269-95.
18. D. K. Lewis, *Convention: A Philosophical Study*, Harvard Univ. Press, 1969.
19. J. Bennett, *Linguistic Behaviour*, Cambridge Univ. Press, 1976.
20. N. Luhmann, "Trust", in *Trust and Power*, Wiley, 1979, p. 71.
21. W. H. Whyte, *The Organization Man*, Simon & Schuster, 1956.
22. K. Boulding, *The Organizational Revolution*, Harper, 1953; F. H. Hinsley, Introduction to vol. XI, *New Cambridge Modern History*, "Material progress and world wide problems", Cambridge Univ. Press, 1962, pp. 32-4.
23. L. Wittgenstein, *Zettel*, (eds. G. E. M. Anscombe and G. A. von Wright), Oxford Univ. Press, 1967, para. 567.
24. L, Wittgenstein, *On Certainty*, (eds. G. E. M. Anscombe and G. A. von Wright), Oxford Univ. Press, 1969, para. 94.
25. L. Wittgenstein, *On Certainty*, (eds. G. E. M. Anscombe and G. A. von Wright), Oxford Univ. Press, 1969, para. 105.

INDEX